THREE PATHS
IN
PHILOSOPHY

Three Paths in
PHILOSOPHY

JAMES COLLINS
Professor of Philosophy, Saint Louis University

HENRY REGNERY COMPANY, *Chicago*

To My Colleagues in Philosophy
At Saint Louis University

PREFACE

CONTEMPORARY philosophy does not constitute a tight unity. Instead, it consists of a sprawling variety of methods and concepts, some of which are in continuity with historically important schools and others definitely born and bred in our own century. Each person who wants to study contemporary philosophy must be prepared to work through this thicket of conflicting positions. The present book is a record of my own journey until the present in trying to understand and appreciate the philosophies of our day. I suggest here that there is some unity amid all the diversity, and that a recurrent pattern of problems is visible in three of the main pathways in contemporary philosophical thinking. They are existentialism, naturalism, and theistic realism. To grasp something about these three philosophies is to acquire a basic orientation for the study of contemporary thought. Since my own position is a type of theistic realism, the critical discussion and evaluations made throughout the book are undertaken from this standpoint. In treating each thinker, however, my aim is first of all to make his mind more accessible to us by examining the questions which bother him and the evidence which encourages him. Only then can some of the leading doctrines in the man's philosophy be fairly and effectively weighed.

The chapters on existentialism try to avoid going over the ground already covered in my book on existentialism. They take a closer look at such questions as whether the existentialists are insensitive to the massive fact and significance of modern science, and whether their own use of art forms tends to disqualify them for theoretical work. There is also the opportunity here to make a comparative study of some influential existentialist notions of religion, which is viewed quite differently by Sartre, Heidegger, and Marcel. Two of the pioneer phenomenologists are also considered: Edith Stein and Max Scheler. Interest is quickening in both of them, but so far the discussion of their thought has not gone to the core problems which really challenge our judgment. In Stein's case, the central issue is the relation of the phenomenological method to the areas of epistemology, metaphysics, and religious faith. As for Scheler, everything else is subordinated to the question of whether or not the transcendence of God can be maintained, if we try to extend his phenomenological method to a description of the religious bond between man and God. The naturalization of God and the divinization of evolutionary process are the results he achieves.

The second major pathway in philosophy considered here is naturalism. It is currently not as popular as the analytic school, but its presence is nonetheless effective. As soon as we press a linguistic or an analytic philosopher far enough to make him declare his assumptions about the scope of human knowledge, we find him invoking the aid of naturalism on what is cognitively accessible to us. Hence it is helpful to examine in a direct and formal way the views of Darwin, Dewey, and Marx on the correlation between man and the rest of the natural world. These three great minds helped to fashion that naturalistic image of reality and knowledge which powerfully, if tacitly, controls so much of the analytic work being done today. This outlook is the nearest thing we have to a common framework of conceptions on man and his role in nature. In bringing this common fund of naturalism to focus, however, it is also necessary to notice and even to underline the serious differences separating the particular approaches of these three men.

In the final part, some questions internal to a theistic and realistic philosophy are faced. They are all facets of one underlying question: What is the properly human manner of developing such a philosophy? I concentrate here on this issue, because upon it hinges the ability of a realistic philosophy of God to constitute itself and function as a contemporary path in philosophy. There is a way of appealing to the ideal of a perennial philosophy and of a Christian philosophy which I find unsound on two counts. It fails to respect the intrinsic requirements of philosophy as a human kind of wisdom. And it also fails to take reflective account of the problems, methods, and evidences of contemporary philosophizing which become apparent from a study of the currents of existentialism and Husserl's phenomenology, naturalism and analytic philosophy. On the positive side, there is a favorable opportunity today for determining the evidential basis in experience for a theistic realism, as well as for doing the detailed work of analysis in respect to both the meanings and the causal relations which are relevant. The actual execution of these tasks depends, however, upon developing an adequate conception of the human manner of philosophizing. Hence in this final section of the book, I try to concentrate upon some basic aspects of the starting point and order which are proper to a philosophically elaborated theistic realism.

With one exception, all of these chapters were written and first published in journals during the decade 1952-1962. They are presented here in slightly revised form, in order to bring out more readily the unity of pattern in my appraisal of these three paths in contemporary philosophy. The one exception is the chapter on Edith Stein, which originally appeared as an article in the same year as her death (1942). It is now recast to take into account her later philosophical writings and relationships. It is a pleasure to acknowledge my debt to the several editors and publishers who have so kindly given me their permission to incorporate all these materials into book form. I have also received welcome bibliographical assistance from the Reverend Edward T. Stevens, S.J. My wife has again helped me deftly and cheerfully in the preparation of the index.

JAMES COLLINS

Normandy, Missouri
February, 1962

ACKNOWLEDGMENTS

I am grateful to the editors and publishers of the following publications for permission to use materials which now comprise the chapters of this book.

CHAPTER

1. *The Commonweal,* 61 (1954), 7-9; *Ibid.,* 68 (1958), 539-542; *The University of Houston Forum,* 1 (1957), 27-30.

2. *The Philosophy of Karl Jaspers,* edited by Paul A. Schilpp (Evanston: The Library of Living Philosophers, 1957), 115-140.

3. *Philosophy and the Modern Mind,* edited by Francis X. Canfield (Detroit: Sacred Heart Seminary, 1961), 20-48.

4. *The Journal of Religion,* 37 (1957), 10-19.

5. *Thought,* 17 (1942), 685-708; *The Modern Schoolman,* 29 (1952-1953), 139-145.

6. *Philosophical Studies in Honor of the Very Reverend Ignatius Smith, O.P.,* edited by John K. Ryan (Westminster, Md.: Newman Press, 1952), 179-207.

7. *Darwin's Vision and Christian Perspectives,* edited by Walter J. Ong, S.J. (New York: Macmillan, 1960), 33-103; *Thought,* 34 (1959), 185-248.

8. *John Dewey: His Thought and Influence,* edited by John Blewett, S.J. (New York: Fordham University Press, 1960), 1-32.

9. *Social Order,* 3 (1953), 207-232.

10. *Thought,* 28 (1953), 571-597; *Cross Currents,* 10 (1960), 162-163.

11. *The New Scholasticism,* 32 (1958), 301-326.

CHAPTER

12. *Leo XIII and the Modern World,* edited by Edward T. Gargan (New York: Sheed and Ward, 1961), 181-209.

13. *International Philosophical Quarterly,* 1 (1961), 235-263.

14. *The Review of Metaphysics,* 15 (1961-1962), 539-572.

15. *America,* 99 (1958), 50-54; *Ibid.,* 102 (1959), 188-191; *Ibid.,* 104 (1960), 371-374.

TABLE OF CONTENTS

EXISTENTIALISM

CHAPTER 1

ART AND THE EXISTENTIALISTS

1. *The Appeal of Existentialism*

THERE seem to be four basic reasons why existentialism has made such a rapid emergence during the past quarter-century. Doubtless, there are other contributory factors, but these will at least enable us to grasp its role and meaning in the present crisis of Western culture.

For one thing, all the existentialists prefer to use the descriptive method rather than the method of strict demonstration or logical inference. Heidegger and Sartre have a training in the phenomenology of Edmund Husserl, whose first canon was that the philosopher must make a careful description of the meaningful context and content of any problem. Karl Jaspers is not a phenomenologist but has remained faithful to his laboratory training in chemistry and psychiatry which put a premium upon a direct and unprejudiced examination of the actual status of things, before elaborating any hypotheses about them. And as for Gabriel Marcel, his long apprenticeship as a practicing playwright has taught him the value of building up one's total conception of a situation from the closely observed details of human life and action.

The deliberate use of descriptive techniques has reaped a double advantage for the existentialists. In a negative and polemical way, they have been able to undercut the case for other philosophies simply by suggesting that we should abandon the endless, futile squabbles over abstract definitions and make a return to the experienced world of human existence. There is nothing quite so persuasive as a demand for a fresh start with the actual things of our experience. The various forms of idealism and logicism were left hanging in mid-air, once existentialism called for a fresh inspection of the very starting point of inquiry. And on the positive side, this appeal for a new beginning on the basis of a faithful description of our living experience fitted in nicely with the growing regard of twentieth-century man for descriptive approaches in all fields. The unparalleled popularity of biographies, sociological and political analysis, and scientific accounts of the world we live in, are indications of a general mood of openness to the real conditions of existence. Existentialism is one more response to this mood—but with a difference—it tries to take account of facts without accepting the arbitrary limits of positivism and naturalism.

In the second place, then, the appeal of existentialism is traceable to the type of situation to which it makes a descriptive return. Many people think that this philosophy is essentially antagonistic toward scientific methods and outlooks, but such is not the case. A good portion of the writings of Jaspers is devoted precisely to this issue, as our next chapter will show in detail. He has made it plain that existentialism makes a fundamental distinction between the scientific approaches as such and the efforts of philosophical scientism to limit reality to what is reported by the positive sciences. The real quarrel lies between existentialism and scientistic naturalism. The former philosophy defends the distinctive and irreducible nature of human existence and its general traits. There is a humane area of facts which cannot be reduced to the rest of nature either in its own content or in the method of dealing with this content.

Existentialism thus supports the ordinary conviction that the concrete, personal existence of man has a unique structure of its own and furnishes a new level of finite reality. For the first time since the rise of Comte's positivism, philosophy is regarded as something other and more than a summation of the sciences or their generalized theory. It is permitted to recognize and deal characteristically with whole areas of evidence which had been banished by naturalism or dialectically transformed by idealism. Coming just at the beginning of an era when men were beginning to realize that the scientific methods are not ultimate and must be regulated by considerations of human dignity, existentialism holds out a hope for an intelligent settlement of the crucial issue of scientific integrity and human values. Even when we find its particular solutions unacceptable, we can recognize its sound defense of the distinctive character of human nature and philosophical inquiry.

As a third ground for the growth of existentialism, we can specify certain human attitudes which had been previously ignored but which have assumed tremendous importance in our time. There have been very careful and nuanced existential analyses of man's anguished dread before his nothingness and his exercise of freedom, the pervasiveness of our awareness of death, the uncertainties of moral decision, and the conflict between individual and society, lover and beloved. For this reason, existentialism is often called a gloomy or pessimistic philosophy, but in our age of anxiety (as W. H. Auden properly names it) a concern about these facts is nothing more than sheer faithfulness to the data of our historical situation. Analyses of this sort are embarrassing to the older sort of progressive positivism and to partisans of well-regimented social utopias. But in reflective minds, they strike a kindred note and bring out into the open the central problems of man which escape the categories of both optimism and pessimism.

Of all these tensions, that between the person and society has received the most attention. Usually, the existentialists are represented as being unqualified individualists, but this charge is based more on Marxian polemics than a reading of the authors in question. For, as Herbert Spiegelberg has noted, the one fact we cannot gainsay is that the existentialists have come solidly to grips with the problems of social existence in the modern world.[1] One may not approve of Sartre's despair over social relations or Camus' portrait of the rebel, but they do throw light upon some important contemporary social attitudes. In their social analyses, Jaspers and Marcel have focused upon some recognizable features of our society: its actual anonymity, its potential reserve for developing personality, and its terrible need for the virtue of trust or mutual good faith. Little wonder that existentialism should take root and prosper, when it has the courage to take as the themes for philosophical reflection precisely the actualities of Western culture today.

This leads at once to a fourth consideration, based on the way in which personal moods and social problems are handled. Because the existentialists employ a patient descriptive method, and because they draw content from concrete facts of human existence, their books are dramatic and compelling.

For instance, Heidegger and Marcel and Jaspers develop the theme of the anonymity of social life by frequent reference to familiar instances. They point to the pitiful way in which a doorman or a ticket-taker submerges his personality behind his uniform and finds his worth in life mainly in his function. Or they call attention to the crushing force of mass opinion, the dictates of the corporate mind, and the subtle appeal to what everyone else is saying or drinking or wearing.

This concrete moral approach is not only readily intelligible to a wide audience of non-philosophers but has a special affinity with the arts. Marcel himself is a dramatist; Sartre is both playwright and novelist; Heidegger has written some pages of sensitive literary criticism, and so has Jaspers. Their thought readily lends itself to embodiment under the various art forms. This enables its message to spread far beyond professional circles. With them, philosophy again becomes a personal activity in which every man can share. The artful dialogue set up between the philosopher and the reader is the first step toward bringing philosophy back from the land of purely formal issues to the common soil of everyday living and thinking and choosing.

2. *The Concern for Art*

Through their close involvement with the arts, especially literature, the existentialists challenge us to revise our image of the philosopher. They accommodate the forms of art to their own uses; their work widens our horizons concerning the approaches possible in philosophy.

Esthetics is, of course, a recognized branch of philosophy in most systems of thought. But the curious thing about the existentialists is that their relationship to literature and the other arts is not directed primarily toward organizing a treatise on esthetics. In fact, the major extentialists have not yet made notable systematic contributions in this field. This is not due to any intrinsic incapacity to do work in this area, although it is unlikely that existentialists would employ the same techniques of measurement and testing which have figured so prominently in the psychological and naturalistic treatments of esthetic problems. The reason is rather that this new and exploratory philosophy is engaged more directly with the art work, and must postpone the specialized questions until the more radical ones are settled. It finds the activity of art to be so close to the heart of its own philosophical inquiry that it must first reflect upon this primary relationship.

The existentialists do not consider philosophy itself to be a form of artistic activity, but they do regard the latter as being highly significant for philosophical analysis. The significance unfolds at two levels: that of interpretation and that of communication. The art work is meaningful, not merely for the restricted questions of esthetics, but for the basic ones concerning man and nature and being. Hence there is a prime obligation on the philosopher's part to take into account

6

the suggestions which come from the artistic experience. Its relevance for metaphysical issues is one of the hallmarks of the existentialist approach in philosophy. The existentialist listens to the creative artist from the outset of the philosophical enterprise, and with reference to the principal themes.

One of the difficulties encountered in appreciating existentialism within a predominantly naturalistic climate in philosophy is precisely its distinctive bond with the arts. It would seem that the existentialist thinker remains too close to life's moods and too reliant upon imagination to achieve philosophical rigor and precision. For the existentialist, however, this raises the question of a pluralism of methods in philosophy and a corresponding difference in the types of clarity and precision attained. He does not surrender his interpretative function to the artist, but he does include the artist's testimony among the primary sources for his own interpretation of human existence.

From the standpoint of communicating the results of philosophical reflection, the existentialist also establishes a unique relation with the forms of literature. He does not insist upon there being only one appropriate way of setting forth his findings, but makes a plea for using the concrete means of art as well as the symbolic forms of mathematics or the terminology of physics. Here again, the very thoroughness with which the existentialist carries out his plan furnishes a stumbling block for many people who associate philosophical sobriety with only one cast of mind and one mode of communication. There is something decidedly disconcerting about finding philosophers who write plays that get produced, novels that get sold and translated, poetry that comes out in print and even between hard covers, and literary criticism that counts with some readers.

Even within American literary circles, however, it is unlikely that the existentialists would feel completely at home. They would probably agree with John Crowe Ransom and the New Critics about the need for distinguishing between the concrete language of poetry and the abstract language of science, between the private and the public aspects of things. But the existentialists would doubtless add that this distinction is made for the sake of finding a principle of unity between the concrete and the abstract. The job for the existentialist philosopher is to explore the dangerous borderland between abstract analysis and concrete expression, with the hope of finding general meaning within the particular beings of experience and art and of finding effective literary modes of communication for his own theoretical investigation.

Because of its twofold concern with the arts both as a source and an instrument of philosophical meaning, existentialism is readily associated with particular styles. Paul Tillich, the eminent theologian, is currently engaged in working out a correlation between paintings and religious outlooks.[2] He suggests that Picasso and Giorgio De Chirico are more akin to the religious spirit than is Raphael, at least for men of our time. The latter's Madonnas may be religious in content or theme, but they lack the religious form or treatment as we now perceive it. On the other hand, Tillich cites Picasso's *Guernica* and De Chirico's *Toys of the Prince* as being genuinely religious in form, even though not in overt content.

Furthermore, he regards these latter paintings as typically existentialist, as disclosing a jagged edge of human life. They keep exploring beneath the surface calm to the point where we catch a glimpse of man's turbulent capacity for disrupting and negating the ordinary ties. The bombing scene portrayed by Picasso introduces us into the middle of the disintegration wrought by human aggression, and reminds us of the fragility of every order of existence. From De Chirico's non-natural relations among otherwise familiar objects, we can share the existentialist conviction that the meanings and relations of our human world depend in large measure upon our own activity of interpretation and the choice of goals.

Puzzled playgoers and reviewers, in company with even more baffled leading men, have characterized Samuel Beckett's tragicomedy in two acts, *Waiting for Godot,* as an existentialist drama. It does have its roots in a soil compounded of the views of James Joyce and the existentialists. The contribution from existentialist topics is apparent in the wholly insecure grip which the two main characters (Vladimir and Estragon) have upon memory and the time-relations, their constant inclination toward boredom and despair, and their fitful lucidities about the human situation.

In response to a cry for help, Vladimir exclaims: "Let us do something, while we have the chance! It is not every day that we are needed. Not indeed that we personally are needed. Others would meet the case equally well, if not better. . . . But at this place, at this moment of time, all mankind is us, whether we like it or not."[3] Here we have the contemporary awareness of individuals as replaceable parts in the workshop, and yet as striving for meaningful and even indispensable action. By expressing in a definite act the responsibility

8

we feel toward others, we may carve out some significance for our personal lives. Beckett leaves unclarified the precise meaning of the situation of *Waiting for Godot*. Each playgoer is left with the responsibility for his own interpretation, just as each of us has to decide upon the sense and direction of his own existence. The only surety is that men are bound together in the common condition of expectation, whether for God or for death or simply for the next sunrise. And at least men can be faithful to their appointment with whatever they regard as their calling and the goal of their expectation.

That existentialism is closely bound up with creative literature is not surprising, given its direct dependence upon Kierkegaard and Nietzsche. Both these nineteenth-century thinkers brought to philosophy an esthetic sensibility and literary skill which belong in the line of Plato and Augustine, Berkeley and Rousseau. Kierkegaard employed many of the literary forms popular among the German Romantics. He used the diary of reflections, the poetic commentary on operas and fairy tales and Bible stories, the psychograph of diverse mentalities, the exchange of letters, and the symposium or feasting-together of alert minds. And Nietzsche found it natural to express his most intimate ideas in lyric poetry, written in praise of nature, in search of the unknown God, and in the cause of resolute decision. Even his major philosophical theory about the eternal cyclic recurrence and the coming of the overman was set forth in poetic language in *Thus Spoke Zarathustra*. Thus there was an historical impetus encouraging the existentialists to tap the resources of literature in their quest for the meaning of human existence.

Jean-Paul Sartre takes a very functional view of his plays as vehicles for his ideas on man and society. Of his four plays printed together in a recent edition, the two older ones—*The Flies* and *No Exit*—move forward with a classic leanness and inevitability which are never quite equalled by the subsequent pieces. In *No Exit*, Garcin complains: "I died too soon. I wasn't allowed time to—to do my deeds." [4] Each of these words carries philosophical significance for Sartre. Garcin is assuming that there is some ideal length of existence to which his own stay on earth did not conform, and that his deeds are somehow extrinsic to his nature. Similarly, the reply of Inez compresses into a sentence Sartre's reflections on the equivalence between oneself and one's actions. "One always dies too soon—or too late. And yet one's whole life is complete at that moment, with a line drawn neatly under it, ready for the summing up. You are your life, and nothing

9

else." The dramatic situation of being enclosed in the boxed-up room of hell is a communicable image for the Sartrean theory that social conflict is the inevitable and graven law of social intercourse. In the play, the beholder also grasps Sartre's meaning for the virtue of lucidity, which is never divorced from the sense of responsibility for one's own character, for the nexus of relations set up with respect to others, and for what may seem like the destiny imposed from without.

In his novels and his parable about "Saint Jean" Genet, the contemporary French playwright who was subjected to severe moral criticism by the community, Sartre is deliberately using literary means to grope forward concretely toward an ethics which has not yet been fully clarified at the analytic and conceptual level. His chronicles about the paths of freedom in France between the two World Wars draw heavily upon the techniques of Faulkner and Dos Passos.[5] He regards the latter as the greatest living novelist, especially in such early books as *1919*. The debt is chiefly for two important points. First, Dos Passos interweaves the social elements of national crisis, popular songs, and commonplace sayings, with the forging of the individual's outlook and responsible choice of attitudes toward the tide of opinion. Perhaps even more impressive from Sartre's viewpoint is the handling of the time factor. He notices that the American novelist portrays even the most vivid and personal acts as past acts, as events which are being reported about from some subsequent perspective. This technique provides the philosopher with a living image for what Bergson and Proust called the essential memorial ingredient in present experience, and the orienting of the present act toward inclusion in the future character of the individual. The temporal moment is a complex and impure affair, an is-which-has-been, but for Sartre this is shown more readily through the novel than through the dense analysis of a Hegelian dialectic.

For Karl Jaspers, literature has always been a major source of inspiration and investigation. As a pioneer in psychopathology, he was one of the first to examine van Gogh's personality and relate his tensions to the general problem of the artist in a technological civilization. The conflict is generated partly because of the artistic vision of values being threatened in our mass society, and partly because of some permanent conditions in existence. The contemporary art work places special stress upon the personal perspective, out of protest against rendering even our perception uniform and standard in size. But like the artistic productions of other ages, it also tries to cast some light upon the enduring meaning of human existence. Thus the crea-

10

tive artist works analogously to the philosopher, but proceeds in a more concrete and intuitive way and without reference to general theoretical issues.

Jaspers looks for the literary exemplar of the existentialist man somewhere between the underground man of Dostoevsky and the harmonious personality represented by Goethe.[6] He warmly admires the latter's factual sobriety, sensitivity to the ways of freedom, and basic openness to all facets of experience.

> You fortunate eyes,
> Whatever you spied,
> Be it as it may,
> It was a beautiful sight.
> (*Faust*)

Yet Jaspers also notes that we have moved beyond Goethe into the world of mathematical physics, non-representational art, and a reopening of the question of a transcendent God. They are factors in our age which affect our notion of man. The existentialist looks for that kind of philosophical rigor and precision which is adapted to the human realities he is most concerned about, and which can clarify the questions of existence within the context of our present age.

One reason Martin Heidegger is the most controversial figure among the existentialists is his ever-growing preoccupation with the work of art, particularly the poetry of Hölderlin. In his zeal for close exegesis of literary sources, he seems to erase every borderline between philosophy and poetic fancy. Nevertheless, he offers some warrant for this direction of his studies. Until the present, philosophy has gone astray by generalizing the categories which hold good only for this or that particular region of things. Even the philosophical terminology is corrupted by patterning itself after the language which fits our technical world of objects. For the renovation of the philosophical language, much can be learned from great poetry. For the poet is actually using language to evoke aspects that lie beyond the range of utility, that engage us as free men, and that break through the limits of the specialized manual to our common tongue as fellow existents.

Heidegger does not ask the philosopher to turn poet or even turn literary critic, but only to develop the habit of listening to the poet and, through him, to being itself. He quotes Hölderlin's saying that "language, most dangerous of possessions, has been given to man . . . so that he may affirm what he is."[7] The philosopher must learn to state in the mode of thought the insights of the poetic concretion, but he can never break the essential bond with the work of art. The

11

Grecian urn, the ode to it, and the well-wrought essay about it are all pointers toward man's ability to enshrine in art-form the humanly significant and permanent aspects of things. The philosopher tries to follow these hints through to their formal expression in thought, agreeing with the poet that we can illuminate man and nature without manipulating them.

Clearly enough, the relation between existentialism and literature is intimate and complex. On the part of the leading thinkers in this school, the association is deliberately maintained. It is not a case of philosophy being transformed unconsciously into something else, but of a group of philosophers who reflectively conclude that it is their responsibility to retain and cultivate one of the traditional alliances. They are convinced that philosophy is being conceived in a one-sided way when it remains closed to the art work or only considers it in terms of the concepts and methods belonging to the logic of science. To grasp the concrete and personal aspects of reality, the philosophical mind must be receptive to the peculiar insights achieved by the forms of literature and other arts. This does not entail any surrender of the proper function of the philosopher, since he must still perform his own work of analysis and generalization, correlation with other aspects and inference to new implications. And in some instances at least, the play or the novel or the dramatic journal provides a means both for communicating the philosophical findings and for exploring the new territory which always confronts the thinker. Gabriel Marcel insists strongly upon this latter function in the philosopher's many-sided relation with art.

3. *The Dramatic Quality in Marcel*

Marcel's genius is as deeply artistic as it is philosophical. He does not confuse these two approaches, and yet neither does he keep them severely isolated from each other. In his own thought and literary activity, he maintains a zone of free interchange between the concrete presentations of the playwright and the researches of the philosopher. His plays display a meditative dimension, while his philosophical treatises remain close to the drama of the person and his choices. Sometimes his plays prefigure the themes which will become central for his speculation, and sometimes they give concrete embodiment to ideas already suggested by his analytic studies. Thus there is a fruitful, organic relationship between art and philosophy in his creative mind. To those who think that philosophy keeps its own identity only by remaining in splendid isolation from artistic interests, this condition is a scandal. But for those who see that the distinction need not rest upon separation from the rest of human experience, the intercourse between dramatic and speculative motifs in Marcel's mind is a fortunate condition for philosophic work.

Marcel's plays pursue the common theme that man finds his vocation in learning to participate in being. This participation is not achieved by dissolving the individual in some vague cosmic embrace, but by gaining awareness of one's personal significance and joining in the community of persons. In dramatic terms, this means a sharp antithesis between the theater of Sartre and that of Marcel. The former sets his stage in the packing-box of hell, with the individual character bedeviled by his past deeds and tortured by the staring presence of other men. For the protagonists in Sartre's plays, there is no possibility of communion with each other or of liberating movement toward the Father of light. Such a possibility is always there in Marcel's dramatic world, not as a sop but as an open path which human freedom is enabled to take. Instead of the room with no exit, the typical setting is found in the home, where there are plenty of doors and windows symbolizing our capacity for becoming accessible to others and for living with each other.

This is not to say that Marcel takes an easy, sentimental view of our human predicament. In an interview, he has stated that his concern in the theater is the presentation "of the soul in exile, of the soul which suffers from the lack of communion with herself and with others." [8] Delicate probing is made of domestic crises to show how they can arouse an awareness of this lack and can suggest acts by which personal communion is creatively brought into being. With Marcel, it is not a question of optimism but of searching into the hidden resources of freedom and making one's belief in God effective for the image of man.

Pastor Lemoyne, in *A Man of God*, has been living for twenty years with his wife on a false basis of stability. In the past, he had forgiven her affair with another man, but he had never clarified for himself the quality of her act of remorse or his act of forgiving. The man's return into their lives forces the pastor to recognize that his attitude has been that of a complacent expert dealing with one of his cases, instead of a husband faithfully loving his wife. In his moral superiority, he has developed an objective and technical relation toward his wife, who in turn has been alienated from him by this professional attitude. Here we can observe in the flesh some of Marcel's typical philosophical themes. The Lemoyne household is split open, because the technical attitude toward an objective case has been substituted for conjugal love on an interpersonal basis of friendship. The wife has grown significantly in moral stature during the intervening years, but this recovery of freedom goes unnoticed by a husband still playing the old role of the competent adviser.

In *The Broken World*, we are permitted to share in another central issue: the effect of death upon human relations. The heroine, Christiane Chesnaye, is moved by a death to recover her selfhood from constant diversion in society. She learns that death need not be a total rupture of personal ties, since it calls forth from her a fidelity whose presence was hitherto unsuspected.

The German Occupation of France also left its deep imprint on Marcel's mind and sensibility. He discovered that suffering becomes meaningful for man by removing the staves which cause the individual to be concerned with himself alone. Especially the evil of racial persecution can serve as the goad for new spurts of social growth, both for good and for evil. Moving beyond the domestic region to that of political and social movements, Marcel's *The Sign of the Cross* explores the effects of anti-Semitism on several souls. The ambivalence of social policies in the face of different human interpretations is shown in the self-criticism aroused in one Jewish person and the discovery of fraternal ties on the part of another.

Other recent plays deal with the many-patterned ways in which obscure and prominent men face the challenge of inhumane social force. This is a direct route to the heart of Marcel's social philosophy and his critique of technology. But at both the personal and the social levels, he relies much less heavily than does Graham Greene upon the criminal act as the means of self-disclosure. And his resolution of a situation is achieved through a fresh human appeal to the common ideals of fidelity and hope, rather than through the simulated shock of theological paradox.

In the contrapuntal fashion of an essentially musical mind, Marcel develops his philosophy around a core of polar themes: art and philosophy, the ordinary man and philosophy, existence and being, society and the person, Christian and non-Christian minds. These are the most significant aspects of his thought for the contemporary inquiring mind.

Even in form, there is some continuity between Marcel's literary and philosophical works. Two of his main philosophical writings follow the journal form, after the example of Maine de Biran and with an intellectual rigor never attained by André Gide. The entries in his *Metaphysical Journal* and *Being and Having* are sometimes gnarled and circuitous, but they allow the reader to follow the genesis of his perplexities and his creative spurts. Marcel permits us to trace the steps leading to his break with idealism, his conversion to Catholicism, and his chiseling of the prime distinctions between mystery and problem, being and having. Like Cardinal Newman, he knows the art of persuasion through telling the story of one's personal quest of truth.

Marcel resembles Newman in another important respect: he permits no discontinuity between ordinary and philosophically justified assent. The real ground of his rejection of airtight systems is not an irrationalist motive, but a fear lest philosophy close itself off from the act of living intelligence. The informal character of his investigations is a means for awakening a sense of the dependence of philosophical work upon the judgments of existing men about themselves and the world of their experience. Philosophy is not a self-priming pump, but stands in radical need of what we can learn as men, not as technicians of a system.

Claudel once observed that the trained philosopher must continually learn how to hear with his eye and see with his ear. Like the artist, he must develop a keen sensitivity to the significance of our daily findings. In Marcel's language, the philosopher has to respect the fore-feeling or presentiment of general meaning that hides in our simplest perceptions and statements. Here again, the artist and the thinker in Marcel reinforce each other. His generous use of descriptions of men, encounters, and frames of mind, is intended to keep his philosophizing in close contact with human experience. To this extent, Marcel grants that he is a kind of radical empiricist, a blood-brother to William James. By preventing philosophy from completing the movement toward becoming a professional specialty, he also preserves its general significance for human life and its capacity to reach God.

Marcel begins his philosophy with the involved self. This starting point is not an involuted psychological state, but the human self considered precisely as being already involved in real relations with a world of existing things and persons. This is the basic realism of Marcel's position. Philosophy starts with the existent in its most concrete form: the incarnate human self as implicated in the actual universe. Because it reflects upon this foundation, Marcel's thought is a philosophy of existence and the concrete. But it is not simply or

15

primarily such, since then it would describe only what we are at the outset and before the work of freedom begins.

In his Gifford Lectures on *The Mystery of Being*,[9] Marcel characterizes his philosophy more precisely as a reflection upon the passage from existence to being. Its dramatic quality derives from concentration upon this transition. Our living situation comprises the structure and relations in which we find ourselves sharing, even prior to making any free choice of attitude. This given factor in our nature is the mark of our creatureliness, our reception of the gift of existence from God. But existential reflection upon ourselves raises the question of the response we will freely make to this situation, the attitude we will take toward our given nature. And the realm of being concerns the free response of man to his existential relations, considered as leading us toward God or away from Him.

Marcel roots all particular dramatic relationships in the primal decision of the human person either to accept or to refuse to acknowledge his participation in being. The closed soul is the atheistic titan. Like the heroes in Camus' novels, he may display great pity and understanding for men, but he stops short of the ultimate recognition of his own bond with God. He fears that such acknowledgment will endanger his freedom and dignity, whose condition he will be more ready to call absurd than derived. By way of contrast, the open soul does not dictate in advance what he must find. He recognizes himself both as a participant in being and as one who shares through a free act. Hence he seeks the freedom and integrity proper to a man of God. Out of this initial refusal or acceptance of God develop the other clashes in existence and in philosophies.

When Marcel calls ours a broken world, he means one in which the social tendencies obstruct this ludicity about the basic question for men, until some shock or crisis permits the question of theism to be posed. The social analyses in *Man against Mass Society* come to focus upon the mass man, as the product of the attempt to evade the mystery of being and its source in our choice concerning God. A dehumanized society is one in which the primacy of being over having is reversed, and hence in which the person is reduced in significance to the function he performs in the world of goods and services. Since another individual can do the same service, the given man has no distinctive worth. Within the technical universe, he cannot claim to be unique and irreplaceable, with the tragic result that he may accept this abstract view of himself as final.

Not pessimism but the search after an opening chink for the intro-

duction of humane values in mass society leads Marcel to meditate
on the mystery of death. He is aware that it can be given an objective
and impersonal description in social terms, and even that it can be
transformed into what Evelyn Waugh satirically describes as a problem in cosmetics and landscaping. Yet he does not accept the statistical and satirical reports as definitive, because of our underground
awareness that more is involved than the technical approach to death.
Instead, Marcel asks us to listen meditatively to these lines from
Rainer Maria Rilke's *Book of Hours:*

> O Lord, give each one his own particular death,
> the death stemming from his own life
> in which he had love and awareness and distress.[10]

Both Marcel and Heidegger point out that there is an aspect of
death which is accessible only to personal introspection. One can ask
for "his own particular death," only if one is aware of it as the meaningful climax of "his own life." Philosophy makes one meditative
neither exclusively about life nor exclusively about death, but about
that integral pattern of free activity which constitutes a significant
personal sharing in being. This is the point at which the rule of
technics is overcome even within its own framework, and the opportunity found for engaging in the personal forms of community.

In his essay on *The Decline of Wisdom,* Marcel has had to face the
charge of hankering after the lost paradise of pretechnical society. He
accepts both the utility of technological organization and the values
of valid power and joy entailed by it. There is no question of reversing
the trend, but only of determining whether the technical or the personal spirit will be dominant in modern society. The very success of the
engineering attitude encourages people to suspect anything which
is irreducible to a technical problem. It is against this universalization
of the categories of objective planning that the personalist philosopher
protests. His positive work is to recall us to our own freedom and responsible way of being.

While other writers have been arguing about the possibility of a
Christian philosophy, Marcel has been philosophizing as a Christian
thinker. Since his position rests upon a study of human nature in its
concrete forms, it can be shared by non-Christians and does not lead
by deductive necessity to Christianity. Nevertheless, Marcel accepts
the basic harmony between human experience and the Christian
revelation, as well as the illumination which the latter casts upon the
personal and social life of man. In acknowledging this help, he also

warns the Christian thinker against any display of intellectual pater-
nalism in respect to his nonbelieving partners in philosophical inquiry.
"Grace should inhabit him," Marcel remarks of the Christian philosopher, "not only as radiance, but as humility." [11] This is a good motto
for anyone working in the intellectual fields within the conditions of
our American pluralist society.

CHAPTER 2

JASPERS' CONCEPTION
OF MODERN SCIENCE

THERE are several highways leading to the heart of Karl Jaspers' thought. One illuminating access to his mind is gained through a study of his distinction between science and philosophy. An analysis of this doctrine is indispensable for appreciating his characteristic approach to philosophical issues. The present chapter deals with four main points: the relation between philosophy and our age of science, the attitudes of Descartes and Nietzsche toward science, Jaspers' philosophical interpretation of the nature of science, and the relation between science and philosophy. From this study, we can see that the existentialists are deeply interested in the nature of modern science and its positive bearing upon a philosophy of human existence.

1. *Philosophizing in the Age of Science*

One often comes away from a reading of Jaspers with the impression that he is not quite sure, in his own mind, concerning the precise relationship between science and philosophy.[1] For, at one moment, he defends the possibility of a separation of philosophy from the special sciences. He points to the profoundly philosophical remarks that emanate from a child, looking at the world in a pre-scientific way. At another time, Jaspers stresses the indissoluble bond uniting science and philosophy, such that the former provides a necessary preparation for the latter. Again, he seems to waver between praise for the pre-Socratic fusion of the two standpoints and a plea for their rigid, systematic differentiation. Thus, we are led to inquire whether or not

19

there can be genuine philosophizing apart from a scientific formation of the mind, and whether it is desirable to make a formal distinction between the scientific and philosophical approaches.

This apparent indecision on so crucial a question can be removed, as soon as we attend to Jaspers' unobtrusive but highly significant use of the temporal qualifier: "today." He admits that, in primitive epochs, philosophical inquiries preceded scientific investigations and that there are still transient gleams of pre-scientific philosophical insight on the part of children in our own time. But as far as the mature mind of today is concerned, philosophical inquiry cannot be carried on successfully, unless the methodology and meaning of the sciences are grasped, at least in their principal features. Similarly, it was quite possible for the early Greek thinkers to merge science and philosophy in a single vision of nature, as well as for the tradition of a "natural philosophy" (coalescing philosophy and the sciences in a single whole) to flourish throughout the classical and medieval periods. Yet these conditions were only possible because science, in its typically modern articulations, had not yet developed. Now that this historical development of the sciences has transpired, however, we cannot close our eyes to it. In our era, the philosopher must recognize explicitly that his method and aim are quite distinct from those of the various modern sciences.

As a rough anticipation of his more detailed distinction between the two, Jaspers proposes that philosophy seeks the meaning of being as such and of the world as a whole, whereas the modern sciences concern themselves about the particular objects and special aspects within the world. Why is it impossible today to ignore this basic contrast or to elaborate a philosophy, without formally attending to it? The fundamental answer is that philosophy is essentially a mode of praxis, an affair of inner activity, a deed in the form of thought.[2] That is why Jaspers prefers to speak of his work as an active *philosophizing*, rather than a static, finished body of doctrine or a *philosophy*. Every practical activity or vital operation is bound up with the concrete conditions of life. In man's case, this means that the work of thought or philosophizing is inextricably associated with, and deeply affected by, the prevailing historical situation. One of Jaspers' chief doctrines is that human existence and all its modes are involved in various situations. He applies this doctrine of situational existence to philosophical thinking, which is a supreme mode of existence and practical human operation. A man cannot engage in this activity, in complete abstraction from the situations of his temporal existence. Man's total involvement in situational being would be called in question, were present-day philosophizing detachable from the historical conditions of modern life.

In both of his extended accounts of the modern age—*Man in the Modern Age* and *The Origin and Goal of History*—Jaspers signalizes the paramount role of the sciences in the formation of post-Renaissance society.[3] He calls the scientific and technological achievements since the seventeenth century the "simply new" factor injected into the mainstream of history. It is their presence which sets off the modern Western world, in a radical way, from previous Western civilization and from the entire Oriental development. The most general description of our historical situation is: the age of science and technology. Hence philosophers cannot divorce themselves from this concrete scientific setting for all activity, and cannot evade the task of interpreting the scientic enterprise and differentiating it from their own. This supposes, however, that the philosopher has at his disposal a precise account of the characteristics of the modern scientific spirit.

As a preliminary contribution toward such a description, Jaspers proposes a distinction between the broad, neutral meaning of "science," and one that is sufficiently limited to convey the distinctive features of the modern approach to nature and man. In the wider sense, scientific thinking is regulated by empirical respect for facts and a concern for rational communication of findings. The scientific mind proceeds in a deliberate, methodical way, and is fully aware both of the method being used and of its limitations. Constant questioning, fresh consultation of new situations in experience, and openness to criticism, are hallmarks of the scientific attitude. Philosophy qualifies as scientific thought in this broad meaning. It welcomes searching questions and criticisms; it roots itself firmly in the soil of existence, to which it must always return; it employs a methodic manner of investigation, and is fully aware of its methodological principles and their confines; it organizes its truths in the light of a unifying principle, so that rational communication among men will be promoted. To this extent, then, philosophy is scientific, without thereby being aggregated among the sciences.[4]

A profound caesura opens up, however, between the specifically modern Western approach in the sciences and the outlooks of the previous ages. There are several unique traits, marking off this new conception of science.[5] (1) Scientific research is animated by the will to know all that is knowable. Consequently, there is nothing too insignificant for careful study, nothing unworthy of investigation. Modern science recognizes no limits to its activity. Every real thing and every sort of possibility provide proper materials for analysis. A drive toward novelty and discovery impels scientific inquiry to explore all the corners of the universe. (2) Correlative to the unrestricted content of science is its unrestricted interrogation of all previous convictions. No belief is too sacred or too firmly established to forbid a radical questioning of its soundness. (3) There is something provisional about all scientific theories themselves. They must submit to the test of fresh experience and experiment, and hence must be prepared for constant revision and even replacement. The scientific attitude includes a willingness to test new hypotheses, even those that seem to contradict facts or outstrip our sensuous intuition of the world. Hence the sciences are essentially incomplete and subject to the law of linear progress, in which each succeeding generation takes a measurable step beyond the position of its predecessors.

(4) Nevertheless, the scientific movement aims at a certainty that is coercive and indubitable. The ideal of mathematical knowledge has exercised a strong attraction over scientific minds, buoying them up with the hope that all fields of scientific work can be impenetrated with mathematical clarity and certainty. The aim of scientific inquiry in the several fields is to bring the objective evidence to a clear condition, where it imposes itself upon the impartial mind, with compelling force. (5) This purpose is promoted by the rigorous way in which scientific methods and categories are applied. A sustained effort is made to universalize the method and categories of a given science, in order to test their scope and cast new light upon familiar situations. Universally valid knowledge is the lodestone guiding every construction of a scientific world of discourse. (6) Viewpoints are not proliferated for their own sake, however, since scientific explanation is also regulated by the requirements of economy and simplicity of means. In regarding an object from every side and with the help of all scientific perspectives, the investigator intends to bring out its systematic connections with the rest of the universe. Even though the object can never be located definitively in respect to all its relations in the cosmos of being, still its position in the cosmos of interrelated sciences can be ascertained. Although the sciences do not achieve a total unity, grounded in a comprehensive knowledge of all reality, they do tend toward a systematic interconnection of methods and categories.

(7) Jaspers defends the speculative character of scientific knowledge. Whatever other ends it may serve, its primary function is to satisfy the will to know all that is knowable. This does not mean, how-

ever, that scientific knowledge is cut off from the practical control of nature, but only that such control depends upon the speculative soundness of the knowledge. Indeed, the practical orientation of knowledge is one of the indigenous features of the modern scientific outlook. There is no historical parallel to the success with which modern science has satisfied human needs. In subjecting so many aspects of nature to human dominion, scientific technology has not only changed the face of the world around us but also profoundly modified the inner life of man himself. Our relation with the natural world has been made more remote in one respect (due to the regimen of machines and the demands of industrial production schedules), and yet in another respect it has been made more intimate (due to increased leisure and perfection of the means of communication and instruments of observation). The tremendous potentialities of technological control over mass societies, for good and for evil, set off our way of human living in a scientific epoch.

2. *The Historical Lesson of Descartes and Nietzsche*

The impact of science and technology has been felt just as strongly in philosophy as in the other areas of human life. In several autobiographical sketches, Jaspers has outlined the condition of philosophical instruction at Heidelberg and other German universities, around the turn of the present century.[6] Philosophy courses were generally confined to epistemology, psychology, and history of philosophy. The latter discipline tended to be a sheerly "objective" recital of what had been taught by thinkers in the past, with no hint that the philosophical tradition was still living and relevant for the problems of modern life. The doctrinal courses were made as "scientific" as possible, in the hope of appropriating to philosophy some of the great prestige of the sciences. Evidence, methods, and proofs were tailored according to the model of the mathematical or biological sciences. Professors vied with each other in presenting philosophy as one science along with all the others or, at the very most, as the summation of the other sciences. For, unless philosophy were shown to be the methodology of the sciences or their highest generalization, it could achieve no respectable standing in the university community.

Jaspers himself remained unconvinced by the scientific pretenses of the reigning philosophies, especially positivism and idealism. In the latter part of the nineteenth century, idealists like Lotze attempted to deal in a scientifically stringent way with the problems of God, the soul, freedom, and moral responsibility. The shaky results of this effort to ape the sciences led many people to deny the spiritual nature of man and his freedom, simply because these latter were not susceptible of becoming objects of scientific demonstration. Positivism profited by this disillusionment with idealism by suggesting that the limits of real being coincide precisely with the limits of scientific thinking. The practical advice was that man should not bother himself about such issues as God, the spiritual soul, and freedom, since they lie beyond the possibility of confirmation or rejection through scientific method and hence can be presumed to be mere fictions of the mind. Both idealism and positivism accepted a common platform: that all philosophical problems can be settled through use of the scientific method. Even Edmund Husserl was not entirely free from this fundamental presupposition.[7] In announcing that phenomenology provides a way of transforming philosophy into a strict science, he simply begged the question of the appropriateness of such a transformation. Jaspers' admiration for Husserl was qualified by the belief that philosophy loses its distinctive approach to reality just as effectively when its main task is to supply the foundations of scientific knowledge as when it is treated as the systematic summary of the other sciences.

Jaspers reports that he wrote his work, *Descartes and Philosophy,* mainly to bring out into the open the historical source of the modern confusion between science and philosophy. Whereas Husserl's *Cartesian Meditations* tried to execute the Cartesian project in a more rigorous and radical way, Jaspers' book casts doubt upon the way in which both Descartes and Husserl conceive philosophical method and truth. Descartes was so impressed by the success of his analytic geometry, that he tried to reconstruct philosophy along the lines of a *mathesis universalis.* Although he distinguished between ordinary mathematics and philosophy, he retained in philosophy the mathematical conception of evidence and certainty. To this extent, he absolutized one scientific method, so that he might revamp philosophy in the form of modern science. Having capitulated to the imperialism of scientism, Descartes was thereafter unable to do justice either to the sciences or to philosophy. Both were eventually the losers by the Cartesian adventure in interbreeding.

Within a half-century after Descartes' death, most practising scientists had abandoned Cartesian physics. For, even though he recognized in advance most of the salient features of modern scientific research, Descartes perverted their meaning, due to his methodologi-

24

cal prejudices.[8] For instance, he hailed the trend toward realizing the unity of science. But, at the same time, he artificially imposed the ideal of a systematic deduction of all scientific truths from a few principles, instead of acknowledging that the idea of unity can be realized in different ways, in different sciences. Although Descartes accorded a definite role to experience and experiment in his theory of method, his actual construction of physics was excessively deductive and divorced from a direct testing of facts. The arbitrary results of his physical deductions were a steep price to pay for vindicating his monism of method and knowledge. Another unfortunate consequence was his lack of insight into the nature of historical knowledge. He was obliged to depreciate the humanities as constituting merely inexact bodies of opinion, since it was difficult to conform them to his mathematical notion of certitude.

Although the consequences of Cartesianism for philosophy were less palpable, they were just as disastrous. In order to obtain clear and compelling evidence in philosophy, Descartes had to reduce the human self and God to the status of objects for scientific understanding. The self or thinking thing was treated only insofar as it served as a counterpart of the body or extended thing. Despite Descartes' high respect for freedom, the latter was definitely endangered through his correlation between mind and body. Spinoza drew the inference that, if bodily states are strictly determined, then mental states are subject to an equally rigid determinism. Universal determinism is the condition under which alone both mind and body can become the objects of clear and cogent mathematical-like demonstration. If philosophy can deal with man's inner life only from the standpoint of what indifferently is evident to all observers, then there must be a methodic elimination of freedom and existential content from the thinking self. Descartes could not rescue freedom and genuine existence by an appeal to the self's relation to God, even though he made a strenuous effort to do so. For he admitted God into philosophy only in the degree that He supported a body of knowledge dominated by objectivity. The Cartesian God was no longer the giver of existence but the guarantor of the criterion of clear and distinct knowledge. This systematic adaptation of the doctrine on God to the unity and objectivity of science undermined belief in His transcendence and thus paved the way for subsequent theories of pantheistic immanence.

In Jaspers' view, then, Descartes was the main source of the typically modern over-evaluation of science. Jaspers refers to this scientism as the "superstition of science." It consists in a theoretical absolutizing of some area of scientific knowledge, which is confused with philosophy, and in a practical tendency to expect everything from science.[9] Since scientific research can pursue an endless course among objects in the world, the inference is made that there are no boundaries whatsoever to scientific knowledge, and that there can be a total scientific world-picture comprehending all reality. On this basis, science is asked to ascertain all values, to decide upon what ought to be done in moral conduct, and to set the ultimate goals for human life. Within this scientistic perspective, philosophy has no distinctive office of determining the norms and ends of our existence: the latter are exclusively immanent and relative ones, which fall completely within the range of the sciences. The only role allotted to philosophy is to supply the general logic of scientific method and of valuational judgments. Individual interpretation and free choice are no longer to be centrally important in either ethical theory or moral practice. Impersonal scientific inquiry and public evidence are to be the sole determinants of the hierarchy of values and actual conduct.

Nietzsche's passionate attack upon the ideal of scientific truth can only be understood against the background of this modern surrender of philosophical functions to the absolutizing of science. Jaspers does not regard Nietzsche as an enemy of science itself but rather as a resolute foe of modern scientism. Science contains one mode of truth but it is not *the* truth, in an unconditional way. Behind our scientific inquiries lies the passion for knowledge, a drive that can be properly assessed only on philosophical grounds. Because the will to truth rests upon a non-scientific basis, science cannot pretend to attain to any absolute truth. Both the ends of scientific work and all its other valuational aspects stem from philosophical commitments, whose justification cannot be undertaken by the scientific method itself. The meaning of science cannot be fully apprehended from within the universe of science itself.

Jaspers gives a metaphysical interpretation of Nietzsche's critique of science.[10] Nietzsche detected something more stirring at the heart of scientific investigation than the scientific mind is aware of: a search after the meaning of being as a whole. There is an essential incommensurability between the dynamism of the search for truth and the actual results obtainable through the scientific method. Science alone cannot quench the deep human thirst for metaphysical truth, which animates the scientific will to knowledge. Even were the scientific description of the world a complete one, man would still be faced with the question of what attitude he is to take toward a world so described. Even though he may desire to do so, man cannot transfer to an impersonal scientific process the responsibility for making a philosophical interpretation of the total meaning of being, and for determining his own individual relation to being.

Yet Jaspers' ironical criticism is that Nietzsche himself is guilty of absolutizing one zone of scientific knowledge into a philosophical whole.[11] Nietzsche has an elusive conception of philosophical truth. Fundamentally, however, he teaches that the scale of human values is to be determined by the relative ability of goals to heighten life itself. The increase of life means an increase in the vigor of the will to power. Jaspers stigmatizes this will to power as a will to illusion, and sets it in essential opposition to the will to truth. Nietzsche associates the will to power with his theory that the universe consists in a grand circle of becoming, which is incompatible with any stable order of transcendent being. But these metaphysical overtones derive from an identification of biological categories with the meaning of being as such. Nietzsche has his own unacknowledged vitalistic absolute, although it is a totally immanent one. He himself falls victim to scientism, when he converts the biological view of process into an unconditioned account of the world, and when he states that sovereign becoming is man's substitute for the permanence of being. In the chapter on Darwin, we will briefly consider how Nietzsche draws a metaphysical inference from evolutionary thought.

Jaspers extends his analysis of the overevaluation of science into a study of contemporary tendencies. When the sciences are cut off from any unifying philosophical principle, they lack a guiding idea that can establish order and hierarchy among them. Consequently, each separate science tries to absolutize itself and impose its perspective upon the other sciences. Jaspers singles out anthropology, psychoanalysis, and Marxism as prime examples of scientistic imperialism.[12] The aberrations of racism in Nazi Germany are attributable to the false intermixture of science and philosophy, at the level of biology and anthropology. Unconditioned truth was claimed for the concept of a pure race, running in the face of both the empirical evidence and the essential boundaries of scientific generalization. Similarly, Freud and Marx mistook their own considerable scientific discoveries for total philosophical explanations. Hence they drew an unbalanced picture of man, as being determined ultimately by unconscious impulses or relations of economic production. On a purely scientific basis, there is no principle of integration which can take account of the findings of psychoanalytic and Marxist research, without erecting them into complete descriptions of the ultimate determinants of human existence. Human freedom and the goals of human life are at stake in the discussion about the relations between science and philosophy.

3. *A Philosophical Interpretation of Modern Science*

Jaspers does not believe that a cultural description of our scientific age and an immanent critique of the sciences are sufficient to establish the proper meaning and scope of science. For the sciences themselves are incapable of seizing upon the fundamental significance of their own form of thought. This is a task performable only by philosophy. The latter is sufficiently close to the sciences to be well-informed about their methods and contents, and yet sufficiently independent of them to take a comprehensive view of them.

Unlike Nietzsche, Jaspers does not regard the will to knowledge as a variation of the will to power. Rather, the speculative quest of knowledge is an authentic and original impulse of human nature. Yet it does suppose the validity of the proposition that the world is knowable. This proposition can be taken in two ways: (1) objects in the world are knowable, or (2) the world as a single whole of being is knowable.[13] Jaspers agrees with the first statement, but denies that the second one is true. The perversion of science into a substitute for philosophy is due precisely to a confusion between these two ways of interpreting the knowability of the world. Because the objects in the world are knowable through the scientific method, the conclusion is fallaciously drawn that the truth about the world as such is also available to scientific understanding. From here, it is only a short step to the further assertion that the real is coextensive with the totality of objects in the world and that, therefore, the only philosophical truth open to man is that supplied by the scientific method.

(1) Jaspers construes in a strictly Kantian way the proposition that objects in the world are knowable.[14] Science (*Wissen-schaft*) is concerned only with knowledge (*Wissen, Erkenntnis*) or what is knowable (*wissbar*). "Knowledge" is not an indeterminate general term, covering every relation between the mind and things. Instead, it connotes one definite sort of thought: that in which a polar relation is set up between the subject and the phenomenal object. An object of knowledge is not being simply as such, but is some particular, em-

pirical mode or appearance of being. Hence knowledge cannot extend to the being of things and must remain content with their objective appearances. Furthermore, knowledge always involves a presentation of the object to the subject. Knowing transpires within the context of the subject-object relationship. This dichotomy governs what can be known about the subject, as well as the object. Knowledge embraces the subject only insofar as it is correlated with the object. It is only the mind as an empirical subject or appearance that enters into the field of knowledge. Just as knowledge is limited to the objective appearances of things in the world, so is it limited to the objective appearances of the knowing subject itself. The latter can be held at arm's length from itself, as it were, and can thus become an object of knowledge for itself. But what is known, here as elsewhere, is nothing more than the objective appearance. Knowledge reaches to the object-being but not to being in an unqualified way, whether it be the being of our self or the being of the world.

These general conditions of knowledge apply strictly to scientific investigation. Although every act of empirical consciousness is faced with some sort of object or counterpart, the scientific mind lays down certain standards for reliable knowledge. The scientific interest is to secure the maximum clarity, logical necessity, universality, and communicability in its determinate object.[15] Scientific inquiry is guided by the ideal of rational objectivity, guaranteed by evidence that is universally valid and compelling in an impersonal way. Yet even the rational objectivity of scientific knowledge conforms to the general requirements of objects of knowledge. The categories and methods employed by the sciences to bring the empirical materials to the condition of reliable objects, known with indubitable certitude, can operate only within the sphere of the knowable. Consequently, they yield knowledge only of the appearances or object-being of things. Within this realm, scientific understanding can obtain some necessary and universal truths, along with many probable and statistical statements. Jaspers intends to show, however, that objectivity is not the sole mode of being and that scientific findings cannot, therefore, be taken as exhaustive of reality.

(2) No limits can be assigned for scientific research, within the field of objects in the world. Endless progress can be made in the more precise and comprehensive knowledge of these objects. Yet there is a capital difference between progressively coming to know more about objects in the world and coming to know the world as such. There are no restraints or limits placed upon scientific research at

the intramundane level, but there are essential boundaries which it cannot trespass.[16] Although it is customary to speak about the scientific view of the world, Jaspers denies that science can furnish an image or system of the world as a whole. The latter is what Kant called a regulative idea, stimulating our search after scientific knowledge. Yet because the world as such cannot present itself to our mind in the form of an object, it falls outside the region of the knowable and thus lies beyond scientific inquiry.

If science can know things in the world and laws about the world, but never the total being of the world as such, then the unity of science cannot be realized through a single scientific method and body of doctrine. Jaspers offers several special arguments in favor of his thesis that the positivistic conception of the unity of science is impossible of fulfillment.[17] (a) From the fact that scientific thought is a mode of knowledge, it cannot avoid the bifurcation of subject and object. The cleavage between consciousness and its empirical objects cannot be overcome by means of scientific knowledge, which is unable to embrace the two poles within a higher unity. There is a scientifically unresolvable tension between the private world of the knowing subject and the public world of objects. The empirical knower may himself become an object of knowledge and thus be included within the objective world studied by the scientific method, but this world still retains its otherness from consciousness-as-such. Even the maximum conceivable objective unification fails to bring all the factors in the world to a total unity of knowledge. This is not merely a factual limitation but an essential boundary of all scientific thought.

(b) Jaspers regards scientific knowledge as something more than a pure methodology. Methods can be taken in isolation, but only for purposes of more exact and orderly analysis. At some point, this isolated consideration must give way, and methods must be restored to the concrete setting of the contents and objects of scientific inquiry. Method is not cultivated in and for itself alone, but always for the more adequate exploration of the objective structure and laws of empirical being. But objects are not homogeneous in their mode of being. Jaspers distinguishes four different domains of object-being in the world: matter, life, soul or consciousness, and spirit. Scientific knowledge is intentional, in the sense that it is directed necessarily toward these spheres of objective being, each one of which constitutes an irreducible world of its own. Because of the intentional character of scientific thought and the basic differences among the four objective orders to which it refers, scientific knowledge can never reach perfectly homogeneous unity, either in content or in method.

Furthermore, there is something endless about scientific research into opaque matter and into the richness of the organism and consciousness. Since only the finite can be expressed in an objective concept, the scientific view remains essentially incomplete and open. The progressive nature of scientific research would be violated, if its findings and methodological innovations could be expressed in a rounded-off image of the world. Such images are due to an extra-scientific desire to convert a science into a philosophical explanation.

(c) Because the several realms of objects are mutually irreducible, there must also be internal and irreducible differentiations in the methods fitted to study them. Inorganic matter, the organism, inner consciousness, and the rational spirit call for different scientific approaches. Each science assumes its own perspective on the world and develops its own proportionate method. Although the method proper to one science gives some insight into the structure of another domain of objects, there remains a need for a method specially fitted to examine the latter domain in its characteristic features. The psychiatric method is not rendered superfluous, for instance, by the physiological study of states of the brain which affect our mental states. Instead of following the tradition of Leibniz and the evolutionists in respect to the continuity between the various objective spheres and scientific methods, Jaspers emphasizes the discontinuities and the need for a new factor in moving from one method to the next. Although he recognizes certain generic traits common to all the sciences (the broader meaning of "science"), he points out that actual scientific work requires several specific scientific methods. There is an analogy between the various levels of meaning in the world, but intrinsic methodological adjustments must be made to pass from one to the other.

The pluralism of scientific methods explains why a given scientific explanation can be universally valid and yet relative, rather than absolute. A proposition may be universally valid and correct within the perspective of a certain science, but its truth is limited to this determinate sphere. Hence it is relative to the method and objective standpoint of the science in question. Thus, while the general constructs of mathematical physics determine something about the structure of all material things, they do not yield an exhaustive account of the nature of organic functions. Mathematical physics neither displaces nor assimilates Goethe's report on the world of living colors or

31

immediate sensuous perception. And from his own experience in psychiatry, Jaspers is aware of the need to keep the study of mental disorders free from the "nothing-but" arguments of philosophical scientism, which seeks to explain these disorders solely in terms of constructs drawn from other sciences.

(d) The absolutization of any one scientific standpoint also breaks down in the face of the distinction in kind between the natural sciences and the humanities. This distinction is not abrogated by observing that the methods of the natural sciences apply to man. The fact of their application is undeniable, but equally undeniable is their limited competence in dealing with human nature. Following Dilthey, Weber, and Simmel, Jaspers underlines the differences between explanation and comprehension as approaches in psychology and psychiatry. The explanatory method seeks causal reasons and objective connections, based upon the constant operation of universal laws of cerebral and mental action. The attention of the method of comprehension is focussed upon the genesis of subjective states of mind and connections of meaning, rather than causality. The natural sciences use the explanatory approach, whereas the humane sciences use comprehension. The latter is historically orientated. It calls attention to those meaningful aspects of human development which cannot be stated in objective, universal causal laws. The humane disciplines pay special attention to the unique correlations of meaning and the unrepeatable sequences of events which actually shape individual and cultural growth.

Yet these arguments do not add up to the conclusion that the various sciences are totally discrete and unrelated to each other. It can only be concluded that the sciences are not united through a single method and mode of knowledge, and hence do not yield a total conception of the being of the world. In Jaspers' terminology, they fail to constitute a *system* of world-knowledge, even though they can be organized into a unified *systematic* of knowledge.[18] Whereas a *system* bases the unity of science upon the unity of the world as a given object and upon a single scientific method, a *systematic* appeals to the non-objective idea of the world and a multiplicity of methods in scientific research. The Cartesian ideal of the unity of science is legitimate, as long as it recognizes that, in our world, the drive toward unity needs to be reconciled with the actual multiplicity of scientific methods and determinate spheres of objectivity. The principle of unity for a *systematic* of knowledge is drawn from scientific understanding itself, rather than from its methods and objects. The understanding employes its categories universally and compares the meanings disclosed at various levels of knowability. Although the world as a whole is never forthcoming as an objectively determined appearance, the idea of grasping its total reality provides a ceaseless stimulation to scientific research. An unending conflict exists between the understanding's demand for total unity of explanation and the pluralizing effect of actual research methods and findings. From this fruitful tension springs not only the drive toward further scientific inquiry but also the desire to gain a fuller acquaintance with the world's reality than the sciences can supply.

There are two false routes by which the human mind seeks to fulfill the need for a deeper grasp on being. One is the way of scientism, which refuses to recognize the essential boundaries of scientific thought. The other is an undisciplined appeal to sheer feeling and purported irrational sources of insight. Jaspers is just as strenuously opposed to the latter alternative as to the former. He grants that there are irrational, passional, and idiosyncratic aspects of empirical being, which the sciences overlook and which are added proof of the impossibility of a complete scientific system of the world. But he denies that these aspects must be approached philosophically by means that are also irrational or purely sentimental. Reason is not only the heart of scientific understanding but also the proper medium of all philosophical insight. Philosophy moves beyond the sciences, but it does not abandon reason (at least in its Kantian meanings) as its principle of discovery.

4. *The Relation between Science and Philosophy*

Scientism and irrationalism bear witness that the human mind seeks to apprehend more about being than the sciences can provide. Truth is wider than the truth about objective events. To know objects is not the same as, and is something less than, to grasp being. But from Jaspers' critique of science, it is evident that our grasp on being cannot be an instance of knowledge, since the latter is confined to the region of objects. We cannot know being as such, even though we may be able to use reason to apprehend it in some non-objective and non-knowing way. Jaspers must now present some evidence to bear out his contention that being is wider than object-being and that truth embraces something more than scientific knowledge.

To do this, he returns once more to a salient point in the previous analysis of knowledge: the dualism between subject and object. The two members of this polarity are not placed indifferently upon the same plane. Descartes' mistake was precisely to think that the self which is correlated with the material thing and with the requirements of scientific objectivity is the total self. This is the source of the naturalistic fallacy, which argues from the fact that man is one object along with others in the world to the unwarranted conclusion that he is nothing else than such an object. But human reality displays itself as a ground of authentic existence and freedom, as well as an instance of empirical being or objective appearance. Free, existential decision does not lie within the range of objective universality, necessity, and certainty. It opens up a vein of being that is determined through the unique and free activity of the individual, who is confronted with moral conflict and uncertainty. Here is a dimension of reality that is present in the world, and yet is something other than the objective appearances of the world.

We have some experience of the inner reality of freedom and human existence. Jaspers refers to this experience as an awareness of the being which man is. Whereas science provides *knowledge* of objects in the world, philosophy rests on an *awareness* of the being of man and the being of the world as a whole.[19] Since this awareness is a form of non-objective and non-knowing thought, it is not subject to the split between the objective and subjective factors in knowledge. Philosophical awareness synthesizes both factors within a single whole of being. We also recognize that man's freedom is not satisfied by a purely immanent union with the being of the world. It seeks to transcend the world and even the human self, in its search after the unconditioned being or the One. Human existence is oriented not only toward immanent contacts with being but also toward transcendence. Thus, we gradually become aware of being as the encompassing. Philosophical thought is a non-knowing awareness of the encompassing reality, considered as the being of the world, the being of man's inner activity, and the being of transcendence or God.

Since scientific thought remains wholly objective and finite, it cannot attain to the encompassing whole of being. This accounts for the distinction in kind between science and philosophy, a distinction which scientific progress is incapable of removing or attenuating. Philosophy draws its vital strength and truth from inner awareness rather than from any sort of knowledge. Hence philosophy has an origin that is intrinsically independent of science. For philosophy to return to its origins does not mean to return to scientific thinking as its source. The wellsprings of philosophizing lie deep within the individual man, insofar as he is a free existent, straining toward transcendence.

Scientific and philosophic progress do not have the same import.[20] The former entails a displacement of previous views, in favor of ever more adequate explanations, whereas the latter leads to a renewal of the continuous tradition of perennial philosophy. Gabriel Marcel expresses the difference as that between solving a problem and contemplating a mystery, and Jaspers would accept this as an apt contrast. There is no question about the improvement of modern physics over its Greek antecedents, which are now studied merely in the spirit of curiosity and historical exactness. But the Greek philosophers are still our masters, and we are privileged to enter into a living dialogue with them and share in their abiding wisdom. Philosophical inquiry does not move from point to point, but tries deliberately to capture the meaning of the source of freedom within us and the tendency of that freedom toward transcendence. Every man, in every age, is capable of becoming aware of the encompassing and thus of exploring the meaning of the origin of being within us and beyond us, rather than moving from one scientific construct to another.

Once having vindicated the essential independence of philosophy, Jaspers is then required to harmonize it with his previous view concerning the practical character of philosophizing. Since the latter is a practical deed, it is indissolubly bound up with concrete historical situations. Granted that our historical era is dominated by the sciences and their practical consequences in technology, philosophy cannot now be dissociated from these dominant factors. Although he does not express himself with all desirable clarity on this issue, Jaspers is advancing a dual affirmation. In its abiding origin, philosophy is independent of science; nevertheless, in our historical situation, philosophy is closely connected with the sciences and even uses them as instruments of its own thought. There is no contradiction in maintaining both that philosophy has an autonomous origin within man's existence, and that it requires science today as its indispensable tool and condition of development. Jaspers complicates the discussion sometimes, however, by stating that philosophy *is* science.[21] The precise sense in which this proposition is meant, must first be clarified, before considering both the dependence and the independence of philosophy in respect to science.

As we have already established, philosophy can rightly be called "scientific," in the broader usage of that term, without confusing philosophy with any of the sciences. Given Jaspers' account of the nature of scientific thought, however, it is now possible to find an even more intimate connection between philosophy and science. Even when "science" is taken in the restricted sense of the scientific methods and objects of knowledge, philosophy can be said to be present in scientific thinking. The scientist, as a human individual, shares in the human spirit and reason. Hence his investigations bear definite traces of the influence of spirit: they seek not only to reach the scientific goal of universal and cogent knowledge but also to convey something more. This additional purpose is to obtain a total grasp upon being, and only philosophy can satisfy this tendency. Although the search for the One and for the totality of being is a properly philosophical impulse, it finds expression in the work of the scientist and thus lends plausibility to the claims of scientism. Because of the presence of a philosophical aim, the sciences respond to the rational idea of the world as a whole and lend themselves to exploitation by scientistic minds. Science cannot fully clarify its own significance, because part of its import is to be an outlet for the philosophical quest itself.

Philosophy and science are distinct but indispensable for each other, especially within our historical era.[22] The greatest service rendered by philosophy to science is a clarification of the latter's structure, its limitations, and its distinction from the philosophical enterprise. Nothing is thereby contributed by philosophy of science to the particular content of the sciences or to the correctness of scientific propositions. But science is enabled to carry on the work of self-criticism, and is saved from making futile inquiries into problems beyond its competence. With philosophy's help, science can restrain the tendency toward absolutizing scientific knowledge and giving the hegemony to some one scientific approach. Jaspers criticizes the view that science is *wertfrei* or indifferent to values. It is such, indeed, in the sense that it cannot set the ultimate goals of moral life and cannot supply the norms for moral obligation. Still, science is not *wertlos* or completely devoid of valuational factors. For, scientific work is sustained by the will to gain knowledge for its own sake. And in a negative way, its progress depends upon a resolute refusal to follow the path of a scientistic absolutization of knowledge. In both respects, philosophy cooperates by strengthening the will of the scientist, so that he may pursue speculative knowledge and avoid scientistic superstition.

Nevertheless, the contribution of philosophy is not wholly disinterested. For, philosophy itself stands to profit by the purification of the

36

scientific attitude. There is a definite sense in which science is the condition and tool of philosophizing, even though the source of philosophizing is autonomous. To appreciate the reciprocal benefit conferred by science upon philosophy, however, something further must be said about the philosophical search after transcendence and the meaning of being as a whole. Although this search characterizes philosophical thought, Jaspers holds that it can never wholly succeed in its purpose. When metaphysics tries to express the meaning of transcendence and the encompassing in the form of thought, it inevitably becomes entangled in antinomies. For, it becomes confronted with the decisive difference between being an existing center of freedom and being ordained toward transcendence, on the one hand, and expressing these conditions in human thought and objective categories, on the other. The realities of existence, freedom, and transcendence are of a non-objective nature, whereas every attempt to give expression, in thought, to our experience of these modes of being must submit to the conditions of objectivity. Indeed, the various modes of the encompassing do not seem to be real, as far as the human mind is concerned, unless they are related to the concrete milieu of empirical being or the world of objective appearances.

Hence philosophical transcendence must be accomplished within the world of objective, empirical being rather than by a withdrawal from it. If the reference to empirical being must be retained in our philosophizing, then the interests of philosophy are promoted by the advance of scientific knowledge of the objective world. This accounts for the close alliance between philosophy and science. Philosophical thought cannot avoid using the categories of objective understanding, so that it may communicate philosophical truth in a clear, universal and rational way. Hence the conditions of objectivity are fundamentally insurmountable for philosophy, which must avail itself of the most highly developed forms of the scientific categories and methods.

Jaspers has a favorite formula for bringing out the mutual distinction and dependence of philosophy and science.[23] Although scientific knowledge is universally valid, it is also relative to some determinate sphere of objectivity; conversely, philosophical awareness is absolute in its origin but relative in its objective expression in thought. Scientific knowledge is not absolute, since it does not convey the total meaning of being and does not fill our lives with an unconditional value, for which we should be ready to die. On the other hand, philosophical awareness is not universally valid and coercive knowledge, since it does not belong intrinsically to the sphere of objective knowledge. Whereas scientific truths can be demonstrated and used as principles of deduction, philosophical truths can only be elucidated or evoked in consciousness. The reality of the encompassing cannot be demonstrated or deduced from something else, since it signifies the origins of being and hence has nothing prior to it. Moreover, the reality of the encompassing cannot be employed as a premise from which any necessary deductions can be made: it provides no blueprint for the conduct of our lives. Freedom, uncertainty, and risk remain the indelible marks of philosophizing.

Given this contrast between coercive, objective, non-absolute, scientific knowledge and free, non-objective, absolute, philosophical reflection, it follows that the philosophical use of scientific categories cannot consist in a direct and positive expression of philosophical truths through that medium. Jaspers' paradoxical view of metaphysics now comes into play, in order to determine the ultimate sense in which science benefits philosophy.[24] As scientific knowledge becomes more perfect, we can see more clearly that the systematic of the sciences cannot actually attain to a complete system of knowledge. This failure of the sciences to achieve a total system of the being of the world provides philosophy with a most significant clue, since it serves as a warning against any identification between object-being and being as such. Out of his experience of the essential boundaries of scientific thought, the philosopher is led to cultivate a form of unknowing or non-knowledge: the inner awareness of being or the encompassing.

Simultaneously, he recognizes the fate to which he must submit. He cannot express his philosophical awareness of being, apart from the objective conditions of thought. Philosophizing is an objectification of a non-objectifiable reality—this is the paradoxical situation of the philosopher. He must use objectifying thought and knowledge, in order to express that which surpasses all objectivity and knowledge: human existence, transcendence, and freedom. Hence he cannot treat the objects in the world and the systematic of the sciences as direct means of expressing his awareness. From the philosophical viewpoint, the world and its objects are so many signs and ciphers, which are not the encompassing and yet which are our only context and instruments for thinking the encompassing as real being, and for communicating our insight in a rational way.

In sum, science and philosophy are engaged in a friendly struggle between different but interwoven ways of thinking. Their conflict is not that between enemies but between brethren, who are engaged in an edifying contest to uncover the truth. Philosophy assists science to remain loyal to the truth about objects known in the world; science helps philosophy to concentrate upon the truth of being and the deliverances of our awareness. The philosopher maintains a threefold freedom, in respect to science.[25] He must have freedom for the unrestricted study of scientific methods and findings. He must also secure his freedom from scientism and every plan to substitute an absolutized brand of scientific knowledge for philosophy. And above all, the philosopher has to maintain his freedom to contemplate the being of the world, of free human existence, and of transcendence. Although he can never bring his awareness of these modes of being to perfect conceptual formulation, he can give it his complete, absolute belief and can freely shape his life in response to its demands.

5. A Comparative Appraisal

One way of evaluating Jaspers' position is to compare it, on a few scores, with the views of American naturalism and theistic realism. Jaspers' own thought can profit by such a comparison with other doctrines; it can also make valuable contributions of its own to the common themes of discussion. Perhaps an intensive study of Jaspers will help to break down barriers and initiate a much-needed dialogue between Kantianism, naturalism, and realism.

Jaspers and the naturalists give different descriptions of scientific knowledge. Jaspers' account fits in well with Newtonian physics and the Kantian philosophy of science. But it does not pay sufficient attention to other theories of science, based upon more recent developments in physics. Thus, whereas Jaspers highlights the ideal of cogent, certain, and universally valid propositions, the naturalists stress the importance of probability and the use of statistical averages. Jaspers regards the latter as a failure to attain the scientific standard of knowledge, whereas the naturalists tend to revise the standard account itself in the light of what can actually be attained by the human mind in this field. Again, Jaspers defends the basically speculative character of scientific knowledge, even though he grants that its practical consequences in technology have shaped the world we live in. From a naturalistic standpoint, however, practice is something more than a consequence of scientific knowledge. The very meaning of the scientific concept or theory includes the practical directions and operations to which the concept leads the investigator. Mutual benefit would result if Jaspers paid more attention to the characteristic procedures of post-classical physics, and if the naturalists agreed to reconsider the question of the relation between speculation and control.

Naturalism does not distinguish as sharply between science and philosophy as does Jaspers.[26] This is in line with the Hegelian parentage of naturalistic thought, since Hegel claimed to overcome the Kantian distinction between science and philosophy, knowledge and faith or interior awareness. Hegel achieved this unification, however, only by universalizing his conception of a single scientific method. Although the naturalists take an empirical and non-dialectical view of scientific thinking, they do retain the Hegelian thesis of a single scientific method. Hence a head-on clash between Jaspers and the naturalists over this issue is unavoidable. Even when the naturalists employ Comte's distinction between the one method and the several techniques or procedures of science, they fall far short of Jaspers' sharp differentiation of methods among the sciences. His vision is directed toward the concretely different ways in which chemists, psychiatrists, and sociologists deal with the same empirical materials, whereas the naturalists look to a general logic of the sciences for confirmation of their monism of method.

Jaspers presents a definite challenge to the naturalistic position, since he argues that the distinction between a broad, general meaning for scientific method and the more restricted techniques is no warrant for concluding to the singleness of the scientific method. He believes that the differentiations required by research in the various sciences affect scientific method itself in an intrinsic way, and cannot be relegated to the region of subordinate techniques and procedures. The questions he raises for naturalism are: whether there is a sufficiently definite and significant content in the broad meaning of scientific method, and whether the procedures of the several sciences involve intrinsic differentiation of method itself.

Jaspers, in turn, could profit by a serious consideration of the naturalistic program of combining a monism of method with an anti-reductionism of content. He has not made this study, because of his definition of naturalism as the identification of being with the object-being studied by the sciences—an identification entailing a most radical sort of reductionism. There is a conflict here between opposing views of what actually constitutes a reductionist standpoint. Naturalism claims that reductionism is successfully avoided as long as one admits the emergence of new values and the fuller realizations of natural traits, without resolving these emergents entirely into their genetic conditions and causes. But Jaspers lays down more stringent requirements for an anti-reductionist philosophy. It is one that refrains both from equating the real with the field of scientific objects and from holding a total evolutionary development of life, consciousness, and spirit from matter.

Naturalism would be unable to meet these conditions of anti-reductionism. For, it is suspicious of any claim that a zone of reality exists which is not accessible (at least in principle) to scientific inquiry, and which can be approached only in some interior and non-objective way. If the real is that which is accessible in principle to the scientific method, then the distinction between being and scientific object-being is broken down. Furthermore, naturalism regards mind as an evolutionary emergent from matter. It attempts to avoid reductionism on this score, by castigating vulgar materialism in a very severe way. On the positive side, however, naturalism does little more than endow matter with a vague dynamism for bringing forth whatever has to be brought forth. It also points to the progress already made in giving a scientific description of religious, esthetic, and moral states. Jaspers' counter-argument is that successful description in terms of another science does not establish causal derivation of the reality under description from the purely material mode of being.

Another area for mutual exploration centers around the problem of values. Naturalists have done considerable work toward establishing a positive relationship between scientific inquiry and the realm of values. They have attempted to reduce normative to factual statements, as well as to furnish a purely naturalistic account of moral obligation. Jaspers seems to be content with repeating the Kantian dichotomy between what is and what ought to be, since this accords neatly with his distinction between scientific objects and modes of being that are grasped through philosophical awareness. In this respect, naturalism comes closer to the approach of theistic realism to the basis of moral obligation, since both philosophies recognize the bearing of factual knowledge on moral decision. There is pressing need for a synthesis between the naturalistic emphasis upon the reference of moral choice to empirical situations, subject to scientific ascertainment, and Jaspers' equally valuable defense of the free individual as the focal center of actual moral life.

Contemporary realists will find Jaspers' distinction between science and philosophy quite instructive. For one thing, there is a signifiant resemblance between Jaspers' position and Jacques Maritain's distinction between the empiriological and the ontological analysis of nature.[27] For both thinkers, the crucial issue is whether or not the discipline is formally directed toward a grasp of being. Maritain maintains that the empiriological sciences deal with sensible being, but only insofar as it is observable and measurable; Jaspers allows that the sciences attain to object-being but refuses them any access to being as such and as a whole. Maritain's conception of empiriological science is more operational and less speculative than Jaspers' view of scientific knowledge. Furthermore, Maritain regards the ontological approach to the world, self, and God as capable of yielding genuine knowledge, not merely experiential awareness and symbolic reference. But Jaspers forces us to consider whether Maritain's proposed contrast between the empiriological and the ontological studies of nature can be rigorously established, apart from the Kantian distinction between appearances and the thing-in-itself. Maritain's contrast is too sharply stated to do justice to the realistic aspect of modern science.

There are two strains of thought discernible in Jaspers' speculations on this problem. One is the orthodox Kantian correlation between knowledge and phenomenal objects. But there is also a tendency to give a more metaphysical interpretation of the object of knowledge. Jaspers refers to the latter both as an appearance and as a mode of being. Yet, granted that what we know in the world is a determinate mode of being and not being as such or in its fullness, he does not show any evident need to equate determinateness or particularity with phenomenality. From the fact that our initial knowledge is particularized, it does not follow that it must also be phenomenal and in no way manifestive of being. A determinate mode of being is still a mode of being and gives knowledge of being under some particular aspect, and not merely knowledge of appearance. Such knowledge is not formally metaphysical, but it can provide a basis for the metaphysical judgment that separates being-as-such from any of its particular, sensible modes. Such knowledge is also not fully exhaustive of the reality of the actual thing, which contains unsounded depths that are not conveyed by our concept of the object or even by our existential judgment about it. Metaphysics is grounded, however, not in a pretended comprehensive insight into reality as a whole but in the human mind's ability to recognize that the existent thing is indeed an instance of being.

Metaphysical realism can make constructive use of several features in Jaspers' notion of metaphysics. Thus, his remark about the indissoluble bond between metaphysical thinking and the context of empirical being need not issue in a doctrine of paradoxical assertions about the encompassing. It can serve as a realistic reminder that metaphysics never ceases to be a human discipline, and hence never ceases to bear a vital reference to our experience of sensible things in the world. This is reinforced by Jaspers' own observation that metaphysical transcendence does not abandon the world but occurs within the world. For Jaspers himself, this reference of metaphysical speculation to the world of objects leads to endless antinomies, since he phenomenalizes the object of knowledge. Yet, if the being of existent things is firmly retained, then the split between science and philosophy, knowledge and awareness, can be healed. Our grasp on being is not an instance of non-knowledge but an instance of knowledge, in which we recognize the act of being which is exercised by the sensible thing and also the presence of this act in nonsensible modes of being. Thus the levels of analogical meaning for human knowledge extend farther than Jaspers' phenomenalism allows him to admit. They include not only our particular sense experiences and the scientific approach to things in the world but also our basic judgments on the meaning of being and the causal relations opened out by a study of experienced things in their condition as existent composite beings.

Jaspers thinks that this analogical treatment of knowledge labors under two defects.[28] First, it reduces everything which the human mind can grasp to the level of the object-form of being, and hence involves a total objectification of knowledge and a reification of being. Second, it places Jaspers, the naturalists, and the realists on the same footing, implying that each can learn something from the others because of their similar nature.

But the first objection misses the point of the suggestion, which is not to reduce knowable reality to the condition of an object, but rather to consider both experienced and inferred realities precisely as existent beings. Whether the existent being in question is to be regarded as a sensible thing or as a personal subject is left for an examination of the particular evidence we have concerning this being. Our knowledge can then be left open to analogical specification in the light of how the beings manifest themselves to us. And by distinguishing "object" in the broad sense of that which is grasped by the human intellect from the narrower meaning of "object," as that which is treated as a scientific construct, we can remove the danger of equating being with the scientifically specified object.

As for the second objection, the theme of this book is that existentialism, naturalism, and theistic realism are different contemporary pathways in philosophy. Yet there is a definite sense in which they are indeed on the same footing. For, they have to submit to the common human condition of drawing their evidence from what we can experience about man and the natural world, as well as what we can infer on the basis of these deliverances. This does provide some common ground for discussion and, I hope, for mutual learning and profit. From such a situation, however, it does not follow that these three philosophies are aspects of one homogeneous doctrine, but only that they are obliged to refer back to some common human experience as their controlling check. For this reason, we need not despair over the fact of conflicting interpretations but can work patiently at governing our own judgments and inferences by this human basis.

CHAPTER 3

THE RELIGIOUS THEME
IN EXISTENTIALISM

ALTHOUGH we rightly regard existentialism as a contemporary philosophy, it is one which has already shown its durability. As a fairly well defined tendency in thought, it has been with us now for a full generation and some of its leaders have been publishing their views for over forty years. The fact of its continued vitality has recently furnished Professor James Feibleman with material for reflection on the general question of the survival value of philosophies.[1] The examples which he cites are existentialism, Marxism, and Thomism, all of which have displayed the quality of continuing to be intellectually attractive under quite different historical circumstances. Feibleman suggests that these philosophies have the capacity for adapting to new cultural situations and showing their relevance to the problems which become urgent under different historical conditions. This is a descriptive account, and it seems to fit the actual cases under consideration. However, the fact that a philosophy can remain humanly important under varying conditions does not mean that its significance can be reduced to a clever method of cultural adaptation. A cultural description of how a philosophy uses the adaptive functions is informative, but it does not settle anything about the validity of the positions argued in that philosophy. These positions and the methods of arriving at them must still be weighed in the light of the evidence adduced in their support.

As far as the English-speaking world is concerned, existentialism is still in the process of being domiciled and related with more familiar ways of thought. Most of the major sources are now available in translation, and there are numerous commentaries explaining their significance. A good deal of the effort at understanding existentialism

45

has been devoted to comparative studies showing its relationship with trends in other fields.[2] Thus we find Rudolf Allers and Rollo May discussing an existential psychiatry, Hazel Barnes probing into the literary forms and attitudes found in existential writings, Paul Tillich using existential categories to express theological doctrines, and *The Chicago Review* devoting an entire issue to what can only be described as a Zen existentialism. These comparative approaches fix our attention upon aspects of existentialism, but it remains something distinct. It is a philosophy, and only as such can it be fundamentally understood and appraised.

1. *The Thematizing of Religion*

One distinguishing mark of existentialism is the stress which it places upon the problem of religion. To acknowledge the importance of religion in human life is a commonplace, but not so common today is the view that it holds a prominent place among the problems to be treated in philosophy. The existentialists do not regard religion as a subordinate issue to be dealt with in a relatively minor way or to be closed off by itself in a special philosophy of religion. Instead, they treat it as one of the major questions falling within the philosopher's responsibility, and maintain that his estimate of it affects quite intimately the bases of his doctrine. Among the existentialists, then, the significance of religion becomes formally thematized and figures as one of the major aims in philosophical work. For quite a while, this emphasis on a philosophical appraisal of religion served as an obstacle against the serious examination of existentialism by American and British thinkers, who tended to classify religious statements as emotive expressions peripheral to the main concerns of philosophy. But the weakening of Ayer's verifiability principle, coupled with the spread of phenomenology and of analytic interest in the language of religion, has brought about a more favorable climate for trying to understand the thematizing of religion by the existentialists.

For grasping why it has become philosophically central, we must notice something about the historical background of existentialism and about its method of investigation.[3] Its remote historical roots lie in Kant and Hegel, both of whom held that a philosophical system is incomplete and fails to pass the test of adequacy until it sets forth the nature of the religious act and its relation with our other human acts. Indeed, within the Hegelian universe one does not apprehend the meaning of philosophy itself apart from a comparison with religion, or reach the climax of the dialectic except by submitting the religious outlook to philosophical analysis. And if we can regard Kierkegaard and Nietzsche as constituting the more proximate setting for existentialism, then the concentration of interest upon the question of religion is seen to be unavoidable. Athough the Danish thinker mistrusted anything that smacked of a system of pure thought, he did recognize some general ways of existence and did make his analysis of the modes of existence culminate with the religious sphere, both natural and supernatural. As for Nietzsche, his basic function as a critical moralist and revaluator was discharged largely through his description of prevailing religious attitudes and his substitution of new pieties for old. Although Kierkegaard and Nietzsche disagreed sharply about the ultimate meaning and worth of religious existence, they concurred in treating an analysis thereof as a prime intellectual duty.

Given this heritage, the existentialists tended from the outset to keep the inquiry into religious existence close to the core of their philosophizing. Another factor in the formation of at least some existentialists was phenomenology, and here the religious orientation of philosophy was not so directly assured. Husserl himself was almost ascetic in his abstention from the topics of religion and God. Although he made some remarks about them, he remained dissatisfied with the phenomenological treatment of them within the context of intentionality. Other phenomenologists, notably Scheler, felt no reluctance about applying their phenomenological method in detail to the religious sphere, even though their results did not always respect the transcendence of God. Scheler's march toward pantheism will be reserved for subsequent analysis. There has continued to be some difference of opinion among phenomenologists about the precise way of studying religion and the type of results that may be expected. But the efforts being made to achieve a phenomenology of religion have influenced the existentialists in their work in this area.

One feature in the method commonly used by existentialists has fostered their investigation of the significance of religion. The categories or tools of analysis which they use are not drawn primarily from the environing world but from human reality in its historical aspects. When men are viewed in a concrete and historical way, their concern about religion is recognized to be a constant trait. Hence there is a primary need to clarify the religious relationship, if one is to obtain an adequate basis in man for interpreting the human and other modes of being. This is reinforced by the existentialist point of departure in the historical situation of Western man, with his long tradition of Judaeo-Christian religious teachings and attitudes. The existentialists do not begin by requiring acceptance of that tradition as true, but they do take their start here in the sense of finding their first descriptive materials in men who have historical religious bonds with the God of theism and Christian revelation. Perhaps it is for this reason that, in the main, the existentialists do not accept the conventional meaning of a philosophy of religion as a search for a religious minimum common to all peoples. Recognizing the religious diversities in East and West, most existentialist treat of religion in terms of its actual maximum complexity rather than of an abstract common denominator.

Whereas all the existentialists accept the thematization of religion, they maintain their independent ways of developing the issue. In examining the respective positions of three leading existentialist philosophers, it will be useful for us to bear in mind an epigraph or brief motto characterizing the religious approach of each one. Sartre's treatment embodies this rule: "Keep looking for the bad faith." In Heidegger's case, our characterization is: "Do not profane that sacred grove." Our motto for Marcel is this: "Remain faithful amid your inquietude."

No man's philosophy can be summed up with justice in a mere tag, but it may serve to focus for us his special view of the philosophical import of religion. In each instance, our guiding sentence is expressed in the imperative mood. The existentialists provide a theoretical basis for their evaluations of the religious relationship, but they do so with some practical aim in view. In regard to religion as well as every other topic, they are both metaphysicians and moralists in their approach. Their study of religion is not purely speculative, but is intended to shape our meanings and existential attitudes and thus also to have some effect on conduct and society. For the same reason, our epigraphs are deliberately metaphorical, in order to convey the existentialists' intent of bringing their analyses of religion into some concrete form of meaning and communication. These analyses can evoke in us an image of how the human inquirer should relate himself to the religious sphere, at least to the extent that he permits his life to be shaped by his philosophical findings. Thus the claims of commitment as well as description are met by the existentialist conceptions of the religious structures in existence.

2. *Sartre: Keep Looking for the Bad Faith*

Jean-Paul Sartre locates his religious position in function of three historical points of reference: Hegel, Kierkegaard, and Marx.[4] He holds that Hegel has constructed the most complete system of knowledge or totalization of philosophy and has defended the actuality of the objective, social modes of being. However, Hegel does not recognize that there is something irreducible and primary about human reality and its lived experience. For this latter insight, we must turn to Kierkegaard as the defender of the specificity of human existence. The human individual is not just another step within the dialectic but makes a founding contribution to the whole process of interpretation. Beyond this point, however, Sartre refuses to agree with the Kierkegaardian description of human reality. He regards that description as too interiorized, too much bound down to the internal states of the individual and, in this sense, vulnerable to Hegel's criticism of empty subjectivity.

Two major questions arise for Sartre out of this schematic comparison. What makes Kierkegaard's treatment of man unsatisfactory, and what basis is historically available for combining the valuable aspects of both Kierkegaard and Hegel? The answer to the first question is that the Danish thinker is seeking to give a religious interpretation of human existence within the context of the Christian faith. Hence he detaches the human existent from both the system of knowledge and the network of social relations, as a necessary condition for directing that existent toward the transcendent God. In Sartre's interpretation, Kierkegaard makes the human individual totally opaque and unknowable, beyond all rational analysis, and detached from all social activities and institutions. The individual is thus emptied of all intelligible content and social responsibility in order to be related solely to God and to be preoccupied solely with his subjective states of faith, despair, and dread. This is the pattern of religious subjectivism which Sartre then generalizes for every effort to bring out the religious significance of human existence.

When the objection is registered that, in fact, religious people are usually concerned about the social order and develop a philosophy of social responsibility, Sartre replies that what they cultivate is a form of religious objectivism proportioned to and springing from their subjectivism. That is, once the religious mind thinks it has arrived at God, it then invokes the sanction of the divine will for its own social plans and its moral precepts. It pretends that the laws of individual and social morality are simply there, in the objective way of things confronting man but not derived from his consciousness. Just as the religious man has to interiorize himself too much in order to maintain the attitude of transcendence, so must he exteriorize himself too much in order to maintain the given social framework and its rules.

Sartre characterizes both these phases of the religious outlook as instances of bad faith. For him, they represent the ways in which the religious mind hides the truth about man from itself, refuses to face up to the truth about human reality and its destiny. The import of the maxim we have assigned to Sartre now becomes clear. He is obliged by his philosophy to take a pathologist's attitude toward religious existence. The assumption in principle is that there must be an element of bad faith underlying every religious affirmation and program, every attempt to attract men toward the transcendent God and to order personal and social conduct by a moral law having a divine sanction. The religious person may be sincere or have faith in his position, but the Sartrean analyst is bound to expose a central refusal to accept rigorous standards of evidence.[5] If it is not discovered at the first examination, then the criticism has to be renewed under some other form with the aim of showing that religious conviction rests on a rejection of lucidity concerning the real condition of man. Sartre will be satisfied with no verdict except guilty when the case concerns the presence of bad faith as the constitutive principle shaping the religious way of existing.

Clearly enough, this criticism hinges upon what Sartre regards as the unblinking truth about man and hence upon his answer to the second major question above, concerning the way of salvaging the sound points in Hegel and Kierkegaard. His answer involves the relationship between Marxism and Sartre's own brand of existentialism. Although he is no slavish follower of either the philosophical line or the political policy of Soviet Russia, he does hail Marxism as the unsurpassable philosophy which best totalizes the demands of knowledge and reality, thought and work. On today's horizon, it furnishes the only possible anthropology or doctrine on the structure and historical reality of man: historical materialism is the sole valid way of viewing the historical process. Sartre repudiates the other existentialists as being mere ideologists of existence, since they seek to develop concrete human values outside of the Marxist context. He describes his own position as developing at the edge of Marxism and as still maintaining a provisional and marginal distinction from the main body of Marxist thought.[6] It remains distinct until the Marxist movement recognizes the need for grounding its anthropology and historical views upon the theory of human reality which Sartre has been elaborating. His theory is intended as the means whereby historical materialism can achieve reflective comprehension about the human project animating all of our historical developments, alienations, and social revolutions. Sartre wants to found Marxism not upon Engels' supposedly objective dialectic in nature but upon the thoroughly human dialectic of man at work in nature.

Sartre calls his own standpoint a monism of materiality, but he is using the words "monism" and "materiality" in a peculiar sense.[7] It is monistic in that it recognizes as real only the active whole constituted by human consciousness and matter, or human enterprise and the material world. This is a type of monism which admits of differentiation within the complexus of man-in-nature, but does not allow the reality of God as transcending this totality. Again, Sartre takes materiality as his foundation, not in the sense of excluding the distinctive activity of human work or praxis, but as encompassing our consciousness and practice entirely within the same natural field of man in his world. This range of reality is humanistic enough to give man a privileged status (at least from our own standpoint) as the questioning, negating, projecting principle at the heart of the matter. It is even broad enough to view man as constantly seeking to transcend himself in the direction of human society and God. But it stops short of allowing the actual being of the transcendent God and the existential value of a religious bond with Him. Understood in this carefully qualified way, Sartre's monism of materiality has a definite kinship with American naturalism concerning metaphysical and religious issues.

Because Sartre depends uncritically upon Feuerbach and Marx for the principle of limiting the real to the active whole of man-working-in-nature, his remarks on God and religion have a somewhat fantastic quality about them. Within his system, the only valid significance for the term "God" is that of designating the basic human project of identifying reflection and matter, history and nature. Since the merger of these components cannot be achieved without collapsing the structure of reality, at least as described by Marx and Sartre, the latter judges that our religious tendency is self-destroying and that man himself is a futile passion, in so far as he continues to strive after transcendence and God.[8] Instead of making a direct inspection of

51

the man of religion, Sartre will approach him only through the prism of his theory about materiality and consciousness. Whether he is discussing worship of the pagan gods, the good Lord of Job and Christian tradition, or the contemporary efforts to achieve sanctity, the outcome of his analysis is predictably the same. His existentialism is pre-set against weighing on their own merit the ways in which the religious commitment has actually shaped our existence.

Sartre sums up his case against religious theism in these words:

Nothing happens to man and objects except in their material being and by the materiality of Being. But man is precisely that material reality by which matter receives its human functions. . . . Every philosophy which subordinates the human to the Other-than-man, be it an existentialist or a Marxist idealism, has ill will toward man as its basis and consequence. History has proved it in both cases. We must choose: man is first of all himself or first of all Other-than-himself. And if we choose the latter doctrine, then we are quite simply the victim and accomplice of real alienation.[9]

Three brief comments can be made on this text. First, there is a descriptive and metaphysically neutral sense in which the materiality of man and his endowing of the material world with human significance must be accepted. But such acceptance does not settle anything about whether the scope of reality must thereafter be restricted to this active relationship of man and his world. In the second place, cultural history renders no clear verdict about the inhumanity of subordinating the human to something other than man, unless we take the subordination in a univocal way to signify a dialectical estrangement of man from his own reality. Such a subordination is a matter of definition within dialectical idealism and materialism, but it is not the kind of subordination actually involved in religious worship within the context of a personal theism. The distinction remains between our relation with a dialectically specified Other-than-man and with the personal God of theistic religion.

Finally, the religious interpretation of existence does not rest upon holding that, first of all, man either is himself or is the dialectically qualified Other-than-himself. What man *is* first of all can be stated in terms of his personal presence and activity in the natural world. As we progressively widen the meaning of our relationships, we become aware of the grounds for acknowledging the transcendent and personal being of God. Our religious response to God does not wipe out our own active presence in nature, but it does bring out explicitly this other relationship of a personal sort. Growth in the religious significance and practical aims of our existence strengthens our hold upon our personal being rather than breaks it through self-estrangement.

3. *Heidegger: Do Not Profane That Sacred Grove*

Martin Heidegger's philosophy is often viewed as a massive attempt to secularize Christian dogma and transfer it to the purely human and mundane plane. Similarities are noted between the doctrine on the Fall and expulsion of man from paradise and Heidegger's remarks on the projecting of man into the world. A parallel is suspected between the Christian opposition of the worldly man and the man of grace and the Heideggerian opposition of the inauthentic and authentic modes of being. Heidegger's views on conscience, our temporal and historical existence, and our orientation toward death, contain some significant theological overtones locating them well within the sphere of Christian influence.

This comparison is helpful for gaining an orientation on his thought and for correcting the opinion that Heidegger represents an unlikely throwback to the purely pre-socratic mentality in philosophy. It is difficult to conceive that his thought would have taken the precise shape it did in fact take, were he not doing his reflection upon materials affected by the tradition of Christian speculation in theology and philosophy.[10] Heidegger himself acknowledges this cultural influence upon his mind, but he also maintains that it is not decisive for the ultimate shaping of his philosophical judgments. Whatever the cultural and psychological origin of the concepts employed in his analysis, he regulates their use by his basic teaching on being and thinking. Consequently, he arrives at a distinctive position concerning the relation of God and religion to philosophy, a position which cannot simply be derived by manipulating the materials received from the centuries of Christian speculation.

Heidegger vigorously repudiated an early attempt made by Sartre to establish a direct filiation between their philosophies.[11] It is significant, however, that the German thinker rejected the atheistic variety of existentialism in such a way that he did not at the same time reinstate either theism or the theory of religion as topics within his own philosophy. It cannot rightly be called an atheistic view of existence, not because it provides a constructive theory about God but rather because it removes from the province of philosophy every argument for and against the being and nature of God.

As Heidegger conceives it, philosophy becomes fully aware of its nature only when it learns to forego both a natural theology and a natural atheology, as being concerned with issues that lie outside its province. This accounts for the remarkable contrast between Sartre and Heidegger on questions of theism and religion. The former's loquacity is countered by the latter's deliberate reticence, at least as far as philosophically grounded statements are concerned. Whereas Sartre deals with such matters in full confidence that his phenomenological ontology can explain the structural meaning of God and religion, Heidegger regards such confidence as an uncritical assumption and refuses to pronounce anything one way or the other on the issues. Methodologically, he keeps his distance and does not find a legitimate basis for philosophy to take any stand on theism and religion.

This policy of separatism or philosophical *apartheid* rests upon three considerations: the nature of philosophy, the history of Western philosophy and culture, and the standpoint belonging to the man of Christian faith. On all three counts, Heidegger feels obliged to refrain from inquiring into the validity of the theistic and religious affirmations, and to do so as a matter of philosophical principle within our historical situation.

The vocation of the philosopher is to pose the question of being.[12] He can do so by provoking wonderment about why there are any particular beings at all, and then by gradually drawing our attention to the difference between inquiries about these particular things-that-are and the question of being itself, in which they share. In its most authentic mode, philosophy seeks to achieve a disclosure of being, as expressed in language that respects its distinction from the whole collection of particular beings or things-that-are. Philosophy is not restrictively metaphysical, in the sense of excluding the other branches of philosophy or of remaining content with conventional metaphysical concepts, but it does interpret and unify its findings in reference to the central question of being.

From this account, it would seem easy to infer that, since God is a being, He comes properly within the sphere of philosophical inquiry. But Heidegger will not accept the inference, if by the term "God" is meant the personal and transcendent God of the Christian tradition. Taking a rapid inventory of the resources of philosophy, he points out that they do not provide any adequate basis for reaching God or even for ascertaining the nature of a religious relationship specified by reference to Him. We draw our categories from the physical world, and hence they do not apply to God unless we are ready to

accept an idolatrous conception of Him as being an object in the
natural world. Even if we take nature to signify the whole order of
things that emerge and endure, the sense of theistic statements is that
God is not an emergent and does not endure in the way that an entity
subject to process endures. Hence He cannot be reached by means of
concepts based upon the objects in nature and proportioned to them.

We may seek to avoid this conclusion by appealing to the distinctive reality of man. Heidegger welcomes our recognition of man's distinctive being, but does not permit it to soften the line of separation.
The existential traits peculiar to man, the free reflective questioner,
are indeed peculiar to him. They set him off from the other things-that-
are, but not in such a way as to identify man either with being itself
or with God. But if man is the place where the question of being is
raised, may he not also be the place where the question about God and
the religious relationship also be raised? Heidegger's reply is that
philosophy raises the first question in such a way that it cannot ask
the second one, understood in a theistic fashion. The goal of philosophy
is to bring about a certain attunement between human reality and
being itself. Indeed, human reality is most genuinely operative when
it attends to being, shelters it as it were in our free reflections, and
searches for the naming words which will announce the presence and
power of being. Human freedom and reflectivity furnish the gateway
for the meaning of being to present itself in the realm of things-that-
are. As a consequence, however, any philosophically grounded meaning of being is perspectival or proportioned to its human gateway.[13]
We have the dignity of searching for the language in which to express
being, but we must also accept the thoroughly limited meaning of
being which will result. From that meaning, we can discover no
philosophical path leading to what religious faith regards as the infinite and transcendent God.

In working out this argument for sealing off the problem of God
and religion from philosophical investigation, Heidegger also invokes
an historical and cultural factor. He does not claim that we are presently in possession of the fitting language for the founding of ontology,
but only that we are aware of the inadequacy of the categories and
language of previous philosophies and are now en route toward an
adequate ontological language and set of meanings. Confronted with
the historical efforts made by European philosophers to attain some
philosophical knowledge of God, he tries to reduce them to a single
philosophical standpoint. Whether it be the prime mover of Aristotle,
the first cause and pure act of Aquinas, or the absolute spirit of

Hegel, the object attained by Western philosophical studies is either an instance of the particular things found in nature or is a way of describing them in their totality.[14] It is something proportioned to the naturalistic categories rather than the transcendent God of religious faith. When Nietzsche said that God is dead, he meant that philosophers were starting to share the common conviction that the old conceptual tools of cause and spirit and dialectical absolute are worn out. They never did serve to reach God, and we are beginning to realize this fact even in our social forms and poetic sensibility.

Heidegger is turning more and more to the poetic witness, not only for encouragement that human language contains the resources for overcoming our forgetfulness about being but also for its illumination of the human religious situation. His favorite poet, Hölderlin, has some lines in a poem entitled "The Archipelago" which compare the flight of the ancient Greeks from their gods to the flight from God in modern society.

> Our generation wanders in darkness, it lives
> As in Orcus, without God. Men are bound to their own tasks
> Alone, and in the roaring workshop each can hear
> Only himself. They work like savages, steadily,
> With powerful, restless arms, but always and always
> The labor of the fools is sterile, like the Furies.
> So it will be until, awakened from anxious dreams,
> The souls of men arise, youthfully glad, and the blessed
> Breath of love blows in a newer time, as it often did
> For the blossoming children of Hellas, and over freer brows. . . .
> But there is light on high, it speaks to mankind even today,
> Full of bright meanings.[15]

Heidegger's special point is, however, that the light which philosophy is able to catch concerning being and the things in nature cannot lead us to God. The philosopher may respect the man of prayer, and may suppose that this religious man is close to God. But the philosopher does not have the warrant to invade the sacred grove, subject the man of prayer to his ontological analysis, and thus reach a conclusion within his own discipline concerning the goal and content of religious living.

Conversely, neither does the man of religious conviction have a basis for influencing the course of philosophical inquiry. As Heidegger views the question, the bright meanings which concern the reality of God and the worth of religion come from faith and remain dependent upon the context of faith. He establishes a sharp contrast between the attitude of faith, accepting a revelation as truly coming from God, and the philosophical attitude of radically questioning every assertion about the real. Commenting on the opening verse in *Genesis*, Heidegger remarks:

Quite aside from whether these words from the Bible are true or false for faith, they can supply no answer to our question [about why there are particular things-that-are rather than nothing] because they are in no way related to it. Indeed, they cannot even be brought into relation with our question. From the standpoint of faith our question is "foolishness." Philosophy is this very foolishness. A "Christian philosophy" is a round square and a misunderstanding. There is, to be sure, a thinking and questioning elaboration of the world of Christian experience, i.e. of faith. That is theology.[16]

For Heidegger, however, the theological mode of questioning always retains faith as its principle, and hence remains disparate from and unrelatable in principle to the philosophical mode of questioning.

This view of the matter is largely shared by the crisis theologian, Rudolf Bultmann, who for over thirty years has been reading Scripture in the light of Heidegger's account of human reality.[17] He does not claim that his demythologizing approach is a philosophical one or that what he does is relevant for reaching philosophical conclusions. He teaches that God does not manifest Himself to philosophical reason in nature, man, or history: it requires the assurance of faith to maintain God's secret presence within the tendencies of human reality, as described by Heidegger. There is no philosophically based natural theology, but the theology based on faith can use the analysis of man to determine the solid core of revealed truth which is significant for our human concerns. Bultmann's fellow theologians wonder whether his criterion of significance permits any initiative and transcendence on the part of the revealing God, whereas Heidegger firmly judges that the resultant interpretation is not relatable to philosophy on any grounds autonomously proper to this discipline. He holds a similar opinion about the work of Scheler and other phenomenologists of religion. Thus Heidegger remains as resolutely opposed to a Christian philosophy as to an atheistic existentialism.

Two interesting points are raised by Heidegger's picture of the philosopher and the man of faith as saluting each other from separate peaks, but never strictly participating in a joint philosophical work. First, we can see that the notion of a Christian philosophy is not uniformly self-validating but needs to be reconsidered in ways that are not purely historical. There is an advantage here, since it shows that the question of faith and philosophy is still with us in a lively form. Heidegger's challenge is whether the man of faith can ever share genuinely in the philosophical enterprise. Everything depends upon the way in which we take the requirement of a radical questioning about being that carries through to the very end. It may mean an actual revoking of the assent of faith, as a matter of methodological principle. In this sense, there would be a contradiction involved in the notion of a Christian philosophy. But the requirement of philosophical investigation may also mean a rigorous adherence to the procedure of searching for the basis in evidence for every statement intended for use in one's philosophy. The man of faith whose work lies in this direction will try to regulate his philosophical acceptance or rejection of statements by the rule of furnishing reasonable grounds, which can be inspected and tested by others. A radical fidelity to this rule and thus to philosophical inquiry can be found in the individual mind along with faith in God, thus permitting a Christian philosophy.

The second noteworthy point is that Heidegger helps to revitalize the theme of the relationship between the conception of being and God. A realistic view is that our metaphysical conception of being depends upon judgmental acts which are originally concerned with the existing being of natural things, including man. Hence God is not to be identified either with the directly experienced existents or with the meaning of being which serves as the subject of metaphysics. We are led to inquire about being, as that which has the act of existing, due to our experience and judgments about determinate, sensible beings. Yet this origin of the metaphysical notion of being does not enable us to say beforehand that the transcendent God lies outside the range or object of metaphysical inference. For we must still ask about the real source of being and of existent things. This question cannot be settled by remaining where Heidegger does, that is, at the point of distinction between the things-that-are and being itself as the theme of our study. Whether or not we are required to accept the truth of inferences concerning God depends upon examination of the specific grounds supporting that distinction. It also depends upon calling into question Heidegger's attempt to melt down all the Western efforts at metaphysics into a single massive fallacy of ignoring that distinction.

4. Marcel: Remain Faithful Amid Your Inquietude

Up to this point, we have seen the rather paradoxical ways in which two of the existentialists thematize religion. Sartre does so by identifying it with man's fundamental tendency toward merging his own lucid questioning and lack of being with a stolid fullness of opaque being—an impossible project which man nevertheless passionately tries again and again to realize. Heidegger thematizes religion by removing it and its theistic basis essentially from philosophical discussion, so that the philosopher as such cannot say whether or not the religious aim of union with God is capable of realization. Two other leading existentialist philosophers, Karl Jaspers and Gabriel Marcel, agree with Sartre that a study of God and religion does fall within the competence of philosophy.[18] Their analyses convince them, however, that we must distinguish between the human act of transcending and the being of God, instead of making the latter just a function of the former. Furthermore, they seek to show that the religious reference of man toward God is not an explosive betrayal of human freedom, as Sartre maintains, but helps to deepen both our personal freedom and our intersubjective relations with other men.

Marcel goes on from here to engage in the delicate task of assessing and moving beyond Heidegger's position, which in many ways is more intricately critical of theism than is the Sartrean doctrine. One of Marcel's earliest contentions was that we are confronted with an initial option of regarding reality either as closed off from every reference to the transcendent God or as being open to that reference. But in the light of the developments we have been describing, he is now aware of two difficulties in this theory of the initial option. For one thing, it fits the opposition between his own theism and Sartre's atheism, but it does not explain very incisively Heidegger's position of not ruling out the reality of God or even our ability to become related in some fashion with Him, and yet of refusing to bring the issue within philosophical range. Another drawback is that it does not deal effectively with minds which claim to be still uncommitted philosophically on the question of God and religion. Such minds cannot be told that the question has already been settled within the terms of their philosophy, but on the contrary they must be given some philosophically specifiable grounds for settling it in some definite way.

Working well within the existentialist tradition to meet this requirement, Marcel returns to the well studied theme of Nietzsche on the death of God, in order to draw from it a fresh meaning. He asks why it is that, while few people have believed very strongly in Nietzsche's prophecy about the coming of the superman and the new order of values, men have been deeply affected by the theme of God's death or the deterioration of religious belief as a powerful social force in the contemporary world.[19] The difference in the reception of these two teachings is that the latter has some descriptive basis in the analysis of modern cultures. Marcel adds, however, that our questioning about the religious relation to God extends to a questioning about the nature of man and the basis of his values: the crisis is humanistic as well as theistic. A point is reached at which we discover the solidarity between our convictions about God and those about man as a free existent and chooser of values.

Marcel uses the analysis of the modes of questioning to correct a misapprehension about his distinction between problem and mystery. It is misleading to say simply that a problem designates the type of question bearing upon man's relations with things, whereas a mystery designates the sort of question involving the relations among persons (whether of a man with his fellow men or with God). This way of taking the distinction transforms it into a sharp dichotomy and overlooks the continuity which can lead us from interrogation about things to that about the interpersonal world of ourselves and God. Mystery and problem are not totally unrelated, since the former comes into view when a problem is followed through to the point of uncovering its roots in oneself and one's convictions about human reality.[20] Thus Marcel is ready enough to speak about problematic man or man considered as persisting in his inquiries until they formally concern his own mode of being and valuing. At some phase in an inquiry about man, we make use of a recuperative reflection, one which attends precisely to our personal way of being and of standing related to other persons. It is here that the religious relation with the personal God presents itself, and here alone that Marcel seeks for the bases of theism. Nothing esoteric is intended, then, when he remarks that the question about God and religion concerns the domain of mystery, since this signifies a proportioning between our method of philosophical research and the personal kind of realities under investigation.

Marcel is now prepared to make the two major moves constituting his chief contribution to our topic. First, there is the polemical move of denying that causality can be validly used to gain knowledge about God. And second, he gives a religious interpretation to human unrest and suggests that this provides the only proper approach to God available in philosophy.

After years of making qualified criticisms of the causal way to God, Marcel now rejects it out of deference for what he calls the philosophical tradition of Plato and especially Kant. What makes him so incisive now on the issue is the prospect of finding here a means to evaluate

Sartre and Heidegger together. Despite their sharp differences about the reality of the transcendent God, the two latter thinkers agree that Nietzsche's dictum about the death of God marked the end of the road for every attempt to reach a transcendent reality through philosophy. On the contrary, Marcel limits the significance of Nietzsche's judgment to mean only the end of a certain way of conceiving God and a certain determinate way of relating oneself to Him. Nietzsche's cultural analysis does not cut off every human relationship in thought and action with God, but only the one which rests upon causality. What has died is general acceptance of the causal argument for God, as well as those practical ways of relating ourselves to Him after the pattern of an effect-to-cause sort of reference. But this does not justify either Sartre's reduction of the whole question about God and religion to a purely immanent and sterile project or Heidegger's elimination of the question entirely from the philosopher's purview. There are other ways of conceiving God and referring ourselves morally and religiously to Him which do not fall within the causal order, and hence which do not come within the scope of the Nietzschean pronouncement.

Within the climate of existentialist thought, then, Marcel phrases his negative conclusion in this way:

It seems to me that we should do away with the idea of a God-Cause, of a god concentrating all causality in himself, or in stricter language, do away with every theological usage of the notion of causality. It is precisely here that Kant has shown us the road, without perhaps being able himself to plumb the consequences of his discovery. It might well be, to resume my line of argument, that the God whose death Nietzsche truly announced was the god of the Aristotelian-Thomistic tradition, the first-mover god.[21]

Behind this criticism lies Marcel's view of the meaning of causality. He takes it in the primary sense to mean an instrumental use of power on the part of man, a human exercise of mastery. Thus cause refers properly to man as the principle of instruments, as dealing with things and shaping his own organism in view of his needs. Every other usage is only a variant of this central meaning, and hence there can be no causal meaning which genuinely transcends the domain of human instrumentality. From this it follows, for Marcel, that causal inference belongs entirely within the field of relations between man and things or organic parts under his mastery. To treat God as a cause would then mean reducing Him to a humanized wielder of instruments or a producer in the noncreative sense. And it would also mean reducing us to the status of tools and objects, which would destroy the personal relationship upon which religious life feeds.

In that event, where can the philosopher turn for aid in his search for knowledge of God? Marcel's answer is that he must reflect upon religious consciousness and examine the concrete modes by which the man of religious faith relates himself to God. If the philosopher does so, he will notice that the religious mind is engaged in liberating itself from every causal representation of God and of our bond with Him, so that religious life can flourish under the sign of freedom and personal participation in being. This provides the philosopher with the clue for his positive reconstruction. He must reforge his categories and other conceptual and linguistic means, so that they will accord more directly with the requirements of religious awareness.[22] He will pattern his approach to God upon a concrete reflective description of the ways in which the religious reference to God is achieved by men. A proper philosophy of God is one that nourishes itself upon the relationship of I-and-Thou or what Marcel terms the invocation of the finite self toward the personal and loving God. The conceptual equipment of the philosophy of God and religion is drawn from reflection upon the actual modes of our religious reference.

The great mass of Marcel's particular investigations are devoted to a descriptive analysis of the threefold process constituting our religious participation in being. The three key operations are reflecting, transcending, and participating as faithful witnesses. Within the religious context, reflection begins as a withdrawal, a break with my conventional engagement in the world of objects, a critical attitude taken toward all the busy functions in which I lose concern for my selfhood. But this negative phase is only a prelude to a recuperation of my personal forces or, in significant religious language, a recollection of myself.[23] What I recover is not the absolute self imagined in the philosophies of absolute idealism, but precisely the questioner at the source of all the questions, the searcher at the root of all the quests of my existence. In a word, the purpose of reflection is to give a man lucidity about his finite and participating personal way of being, rather than to beguile him with the dreams of absolute self-sufficiency or absolute objectivity.

The reflecting self serves as the springboard for transcendence. This image can be misleading, however, since transcending does not involve any spatial removal or abandonment of experience, but rather an inward journeying.[24] We learn to regard ourselves in a new way, not just as agents dominating a world of things and functions and not even as reflective questioners doing no more than raising the questions. Transcendence signifies our acts of discriminating among the questions, stressing those which bear upon the personal source and goal of our being, and thus orienting our attitudes and practical commitments toward God.

The fruit of transcending is given in participation. Here, we explicitly recognize and freely accept our bond of being with God, our dignity of being-alone-with-and-toward the personal God. Marcel has concentrated upon the concrete expressions of human participation in the modes of faith, prayer, and witness.[25] On the basis of his analysis of them, he concludes that Sartre and Heidegger have misread the human situation in conceding a relationship of human freedom only to being in some finite and nonpersonal meaning. These religious modes of human participation open up the human self to the initiative of the divine personal self. For the religious person to remain faithful means to adhere freely to its engagement with God and other persons, to retain these personal bonds under the temporal conditions of distraction and erosion and inquietude.

One traditional approach which Marcel incorporates is a form of the argument from the desire for God, based upon a study of human inquietude.[26] It has the advantage of providing a religious context for the existentialist analyses of anguish, as well as of distinguishing a psychologically draining anxiety from a fruitful unrest. It also enables him to draw upon the rich historical sources of the theme of man's restless search for God, as developed by Augustine, Pascal, and Kierkegaard, without compromising himself on the issue of a causal inference. This he does by limiting the meaning of causality to physical efficiency and that immanent sort of teleology which concerns the use of things and the health of the organism. Because the theme of inquietude is a constant one in human history, especially under the impact of the Judaeo-Christian revelation, it furnishes an intersubjective basis in human reality for the religious reference of our being. And finally, Marcel is intensely interested in this expression of our religious orientation because it helps to define the conditions under which the the religious man relates himself to God. The demand of the religious call is that we remain faithful witnesses to our spiritual bond with God, while nevertheless retaining our human mode of inquietude in history.

One of the sources on this topic whom Marcel might well have consulted is Cardinal Newman. The latter tells us that "to be at ease, is to be unsafe. . . . [A religious mind] is ever realizing to itself Him on whom it depends, and who is the centre of all truth and good." [27] The person who is too easily satisfied and unconcerned about his life runs the risk of losing that culminating mode of human reality which consists in fidelity to God and constant search for Him. Newman is significant here in another respect. Although he himself prefers the way of conscience to God and stresses the heart's restlessness until it comes to God, he is much more cautious than Marcel about the causal argument. He does not reject this other way to God, but assigns it to metaphysics as a discipline distinct from his own approach of personal reflection. Theistic realism is sufficiently complex to include both the causal and the personal-reflective ways to God.

Furthermore, Newman suggests that there is a personal meaning for causality, not merely in the instrumental sense that it is a power exerted by a person upon things but in the more pertinent and philosophically adequate sense of characterizing the creative relation between the infinite person, God, and the finite persons to whom He communicates being. For Newman, causality has to be rescued from the univocal use of it to designate scientifically determined relations among physical objects. In its most proper significance, it refers rather to the free sharing of being and the ordering of actions and ends within the interpersonal community. Its reality is founded upon the living operations of mind and will, both in the creative giving of life and a moral order by God to men and in the spiritual relations among men. The proper context for the causal relationship is a creative, personal, and providential one for Newman. Hence he cannot agree with Marcel that to call God a cause is to degrade Him to the role of an artificer or to reduce men to mere tools and impersonal objects of fabrication. Hume's problem about applying the personal meaning of causality beyond the human sphere is a serious one, but it is better to face it through a more careful analysis of the components than through a denial of causality to God and personal agency. Realistic theism accepts the challenge of integrating personal meaning and causality, rather than setting them in uncritical opposition.

In his actual practice, Marcel himself refers to God in ways that would be considered as causal anywhere else than in his definitional framework. God is not an instrumental producer, but He is the creator of all beings. He is the infinite person who communicates being to us, and we are participants in being from Him. We also seek His personal presence as the goal of our desire, as the only way of bringing our inquietude to its proper fulfillment. Not only these usages of Marcel but also the history of Western reflection on the causal question indicates that the whole issue is more complicated and the developments more far-reaching than he will allow. This history of the causal problem shows, for instance, that St. Thomas does not merely adopt unchanged the Aristotelian notion of the first mover. Both the revealed doctrine on creation and his own philosophical reflections upon the intimate bond between creative causality and the communication of the act of existing obliged Aquinas to revise the theory of cause in some important ways, all of which helped to respect the personal aspect of causal action. And the cautious example of Newman indicates that we are still confronted with the need for rethinking causality in an analogical way which is suitable to the communication of being from one person to another. A sense of the continual reinterpretation of such a basic relation as the causal one animates the English cardinal's remark that "the whole system of what is called cause and effect is one of mystery." [28] An urgent task for theistic realism today is to bring out the precise significance of the causal relation when it concerns a communication and ordering of being in that particular domain which Marcel designates as the order of mystery or interpersonal act.

Marcel himself doubts that even an analogical reinterpretation of causality can liberate it from its mechanistic connotations and provide it with a metaphysical meaning equivalent to God's generosity and free giving of being.[29] He thinks that the causal explanation is irremediably bound down to a materializing, reifying, empirico-technical treatment of the related beings, whereas the religious relationship is found in the communion of spirit with spirit. The religious bond is apt to disappear when we talk in retrospective, historical terms about God as having caused the world in some remote past, or when we say that God caused a certain physical evil as a test for someone in the way that an experimenter or researcher might produce an effect to test a material.

Two issues are involved here: the appropriateness of our ordinary causal talk about God and ourselves, and the analogical meaning of causality as applied properly to God. On the first score, Marcel has an ample basis for criticism. As our later analysis of linguistic theism will bring out, we do speak carelessly about God, as though His causality occurred long ago and not in the present, or as though He had to work externally upon us in order to discover our moral qualities. Yet the defect here lies in a failure to make our language responsive to the meaning of divine creative causality, rather than in the predication of causal activity to God. Our ordinary talk on religious matters often remains insensitive to the intimate and abiding personal presence of

God which is involved in His creative causation or giving of the very being of human reality. The solution does not lie in opening a cleft between the causal analysis and the religious attitude, but rather in realizing that the proper meaning for divine causality is the giving of being through a free, personal act of love. In the light of this meaning, St. Thomas gives a causal interpretation to the remark of St. Augustine that God is more intimate to me than my own self. There is an ultimate agreement between the religious awareness of God's immanence and respect for our freedom and the view of divine causality which makes it consist in His personal giving of the act of existing and the entire being of the finite reality, respected in its own way of being and acting.

5. *Conclusion*

Where do the existentialists leave us in their treatment of the theme of religion? Precisely where they want to: as individuals responsible for our own interpretation of that aspect of human existence. The existentialists do not impose a decision upon us about the nature of religion, and they do not even confront us with a uniform final answer of their own. Their achievement lies in another direction, and it is twofold. The first result is to make the questions dealing with man's religious relationship important ones, not only for a specialized philosophy of religion but for the whole tissue of philosophical inquiry today. In the second place, they present us with a wide spectrum of possible positions which can be taken on religion from a starting point in philosophy. Their positions are by no means exhaustive alternatives, but they do sharpen many of the issues involved in any discussion on religion and thus invite us to make our own reflections about it.

At a descriptive level, there is some measure of agreement among the existentialist reports. They all regard the religious aspect as a major and constant feature of our human existence, whatever one may think about its truth-claims. Moreover, they concur in describing its reality as personal, relational, and active. It engages a man precisely in the zone where he is a free, personal self, rather than an interchangeable part or link within the world of things and functional services. To call a man religious is to predicate something relational about him, to specify his becoming involved in the interpersonal community. Moreover, the act whereby a man relates himself in a religious manner is a free one, at least as soon as an individual becomes mature enough to realize his responsibility in the matter. The existentialists also agree that the free act whereby the religious relationship is established can be further specified as an act of faith in respect to the transcendent. Whether or not it be contrasted with natural and philosophical knowledge, religious faith is taken as signifying the proper act of orienting the human existent toward what it regards as a transcendent reality, namely, one which is distinct from and more richly actual than the universe of human selves, cultures, and material objects. There is an active or practical quality to this orientation: it involves not only the mind but the practical concerns of the person and often of the community of believers.

Another common premise shared by the existentialists is that, in our human world of widely diverse religions, the Judaeo-Christian tradition conserves the most values and achieves the highest unification. Consequently, religious transcendence is usually interpreted by them to mean a reference of the human person to the transcendent personal God. The intentional meaning of religious faith is only fulfilled through a reference to a personal being which is other than the human self. Hence the I-and-Thou pattern is accepted as characterizing the human existent's relationship with the transcendent reality. The practical commitment characteristic of the theistic religious response provides another piece of testimony, since it intends to be a response to the holiness and the demanding initiative of a personal God, not merely of an ideal standard.

Where the existentialists part company is over their evaluation of this description of the religious situation. Sartre will call for a reconsideration of every statement in the description, in order to show that the whole religious structure leads to frustration rather than fulfillment. Heidegger will put a large set of parentheses around the entire matter by declaring it outside the bounds set for philosophical inquiry. Marcel will use the description as a basis for uncovering some enduring traits of participating being and its real ordination to God. Jaspers will agree, but with the proviso that the entire surge of religious transcending rests upon a philosophical and thoroughly naturalized act of faith.

This division of opinion is not reducible simply to a question of priority. The problem is not merely that of agreeing with Sartre and Heidegger to develop an independent theory of being first of all and then to take a stand on religious assertions, or of agreeing with Marcel and Jaspers to take account of the religious reference of man from the very outset of one's study of being. In point of fact, all the existentialists have colored their study of being and human action with their strong convictions on the meaning of Nietzsche's pronouncement about the death of God and effective religious belief. Their reaction to his dramatic thesis has had a powerful influence upon their fundamental views on the nature of philosophy, the range of our investigation of being, and the soundness of religious faith. We cannot set an impossible demand that they should erase this influence. But it is reasonable to ask that some measures be taken so that their philosophical positions on religion will not be basically predetermined apart from argumentation.

To avoid such a result, I would suggest in conclusion the following five points of method. First, a firm distinction must be kept between cultural estimations and philosophical theories about the nature and compass of being. Cultural estimations remain notoriously contingent and, even when made by great minds, ignore many factual situations and latent resources of man. The cultural appraisal can include a description of the current condition of religious belief, but such a description is not definitive about either the validity of the religious affirmations themselves or their capacity for attracting minds under fresh historical conditions.

Second, there is a capital difference between giving an *initial* account of the conception of being by reference to our direct experience and then converting the experienced component traits into the *sole* marks of reality. The latter method decides beforehand that the concept of the real will include only the various modes and relations of some favored constituents, such as Sartre's dyad of matter and the human project. In this approach, the extent of our inquiry into being is limited by what we introduce at the outset into a controlling concept of being. Such a procedure would make it purely a matter of initial option whether or not to include God and our religious relation to Him in the order of reality. But the philosopher demands some grounds for regarding the terms of a relation as real, and hence it is more reasonable to begin with the experience of things and the judgmental acts in which we affirm them to be real. Without identifying the scope of our knowledge with that of being, we can nevertheless agree to give philosophical certification only to those things coming within our experience or judged to be required in order to explain that experience satisfactorily. This procedure leaves the inquiry into being open, not in the sense of sanctioning everyone's assumptions but of regulating the judgment of reality by the specific considerations of the case. Thus a theory about God and theistic religion is not banished *a priori* from philosophy or treated as a mask of bad faith, but is entertained for the sake of testing its basis.

In the third place, it is sound practice to undertake an independent descriptive survey of the several fields of human experience, including the religious realm. Its purpose is to determine as carefully as possible the structures and operations involved in these different fields. We inspect these structures and operations as they present themselves in human existence and symbolic expressions. This descriptive analysis is not sufficient by itself to settle all the philosophical questions, but at least it supplies some determinate material and some ways of controlling the philosophical inferences.[30] A descriptive study of religious experience, for instance, does not decide the problem of religious diversity and does not rule out the naturalistic view that such experience concerns only the aspirations of man. Religious experience alone does not settle between rival truth-claims built upon an interpretation of it. But it does manifest definite patterns and does engage certain definite human acts. Any philosophical theories about the religious aspect of our existence which violate or fail to take full account of the patterns and acts found here, are lacking in explanatory adequacy. It is not necessary that the philosophical instruments used to study God and religious relationships be drawn in the first place from a specifically religious context, but it is necessary that they prove their capacity to adjust to the requirements of inquiring about the transcendent God and our reference to Him.

A fourth point suggested by our study is that the descriptive treatment of religious existence needs to be integrated with the knowledge gained about God and man through causal inference and the analogical predications employed in such inference. A critical blind spot in many existentialist and phenomenological accounts of religion is their conventional acceptance of a bifurcation between the causal and descriptive methods, or between causal and meaning-directed analysis, with the study of religion committed entirely to the latter method. Sometimes, the reason for making this restriction is an unspoken belief that there is no philosophical way of justifying the causal inference to God in the face of the Humean and Kantian critiques. To this is often added a consideration drawn from the doctrine of Husserl, which will be examined later on in this book, concerning the reduction of existential and real causal factors. Husserl views causality mainly in physical terms and subjects it to a reduction, so that it will not infect the domain of personal relations and meanings. But this does not dispense us from recovering a more basic conception of causal activity as a free and personal giving of being. Until that is done, however, a purely descriptive emphasis upon the intentional reference of religious experience to a transcendent being will not overcome the naturalistic and empiricist comment that both the religious act and the religious intentional object are traits characterizing the imagination and moral aspiration of man-in-the-natural-totality. For a theistic conception of religion not merely to be depicted but to be given a philosophical foundation relevant to all these critical movements in modern philosophy, the descriptive phase in the study of religion has to be incorporated within a reflective causal approach to the personal bond between man and God. To do so, theistic realists must work out the personal import of causality in the relationship of God and man.

Finally, the example of the existentialists shows that a philosophy of religion does not stand alone and is not itself a primary discipline. It fits into the movement of philosophical inquiry as a second-level teaching, a reflective unification of knowledges which are originally established in the course of other analyses. Underlying the existentialists' theory on religion is their doctrine on being and the beings in the world, their study of human reality in its freedom and capacity for establishing intentional relations, and the direct description of the domain of religious experience as a kind of intentional meaning and operation. With suitable changes, this is the foundation in direct knowledge required for any philosophy of religion. Especially in the case of a theistic philosophy which admits some inferential knowledge about God and which examines human moral life in its reference to God as our ultimate goal, there is an opportunity for developing such a reflective discipline. It is not entirely satisfactory to reduce the philosophical study of religion to a short paragraph in a treatment of justice toward God. Not only the empirical materials on human religious life ask for a philosophical scrutiny, but also the various philosophical analyses bearing on the man-God relation demand a distinctive unification and emphasis. The existentialists quicken our appreciation of the need to do some work in the philosophy of religion which will illuminate the theistic view of man and God.

CHAPTER 4

FAITH AND REFLECTION

IN KIERKEGAARD

THE GREAT masters of Christian thought lead us back eventually to the relation between faith and natural reason. Their preoccupation with this problem is not an accident, for it expresses the abiding concern of the Christian mind with the impact of divine truth upon human reality. Different aspects of the tension between faith and reason come to the fore in response to the various historical conceptions of God and man. It is one of the sure marks of Kierkegaard's authenticity as a Christian thinker that he should be engaged constantly with this issue.[1] From his early years as a theological student right down to the bitter years of public strife, he never ceased probing into the connection between faith and reason. He made this question a central focus in his general program of restoring the genuine meaning of the basic Christian terms. By attending to his views, we can discover certain aspects of the modern problem of religion which the existentialists do not face with equal clarity.

It is noteworthy that Kierkegaard himself does not usually formulate the problem as that of faith and reason. It is more customary for him to speak about the relation between faith and reflection or between existence and pure thought. This is not an insignificant terminological shift. Rather, it indicates his sensitivity toward the actual way in which the problem was being posed in his own day. Given the attempt of the Hegelian philosophers to reinterpret faith and reason in terms of an idealistic theory of pure thought and dialectical reflection, Kierkegaard had to make a new formulation of the perennial Christian theme of how faith stands related to our natural understanding. Three phases in his analysis of faith and reflection call for special inquiry. What relations obtain between faith and reflection and

71

the first two spheres of existence? How does Kierkegaard's opposition to Hegelianism affect his view of faith and reflection? Does some sort of reflective activity persist even at the level of Christian faith or the religion of transcendence? Once these questions are examined, some responsible conclusions can be drawn about the relevance for us of Kierkegaard's work.

1. *The Spheres of Existence*

Many people still find it easier to read about Kierkegaard in secondary studies than to persevere with the sources. One reason for their reluctance to risk a throw with the Danish Socrates himself is the widespread opinion that he abounds in ambiguities and contradictions, whose import can be unraveled only by the experts or dons. There is some basis in fact for this prejudice, due to Kierkegaard's use of pseudonyms and his technique of indirect communication. But even had he composed all his writings in the direct manner of his religious meditations, a residual difficulty would still remain. His mind is many-leveled in its structure and, to enter into communication with it, the reader must learn to hold several perspectives simultaneously before him. This mature use of intellect certainly runs counter to some prevailing currents in modern education which accustom people to think along one groove and to forsake the rigors of comparative analysis. The reader who is trained to drain out the rich diversities of meaning and flatten out the problems of human existence will find Kierkegaard obscure and confusing even in his best passages.

Yet the remedy does not consist in denuding him but rather in enlarging our own vision to include the several reaches of human freedom. Fundamentally, Kierkegaard is forced to recognize several meanings for human life and its basic language, only because of his fidelity to the ways of freedom. Men give different interpretations to their modes of existing, and they use the common human terms to express different scales of value. Responsiveness to this situation overrides any inclination on Kierkegaard's part toward sheer virtuosity of style and dialectical complexity of thought. Analogous and conflicting meanings are found in his writings mainly as a consequence of his study of human freedom and its modes of expression. Still, he does not abandon us to a condition of moral and semantic anarchy. His theory of the three spheres of existence is an attempt to do justice to the actual diversity and yet achieve some unity, in the light of a

Christian evaluation of man and existence. He bids us make a constant comparison between the esthetic, ethical, and religious ways of appraising human life and expressing its ideals. He keeps us alert to the alternatives of human freedom in approaching the central issues of existence.

The educative effect of entering into dialogue with Kierkegaard is immediately apparent when one tries to discover his position on faith and reflection. His prime concern is not to lay down a definition of them and then measure the distance of other doctrines from his own. Since he is considering faith and reflection existentially or in respect to the uses of human freedom, he takes an inductive and practical approach. He describes their role within the different spheres of existence, so as to remove the impression that the problem is a purely speculative one having interest solely for professional theologians. By uncovering the presence of some sort of belief and reflection in every mode of existence, he establishes the broadly human importance of determining various contextual meanings for belief and reflection. In this way, he makes us concretely aware of the analogous ways in which men relate them and of the persistent tension between the two in all the stages of existence.

In the initial or esthetic sphere, faith signifies a man's immediate attachment to life, his animal conviction in the reality of the world and perhaps of its supreme principle. Kierkegaard was unwilling to base religion upon faith in Schleiermacher's meaning of a spontaneous feeling of dependence upon a primal source of being within the universe; for such a faith is a purely natural and determined act, whereas religious faith is a gift from God and a free response of man. Furthermore, this spontaneous attachment to the universe and its absolute principle is a naive and uncritical attitude, which stands in need of rational justification and extension. It is destined to be transformed into something more perfect, into a philosophical explanation which may well be of a pantheistic sort. This marks off esthetic faith definitively from the religious faith of the Christian: the latter is not an immature point of departure but the goal of all the strivings of existence. It is not a moment within reason's own development but a reach of decision and truth beyond reason's proper scope.

This critique is valuable today, when many people defend religious faith primarily on the ground that faith is required in every practical act and even in the scientific outlook. Kierkegaard has no quarrel with such an argument, as long as it pretends to be nothing more than a suasion directed against a naive sort of rationalism. This approach breeds confusion, however, if the radical difference between esthetic and religious faith is overlooked. There is no direct transition from our working animal faith to religious faith. Hence Kierkegaard protests against the inference that Christian faith must be subordinated eventually to scientific and philosophical knowledge. Such a naturalistic inference is based upon an inadequate study of the different existential conceptions of faith. Religious faith will pass away, but only to the eternal vision of God and not to temporal forms of knowledge.

There is also a type of reflection found in the higher degrees of esthetic life. At its peak, the esthetic mind is dedicated to a refined pursuit of pleasure in its most exquisite moments. A person of this sort is constantly surveying the possibilities for his own temporal ease and enjoyment. In some degree he overcomes the original blind attachment to vital forces and achieves a certain reflective grasp of himself. But esthetic reflection is an inwardness lacking in the ideal principle, since it does not relate the self to any permanent standard of social conduct or to the demands of God. It is a defective sort of self-understanding, since it isolates a man from his responsible connections with others. This type of reflection stresses an imaginative toying with possibilities at the expense of the ability to make decisions concerning the actual world. Out of such reflective acts are born the everlasting playboy, the self-centered epicure, and the sterile doubter.

The careful Kierkegaardian descriptions of these human types should make us cautious about lending indiscriminate praise to the reflective mind. If the educational process aims only at arousing reflectiveness in students, then it falls short of its full purpose. Education must include a comparative and critical inspection of the different ways in which men can become aware of their nature and destiny. There is an educational responsibility to provide at least the evidence for making an independent appraisal of the various types of reflective existence. "Reflectiveness" is a polyvalent term, which does not carry with it its own inherent justification. Kierkegaard agrees with Socrates that the unexamined life is not worth living, but he adds that some ways of conducting the self-examination of one's life are worth more than others. His position is realistic, since he does not allow the general praise of reflective living to overshadow the fact that men become reflective in conflicting ways, which need to be evaluated.

Indeed, from the dynamic standpoint of personal development, he recommends ethical reflection as a means of overcoming the defects of both esthetic faith and esthetic reflection. The ethically grounded individual subjects our vital allegiances to a careful critical scrutiny and, at the same time, raises the level of reflective concern from momentary personal pleasure to conformity with universal moral law. Ethical reflection drives home two ineluctable facts of our human situation: the individual's distance from the moral ideal and the need for a free decision to attain the eternal ideal. It dissolves the esthetic dream that the individual man naturally coincides with the conditions of his enduring happiness, and that there is some technique available for eluding the strenuous test of moral freedom.

In bringing the individual into a more demanding relation with the moral standard, the ethical mind is critical of the purely esthetic mode of reflectiveness. The latter attempts to evade the norm of eternity. But ethical reflection assures us that man is a prisoner neither of time alone nor of eternity alone. He is a temporal being whose spiritual center impels him toward eternity. The decisive function of ethical reflection is to make us aware of eternity as the goal of our temporal freedom and the measure of our moral striving. Freedom is dedicated to aims that are not wholly temporal and self-centered, as the esthetic mind pretends.

How, then, does ethical reflection bear upon the reality of faith? Kierkegaard does not provide a perfectly clear answer to this question. After portraying the knight of ethical faith as bearing the banner of eternity in the thick of temporal strife, he becomes dissatisfied with his own symbolism. The cause of Kierkegaard's uneasiness is not difficult to locate. Ethical insight is a mode of natural knowledge. It requires a disciplined will to attain, but still it can be acquired through our unaided efforts. Kierkegaard could not say simply that esthetic faith is overcome by ethical reflection, without seeming to imply that natural knowledge and effort are unconditionally superior to faith. Yet he could not remain content with an ethical faith which is nothing more than a practical expression of the hope generated by ethical reflectiveness. For then there would be nothing transcendent and freely donated by God in faith: it would be reduced to a purely natural extension of our knowledge of moral ideals.

Kierkegaard's hesitations are sometimes more illuminating than his firm assurances. In the present instance we can see how important it is to discriminate between the several meanings of faith. There is a legitimate sense in which one can have ethical faith. This is the individual's confidence in the integrity of his moral ideal and the social group's confidence in the practicality and humaneness of its social aims. In Kierkegaard's view, such faith is the offspring of natural insight and does not lead necessarily to a religious outlook. It is only mixing the categories of life to identify religious faith unqualifiedly with our passional adhesion to personal and social moral ideals. What John Dewey describes as our common faith is an instance of ethical faith or social dedication to an ideal ascertained by ethical reflection and scientific techniques. Although it is a definite type of faith, it remains distinct from what Kierkegaard regards as the religious and Christian modes of faith.

Ethical faith partakes of the limitations of ethical reflection. Kierkegaard calls the latter "the first reflection," insofar as it introduces the ideal norm into human motivation. But ethical reflection does not determine whether the moral law is itself grounded in a personal God, to whom we owe our primary obedience. The person-to-person relationship upon which religion rests cannot be established solely by means of ethical reflection and faith. Despite its emphasis upon decisive action, the ethical mind is likely to become lost in endless reflection upon the unconditional demands of moral law and the inadequacy of our human resources. This paralyzing comparison between the moral norm and particular human actions brings the purely ethical life to a standstill through what Kierkegaard refers to as an "overdose of repentance." The curious feature of this repentance, however, is that it does not concern past deeds so much as future attempts to satisfy the moral standards. Ethical reflection leads to a sort of despair, precisely because it leaves out of account the ultimate relation between the personal God and the individual man as a sinner open to personal redemption.

Beyond both ethical reflection and ethical faith lies a "second reflection or double reflection," which is a movement of mind bringing the eternal moral law into personal relation with free, finite individuals existing before God. But such a reflection can operate only within the mode of existence constituted by religious faith.

2. Beyond Idealism

Before examining religious faith and reflection in themselves, some mention must be made of the idealistic philosophies of religion which provided the negative background for Kierkegaard's thought. Although he had read Hegel's lectures on this subject, his main concern was with the more popular expositions of philosophy of religion by men like Martensen and Erdmann. They rendered the formulas of Augustine and Anselm unavailable to Kierkegaard by adapting them to the exi-

gencies of the idealistic program. The desperate note which sometimes sounded in Kierkegaard's discussion of faith and reason resulted
from the seemingly successful appropriation of all the terms and formulas of traditional Christian thought by the absolute idealism of the
nineteenth-century Hegelians on the right wing.

The venerable maxim "I believe so that I may understand" was
interpreted, for instance, to signify that religious belief is the first
step on the road to a total philosophical system of knowledge. Faith
can be taken in various senses: as Schleiermacher's immediate feeling
of dependence, as Jacobi's intuition of the divine, or as Hegel's absolute content under the form of feeling and representation. In whatever meaning assigned to it, however, faith connotes an undeveloped
condition whose inner dynamism demands completion and transformation into philosophical knowledge. The perfection of man's relation
to God is found not in the half-way house of religious faith but in
the terminal edifice of the philosophical system, where scientific insight is at last attained concerning the proper relation between man,
nature, and God.

Hegel himself claimed that the ideal content of faith is final and
that Christianity is true, revealed religion. But he reserved for philosophy the privilege of embodying this content in the only ultimately
adequate form as scientific knowledge. The impetus of the spirit does
not culminate in the Christian faith but—at least for the few who can
apprehend it—in the philosophical knowledge of idealism. What is
the principle of distinction between believers and knowers, between
those who remain satisfied with the penultimate religious expression
of the spirit and those who press onward to its final actualization in
philosophy? Hegel's answer highlights the distinction between reflection and reason or pure thought. Relying upon finite *reflection*, the
man of faith perceives the contrast between the finite and the infinite
and also regards it as a hard-and-fast distinction. The attitude of faith
and religious worship supposes a permanent otherness between God
and the human spirit. For its part, philosophical *reason* recognizes
the partial validity of this distinction and nevertheless denies that it is
ultimate. From the comprehensive vantage point of pure speculative
thought, the underlying identity of finite and infinite spirit is seen.
Philosophy of religion is nothing other than the purifying of faith, the
dialectical removal of the veil obscuring the identity of the finite and
the infinite. Thus for those who succeed in transforming finite reflection into the absolute truth of reason, faith itself becomes transformed
into speculative philosophy or scientific theology.

77

What is most significant for our present inquiry is the correlation established by the Hegelian philosophers of religion between faith and reflection, as distinguished from speculative certainty and reason or pure thought. If the contrast had been drawn simply between faith and reason, Kierkegaard might well have embraced a sheer fideism or an irrational voluntarism, in order to save Christian faith from engulfment in philosophical reason. Instead, the idealists paired faith with a type of reflection which is committed to the irreducible difference between God and the finite individual, as well as to the unqualified need for religious worship. This suggested to Kierkegaard that religious faith must retain its integration with some sort of reflective activity rather than cut itself loose from all connection with reflection. His close involvement in the post-Hegelian movement not only made him suspicious of the claims of idealistic reason and speculation in the area of religious faith but also led him to correlate religious faith with the factor of reflectiveness and objective reference. Finite reflection is constituted not only by a subjective attitude but also by an affirmation concerning the actual being of God and man.

3. Religious Faith

The position of Kierkegaard in respect to the spheres of existence and the idealistic philosophy of religion provides the indispensable background for understanding three of his well-known descriptions of religious faith: (1) he refers to religious faith as the absurd or the paradoxical; (2) he calls it an immediacy after reflection; (3) he characterizes it as becoming contemporaneous with Christ. The first description marks off religious faith from Hegelian philosophies of religion; the second one differentiates it from the first two stages of existence; the the third one brings out the specific character of Christian religious faith. It is clear that all three aspects of religious faith entail a certain view of the nature of religious reflection.

1. In scanning the texts where Kierkegaard refers to religious faith as a sacrifice of the intellect and an acceptance of the paradoxical and absurd, one must pay careful attention to the context. The most incisive statements of this view are found in his early *Journals,* when he is undergoing the crisis of Romanticism, and in the works pseudonymously attributed to Johannes Climacus. The latter represents what today might be called the standpoint of cultivated secularism. Johannes Climacus is by no means hostile to the religious outlook. He makes

a sincere effort to understand it and differentiate it from other attitudes. He describes religious faith sympathetically but from the outside, as seen by a non-believer. Hence he is more successful in stating what it is *not* than what it is in positive essence. Somewhat humorously, he points up its striking contrast with idealistic philosophies of religion. If they embody the consistent whole of systematic truth, then religious faith is absurd in its stress upon the individual, his sin, and his otherness from God. If certitude comes only from dialectical, necessary demonstations based on the identity between the subject and the object, the finite and the infinite, then religious faith is supremely uncertain, unobjective, and paradoxical. For it insists upon the contingent, the given, and the irreducibly finite, to the point where they cannot be demonstrated by means of dialectical incorporation into a total system.

Speaking in proper person as a believer, Kierkegaard indicates the basic ground why religious faith cannot be assimilated to any "rational truth," in the idealistic sense. Such assimilation depends upon some sort of dialectical identity between the divine and the human spirit. In this particular sense of rationality or conceptual adequacy, theism and Christianity belong outside the pale of rational truths and certainties. Moreover, the distinctively Christian religious faith rests upon the Incarnation, which is a free union of the temporal and the eternal in the person of Christ. This union is not subject to any necessity and demonstration. Similarly, the act of Christian believing remains free, in the sense of not being coerced by any philosophical inference or dialectical development. It is not the intellect alone which leads to faith, since freedom always includes an act of passion or will.

Kierkegaard sometimes speaks as though the intellect were positively excluded from the act of faith. Yet all that his opposition to idealism and pantheism requires is that faith be not regarded as the necessary outcome of a demonstrative argument or a dialectical process. He has used the weapon of intelligence to defend the irreducible distinction between the finite individual and God. This suggests that there are other ways of viewing the intellect than the one dictated by the presuppositions of Hegelianism. It also opens up the possibility that a philosophical theism may establish the truth of God's actual being and nevertheless refuse to subordinate divine freedom, historical contingency, and the act of Christian faith to a necessary dialectic. Kierkegaard explores the ways in which the solitary individual can make this refusal, but he leaves unexamined the ways in which a constructive philosophical doctrine can be based on the same refusal. To this extent, he remains the victim of the idealist interpretation of the history of philosophy.

2. The description of religious faith as an immediacy after reflection is indigenous in Kierkegaard's own theory of the spheres of existence. His intent is neither to exclude reflection entirely from religious existence nor to identify the latter simply with immediacy, but rather to specify the precise relation between religious faith and the various sorts of immediacy and reflection. Religious faith is not to be confused with esthetic immediacy, in which the spontaneous awareness of God is fused with a feeling for life and one's own well-being. To reach the truly religious standpoint, the act of reflection must intervene decisively in various ways. Esthetic reflection enables one to become aware of the innumerable imaginative possibilities for the self and the boundless region of inwardness. The maturing self must also submit to the discipline of ethical reflection, which measures the immediately given situation by a norm and underlines the distance between imaginative possibilities and the free act of moral decision. Nevertheless, the values of immediacy or attachment to the actual cannot be emptied out through the operation of reflection. Religious faith is a mode of immediacy, insofar as it involves a total practical commitment to an actuality other than human thought. Yet the actuality to which the religious believer is committed by his faith is that of God and not of the finite self or a separate moral ideal.

The manner in which religious faith comes "after" reflection has to be carefully determined. The two varieties of reflection directly concerned are the esthetic and the ethical, to which may be added the non-existential reflection of the idealist systems. Religious faith is after these types of reflection, in the sense that it does not precede them as a prologue or as a nascent state tending to become transformed into them. Viewed in the perspective of the stages of existence, these reflective activities are subordinate to the act of religious faith. And yet this faith does not come after them in the way that a conclusion follows from its premises or a dialectical synthesis from its prior phases. There remains a radical discontinuity between every philosophical reflection and the act of religious faith. Kierkegaard expresses this discontinuity by the metaphor of a leap. No matter how intense and thorough the preparatory work of esthetic and ethical reflection and how penetrating the philosophical analysis, the believing mind is not carried over by their momentum alone to the commitment of faith. It requires a leap, a free intervention of the will, a practical insertion into existence at the point of its intersection with eternity.

80

Once having made these qualifications, Kierkegaard is freed from any need to maintain that faith follows after reflection in such fashion as to exclude it entirely. He states explicitly that reflection is good in itself and capable of being redeemed in the religious sphere. He calls for a religiousness sufficiently powerful and supple to control the great forces of reflection. There would still remain an unalterable opposition between religious faith and the idealistic dialectic which tries to churn God and the universe into a common process. But the central energy of human reflection can be made to build up one's inwardness and dedication to existential truth, thus serving the ends of the life of faith.

In his religious discourses Kierkegaard sketches the operations of religious reflection or ethicoreligious conscience. The conscientious man does not spurn the objective findings of the sciences concerning nature and man's place therein. But he is anxious also to consider the subjective, practical relation of man to other realities through the use of freedom. Religious reflection is that second sort of reflection required to bring ethical norms into relation with the individual self and the personal God. Once it comes into play, there is a reintegration of ethical reflection itself within the ambit of religious existence, whether of the common human sort or the distinctively Christian religiousness. Hence the religiously reflective individual has a grasp upon the ethicoreligious truths of existence: he perceives himself as an individual and a sinner existing before God and standing in need of his aid. Reflection is here no enemy to action but its essential condition; for it makes a man heedful of those concerned truths which govern the religious disposition of his freedom.

We are given no straightforward answer by Kierkegaard to the question whether esthetic and religious reflection can be similarly harmonized. He felt it to be his doom, and not his glory, to be a poet as well as a thinker. The poet or esthetically reflective mind grasps an ideal in its imaginative possibility and then proclaims its worth in persuasive words, regardless of his own practical relation to this ideal. Kierkegaard was sensitive to the opportunity for hypocrisy on the part of a religious poet, who might arouse others to the demands of religious faith, without himself conforming to them. And yet he acknowledged his vocation to be that of the poet of the religious, the poetic reflector of religious existence. To avoid dishonesty, he tried to combine a severe reading of the Christian ideal with an insistent reminder that he himself was only a striver and pursuer. He also came to recognize that the religious witness embodies another way

81

of communicating religious truth to others, since the witness may be quite lacking in poetic genius and yet be powerfully persuasive through his example. In his personal life and thought, however, Kierkegaard never quite succeeded in reconciling the mode of communication proper to the religious witness and that of the honest poetic reflector of religious existence.

3. The final note of religious faith as a becoming contemporaneous with Christ helps to resolve the difficulty of esthetic reflection in the religious sphere. The attitude of the man of faith is one of constant *becoming* or striving to follow Christ, but it includes no claim to *being* in a state of perfect conformity with the truths he confesses. Hence, in presenting the Christian way to others, there is an inevitable disproportion between the demands of the following of Christ and the life of the Christian exponent, whether he be poet or witness. Because it is a process, the act of faith has a temporal aspect to it. But it does not consist either in going backward in time or in moving toward an indefinite future. We make our encounter with the Lord of time and history in the instant or act of believing itself. The contemporaneity consists in the mutual response of freedom between the finite individual and the God-Man, in whose divine person time and eternity meet in a primary way. Christian religious faith is distinguished precisely by the authority of Christ, who alone can rightfully place an unconditional demand upon the personal freedom of man. The special inwardness of the Christian man of faith consists in his practical commitment to the actuality of the Incarnation, with which he is constantly striving to conform his thoughts and deeds.

Because of his own intellectual situation, Kierkegaard deliberately stressed the act or subjective *how* of faith over the content or objective *what* of faith, without excluding the latter. Today, however, we are no longer in danger of supposing that Christianity is demonstated by some philosophical system. Indeed, since Kierkegaard's time the trend has been in the other direction. Naturalism has raised the suspicion that no philosophical approach to God is possible and that no rigorous mind can accept the Incarnation as a strict truth. Hence, many religiously inclined people are timid about acknowledging any role of the intellect and any intellectual content in religious faith. In view of the changed atmosphere, the contemporary function of the Socratic gadfly would seem to be to stress the *what* of faith and the function of intellect in the act of believing. And yet this should not be done in such a way as to lose the gains undeniably made by Kierkegaard.

4. *The Principle of Interplay*

There seem to be three main gains obtainable from a study of this conception of faith. First, Kierkegaard has taught us to recognize that faith and reflection have several depths of meaning. After sharing his company for a while, we are not likely to pass uncritically from one usage to the other or to make altogether loose comparisons. He has disclosed an abiding human need for the different sorts of faith and reflection at various phases in the growth of the self.

In the second place, he has brought out the distinctive nature of religious faith and reflection. One would have to be entirely unmindful of Kierkegaard's work to attempt the assimilation of them to other existential attitudes or to any philosophical doctrine. One may perhaps develop a philosophy of religion in the descriptive sense, for this is what the pseudonymous Johannes Climacus does. But the descriptive approach to faith and reflection never leads to the subordination of the act of faith or the truth of the Incarnation to some philosophical system.

And, finally, Kierkegaard has made us all his debtors by connecting Christian religious faith with the actuality of the God-Man and of man as fallen and redeemed. Instead of following Hegel's lead in reducing the Incarnation to our need to believe in a concrete way, he suggest that the person of Christ in his divine and human natures provides the essential condition for our act of faith. This does not render any the less important our inward appropriation of existential truth. But it does bring home to us the fact that there is something— or, rather, a divine-human someone—to appropriate and build ourselves upon. Yet we should not use the language of unmitigated appropriation but rather that of love. For the reflective man realizes that faith is quickened only in love or the giving of person to person through free interchange. It is the finalizing goal of this interplay between all the factors of religious existence which Kierkegaard indicated in his remark that the most complete subjectivity coincides with the most complete objectivity. Men can at least aim at some remote analogue of the divine way of joining subjective intensity with objective vision.

Perhaps it is in the notion of interplay or existential tension between the several factors of faith and reflection that Kierkegaard is of supreme relevance for us today. Paul Tillich has been exploring the points of conflict and possible reconciliation between the attitude based on biblical religion and that fostered by the search after ultimate reality. Kierkegaard's contribution is to bring out that there are several ways in which one can engage in reflection. If the attempt to supply a general theory of being is undertaken in a spirit that renders impossible a distinct revelation from God or that reduces the responsibility of will and decision to a purely speculative system, then there is bound to be conflict with Christian religiousness. But there are other routes for the inquiry into being to follow. Kierkegaard's analysis of the various types of reflection and of their relations to religious and moral faith suggests that the personal attitude of the thinker is decisive for the relationship. Our task today is to examine the possibility of engaging in a general intellectual study of the real, without severing the bond between reflection and action or clouding over the openness of reflection to revealed faith.

CHAPTER 5

EDITH STEIN AS A PHENOMENOLOGIST

TODAY, we know Edith Stein primarily as a heroic and saintly human person. She was one of the numberless victims of Hitler's war of extermination against the Jews, but her story remains to encourage us about the nobility of the human spirit and the strength which one receives from religious faith. As a Catholic nun of the Carmelite order, she left her testament in religious reflections on the Christian life and in a study of mysticism as being the living science of the cross. In her religious and educational writings, Edith Stein made personal use of a phenomenological method. She also employed this approach in reinterpreting the classical and medieval metaphysical doctrines on finite beings and their relationship with the eternal being of God. The purpose of the present chapter is to probe behind the religious, metaphysical, and educational achievements of Edith Stein to her understanding of phenomenology as a tool for working in these areas. Our interest is in her own basic formation in phenomenology and the contributions which she made directly to its advance during the period between the two World Wars.

She was one of the first students to receive the doctoral degree in philosophy under Edmund Husserl, after he assumed his chair at the University of Freiburg in Breisgau. Her 1916 dissertation was written on the problem of empathy, a psychological concept recognized to have some bearing on phenomenological problems.[1] Husserl had criticized the experimental side of Theodor Lipps' concept of empathy, but for a while he was inclined to accept a revised version of it as being part of our original equipment. Empathy held some attraction for Husserl when he began to consider some difficulties in his view of the self as a monadic center of pure consciousness.[2] There was a possibility that empathy might be the effective means whereby the transcendental ego could relate itself to other subjectivities and the world

85

of nature. Then the ego could overcome any solipsistic isolation and take its place in a phenomenologically verified community of selves. In her dissertation, however, Edith Stein refused to accept this rather easy solution for a problem which was to bother Husserl down to his final years.[3] On the other hand, she admitted that we do have experience of other subjects and that its explanation can only be found in a nonpsychologistic analysis of the structure of the human person. Thus her dissertation served her, as such an exercise usually does, mainly to raise some problems and set the course for later investigations.

After the first World War, Edith Stein had the advantages afforded by her position as Husserl's assistant. She had access to his still unpublished manuscripts and discussed the problems which were then uppermost in his mind. This close association between master and learner was reflected in the topics which Edith Stein chose for her own work, since most of them concerned the social relationships of the individual person. Although she became increasingly critical of the epistemological framework which led Husserl eventually to his principle of transcendental intersubjectivity, her findings on the question of interpersonal communication throw some valuable light on the social aspects of phenomenology. They also establish some of her own basic convictions which were later to be given more concrete form in her educational and religious writings.

Edith Stein's first two essays, published in Husserl's *Annual* for 1922, dealt with the social relationship as a phase of the phenomenological foundation of psychology and the humane sciences.[4] This approach is a reminder to us that Husserl's critique of psychologism did not blind him to the need for giving a foundation to the humane sciences and hence that the later French phenomenologist, Maurice Merleau-Ponty, was building upon a long tradition when he specialized in this area. Stein concentrated upon two related issues. The first was an effort to awaken a phenomenological meaning for causality, as considered in terms of the individual human agent. Later, she extended her inquiry to include the various forms of community life in which persons become involved.

1. *Restoring Human Causality*

In his attack upon psychologism, Husserl had objected to the extension of physically based causal concepts into the sphere of pure consciousness and rigorous knowledge. He pointed out that connections of meaning are not the same as connections established on the ground of associative habits, as Hume had claimed. But Edith Stein wondered whether there is any other concept of causality than the physically based one, and whether it can be defended against Hume's criticism. She was dissatisfied with merely contrasting meaning and causality, since there may be a type of causality which respects the realm of meaning and has its foundation in the same source where we have our meanings. We have already seen the relevance of this topic for evaluating the existentialist views on religion.

Hume's account of causality is not effectively overcome by Kant, because he changes the terms of discussion from the human experiences to the *a priori* categories which are supposed to render them possible. It is better to show that Hume psychologized the causal bond only because of his failure to keep looking at the phenomena bearing on the matter. Edith Stein notes that Hume's explanation in function of customary expectation rests upon his previous epistemological postulate, taken over from rationalism, that wherever the connection is not analytically necessary it does not refer to any real causal linkage. It is this presupposition which prevents him from finding in the phenomenal process anything but a sequence determined by associative paths. The only way to remove the Humean position is to return to a steady description of the relations we experience. The causal relation is not primarily a question about logical kinds of connectives but one about what appears in the original living stream of human experience.[5] Edith Stein returns to our perceptual and reflective lifeworld for a meaning of causality that is not drawn from physical science but from our human way of being and acting.

We can experience and analyze the causal process, as soon as we recognize the active presence of the self in our conscious life. The self is not a bundled summation of our perceptions but the living source of our acts of perceiving. The description of our psychic life is left incomplete, if it is confined to our actual experiences as facts and is not prolonged to include the self as the active principle constituting those facts into a meaningful pattern. Within the evanescent stream of life, sense and direction are achieved through the causal influence of the self and its several permanent powers or capacities.[6]

In her analysis of empirical consciousness, which is not simply evacuated by the process of reduction, Edith Stein distinguishes between a relatively passive and a relatively active aspect. Insofar as our empirical life involves some receptivity and ordination to the natural world, the kind of causality undergone is best described in terms of physical determinism. Hence in stressing the causal activity of the self, Edith Stein does not intend to eliminate any of the relationships which are regarded as causal either by classical mechanism or by later physical and psycho-physiological theories. She admits the usefulness of treating the psyche as a regulative mechanism having a determined quantum of energy. But this cannot be the complete or the decisive interpretation of our way of experiencing and acting.[7] Even when physics suggests that probability rather than completely determinate predictability governs the relations among events, there is need for another interpretative principle at the level of our conscious life and activities. The psychic field presents itself as a qualitative continuum in which the initiative is increasingly taken by the inquiring and desiring self.

Analysis of human experience shows not only a determination by physical conditions and unconscious forces but also an influence in the order of apprehended meaning and sought purpose. This is a sign of the causal presence of the self, whose influence is purposive and not modeled upon physical forces. The moral philosophers can help us here, since in every age they have distinguished between the actions which merely are done by a man and those which can rightly be called human. For, the truly human actions are those which embody an intent and belong within a pattern.

At this point, Edith Stein suggests that *causality in the purposive sense* and *intentional meaning* are complementary principles in our properly human living experience, rather than opposed domains. This is the only way to make an effective criticism of the Humean notion of the flow of experience as consisting of inherently discrete pellets of perception or sense data, which are bound together only by the beliefs which customary association imposes on us. The actual human agent can at times relate his actions in a meaningful and liberating way: he can grasp the grounds and aim of a proposed action and relate this particular pattern of conduct to a broader frame of meaningful existence. Properly human actions take their origin in the purposive self, and are related to each other on the basis of the meaning and mutual implication intended for them by the self. Where the self is directly and properly involved in human actions, all other considerations become subsidiary to the relationship of a proposed line of conduct to the meaningful unity for which the self is striving. This is the sort of causal actuality which comes within our experience, and which phenomenological description refuses to disintegrate either by identifying causality with physical intervention or by treating our original perceptions as atomically separated islands.

By resisting these two latter procedures, Edith Stein was also able to bring out the link between meaningful causality and freedom. At the distinctively human level of conduct, the agent seeks to will one act on the basis of another act or with respect to some general conception of his life which he attends to, at least implicitly. The causal role of the self is not that of a physical agent emitting energy units but of a striving principle of meaningful actions. The self is the originative and free source of actions which belong precisely in the domain of meaning and which are laden with intent.

Human actions refer to the world of objects as being meaningful and perhaps desirable for the agent. We are confronted with things, not as so many unknown x's of classical modern epistemology, but as motivating realities which challenge our effort to attain an adequate pattern of significance and value. Since the causal operation of the self opens out this face of things to us, human volition cannot be explained away successfully by Hume's univocal continuum of associated perceptions and passions. Edith Stein wants to extend the recognition of newly emergent levels of being from the biological order to that of human conscious life. The unity which arises from incorporating a particular action and object into a wider pattern of motivated and willed acts is a new sort of complexus in the field of activity.[8] This unity belongs in the region of our free acts, where the self is meaningfully dominant and where its deeds come to be under its own rational control.

Edith Stein rehabilitates the term "will" to designate the self insofar as it is causally operative in developing its meanings and style of conduct. The decisive act of will is required so that the practical motives can become effective, and not merely possible, aims of action. For most people, the experiential basis for acknowledging something immaterial and transcendent in man is furnished by their desiring and deciding activities, which they recognize to bring in a factor that is not entirely shaped by external nature and the objects of sense inclination. A man does not always act solely in respect to the attainment of sensible objects, taken by themselves. Sometimes, he recognizes that their meaning as motivating realities must be related by himself freely to other considerations. These other and often dominating considerations affecting our choice concern the individual's relations with other subjects or centers of freedom.

Rather briefly, toward the end of her study on causality in the individual man, Edith Stein observes that the other subjects or causally operative selves include both our fellow men and God. She describes the religious act as having a distinctive intentional structure, a point which we will also have to consider presently in connection with Max Scheler. From her perspective, the typical quality of the religious act is its trustful surrender to and rest in the personal God. She relates religious worship closely with a sense of freedom and spiritual rebirth, of being able to rely upon a personal and good source of strength distinct from ourselves. Divine causality is thus a requirement, not a disruption, of human development. Paradoxically, our individual growth depends upon our ability and willingness to turn to God and our neighbors for help in achieving the meaningful unity of our personal existence.[9] That is why the reality of other selves arises not primarily as a problem in epistemology and transcendental phenomenology but as a personal and moral one concerning the active development of the self.

2. *The Self and the Community*

Edith Stein approached the question of social life in terms of the well known distinction between community and society made by the German sociologist, Ferdinand Tönnies. He viewed a community as a natural, organic grouping of individuals, whereas he described a society as a somewhat artificial union resting upon an act of rational deliberation. Edith Stein was not fully satisfied with this account, because it placed the emphasis upon the matter of origin rather than upon the present intention of the individuals participating in these social forms. Hence she suggested the following distinction as a preliminary step. When one man regards himself precisely as a personal subject and regards other men as objects, the result of their mutual efforts at understanding and common effort is a *society*. On the other hand, when one subject recognizes others precisely as fellow personal subjects, then they are able to live together in a *community*. This contrast should not be applied too rigidly, however, since in most of our social groups there are both societal and communal features present. The distinction is helpful mainly to detect the dominant quality in a particular human association, rather than to serve as a criterion for determining any pure instances.

One use to which Edith Stein puts this distinction is in guiding her description of the kind of leadership to expect, when a human group becomes predominantly a society or a community. The intentional relationship between the leader of a society and its members is most favorable to exploiters and dictators, since they can treat the members as objective instruments of policy. The exploiter looks upon those with whom he is associated in a society as so many means to be used objectively for the ends he proposes. But his ability to objectify the members of his group is eventually bound within some limitations. He does have to make due calculation of the effect of his rule over them. If only to advance his exploitive purposes, then, he must recognize that they have a personal, subjective reality, that they are centers of interpretation, and that their meaningful attitudes are really present even when he chooses to run roughshod over them.

Thus even the industrial exploiter and the political dictator bear reluctant witness to the truth that society is not the unique and self-sufficient form open to men seeking a social development of themselves. To treat other individuals as impersonal tools, one must ape in some way the understanding among persons upon which community life rests. Perhaps the reason why Edith Stein does not want to accept a doctrinaire opposition between society and community is that it obscures this open relationship between the two, and hence quenches the hope for extending the realm of communal ties. She is also aware of the special problem facing the genuine leader of a community. The leader or leaders do have to make a careful, factual study of the members of the community with their needs and resources, the problem being to do so without treating the members purely as objects and thus losing the communal quality. Stein recommends that any program for the community should contain safeguards against using it for the private advantage of those in power, and that it should draw directly upon our personal experience of working with such community members as friends and family.

From the phenomenological standpoint, however, there is a difficulty about showing how an ego which is constitutive of its conscious life can ever have this communal experience with other such egos. Edith Stein does not try to resolve this question in the reductional terms in which it is framed. Instead of working out from a theory of the transcendental ego, as does Husserl himself, she returns to an analysis of the actual community life which we have. And here she distinguishes three components: the subject of the communal experience, this experience itself, and the living stream which unifies the experience.[10]

There is a sense in which we can speak of the social subject of our group experience, a subject which embraces a multiplicity of individual selves. The trust which I feel toward our leader is not mine alone but belongs to the whole group: what we experience is our trust. In this sense, there is a social self or subject of experience, which we sometimes refer to as the community spirit or the tone and temper of a community. In the same vein, we distinguish between what befalls an individual, even regarded as a member of the community, and what happens to the community as a social reality. But Edith Stein warns against concluding that the subject of the communal experience is an independent structure. The experience of the community as well as that of its members springs ultimately from the individual selves constituting this group. In them is rooted the unifying intention of seeking a common object and realizing a common pattern of meaning which constitutes the actuality of the community.[11] There is a social subject in the degree that there is at least an implicitly intended common goal of activity, affecting the meaning of existence for many persons. Individual selves contribute in their various ways to the lived experience of the community. In and through the actual participation of the members in the unity of goal and unity of meaning, the community has its own social experience.

Whereas totalitarian social philosophers would go on to attribute a super-individual consciousness to the subject of communal experience, Edith Stein holds that there is no ground for drawing that conclusion. She grants that the community lives and *experiences* in and through its members, but not that it can *reflect* upon itself when they reflect upon their experience. Hence the community is not a superior self, in any real and rigorous sense. Only the individual human persons can reflect upon the communal experience, and hence only in them is the structural being of selfhood properly realized. There is an experience belonging to the whole community, but the constitutive source of this experience lies inalienably in the individual selves who jointly intend this shared life.

Once this limitation is firmly established, Edith Stein is able to move ahead with a study of the community. It does not consist merely of an additive mass but is a distinctive reality, born from the commonly intended living experience of many persons. Its members enter into the community in a differentiated way and sustain its different operations. Although the community is not a free reflective self, it does bear certain responsibilities and opportunities for the use of power which the individual members can only realize in this cooperative way. The members are enriched in personal growth through their acceptance of the common intent of community life. But they must come to be sufficiently reflective about their communal experience to recognize that the personal free self should never allow itself to be totally exhausted in its social functions and pursuits.[12] Social tasks are not self-sustaining ends in themselves, and they wither away in our hands when we devote all of our energy to them and forget the personal springs from which their structure arises.

To bring out even more forcibly the personal basis of communal life, Edith Stein returns to the distinction between society and community, now adding to it the concept of the mass. The latter is a grouping of men solely on the basis of their place of birth or their occupation or some temporary sentiment, but without the organizing presence of a reasonable social pattern. Just as animals run in a herd, so men can join in a swarming mass without achieving a commonly intended purpose. The perfection of a society is that it does involve a union of men for a reasonable social goal. But this goal is something distinct from the personal reality of the members of the society, and does not engage them as free selves. More of a demand is placed upon us as members of a community, since here the ground and goal of the social intention should be the personal realization of those who are participating in it.[13] Edith Stein is as sharply critical of the drift toward anonymity in modern European social life as are Gabriel Marcel and other existentialists. If personal freedom is not enhanced by the social arrangement, then it is no more than a featureless mass or a mechanized society devoted to subhuman ends.

The final theme in Edith Stein's analysis of the community is the need for *restraint* on the part of the community. As a humane social form, it is not omnicompetent and cannot totally absorb the personal life of men. The social instruments for limiting human societies and communities do not destroy their nature but keep them balanced and helpful to men. Stein adds that acceptance of limitations in the exercise of social power not only promotes the human benefits but also brings out the finite character of every community and society on earth.[14] The limited community not only encourages us to use our personal freedom but also permits us to devote ourselves in a proper way to God. One of the fruits of self-restraint in the earthly community should be the freedom for transcendence or the search for the City of God.

3. *Analysis of the State*

Husserl's *Annual* for 1925 contains a long study by Edith Stein on the nature of the state.[15] Here she applies the conclusions of her previous investigations to the particular case of the civil community, and develops some new points. Writing at a time when totalitarian philosophies of the state were growing powerful in the practical order in Russia, Italy, and Germany, she seeks to work out a phenomenological path between the extremes of statism and individualism. She is more openly and pointedly critical of totalitarian and racist trends in Germany than were most of the phenomenologists writing during the nineteen-twenties.

Since it is lacking in purposeful motivation, the mass cannot constitute itself as a civil community. But the state does get founded on the other two social forms: community and society. Stein regards the state, at its best, as being a community which also involves many societal elements. This is another reason why she does not accept a sharp dichotomy between community and society: the sound civil community must take advantage of the rationalized procedures of a society, while nevertheless subordinating them to the interpersonal life of the members of the community. Locke and Rousseau were in error when they treated the state chiefly as a society and gave it an origin in a social contract or deliberate act of will. Like other communities, the state has a natural origin, in the sense that it builds upon existent social groupings and does not usually depend upon a contractual act.

We can keep our perspective on the state by refraining from treating it in isolation, like Hobbes' mortal god or leviathan. The state is an intermediate form of community, finding its context by reference to the smaller domestic and friendly groups and the all-embracing union of the world community or humanity. Edith Stein differentiates the state from the smaller groups by the note of sovereignty, since the state can make, interpret, and enforce its own laws. But she adds that the various smaller groups constitute public spheres of life which do not depend on civil enactment for their existence, and which should not be annihilated by the civil community. Like every other community, the state must exercise self-limitation in respect to these public spheres and also in respect to the requirements of the world community. Stein would agree with John Stuart Mill that self-restraint of civil power is no defect in the authority of the state.[16] On the contrary, limitation of civil power and promotion of the freedom of its citizens are the functional conditions whereby the state maintains itself as a proper form of community life.

Even though she employs the unwieldy concept of sovereignty as the distinguishing note of the state, Edith Stein is on her guard against any absolutism based upon racism or a folk mystique. An irrationalist form of state absolutism sometimes results from considering the state as a community having organic natural origins, in contrast with the rational decision or the social contract at the base of a society. But Stein has already pointed out that the unity and distinctive experience of the community are due to the participation of its members in a common purpose, which is intelligently as well as affectively apprehended and accepted. What is natural for man as a communal being is precisely that he make an intelligent appraisal of his situation and use his power of reflection in determining and developing the various communal forms of life, including the state. Furthermore, there is historical evidence that a people may retain its communal way of life even under foreign rule, even when it does not also exercise civil power over itself. Edith Stein finds no contrary evidence requiring the state to achieve its unity of existence and power by confining itself to some single folk or some single race.[17] It can embrace several folk-communities and racial groups (if these latter can be distinguished within the human pool), or else it can serve as a communal instrument for groups of people who are not joined together on any basis of folk or race.

Following the personalist bent of her social analysis, Edith Stein looks to the structure of the human person rather than to the formal and somewhat barren concept of the state itself for reasons why the state is usually developed within the context of some already existing communities.[18] The need is a mutual one. The social values which are created in the family, the work group, and other intermediate communities are usually best protected and fostered under a common public law. For its own stability and acceptance to people, civil power in turn ordinarily supposes a vital community and social solidarity of the people, as they engage in various communal and societal forms. The rhythm of personal existence is a complex one, and we learn the discipline of social life by participating in many kinds of communal existence. The bare relationship of individuals to the state is an abstraction which does not take account of the plural community life in which we freely develop. Other sorts of community life can legitimately make more intense demands upon us than the state. For our relations with family, friends, and other associates are essential for realizing our personal and interpersonal capacities.

Within its legitimate sphere, however, the state must be served not only by the external fulfillment of appointed tasks but also by our interior adherence to the common intention of its citizens. Edith Stein does not accept the purely penal theory of the nature of civil law. If a civil servant employs his office for his private interests, he not only violates public regulations and accepts the penalty but also violates his conscience and delivers a thrust against the spiritual foundation of the civil community. His act tends to make that community a mere object serving his own ends, and thus he severs himself morally from it and tends to weaken it to the extent that he could have made an honest contribution. This requirement of a personal moral adhesion holds for any legitimate kind of state. Edith Stein does not think that there is any absolutely best form of government or that the practically more desirable form can be decided simply from analysis of the idea of the state.[19] Each arrangement has to be weighed in the light of the particular social circumstances, and in most instances it is healthy to be confronted with several political alternatives.

Although Edith Stein treats the relationship between the person and the state as a moral one, she criticizes the view that man finds his supreme moral vocation in his life as a citizen of the state. Whereas Husserl opposed subjective idealism mainly on epistemological grounds, Stein's opposition to German idealism centers here upon its ethical exaltation of the state. According to Fichte and Hegel, the state is the realization of ethical actuality and of the striving of history for freedom. But there are three defects in this conception of the state.[20] First, if the role assigned to the state is due to its position in a dialectical process, then the problem of freedom within the dialectic of history applies with special acuity to the state itself. There is an inherent necessity in the phases of the dialectic which militates against a freedom based upon personal choice. If the ethical supremacy of the state is due to its function in the unfolding of a dialectical process in being (not just a dialectical method of interpretation), then the ethical order is not rooted in the personal, free agents. In the second place, we may well speak about an unfolding simply as a development, without connoting any ideal necessity in the process. But then we must add that what actually develops is not freedom-in-itself or history-in-itself but the human reality of persons and interpersonal communities. The state is one form of communal existence, and as such it cannot be regarded as a summating self. There is social responsibility and social freedom in the state, but only within the conditions already specified for the interpersonal subjects of communal experience. Finally, it is undeniable that human freedom is bound up for better and for worse with the ways in which we dispose civil power. But a fully contextual view of the state shows that the historical aspects of freedom reach farther than the state, which is itself ordered to the welfare of humanity or the world community. For a full conception of moral freedom, we have to see the life of the personal existent in plural relationship with all the kinds of community and also in relationship with God as transcending all human communities.

One reason why Edith Stein refuses to locate man's ethical vocation in his civil life is to permit our religious transcendence to develop in freedom. Part of the self-restraint required of the state as a human community is that it should not demand its citizens to regard it as their supreme ethical good. The state is not itself the bearer of religious values, since it is not a self and does not have any independent capacity for reflection in the religious mode.[21] The state can indeed encourage or hinder man's community with God, and this is the ground for the long and troubled history of the church-state relationship. This history suggests that we should stress both our moral obligations toward our civil life and also our resolve not to burden the state itself with an absolute ethico-religious significance.

4. *Husserl and St. Thomas*

In the special volume issued in 1929 to celebrate Husserl's seventieth anniversary, Edith Stein contributed a comparative essay on Husserl and St. Thomas.[22] This was her first extensive statement of the results of a detailed study of the Common Doctor which she made following her conversion to Catholicism in 1922. She felt that there was a substantial intellectual continuity between what she had learned as a phenomenologist and what she discovered with the aid of religious faith and Thomistic philosophy. Her aim in this essay was to specify some of the major points of agreement and difference between the two masters of her intellectual life.

Granting the great historical distance between Aquinas and Husserl, there is nevertheless a marked similarity in their attitudes toward philosophical work. For both thinkers, philosophizing is not a pleasant pastime ruled by our passing moods and fancies but a way of attaining scientific knowledge, a precise method of thinking which yields a body of systematic and certain truth. This likeness must be recognized, even when we realize that the model for scientific knowledge is more theological with Aquinas and more mathematical with Husserl. They also agree that the philosopher's situation is deeply affected by a long tradition of Western philosophy, and that his vocation is to rethink the origins and discover afresh the springs of evidence in that tradition. Both thinkers regard the universe as being intelligible and as challenging man to trace out the intelligible connections and determine the necessary structures of meaning concerning the world.

Aquinas and Husserl share a basic confidence in the ability of our mind to carry on this philosophical work. But the distinction between natural knowledge and that obtained through supernatural revelation is more important for the Thomistic outlook than for the Husserlian. The validity of this distinction is not denied by Husserl, but neither does he regard it as being relevant to his philosophical studies, which rely upon what can be ascertained by reason taken in its essential natural functions. Viewing reason in this way, he sees no point in setting limits in principle to the efforts of the human mind to encompass all meanings. Yet Husserl does grant that the attainment of certain knowledge through philosophical analysis is an endless task, an approach in the direction of an ideal completeness of truth that we never fully possess.

Aquinas agrees with this judgment about the essential openness of philosophy to further insights, since this corresponds to the temporal condition of man. Where a difference crops up is over the question of divine knowledge. As far as God's own knowledge is concerned, Aquinas holds that we can truly ascertain that He is in perfect actual possession of the truth, whereas Husserl abstains from making any philosophical pronouncements bearing upon the being and knowledge of God. Thus as far as Husserl will go in philosophy, the complete grasp of truth remains an ideal to be sought and not an actuality to be acknowledged as already present anywhere in being.

When we take the doctrine of Aquinas as a whole, it is thoroughly permeated by revelation and theological reflection in a way that remains quite foreign to Husserl's conception of philosophy. The latter does not regard faith as a more certain way to truth, one which preserves reason from many errors and reveals to it even some truths which it might have discovered through its natural power. For Husserl, philosophy cannot show that there is any duty on the part of human reason toward supernatural faith, and philosophy does not look forward to finding its fulfillment in a rational investigation of revealed truths. This does not mean that he is opposed to revelation and supernatural faith, but rather that he accepts the complete modern separation of philosophical reason from the influence of the supernatural. Philosophy simply prescinds from faith as a response to the transcendent God. There is a Husserlian theory of belief, but it belongs to the analysis of rational natural knowledge, which sets its own methodology and justifies its own doxic or conviction-yielding acts in an immanent way.

As Edith Stein sees it, the most serious difference between Husserl and Aquinas beyond the question of the relevance of revelation to philosophy concerns the theory of reductions in philosophy. She herself uses an eidetic reduction in order to bring out the essential structure of the community and the basis of causality. But she stops short, and maintains that Aquinas would also stop short, at the final transcendental reduction of the acts of consciousness and their intended objects to the pure immanence of the ego. Her reluctance is due partly to the ambiguity in Husserl's remarks about how the pure transcendental ego constitutes the world along with its own meanings. Even granting that Husserl does not mean that the constituting act is a making or creating of the objects in the world, he does speak as though both the act and the object of knowledge are totally immanent structures within the intentional life of the constituting ego, which thereby attains to a certitude beyond the reach of doubt.

But this total immanence lies beyond our human condition. The transcendental reduction supposes as the condition of philosophical certitude a situation which is properly found only in God's self-knowledge. Hence in all of her phenomenological studies, Edith Stein remains as close as possible to what Husserl calls the empirical ego and its intended essential structures, without trying to found her results upon a relationship between the empirical and the transcendental ego. She also agrees with St. Thomas that the human intellect is ordered to a reality which it knows to be existentially as well as intentionally distinct from itself.[23] The difficulty about Husserl's transcendental reduction is that it removes this indelible mark of our creaturely dependence, even though it seeks to maintain the distinctive structure of the empirical ego. Later on, I will attempt to make a more detailed analysis of how Husserl's conception of man is affected by his theory of a reduction to the transcendental ego.

Stemming from this fundamental issue is a contrast between Husserl's conception of ontology and Thomistic metaphysics, at least as Edith Stein views it. In the Wolffian tradition, Husserl admits that there are several regional ontologies of both a material and a formal sort, dealing with the different kinds of objects. But he considers them to be essential sciences which do not draw their certitude from the contingently grasped actualities. The entire world of contingent facts and acts is retained in its essential content by Husserl, but it does not provide the basis for his judgments about their being. Here, he comes into sharp conflict with the Thomistic view of metaphysics as a science basing itself upon the actual world and the knowledge grounded in this world. Thomistic metaphysics organizes itself around the analysis of contingent actual beings, as its certitudinal foundation, and the inference to God as its goal.

At this point, Edith Stein was touching upon the crucial issue which was henceforth to confront her in all her philosophical investigations. She was coming to orient metaphysics toward experienced realities and God, or finite beings and the eternal being. Could she accept this way of shaping philosophy and still use the phenomenological method? Clearly, she could not do so without rethinking that method and submitting it to considerable modification. Husserl's primary concern was not for a metaphysics of God and finite beings but for a transcendental phenomenology answering the question: How is a world which I can immanently investigate constituted for consciousness? [24] Taken as a whole, his method was designed to deal with the intending subject and its constituting acts and objects. Edith Stein's judgment was that a philosophy so centered cannot emerge from the immanence of purified conscience to which the transcendental reduction leads. But she did not conclude that the phenomenological method is so bound up in solidarity with Husserl's philosophy that it cannot serve any other philosophical aims. Much of her later work was devoted to showing that the phenomenological method is not just a global whole, that some aspects of it are useful for metaphysics, and that the only way to back this up was to make some actual use of these aspects in the context of a philosophy ordered to the study of finite acts of being and the infinite being of God.

Even in 1929, however, she felt that her task would be eased by clearing up some misconceptions about the Husserlian theory of our grasp of essences. There is a broad similarity between phenomenology and Thomism on three related points. [25] First, all human knowledge begins with sense perception. Whatever their differences on the metaphysical import of the sensible world or its precise way of contributing to philosophical knowledge, both Aquinas and Husserl treat our perceptual acquaintance with objects as basic and controlling. Next, they agree upon the need to make an intellectual elaboration of the perceptual data. We have to submit them to analysis, variation, and some kind of inference in order to reach their essential meaning. The Husserlian grasp of the essence is not a direct and effortless view, for otherwise there would be no need for the discipline of philosophical method and the careful analysis of the sense qualities. In the third place, there is agreement that intuition under human conditions is not purely active and does not sheerly produce its objects. Even though Husserl extends the scope of intuition beyond the range admitted by Aquinas in order to include our knowledge of essences, he does so without denying the distinction between directly given truths and those arrived at in a mediate way. Insofar as the phenomenological method concerns our search after the truth of essential structures, then, it can be used in the reconstruction of philosophy along broadly Thomistic lines.

5. *Finite and Eternal Being*

As Edith Stein's philosophical thought actually developed during the nineteen-thirties, however, it was not rigidly Thomistic but showed the deep influence of her readings in St. Augustine, Dionysius, Duns Scotus, and St. John of the Cross. Despite constant harassment from the Nazis, she managed to prepare for press her major philosophical treatise, *Finite and Eternal Being*.[26] The book was written in 1935-1936, and was already set up in type at Breslau when the order against publishing any non-Aryan writings was issued by Hitler. Hence the book was not actually published until 1950, in the Louvain edition of her writings.

She conceives of her masterwork as being both an essay in perennial philosophy and an effort at achieving an understanding between Aquinas and Husserl. She does not give a normative, doctrinal definition of perennial philosophy, but regards it as the persevering efforts of men throughout history to arrive at the truth of being. This is the prevalent meaning for perennial philosophy among phenomenologists and existentialists today, and we will analyze it somewhat closer in a subsequent chapter. Edith Stein does not pretend to have achieved a complete reconciliation between Aquinas and Husserl, since the points of difference which she had already noted are fundamental and remain in force. Moreover, in this mature work, she does not claim that her own position rests upon an integral acceptance of either philosopher, or even upon a selective blending of the two. But she does believe that both of them have aided her toward discovering the meaning of being, both as finite and as eternal.

Her method here is to begin with analysis of Aristotle and St. Thomas on the great metaphysical topics: act and potency, essential and actual being, substance and accident, matter and form. The approach is primarily analytical and doctrinal, without much concern for historical discussions. After presenting the positions contained in these classical sources, Edith Stein attempts her own reworking of the problem with the help of phenomenological procedures. However, the phenomenologists whom she most frequently cites are those who stressed the realistic and object-oriented aspects of phenomenology, rather than those who follow Husserl himself in the transcendental idealist phase of his philosophy. Thus in natural philosophy she relies heavily upon the work on matter and life, space and time, done by Hedwig Conrad-Martius, whereas in metaphysical and psychological areas she makes considerable use of Alexander Pfänder and Jean Hering.

In addition to the Aristotelian and phenomenological traditions, however, Stein also brings in some considerations from Catholic theology and especially her favorite mystical sources, St. Teresa of Avila and St. John of the Cross. Her precedent for attending to revelation is St. Thomas, and for studying the mystics is Jacques Maritain. Her aim is to make a contribution to Christian philosophy with the aid of these various sources.

On every major issue treated, there is a systematic comparison made between classical philosophy, the Christian outlook and phenomenological method. Edith Stein's treatment of act and potency is typical, since she approaches this problem both in the more traditional way, which rests on a study of sensible things in motion, and in phenomenological terms of our own self-experience.[27] Here, she continues the pattern already set in her earlier treatment of causality. The fruitful suggestion is made that all of the basic metaphysical concepts have to be reinterpreted so as to include the distinctive evidence of our *personal experience*. There is no question for Stein of eliminating the analysis of the sensible world but only of adding the quite distinctive and irreplaceable way that finite being manifests itself in our personal and conscious existence. Since the intentional or object-intending nature of our experience is a basic phenomenological thesis, she shows in practice how the acts of our inner life can be examined for metaphysical purposes without undermining the reality and importance of the material world and the analyses made primarily in function of it.

There is a balance in Edith Stein's approach to metaphysics which is lacking in some other efforts to reconstitute this science on a phenomenological basis. She does not propose any doctrinaire opposition between material things and human experience, and hence she does not lay it down that act and potency, substance and causality, are incompatible with a metaphysics of human meanings. What she does ask very sensibly is that our reworking of these metaphysical bases should take into account the human aspects as well as those which refer mainly to the sensible world of things.

Edith Stein's main philosophical treatise is a highly personal reformulation of the sources. It cannot properly be said to achieve an integration between Aquinas and Husserl, taking each man in his full philosophical import. There are four factors which prevent her from making any such comprehensive synthesis. The first one lies in her failure to make a historical study of St. Thomas himself (as distinct from "Thomistic" textbooks), in order to ascertain from all available texts his precise meaning on metaphysical issues. The purely analytic approach has some doctrinal advantages, but ultimately it leaves us uneasy about Stein's references to Aquinas and other philosophers. She does not see the intrinsic philosophical interest to be found in studying the historical relations between Aquinas and Aristotle, as well as between Aquinas and the other medieval thinkers. Especially on the question of essence and existence, she could have profited from a reading of Avicenna and from a historically oriented introduction to Duns Scotus. Scotus is indeed appealed to as a counterauthority against Aquinas on many questions, but the opposition remains very abstract and does not take account of the systematic contexts within which these two thinkers operated.

The second consideration is closely related to this last point. Edith Stein states her disagreement with St. Thomas on a number of important questions.[28] The principle of individuation is located in the form rather than in signate matter; a spiritual matter is placed in angels, who are pure spirits but not pure forms; all creatures (and not only men) bear the image of God; universals have an irreducible nature of their own. She states that she sides with Duns Scotus on these points. But in fact, her judgment is guided by her own conception of being.

She views finite being ultimately in function of the *unfolding of meanings*.[29] This is consistent with her contention that the pure forms or meaningful essences arrived at through phenomenological analysis of experience are metaphysically more basic than either the act of real existing or the conceptions of our mind. Stein uses the broad term *Existenz* to include both the unfolding of meaning in the world of space-time empirical being (*Dasein*) and the determinate existence of ideal objects, such as mathematical natures.[30] The latter are not actual, in the sense of existing and operating under space-time conditions of empirical being. But they do enjoy an independent, subsistent meaning that is reducible neither to actual spatio-temporal existents nor to our thoughts, but only to the divine mind. God alone is fully actual and meaningful, but His being must be kept distinct from that of the existential order in the above two senses. In respect to pure essences, moreover, His main work is to provide the ground of their unity and order. Nevertheless, Stein repudiates the pantheistic interpretation which we will find Max Scheler to advance.

Edith Stein is convinced that we can move philosophically from a study of finite being to God, from composed beings to the uncomposed actuality. Her description of act and potency, essence and existence, matter and form, is intended to provide a detailed account of the structure of composed beings. But the composition is nowhere conceived in terms of mutually uniting principles of being. The components are treated as parts, layers, and levels in the constitution of finite being. In that way, these components can be treated separately as objects intended by our distinctive acts of meaning. In order to make the actual transition from composed finite beings to the eternal God, however, Stein finds it difficult to use efficient causality in analyzing her layered conception of finite being. Hence she relies mainly upon what Plotinus, St. Augustine, and the mystics tell us about the orientation and hunger of the soul for God.[31] This is basically the yearning of temporal selves for the eternal actuality of God, and fits in with her earlier stress upon a purposive personal notion of causality.

There are some indications that Edith Stein was in the process of subordinating all of the key metaphysical concepts in Aristotle and Aquinas to a theory of being that is much closer to Heidegger. In a brief note, she agrees with the latter thinker that temporality is the distinguishing mark of finite being as such, rather than the composition of essence and existence. That is perhaps why she views finite being chiefly in terms of the unfolding and the being-unfolded of meanings, and why she refers to God most characteristically as the eternal being. However, she explicitly disagrees with Heidegger's remark (in *Being and Time*) that time provides the gateway to a grasp of the general significance of being, since this would reduce the humanly apprehensible significance of being entirely to temporal and finite modes of being.[32] Edith Stein might have accepted Heidegger's later position that we must take the standpoint of being, in turn, in order to learn the secret of time. But then she would ask whether the meaning of being is enclosed within the finite and temporal order or whether we do not have to trace finite beings to their roots in the eternal being, as the condition for reaching the full significance of being as such.

The two remaining reasons which prevented her from uniting Aquinas and Husserl in the spirit of her earlier commemorative essay are highly contingent ones, bearing upon her relation with Husserl himself. For one thing, she was no longer directly associated with him during his amazingly productive later period, when he was exploring so many new paths and giving fresh developments to his old themes. Edith Stein realized that she was not in a position to assimilate all of these findings, compare them with relevant teachings in Aquinas, and then reach her own conclusions on a large scale. And finally, even in *Finite and Eternal Being* she methodologically confined the discussion to metaphysical issues. She did not feel prepared as yet to deal with those problems of knowledge which she had previously specified as being so important in comparing Aquinas and Husserl. Precisely how to integrate her conception of being with a doctrine on knowledge remained as a project for future work. But she was not given the peace and leisure to carry out a study of these further questions. We are fortunate to have the fruits of the actual work she was able to do in phenomenology and metaphysics.

CHAPTER 6

ROOTS OF SCHELER'S
EVOLUTIONARY PANTHEISM

1. *The Problem of Max Scheler*

In Europe and America, the philosophy of Max Scheler (1874-1928) is undergoing a remarkable and paradoxical renascence. He has been hailed by diametrically opposed groups as a saving guide in the midst of intellectual chaos. His emphasis upon philosophical anthropology as the basic, unifying discipline has met with renewed approval in the wake of the second World War and its shattering effect upon European humanism. Many searching individuals have turned also for religious support to his speculation about God as a component in the travail of mankind. Scheler's "partnership pantheism," in which God realizes Himself by means of human efforts, has exercised the same attraction as the evolutionary notion of a finite developing deity. Man is no longer alone and worthless, if he can be shown to be a co-worker with divinity in the furtherance of cosmic ends.

The paradoxical feature of the Scheler revival is the sponsorship that it has also received from Christian thinkers. Although they repudiate the pantheistic developments of his later years, they accept a good deal of his philosophy, especially that portion which was conceived during his Catholic period, 1916-1922. Since this period also coincided with Germany's first military defeat and the attempts at spiritual as well as national rebirth, it is felt that Scheler's Catholic essays have an analogical relevance for the present generation. An attempt is being made to recapture the compelling inspiration and confident religious tone of Scheler's book, *On the Eternal in Man*, which seemed to announce the return of Christian intelligence from cultural banishment. George N. Shuster, then a student in Germany, reminisces that this book "seemed to not a few of us younger Catholics just the book we had been hoping for." [1] And a study on Christian philosophy in modern Germany holds that "without him [Scheler], Christian philosophy in the Germany of the last decades is unthinkable. . . . With his book, *On the Eternal in Man* (1921), he became the great herald of a religious renewal." Today, many Christian philosophers in Europe and America feel also that Scheler can aid in an intellectual recovery of the great philosophical themes, through his personal adaptation of the phenomenological method to metaphysical, ethical, and valuational questions.

Thus different aspects of Scheler's mind are being rehabilitated, now in the interest of pantheism and now of traditional theism, when it seeks a new mode of presentation. Inevitably, the question must be reopened as to why he made such a violent about-face, repudiating his belief in a transcendent God and advocating propositions about an immanent deity which he had previously branded as contradictory and foolish. At the time of his death, a number of his friends and colleagues sought to clear up this enigma, which scandalized so many people. It was agreed that Scheler's mind was excessively volatile, impulsive, and given to contradictory veerings from one extreme to the other. He was often guided by emotion and passing suspicion rather than by sober analysis and consistency. He took a romantic delight in experiencing conflict and contradiction within himself. Psychodynamically, it might have been predicted that his temperament would lead him from the authority of the Church to a kind of theosophical piety of his own contrivance.

Most Catholic writers accepted this psychological explanation, as advanced by Dietrich von Hildebrand in *Hochland*.[2] They stressed the flaw in Scheler's personality which led him to prefer the novel to the perennially true, the convenient to the universally just. But a sharp dissenting opinion against this common verdict was entered by Nicolai Hartmann, in his necrological notice in *Kantstudien*.[3] Hartmann agreed with many of Scheler's major conceptions, including his objective ontological orientation and his theory of realms of ideal being. He contended that Scheler's intellectual restlessness only illustrates the principle that a blind impulsive urge lurks at the heart of things, and that conflict is indeed the father of all. From the standpoint of Hartmann's own atheism, the contradictions in Scheler's life only mirror the contradictions in reality. Scheler was rightfully honoring the truth of the moment by changing his tack so often. His was the honesty of a man seeking desperately to believe in some kind of God, in a world that is actually godless.

It is unlikely that either a purely psychologico-moral explanation or one based on the atheistic hypothesis can provide a conclusive answer. Both approaches assume, however, that the gap is extremely wide between the theistic and pantheistic periods of Scheler's development. Yet there are certain facts that oblige one to distinguish carefully between the full range of theistic positions and Scheler's earlier conception of theism. He himself always stressed his differences with at least Thomism in matters of natural theology. In turn, his early Thomistic critics frequently charged him with holding views that were at least implicitly ontologistic and pantheistic.[4] Even before he himself became aware of these further consequences, his Thomistic opponents were urging him to clarify his doctrine on man's relation to God, in order to remove what seemed like a tendency toward their ultimate identification. This suggests a much closer and more continuous relationship between the two phases in Scheler's theory of God than is usually suspected.

No more definite statement can be made on the basis of these first Thomistic critiques. With one notable exception, they were directed primarily to Scheler's ethical system and theory of values, his notion of theology, and his attacks on the Thomistic proofs of God's existence.[5] Insufficient attention was paid to the Schelerian conception of philosophy as such, and hence to this theory of metaphysical reasoning. This neglect was due, in turn, to a certain insensitivity toward areas of conflict that were less apparent but perhaps, in the long run, generative of the deeper cleavages of his later years.

Scheler furnishes one of the few clear-cut modern instances of the essentialist way of thinking and the dangers to which it is often exposed. Even during his Catholic days, his doctrine was poles removed from a philosophy of being that rests squarely upon the act of existing as the ultimate perfection of being in all things. His difficulties concerning the role of existence in metaphysics supplied the goad that eventually drove him from an uneasy theism to a more congenial pantheism. To this extent, his principles remained abidingly the same throughout the tremendous moral and intellectual upheavals of his life. To Scheler, the difficulties involved in seeking an existential basis for the doctrine on God and religion always seemed to be insuperable.

What complicates the problem of metaphysical essentialism here is the influence of phenomenology upon the general outlook. Scheler was one of the first and most successful phenomenologists, collaborating with Husserl in the publication of the *Annual*, even though their methods remained quite divergent. His phenomenological studies on value, love, sympathy, *ressentiment*, and the sociology of knowledge were pioneer and permanent contributions. Along with Pfänder and the Munich school of phenomenology, he stressed the objective reference of phenomenological description. He went on to consider its bearing upon questions of real being. Scheler's philosophy indicates one of the ways in which a phenomenological method can be adapted for making inquiries into metaphysical matters. His philosophy takes the shape of a phenomenological essentialism, in which it is difficult to preserve the integrity of the actually existing being. Thus it furnishes an instructive counterpoint to the existentialist versions of a phenomenological ontology.

There are some definite literary landmarks charting the course of Scheler's speculations on God and man.[6] The point of departure in the Catholic period is provided by two essays in *On the Eternal in Man:* "On the Essence of Philosophy and the Moral Condition of Philosophical Knowing" and "Problems of Religion." The latter essay cannot be properly evaluated without the background provided by the former. The inadequacy of many scholastic attacks upon Scheler's early theory of religion results from a failure to trace his reasoning back to its methodological basis. At the other arm of the compass are his two posthumous publications: *Philosophical Perspectives* and *Man's Place in the Cosmos*, both of which rest openly upon the identification of man with a self-realizing deity. The most striking result of a close study of these books is the uncovering of a large amount of common doctrine. Something of the arbitrary character of Scheler's evolution is thus removed, and at the same time an instructive example is given of the hazards of metaphysical essentialism, when allied with phenomenology.

2. *Philosophy and the Sciences*

Scheler's relations with Edmund Husserl, the founder of phenomenology, are intricate and difficult to unravel. For every point held in common, Scheler advanced another in disagreement; or rather, he found himself to be both in harmony with Husserl and at odds with him on the very same issues. A good example is the question of whether philosophy is a science. In 1911, Husserl issued a famous programmatic statement to the effect that phenomenology's purpose is to make of philosophy a rigorous scientific discipline.[7] In his own method, he saw the only adequate means for completing the Cartesian transformation of philosophy according to the pattern of mathematics and logic. Scheler agreed with this ideal only in a highly qualified way. If by "science" is understood the Platonic *episteme,* a sure grasp of ideal forms, then philosophy is supremely scientific. But following the same usage, the disciplines that are referred to customarily in our day as "the sciences" fall within the sphere of opinion, the Platonic *doxa.* Since there is no reasonable hope that Plato's use of these terms will ever again become current, the modern meaning of science must be followed. In this latter sense of the word, Scheler denied that philosophy can or should be included among the sciences.

Although he deemed his opposition to Husserl on this score to be more verbal than real, it actually opened up a considerable chasm between the two phenomenologists. Scheler's underlying intent in making this correction was by no means merely linguistic. He wished to safeguard the autonomy of philosophy against positivistic attempts to assimilate it to the special sciences as being their center of synthesis. He was not satisfied that Husserl's well-known resistance to this imperialist tendency of positivism was doctrinally well-grounded. To the usual objection that a nonscientific philosophy would open the door to every manner of enthusiasm and unwarranted assertion, Scheler replied by distinguishing between the logical rigor of one's canons of evidence and reasoning and the technical exactitude of laboratory procedure. Philosophy should not try to ape the sciences in respect to mathematical exactness, but intellectual rigor is by no means a monopoly of what we today call the sciences. As we have seen, this distinction between exactness and rigor helps Jaspers to criticize the Husserlian conception of a scientific standard in philosophy, and it is used for a similar purpose by Martin Heidegger.[8]

Characteristically, Scheler overstates the case for the autonomy of philosophy by declaring that it alone can gain rigorous evidence (scientific status, in the older terminology) and that the special sciences, deductive as well as inductive, are restricted to the realm of opinion and probability. His reasons for this drastic verdict are based not on an analysis of empirical methods and the use of statistical frequency but, Platonically again, upon the spheres of reality under consideration. Like Husserl, he establishes the closest linkage between the natural or commonsense attitude and that of the scientist. Using terms which have since become popular with the existentialists, Scheler describes the natural outlook as one based on an identification between the immediate pragmatic milieu and the world at large. The untutored mind regards environing being (*Umweltsein*), which ministers to human needs, as equivalent to mandane being as such (*Weltsein*).[9] The sciences criticize this assumption only in a relative degree. They seek to broaden the horizon of human environment, but they still regard nature primarily as it affects human interests and is subject to human control.

Because of this practical orientation, the sciences cannot extend beyond purely relative modes of being. They treat of being only insofar as it bears upon our vital instincts. The satisfaction of the latter provides an ontic criterion for scientific research. Man's biological structure becomes the center of relevance for scientific findings. The scientific world is thus the generalized pattern of the human milieu and retains an ultimately biological reference. Hence the structural forms of the scientific world are universal only within the context set by the natural outlook and the drive to extend our control over nature.[10] Because the sciences cannot emerge by themselves from this totally relative approach to being, they cannot acquire that insight into being as such and the essential structures of being which constitutes philosophical truth. The several forms of evolutionism and naturalism are affected by this restriction.

This limitation is also seen in scientific methods, which rely widely upon observation and induction from the empirical events. Scheler agrees with Husserl that the inductively sought material content of experience is infinite and properly inexhaustible. Hence scientific propositions dependent upon this procedure are provisional, subject to revision or complete displacement, and hence only probable in strength. The sciences are too intimately bound up with contingent, existential modes of being to overcome the hypothetical character of existential apprehension.

Scheler even attempts to extend his account to the mathematical sciences, in which the deductive method predominates. He fails to specify the exact sense in which mathematically organized thought is also pragmatic and hypothetical. Instead, he falls back upon the time-honored, but arbitrary, German idealist distinction between understanding and reason. The deductive as well as the inductive sciences are functions of understanding, which is taken not in the Kantian manner, as a constitutive principle of genuinely universal and certain knowledge, but in the Hegelian sense of a cognitive attitude restricted to the relative and provisional appearances of being. No special justification of this pejorative use of "understanding" is offered by Scheler.

It fits in conveniently with his dichotomy between science and philosophy, and hence it is accepted without further ado.

That Scheler is not entirely satisfied with this solution, however, is indicated by his insertion of a significant qualification. He admits that some scientific research is conducted in a quite theoretical and objective spirit, seeking truths which need have no bearing upon our welfare, even though they do not surpass the level of finite, contingent being. Furthermore, many mathematical propositions and some "natural laws" contain factors which are not at the mercy of further empirical findings. In such instances, he allows that scientific thought supposes and makes application of (but does not originally generate) the definitive essential insights proper to philosophy. Philosophical reason has an office to perform in regard to the understanding, lending it something of the absoluteness and universality of essential patterns.[11] With this help, the scientific mind can try to view the contingent world in its permanent connections. Thus the philosophic grasp upon the essential forms of being supplies the basic presuppositions and axioms for all the sciences.

Scheler's purpose in making so severe a delimitation of the sciences is not merely to secure the liberation of philosophy from the position of a handmaid of the sciences. In addition, he seeks to determine something positive about the nature of philosophy and its starting point. The drawbacks of the commonsense and scientific standpoints can be reduced to two major items: (1) they are confined to a view of being as relative to the human organism and its needs; (2) they are subject to the contingencies of empirical existence. By way of contrast, this suggests the criteria governing philosophical investigation. It must try to apprehend being in the absolute sense, that is, out of an interest in what it is in itself rather than in what it contributes to our needs. And philosophy must try to shake itself loose from the contingent existential order, so that it may contemplate the world in its essential purity of structure. Only in this twofold way can the commonsense equivocation between the world about us and the world as such be removed. Lest it be inferred that this critique of the ordinary outlook is a step toward esotericism, Scheler adds that the movement toward the absolute and the essential order can be performed in principle by any individual.

But to be actually undertaken, this philosophical movement of the soul supposes a moral condition. Scheler is quite aware of many of the pitfalls surrounding this question of the moral disposition required for philosophizing. Yet he warns, in the Platonic-Augustinian tradition, that one must philosophize with one's whole soul, that the entire man must be engaged in this sublime activity. He defines the philosophical attitude as: "a love-determined movement of the inmost personal Self of a finite being toward participation in the essential reality of all possibles." [12] Because philosophizing is an engagement of the entire person, it springs from an act of love, which determines the orientation of a man as a whole. But the peculiarly philosophical sort of participation is in the cognitive order: although impelled by love, the philosophical act itself is one of knowing. Hence the moral prerequisite should not be confused with the actual development of the specifically philosophical manner of participating in being. Kant's doctrine on the primacy of practical reason does not successfully avoid this confusion.

Scheler's chief originality in regard to the nature of philosophy lies in his analysis of the presupposed moral factor. In *On the Eternal in Man,* he refers to it as an upsurge or a moral elevation of the person.[13] It is a flight of the alone to the Alone, of the finite personal center of act to the infinite, personal center of act. At least in this early passage, Scheler dissociates himself from Plato and Plotinus by insisting upon the personal nature of both poles of the movement. Moreover, he regards the emphasis placed upon the act-character of persons as a corrective of the Aristotelian-Scholastic doctrine on substance. He accepts uncritically the modern commonplace that the substantial principle is passive and inert. Consequently, he denies any substantial basis for the series of personal acts in God and man. This places the unity of the person in jeopardy and renders inexplicable its ability to set a permanent goal for its acts.

The mind's prephilosophical soaring can only transpire on condition that the fetters of the natural-scientific world are broken. At this point, Scheler makes a crucial decision. He identifies the finite existential aspects of being with the psycho-physical setting of the human person and its practical concerns. They are made to stand and fall together as an integral whole. The very reason why the mind is tied down to a purely relativistic conception of being is also why is it endlessly involved in probabilities. In both cases, the mind's ascent has been hampered by an excessive attachment to the world as existent. Only when this bond is sundered—as much as is humanly possible—can the personal core of man begin to breathe the atmosphere of the absolute and hence begin to philosophize. This detachment from the realm of contingent existence is not confined to an intellectual abstraction or a methodic suspension of belief. It is fundamentally a sort of moral ascesis, a divorcement of one's actual center of adherence from relative existents, a loosening of the real allegiances that moor the human person to the world about him. These moorings are to be cast off, not merely lengthened. They are to be repudiated as genuine points of departure for philosophy, rather than employed as the basis and first moment of the elevation.

Although in 1921 he was somewhat hesitant about subscribing to the Platonic notion of philosophy as a dying-away to the senses, Scheler displayed no reluctance on this point at the end of his career. *Man's Place in the Cosmos* advocates unconditionally the radical philosophical asceticism which was present in germ in the earlier work. Now, Scheler is certain that a break must be made with the instinctive urges and, consequently, with the senses and their affirmation of contingently existing modes of being. Sensation has no cognitive value in philosophy, since it is of merely practical, self-centered import. In his colorful style, Scheler calls man "the being-who-can-say-nay [*der Nein-sagenkönner*], the ascete of life, the eternal Protestant against all sheer actuality." [14] He agrees with Schopenhauer that man is the being who can give a strong *Nay!* to the will to life. Although Scheler does not regard the life-impulse as intrinsically good or evil, he does subscribe to Schopenhauer's initial denial of this urge as a condition for mounting to the region of ideas and essences.

Furthermore, he accepts Schopenhauer's voluntarist interpretation of "actuality" or "reality." [15] These terms designate something met with in the appetitive order rather than in the cognitive, and hence something that can be treated only by a resolute act of will. The real is first and properly grasped as a resistant force acting against the urges of one's own life. This resistance is conveyed by the senses, which tell us that the world about us is actual and existent. Their report is exclusively practical and extra-philosophical, and given actuality is of the same sort. Schopenhauer suggested the need for an "irrealization of real being," a process of neutralizing its actual, existent factors so that the mind can rise to the level of ideal essences. In this de-actualization or separation of essence from its existential setting, Scheler sees the indispensable condition of philosophy and the constitutive act of the human person. Man is *the grand irrealizer of being* —a formula which also appeals to Sartre. Man distinguishes himself from other beings in nature only by this ability to set the actual order at nought, disengage the pure essential forms, and study them without distraction in their permanent connections.

By establishing this equation between the actual as the vitally resistant and the existent as sense-grounded being, Scheler also hopes

114

to join the voluntarist-ascetic tradition with phenomenology. In a single breath, he mentions, Buddha, Plato, and Husserl as his sources. He cites with approval the Buddhist technique for withdrawing from the reality of the actual world and empirical self. This method is transferred into the philosophical sphere as a suspension of the actual traits of things through a radical displacement of sense perception and its existential significance.

Is this technique the same as Husserl's phenomenological reduction of actuality and the natural attitude by way of placing existence within brackets? Scheler's constant answer over two decades is that the process of detachment and irrealization includes and surpasses Husserl's method.[16] He admits that Husserl is on the right track in resting his philosophy upon a suspension of the existential co-efficients. Only when they are placed in abeyance and deprived of their force, can the mind gain that essential insight which supplies philosophy with its strong meat. But as a more radical basis than the famous Husserlian reduction of the natural attitude behind the sciences, Scheler advocates an ascetic detachment through an act of will, releasing man from the hold of actual pressures or from what the poet Schiller calls our anguished dread before the earthly. More must be withdrawn than belief in the existential judgment. This judgment (expressed in the proposition, "A is real") would contain a purely formal and empty predicate, "real," were the latter not first filled or given content through the sense experience of resistance to the vital impulse. Now if existence is precisely this resistance (and Scheler never questions this major assumption), then the process of bracketing must first of all be one of enfeebling our vital attachment to the real order presented through the senses. Consequently, Husserl's claim to have founded a wholly presuppositionless philosophy is placed in doubt. Scheler argues that the logical loosening of essences from belief in their existential context rests upon a more radical, ontologico-moral reduction of the existential to the essential, the contingent to the necessary.

Scheler's version of the autonomy and presuppositionlessness of philosophy rests on this primary act of detachment from the actual world. Only when the contingent interweaving of the knowing operation with the psycho-physical organism is split apart, does the mind cease to be hemmed in by the conditions of common sense and scientific knowledge. It attains the distinctive standpoint of philosophy after making a break-through, not so much *to* contingent actuality as *beyond* it to the essential structure of the world. This is Scheler's interpretation

115

of the famous phenomenological slogan: "Back to the things themselves!" The return to things is made only when they are regarded in their essential constitution, unclouded by the concerns of existence.

Nevertheless, Scheler refuses to accept the world-denying stand of Schopenhauer and Buddhism as ultimately valid. He does not regard contingent existence and the instincts as intrinsically evil, but only as hindrances to the intitial ascent of the philosophical mind to the being of the world as ordained to the absolute. Hence he envisages an eventual return of the philosopher to the actual world in order to reconstitute it from the perspective of the absolute. Like Husserl, he is prepared to find a place for finite existence, just as long as the incorporation of existential modes is carried out upon his own terms. Whether this project can be successfully executed is the major question evoked by a study of Scheler's metaphysics.

3. *The Nature of Metaphysics*

In practice, Scheler tends to equate the best form of philosophy and metaphysics. Philosophy remains distinct only insofar as it includes a phenomenological reflection upon the basic attitude constitutive of metaphysics. The negative aspect of the metaphysical attitude has been examined, but we must now state its positive features. Indeed, there is an exact correlation between the "de-actualization" of reality and the "ideation" or apprehension of essential forms. The mind can perform the latter operation only after it is clearly distinguished from natural and scientific cognition. Existential and essential knowledge are completely different. Existential knowledge is hypothetical, endlessly augmentable, and constantly threatened with overthrow. In refusing to base one's ultimate philosophical constructs upon this type of cognition, one clears the path for an intuition of essences. Rigorous evidence is acquired only at the essential level, since it is only here that truths are definitive and certain in an *a priori* way. An essential insight may be lost and recovered; other insights may be added to it; but it has an atomic integrity within itself whereby it must either be known in full or not known at all.

Scheler attempts to reduce the essential intuitions to three primary ones, which constitute the broad basis for all philosophizing.[17] (1) The first evident insight is based on the mind's wonder that something is rather than is not at all. Why should the world and myself with it, have being instead of nothingness? This is the same question which

116

made Schopenhauer, Schelling, and Heidegger react with philosophical wonderment. Scheler grants that this wonder, which Aristotle deemed the beginning of wisdom, can be expressed in the proposition: "Something is." But since this is suspiciously like the Thomistic first existential judgment, he prefers to reformulate it in the form: "Not-nothing is," or "there is not nothing." The advantage of this second formulation is that it rests upon the recognized possibility of the nonexistence, nonactuality, of the world that in fact is. It places the accent upon the revoked possibility of non-existence rather than upon the acceptance of actual, given existence. Hence it accords well with the revocation upon which the philosophical grasp of essence rests.

(2) The second evident insight, consequent at once upon the first, is that there is an absolute being, upon which all non-absolute beings depend for the reality they have received. In other words, the being of *ens a se* or the self-sufficient absolute is the second intuition following on the mind's liberation from the actual world. Retrospectively, this casts further light upon the first axiom, which is really an affirmation that something dependent and relative has being or that something dependent and relative has not been reduced to nothingness. Thus understood, the first Schelerian intuition is even farther removed from the spontaneous affirmation of the existent thing which grounds Thomistic metaphysics. Why the beings around us should be regarded as contingent, relative, and dependent is never justified. Almost an entire theory of being is smuggled by Scheler into his unconditionally first judgment. He is forced to employ these tactics in order to rule out a metaphysical establishment of these points and hence in order to show the need for, and primacy of, a religious intuition of being as dependent upon the absolute. This is why he calls the real distinction between essence and existence a religious view of things: his metaphysics accepts as a first principle a statement about contingent being which requires either a philosophical foundation (which he does not allow) or a religious sanction. Without this recourse to a prior religious intuition, there would be no reason for asserting that an absolute being is "demanded" at the very outset of metaphysics.

(3) Finally, it is evident that in all beings other than the absolute, there is a real distinction between essence or whatness and existence or thatness. Since this is a primary datum, Scheler does not tarry to argue out the case or settle fine points of dispute. The distinction is a real one in finite beings and only a logical one in God. It is not conceived in terms of mutually proportioned principles of being. Scheler's phenomenological description of whatness and thatness, as well as

his interest in a sharp contrast between essential and existential knowledge, makes this distinction at the created plane one between different levels of being, rather than between mutually required co-principles of every finite being.

With the aid of these three fundamental axioms, metaphysics is equipped to explore the realm of essence. Nevertheless, a difficulty crops up at once in connection with Scheler's theory of essential insight. The problem is one that has been haunting modern philosophy ever since Descartes proposed to base metaphysics on a series of intuitions of simple natures. In order to join these atomic intuitions together for the purposes of inference and unified knowledge, relations between the simple natures must be included among the primary objects of intuition. Now as Spinoza was quick to point out, this is only an *ad hoc* device unless the simple natures have real, organic unity in an absolute nature.[18] Husserl and Scheler are both concerned about this objection, the former developing his theory of the world and the latter moving in a pantheistic direction in order to meet it. Scheler defines philosophy as intuitive understanding of essences, their connections and synthesis, and their relation to the absolute being and its essence. The moot point is whether the absolute being is identical with the immanent concatenation of essences or whether this internal unity is an effect bearing reference to the absolute.

During his Catholic period, Scheler favored the latter part of the alternative. The purpose of metaphysics is to grasp the world as an essential whole and to point at least in the direction of the primal ground or principle of the world. Kant had developed the notion of the world in general as a comprehensive unity. His shortcoming was to have interpreted experience in too narrow a way, as sense experience alone. Only if the sensibly given is made coextensive with the whole field of intuitive data, do the Kantian strictures against metaphysics have a telling effect. Scheler cites the phenomenological studies of many levels of data as proof that experience is wider than the sensuous mode of experience. Essences are given to us in a distinctive intuition, precisely when sensuous conditions are set aside. Since essential truths hold even for cases that go beyond sense experience, Scheler believes that his ontology of essences marks a revival of metaphysics as valid philosophy.

The metaphysician seeks not only to trace out the structural connections among essences but also to view them as converging upon a common point of intersection. As relative essences constituting the world, they give common indication of the need for an absolute ground of the world, or *ens a se*.[19] This is the high water mark of Scheler's concessions to metaphysics. Immediately, he begins hedging and qualifying his admission, so as to bring it in line with his favorite thesis about religion and metaphysics.

He denies that there is any sense in which religion, supernatural or natural, rests upon metaphysics or even upon a natural causal inference to God's existence. Both disciplines are autonomous, even though they confirm one another and bear mutual reference through the neutral reality of *ens a se*. Because they refer to different intentional objects (religion to God as salvation, metaphysics to the absolute as supreme being), there can be no founding of religion upon metaphysics. The entity in which these diverse intentional objects are grounded may be one and the same supreme reality, but no analytic transition is possible from the one aspect to the other. Each approach may affirm the same set of propositions, but with a different order and a different end in view. The formal or intentional distinction between the metaphysical and the religious ways of viewing the absolute reality prevents acceptance, above all, of the Thomistic synthesis of the two within a single body of Christian wisdom.

This polemical intent leads Scheler to restrict the competence of metaphysics to a determination of intramundane essences and their direction to the absolute. He does affirm that metaphysics has "absolute knowledge-evidence" about two propositions: that there is an *ens a se* from whose essence its existence necessarily follows, and that this *ens a se* is the first cause.[20] (Scheler is careful not to refer to the metaphysical absolute as God or to call it a creator, since these insights are reserved for the independent religious intuition of God.) But the strength of this double admission is watered down at every subsequent stage. This is due, basically, to the fact that Scheler has had to rule out any causal proof starting from sensible existents.

Scheler's metaphysical procedure is to determine an absolute essence from which the act of existing necessarily follows. He denies the possibility of the Thomistic a posteriori proofs about God's existence precisely because he holds that one must already have found the essence before attempting to show its existence. It is the real and not the nominal essence that must already be in one's possession, and it must be seen clearly rather than in a confused way. To attain the essence itself, one must either make inference from another instance of the same kind or acquire the essence through direct intuition. Since the former route is impossible in the case of the unique infinite being, a direct intuition of the divine essence is man's sole resort. This act is exclusively religious, and in this sense a religious supposition is necessary before there can be any talk about a metaphysical demonstration of God's existence. The center of metaphysical intuition is rather the essential structure of the world. The lines of essential interconnection and synthesis point toward a primal absolute principle of the world, but they do no more than point a direction without actually taking us to the God of religion.

Hence it is not surprising to learn that the Schelerian absolute is, from the metaphysical standpoint, only an ideal limit. Metaphysics is not empowered to reduce the network of essences any further. It cannot specify, for instance, that these forms are divine ideas or eternal truths residing in the divine mind, since it cannot validly make the final grounding of the totality of essential structures in an existent absolute subject. But, it may be asked, why should it be counted an imperfection in this system of pure essences not to be able to make a valid existential judgment about the absolute being? Scheler supplies no clear-cut answer to this query, since he is too engrossed in his running attack upon what he took to be Thomistic natural theology to work out his own positive stand with all desirable thoroughness. But certain incidental remarks provide a clue to his mind on this central issue.

Scheler was mortally afraid of losing complete hold upon existence. He reacted vigorously against some of the dangers of a pure theory of essences and a defiant acosmism. Some accommodation had to be made for existence within his ontology of essence. But the difficulty is how to honor existence and at the same time set off metaphysics from the sciences primarily on the ground of a philosophical apprehension of essential structures, completely free from the conditions of actual existence. When there is question of the distinctive standpoint of philosophical metaphysics, it is said to be an essential rather than an existential kind of knowledge. But this statement is subsequently modified to mean that metaphysics is not confined to modes of contingent existence but can move beyond them. In transcending the given order of natural existence, metaphysics nevertheless retains a twofold, tenuous relation with the existential. Initially or in the genetic order, it must receive its essences from the actual world, even though it apprehends them only by negating this world of existents. Terminally or in the teleological order, it at least aims at securing existential judgments concerning the essential configurations and their total unity as the world. In these two respects, metaphysics is not free from existence, but bears reference to the really existent.[21]

Without ever fully clarifying his position, Scheler is thus groping toward a distinction between two sorts of real or existential knowledge. The natural attitude as developed by the sciences constitutes an imperfect *initial* sort of real knowledge, one subject to all the defects of cognizing immediately given existence. Religion, on the other hand, provides a real knowledge of a perfect *terminal* sort. It rests on an intuition of the divine essence, which lies beyond the distinction between essence and existence. Hence religious intuition, in apprehending the highest good, apprehends that essence alone whose existence must flow from its essence. Because the divine essence is the highest good and independent of all other beings, its existence must follow and be known to follow. Scheler never doubts our ability to know the divine essence sufficiently to grasp intuitively the necessary relation between essence and existence. Hence he remains uncritical on the main issue concerning the need for proof of the statement that "God exists." Instead of respecting the inferential character of human knowledge, he stresses the objective truth that, in this privileged instance, actual existence is not contingent or bound up with the human organism's urges and needs. This intuitive truth about God's existence is a perfection rather than a defect. It marks the primacy of essence over existence in such a way that the existential factor is subordinated without being suppressed. At least, this is how Scheler would like the matter to appear.

The position of metaphysics can now be appraised as maintaining an uneasy compromise between these two sorts of existential knowledge. By its empirical roots, it is bound to the natural-scientific relation to existence; by its aspiration it seeks an analogue of the religious relation to absolute existence. Yet it remains an autonomous discipline, poised between the world and God, between ordinary existential knowledge and intuition of the divine actuality. Metaphysics is a mixed science, as far as certitude and evidence are concerned. Its major premises are supplied by intuitive acts directed to essential patterns. To this extent, its propositions are strictly evident and valid a priori for all instances. But its minor premises have their source in inductive experience. The essences are presented to man only in the context of contingent actuality. Because of this necessary reliance upon the experiential world, metaphysics partakes of the probable and hypothetical nature of commonsense and scientific thinking.[22] This is the significance of two qualifying remarks made in passing. Scheler requires philosophical metaphysics to break *as much as* is humanly possible

121

with the context of contingent actuality; thereby, metaphysics can become as presuppositionless *as possible*. A total severance is impossible.

As compared with religion, metaphysics fails to achieve the purity of strict evidence, absolute certainty, and eternal, definitive truth. There are numerous drawbacks, therefore, against any project of founding religion on metaphysics. It would be foolish to found the more perfect upon the less perfect and thus to give religion a shaky and incongruous underpinning. The more metaphysics tends to the absolute, the less reliable it becomes. This results from a growing disparity between its formal side and its material side, as it mounts the scale of relative beings en route to the absolute. Its formal propositions are universally applicable, at least within the range of relative essences and their directional intimation of the absolute essence. But the entire material content of metaphysics is drawn from contingent actuality. Hence in dealing with the absolute being, metaphysics has at its disposal only some purely formal and essential determinations. There is no possibility of an intrinsic and existential metaphysics of the absolute, not to mention an existential metaphysics of God.

Most metaphysical propositions about the absolute are merely hypothetical and probable, because of their necessary reference to the contingent findings of the sciences. In fact, the hypothetical character increases and the probability decreases in proportion as metaphysics seeks to surmount the essential constitution of the world, in an effort to determine the nature of the primal ground of the world. It has been allowed previously, to be sure, that metaphysics can ascertain the being of the *ens a se* and the fact that it is the first cause. Scheler adds, however, that these are the two most formal propositions in metaphysics. Looked at more critically, they are merely formal propositions, barren of existential content. They designate the absolute only in its essential aspect and are powerless to support any transition to a real affirmation of an infinite act of existing. Only purely formal and analytic inferences are available to metaphysics at this level, since it is wholly bereft of intuitive content bearing on the non-relative being. Indeed, these most formal statements refer rather to the immanent Logos or integrating essential pattern of the world than to the essence of the transcendent being in its own reality. The metaphysical absolute remains wholly immanent in content. Metaphysics developed along these essentialist lines may confirm, exhibit, and indicate the reasonableness of religious belief in God, but the transcendent significance of metaphysics comes from religion alone.

4. *Idolatry of the Relative*

Certain aspects of Scheler's outlook were bound to collapse with his loss of the Catholic faith, since they supposed the truth of supernatural revelation. Without this supposition, the tremendous exception to the human mode of cognition made in favor of religious intuition had no footing. Granted that psychological and moral causes hastened the destruction of his faith, nevertheless, certain internal difficulties and dangling lines of inquiry in his earlier synthesis should also be reckoned with as furnishing motive forces in his transition to pantheism. Perhaps the most revealing words of self-confession penned by Scheler are contained in some notes written in April, 1928, a few weeks before his death. "The questions: 'What is man? What is his place in being?' have occupied me since the first awakening of my philosophical consciousness more essentially and centrally than any other philosophical question. . . . I had the increasing good fortune of seeing that the major share of all the philosophical problems that I previously treated, were coinciding more and more with this question." [23] This was the introspective discovery made after 1922: Scheler sought to bring his entire philosophy into conformity with this recognition of the absolute primacy of philosophical anthropology.

There are a number of sure indications in *On the Eternal in Man* that the problem of being must coincide eventually with the problem of man's being, in the sense of anthropological pantheism. The internal requirements of his doctrine on the existence of God can have no other issue. Similarly, his manner of reconciling the absolute of metaphysics and the highest good of religion foreshadows the same conclusion. These two developments converge upon a common outcome: the realization of the godhead in and through man.

The metaphysical effort is brought to a sudden halt with the determination of a world-ground, an essential and intelligible nexus for all particular formal structures. The metaphysical striving after existential truth is futile, since it is a process of breaking free from naturally given existents and then pointing in a merely formal way toward the absolute existent. In this predicament, Scheler must appeal to the religious act as being capable of an immediate ascent to a realm of essence and existence open to it alone. Religion is not simply distinct from metaphysics but is supposed by it within the order of metaphysical inquiry itself, as far as existential grounding in the absolute is

123

concerned. The only reason why one feels the need for a metaphysical demonstration of God's existence is because the truth has already been given in religious intuition. Scheler does not explain why this further verification is required: it is just as puzzling a fact as the persistently existential orientation of metaphysics in general. In any case, religion supplies what metaphysics lacks and yet requires. Everything depends, therefore, upon the way in which religion makes this prior apprehension of God's existence.

Scheler becomes deliberately hazy in his description of the religious way to the existing God. He wants to avoid open conflict with St. Paul's saying that the invisible God can be known from the visible things in the world. Hence he speaks of the basic religious movement as an inference, yet adding that it is a noncausal perception of God's symbolical presence in nature and man. In this way, the Vatican Council and Kant are supposed to lie down in amity. In language more native to his own manner of thinking, however, Scheler refers to the existence of God as something that must be "determined," "agreed upon," or "understood" to follow from the intuited presence of unconditioned value.[24] The latter is what is ascertained directly by religious apprehension, and from it there follows—by human agreement—knowledge of the existence of the supreme good. Now, either this agreement on value is sheer convention or else it conceals a complex set of metaphysical assertions about the relation between independence and existence, as well as between value and existence. Scheler does not clarify his position on this difficulty. It is likely, however, that his interpretation of the religious act is controlled by a definite metaphysical tradition of the primacy of the good. Although he champions the complete independence of religious intuition, his actual descriptions are covertly specified by a metaphysic of the good as the principle of existence.

Thus the problem of God's existence is narrowed down to that of an absolute good. The human spirit cannot be satisfied by the finite values realized in the world. It transcends them in its yearning for a completely unlimited good. Its fundamental "intention" or objective desire can only acquire fulfillment and content by the gain of an absolute good, which has independent being. The reality of the highest good is required by the peculiar nature of the religious act. It not only ranges beyond the finite order but also demands a real, personal response from its only adequate object: the supreme good and salvation of the soul. Hence Scheler regards it as a synthetic axiom of human religious consciousness that the absolute and independent plenum of value must also possess existence, since only on this condition can the appropriate religious response on the part of the object be forth-coming.[25] Man's peculiar religious needs require the existence of God.

Scheler is at once confronted with the objection that he is following the immanentist approach of Modernism and hence is basing his demonstration solely on subjective wishes. Two points in his reply are of special importance. He notes, first, that desires or wishes as such belong to a wider, neutral class. What makes them specifically religious desires is nothing other than the religious act as directed to a distinctively religious object. This answer avoids one difficulty by raising another one. For, religious acts of apprehension themselves fall within the wider class of cognitive acts. Hence some justification in the *cognitive* order must be offered for supposing the existence of their intended objects. It is possible to associate desires with groundless claims to religious knowledge, and then the wishes themselves must be adjudged groundless religious desires. Scheler is apprehensive lest the application of common epistemic tests destroy the distinctiveness of the religious attitude. It is, however, an ordinary human procedure to distinguish between theoretical proof of some reality and the prac-tical consequences that may flow from such a recognition, even though they do not flow with necessity. The religious relation of a man to God may be in closest continuity with our knowledge of God's ex-istence, without thereby removing the need for a distinctive disposition of will, enforced by the moral virtue of justice. Scheler mistook the retroactive effect of a man's practical disposition of religion upon his entire theoretical outlook for a completely independent way of knowl-edge. He did not see that a worshipful attitude may spring from knowledge gained through natural and metaphysical inference, as well as from our faith in God.

Secondly, Scheler argues that the existence of the supreme good is assured because analysis of the religious act regards this act precisely as existing in men. Since the start is made with the religious tendency as an existing fact, the conclusion bears upon the supreme good not only as the intentional object but also as the existing cause of this act. This is difficult to reconcile with Scheler's other statements about the independence of the religious act from any exhibition of the ex-istence of either the outer world or one's own self. It also runs counter to his sharp contrast between the biological and the religious meanings of existence. More and more, Scheler is forced to reveal the *human* foundation of the existence attributed to the unconditioned being. Al-though philosophy must make a break with given existential conditions, the existential act is restored in the religious sphere by virtue of man's self-dedication to the perfect good. This leads Scheler to say that actuality gets its value, sense, and significance, in and through man's function of leading things back to God as their root and essential meaning.

This implies that there is at least a concordance between the religious God and the metaphysical absolute. Since no analytical inference can be made from the one to the other, Scheler is compelled to account for their broad agreement in terms of the human subject. We can have a priori certainty on this point only because of the unity of human consciousness and the human spirit, from which both religion and metaphysics take their rise. In this conclusion, Scheler follows the lead of Kant in locating the reconciling principle of knowledge and faith within the structure of the human subjectivity, as the common source of diverse objective intentions. Religion as well as metaphysics is being thoroughly anthropologized.

The human contribution is, indeed, preponderant in this instance. For the common X, which is diversely intended by religion and metaphysics, is intrinsically indifferent to these different sets of determinations. In itself, the one identical Real is neutrally capable of being denominated the metaphysical highest being or the religious supreme good. Whereas St. Thomas would require that God be infinite in being and goodness, Scheler allows the godhead to remain undetermined within itself. At least in regard to our mind, the divine is a possible reality or a last logical subject, capable of receiving religious and metaphysical predications quite indifferently. Scheler's impersonal "divine" object is only called God from the standpoint of our religious drives, and only entails existence as being the absolute condition for satisfying these drives. At the same time, this *ens a se* is specified metaphysically as the correlate of all possible essences in the world. The unity of the human spirit alone assures us that the religious act-center and the metaphysical world-ground or Logos are one and the same reality.

During his Catholic period, Scheler could reassure himself that the divine neutrality is in reference to our cognition and is a bulwark against the pretensions of Wolffian natural theology, which he regarded as the prototype of all philosophical discussions about God. But insofar as he acknowledged some religious and philosophical propositions about God to be true, the theory of neutrality came to have an import for God's being as well as for our knowledge of His being. The ontological consequences of Scheler's position are two: (1) the presence of a deep-seated dualism in God as well as man, and (2) the reciprocal need of man and God in reconciling the extreme poles in some concrete synthesis. These inferences appear in hesitant but unmistakable outline even in *On the Eternal in Man*.

The *ens a se* is both a center of act and life and the nodal point of essential structures. This corresponds to the vital and noetic aspects of human nature. Although he spurned Eduard von Hartmann's "redemption of God through man," Scheler nevertheless began to make some general pronouncements about life and mind which were applicable to God as well as to man. Man's task is to follow the way of the spiritualization of life, which is at the same time the impregnation of spirit or mind with power.[26] Mind by itself is impotent; life by itself is blind and destructive. The forces of life as well as the ideals of spirit surge out from God to man. In the human breast, the elevation of life and the activation of spirit take place. Concrete actuality is now no longer an imposed datum but a product of the human struggle with this dualism.

Thus even the man-centered terminology of *Man's Place in the Cosmos* was anticipated by a decade. It was only necessary for Scheler to remove the disturbing religious thesis that God has a kind of supernatural actuality and existence beyond the world. If, as Scheler so often insisted, metaphysics attains only truths about the world and its essential structure, then the divine Logos has the world immanent in itself and does not merely furnish the indwelling form of the world. Conversely, the instinctive urge of life in God achieves realization only in the finite, historical world. God is now viewed as the highest tension between mind and vital impulse. As mind, God is the world-ground or Logos, which has no original creative power. The latter comes from the vital-impulse side of the divine nature. The divine essence or ideal region of being is actualized only in temporal process.[27] Only in and through man and human history does the godhead acquire genuine existence. The finite world must be taken as the body or concrete actualization of the Logos, which in turn illuminates the dark recesses of instinct and life in God.

What Scheler formerly called the neutral divine *ens a se* or indifferent Real is now referred to as the impersonal primal ground of divinity. It is the atemporal wellspring from which stream forth life and mind, instinct and Logos. These two poles are not complete in themselves. To gain perfect actuality, a process of becoming must be undergone. The entire course of the universe constitutes the self-realizing of the godhead. Man's special place in the cosmos is to be the conscious seat where the integration of life and mind can be deliberately undertaken. In man's self-development, God also becomes Himself. During his final, post-Catholic period, Scheler confesses that this is the insight he learned from Spinoza and Hegel, combining it with the vitalism of Schopenhauer and Bergson. Man develops in proportion as he vitalizes mind and spiritualizes life. The Freudian notion of sublimation is appropriated by Scheler to cover the conquest of instinct by naysaying mind and the reciprocal empowering of mind by controlled instinct.

Scheler's early problem of dualism is never fully resolved, however, even after the suppression of God's transcendence and immutable actuality. Metaphysics and religion remain just as far apart as before, since the former continues to approach the primal ground cognitively as mind, whereas the latter approaches it affectively as life.[28] In Scheler's final phase, religion degenerates into a somewhat craven search after security and shelter, an imaginative flight from the possibility of nihilism opened up by metaphysical speculation on being and the nought. Within man himself, a split develops between mind or person and the everyday empirical self, which is the psychophysical unit.

Above all, Scheler never explains how the process of de-actualizing our empirical existence and life-urges is to take place. For the initiative is supposed to be taken by mind, which he describes as intrinsically powerless. Whence does it receive the power to turn against life, initiate acts of choice, call forth and regulate its representations as a check and guide to the forces of life? Scheler replies that it performs these functions in its capacity as will. To have this capacity, however, means that there is an active, powerful aspect of mind which can originate acts of denying, suppressing, coordinating, and leading. These operations indicate that mind has a native vigor of its own, even though these powers, as found in man, must cooperate with vital forces in the incarnation of spiritual values. There is no need to contrast power and purpose, simply because some excessively abstract thinkers have underplayed the role of the vital and the carnal in human history. There is still less justification for attempting to right the balance in the human scale by injecting tensional process into God.

Scheler once wrote that every man must believe either in God or in an idol. "The relativist is the absolutist of the relative."[29] Hence Scheler defined an idol as an attempted absolutization of the relative. His own intellectual history was a journey from worship of God to idolatry of cosmomorphic man. This Odyssey was due in part to his insatiable appetite for new viewpoints: he defined man in his own image as *bestia cupidissima rerum novarum*. But Scheler also provided in advance a criticism of his own later definition. It is valid in all cases except the religious, where the man who always yearns for novel beliefs is as self-depleting as the heretic.[30] In the case of religious life, the motto always is: Back to the origin! But Scheler came to mistake the origin as a theosophic primal abyss of deity, wherein God is constantly in the making, with man's help.

Unfortunately, Scheler left no way open for extricating himself from his final position. It was a miasma quickly exploited by the lay theologians of the Third Reich, who liked to describe God as the developing form which man carries within him. Scheler's initial philosophical withdrawal from actual existence left him a prey to such phantasmagoric thoughts. He wanted to make this withdrawal, not in a Buddhistic frame of mind, but with the intention of refashioning the given materials of life according to a better, essential pattern. But he cut himself off so definitively from the experienced being accessible to man that there was no point of insertion left for making his proposed redemptive return.

Scheler's protest against actuality is so complete that there can be no question of regaining contact in a human way, no matter how exalted the motive for the break. There is a fanciful sort of exaltation, that of Scheler's "eternal Faust," which involves a disregard for the conditions of human existence and ethical order. Only God is beyond finite actuality in the way Scheler wants man to be beyond and above it. That is why both Scheler's God and his higher man remain abstractions caught captive in his own asceticism. It is true that they are realized in strict correlation, but that process of realization remains an abstract and imaginary one. It is only within Scheler's Faustian imagination that this twin birth of God and man transpires.

Scheler burdened down the phenomenological reduction with metaphysical functions it is not designed to perform. He transformed his analysis of moral attitudes, at which he excelled, into a metaphysics of God and man.[31] His empirical, moral starting point is an unassailable one. Man ought not to be satisfied with conventional conduct. He should step back from it in order to view it against his standards of an ideal personal and social way of life. Nor can he simply follow his instincts and drives wherever they prompt him to go. He must rise above the sheerly impulsive level by an assertion of his freedom and a pursuit of only those ends which have been critically tested and approved. As the existentialists are fond of saying, man must fashion his own character or "soul."

The phenomenological reduction is an appropriate way of gaining an exact description of the various situations and motives involved in the ethical growth of a free personality. This is one of its legitimate uses. But Scheler converted a reduction originally made for purposes of description into a reduction for purposes of metaphysical explanation and actual moral reform. Hence he became involved in an ambiguous use of the word *actuality*. It meant for him both the established order of personal drives and social conventions and the very act of existing. He capitalized on this ambiguity in a systematic way. Because it is true that we should not merely take the given drives of the individual and the conventions of society for granted, he argued that we should not accept the order of existing being as a valid source of philosophical evidence. He moved imperceptibly from a moral rejection of conformism to a metaphysical and epistemological rejection of real being in its actual evidence. This is an illicit transfer of asceticism from the moral to the theoretical sphere. Scheler argues that there is something ignoble about submitting to the giveness of existent being, a kind of ethical servility and cowardice. He would persuade us that we should give to real existent being in the theoretical order the same triumphant and meritorious *nay* that we are inclined to give to selfish impulse and herdlike conduct.

This is the kind of asceticism that is unholy for man to practice. Indeed, he cannot practice it anywhere else than in his own fancy. He may dream about returning to the actual world with the compelling power of essences but, to use a significant phrase drawn from everyday parlance, "his dreams will never materialize, never come true." The impotence of any theory that claims divinity for man is verified in Max Scheler's philosophy. For his final words of advice are more reminiscent of the Lord Buddha than of a world-shaking Tamerlane.

Man's highest and most successful act, Scheler affirmed, is the formation of ideals, the gathering together of various intuitions of essences into an ideal totality. But the contingent, historical, existential aspects will always remain unharnessed and unexplained. They fall outside the range of philosophical activity. In their regard, man can only assume an attitude of resignation: he must suffer what befalls him in an existential way. Thus his intelligence and practical control are never restored to an effective relation with the actuality they once ascetically renounced. By this renunciation, Scheler destroyed the conditions for working out an adequate science of being and human conduct. In the end, his remarkable powers of analysis and description stood in the way of his projects of reviving religious life and supplying a philosophical anthropology. He was left with a gnosis which, unlike wisdom, was unwilling to dwell among men and find its joy among existent beings.

NATURALISM

CHAPTER 7

DARWIN'S IMPACT ON PHILOSOPHY

DARWIN's *Origin of Species* records one of man's decisive penetrations in his persistent effort to understand the world and himself. We are different because of its transforming presence, its capacity for unifying the data and theories in biology and for impelling the evolutionary theme into the central position it now occupies in all regions of human thought and sensibility. There are no living sciences, human attitudes, or institutional powers which remain unaffected by the ideas that were catalytically released by Darwin's work and the great efforts at generalization to which it gave impetus, direction, and prestige.

To acknowledge the massive cultural importance of Darwin's own biological findings and of the general evolutionary outlook which it encouraged is not sufficient to dispense us, however, from the usual tasks of careful analysis and critical sifting in the various fields. The human mind is not a mass of seaweed which must simply surrender itself to the prevailing tides: the work of careful discrimination and critical assessment has to continue even at the time when the contemporary mind is keenly aware of how deeply it is permeated by evolutionary ideas. The need for reflection upon Darwin is perhaps greatest in philosophy, since it is here that we study the transition from the *biological theory of evolution to evolutionism* or the general interpretation of man and the universe in comprehensive evolutionary concepts. This transition is sometimes accomplished insensibly in particular areas of thought where full attention is not paid to questions of method, theory-construction, and the validity of appeals to analogy. But the philosopher's business is to deal with such topics explicitly and to study them in the concrete case of applying biological evolution to all other regions of knowledge and interest.

Moreover, the internal growth of philosophy itself during the past hundred years has been strongly shaped by the current of evolutionism. We must continue to agree with the estimate of the *Origin of Species* made over two generations ago by Josiah Royce: "With the one exception of Newton's *Principia,* no single book of empirical science has ever been of more importance to philosophy than this work of Darwin's." [1] For an understanding of philosophy in its own domestic history during this period, then, we have to examine the various ways in which philosophers responded to the evolutionary theory and sought to give it the function of a universal explanatory principle. Discussions centering upon this issue bring us to the heart of many philosophical achievements and tendencies that determine our present standpoints. The evolutionary premise is none the less real and influential for having attained the privileged status of an accepted framework for contemporary philosophical inquiries.

1. *From Physico-Theology to Agnosticism*

Darwin's story is seldom retold without including a dramatic foreshortening of the whole question of evolution and theistic religion. [2] The famous 1860 encounter at Oxford between Bishop Wilberforce and Darwin's bulldog, Thomas Huxley, resulted in the utter deflation of the former and in the latter's memorable vindication of the seeking and telling of truth in scientific questions. This meeting is often made to do the work of a definitive symbol for an agelong conflict between science and religion, at least a religion having a basis in theism and Christian revelation. When the symbolic transformation of the incident occurs, it then becomes difficult for anyone thinking in these terms to consider it at all likely that theists may still have some good grounds for their assent to God and to man's service of religion. In this common situation, the question of God and evolutionary thought becomes unavoidable. And equally unavoidable is a preliminary historical analysis of the typical views on God which were contested by the early Darwinians. Just as one cannot properly evaluate the customary easy appeal to Kant in ruling out a metaphysics of God without examining the historical circumstances shaping the Kantian conception of natural theology, so one cannot effectively deal with the symbolic use of the Wilberforce-Huxley encounter without analyzing the prevalent approach to God which the first generation of Darwinians found inadequate.

The Victorian crisis of unbelief, as induced by evolutionary controversy, has a definite but severely limited significance as far as the

136

underlying philosophical issues are concerned. There can be no question here about an undermining of natural theology as a whole, since the whole range of the philosophy of God does not enter into the actual dispute. There are definite ways of developing a philosophical approach to God which simply do not get explored and weighed by the principal Victorian evolutionists and their theistic counterparts. Newman and his way of individual assent, for instance, stand entirely apart from the two groups actually at odds, and the same can be said about a realistic causal inference from finite sensible being to God. Yet what gives dramatic intellectual importance to the Victorian quarrel is that it does indeed mark the end of the road for one widely accepted route to God: that of physico-theology.

This approach is developed scientifically by Mersenne and Boyle in the seventeenth century, achieves popular form in William Derham's Boylean Lectures of 1711-1712 on *Physico-Theology,* and finds its classical expression as a teaching instrument in William Paley's manual titled *Natural Theology* (1802). There is a fate about these titles themselves. Whereas in his first *Critique,* Kant located the current design argument within a physico-theology, at the outset of the nineteenth century the latter became identified in England simply with natural theology. When Newman at Oxford and Darwin at Cambridge did their required reading in Paley, they were being introduced to all that remained effective at the British universities of the rich variety of ways in natural theology.[3] The latter had contracted itself to what was in effect a physico-theology, and Newman almost alone of his generation was able to make the proper distinctions and to develop a philosophical approach to God that was not reducible to physico-theology. In large measure, the Victorian crisis over evolution arises out of a failure on the part of men like Darwin, Huxley, and Wilberforce to see that the Derham-Paley position falls pitifully short of encompassing all the resources of the philosophy of God, and hence that it does not deserve to be treated as natural theology without qualification.

Although the Greek and Christian traditions have always appealed to the traces of divine order and providential governance in the visible universe, this general appeal takes its specifically philosophical meaning and cogency from the particular intellectual context within which it functions and by which it is qualified. The novel feature of the Derham-Paley argument from design is that it conforms with the requirements and limitations of modern classical mechanics. The mathematically formulated laws of Galileo and Newton concern the motion and position of macroscopic bodies. But they are not framed to give any understanding of the essential structure of material things, their existential composition and causal dependence in being, or their finality as based upon an act-potency analysis of their principles of being. Physico-theology accepts these restrictions of explanation, and hence does not furnish any inferences to God that are based upon the metaphysical considerations which fall outside the scope of Newtonian mechanics. Operating within the phenomenalism and constructural method set by this scientific viewpoint, the appeal to order in the universe takes on a definite hue and shape. It does not deal with the intrinsic finality of agents but confines itself to a study of the design and extrinsic relations exhibited by component parts of the world machine.[4] Within this historical situation, the appeal to cosmic and organic order becomes a design argument and foregoes any metaphysical basis in the study of the finality of finite agents.

The specifying influence of the phenomenalistic and mechanistic context accounts for two special traits of the arguments employed by the physico-theologians. In the first place, great stress is laid upon the analogy of the workman and his product as a way of understanding and accepting the relation of God to the whole universe and expecially to the organic sphere. Analogy now takes on a separate career of its own. It is no longer founded upon a direct metaphysical analysis of the need for a causal act to account for composed existents, but instead it becomes an independent basis for leading us to the designer of things. The design argument is based upon a maker-analogy which is liberated from a study of causal dependency in being and hence which seeks to convince us on the strength of the analogy itself. It is because of the analogy of making that we are asked to accept the maker as the actual cause. The only kind of causal activity which God can have within this perspective is of a making sort, and the only ground for requiring this activity is the persuasiveness of the analogy itself. Such an autonomous maker-analogy is particularly vulnerable, since it does not clarify the meaning of causation, the possibility of applying the making activity beyond agents within material nature, and the degree to which an independent comparison can be made between the many, finite cases of making which we do experience and the unique, presumably unconditioned sort of making which belongs to the divine designer. These are precisely the points at which Hume and then Kant attacked physico-theology and forced it to retreat from claims about a design for the entire universe to those for a design of organic things.

Here, however, the second characteristic of the design argument

138

becomes prominent and ultimately undermines the position itself. For this approach to God rests upon showing some deficiencies in the mechanical system, some instances of motion and adaptation which require the intervention of an intelligent agent over and above the mechanical forces at work in nature. The maker-analogy is to be accepted mainly for the negative reason that we cannot account for certain aspects of the world by means of the scientific principles now at hand. But as both Laplace and John Stuart Mill point out, this kind of reasoning places our acceptance of God upon a temporary basis which disappears as soon as the scientific explanation is sufficiently rounded off to include the facts in question. Without fully realizing what they are doing, the physico-theologians are simply formulating in theistic terms a challenge for science to fill out its own explanation and thus render belief in God otiose or at least founded on some considerations other than the shortcomings of the scientific analysis at some particular phase in its history. This is what Kant means when he says that the "God" of physico-theology is only a limit-idea for scientific explanation, and what the story about Laplace conveys in stating that there is no longer any need for the hypothesis of God in celestial mechanics.

With Paley, physico-theology made one last effort to reach God within a phenomenalistic and mechanistic framework or (as the subtitle of his book phrases it) to furnish "evidences of the existence and attributes of the Deity collected from the appearances of nature." Yet this way of thinking had only maneuvered itself into the negative position of invoking God as a means of filling in the lacunas in the scientific account of the earth and organic adaptations. It could only be expected, then, that the great development of geology in England during the first half of the nineteenth century would also be the story of a constant retreat made by theists, many of whom were themselves prominent geologists.[5] A rearguard action was fought by the defenders of catastrophism, which explained the fossil record by appeal to a series of divine interventions bringing one organic world to a cataclysmic close and replacing it by another. Through the work of Hutton, Cuvier, and above all Sir Charles Lyell, the uniformitarian view finally prevailed, opening up for our minds the vast stretches of geological time and the constant operation of uniform natural forces. We can now see that the time-scale used by the physico-theologians was pitifully inadequate, that species did become extinct, and that constant natural factors could account for earth strata and their adaptive relations as successfully as for the formation of the stars.

By the time Darwin was bringing his theory about the origin of organic species to maturity, the case for physico-theology was also rapidly shrinking to the region of living things. Here at least, it seemed quite clear to Paley and his countless readers that divine agency is needed to account for adaptation in organisms. If anyone balked at being able to trace the connection with a designing mind as readily in the organism as in the watch, he had a confident reply. "In the animal, we trace the mechanism to a certain point, and then we are stopped; either the mechanism becoming too subtle for our discernment, or something else beside the known laws of mechanism taking place." [6] But Darwin simply refused to stop at the threshold of organic nature. He chose to enlarge our knowledge of the range of mechanism at this point and, in doing so, he could only conclude that he was also sapping the resources of physico-theology, which he identified with natural theology as a whole. In his study of competition and natural selection, chance variation and indefinite divergence of forms, he felt that he had found the instrument for piercing the subtlety of the life process by means of mechanical forces, without appealing to a special creative act for each natural species. The design in organisms is undeniable as a descriptive fact of adaptive relations, but the explanation of how it is brought about through chance variation and other natural factors remains at the level of the immanent mechanism of nature. There may be a supreme contriver of living things, but we are no longer coerced by deficiencies in biology to say that there must exist such a divine designer.

In his historical situation, Darwin could not avoid viewing every successful new step in his explanation as being correlated with the last few steps remaining in the case for God drawn from the appearances in nature. He himself never drove home aggressively the ruin of physico-theology and only worked out its negative implications for his own religious view in a gradual, unemphatic way. He drifted slowly and painlessly from the passive theism of his early days to the *Origin of Species'* concluding remarks on a vaguely supposed superintending power, and finally to the complete agnosticism and indifference which marked his last years. Darwin's original hold on the theistic conviction had depended on the atmosphere of physico-theology, and as this state of mind gradually faded away before the advances in geology and his own evolutionary biology, it was not replaced by any other living way to God. For him, then, the disappearance of the grounds for Paley's design argument meant the disappearance of all reasonable evidence for the reality of God, and hence his interest simply turned in other directions.

In June of 1860, however, Darwin was still cautious enough about drawing any agnostic implications from his theory of organic evolution to make the following long reply to the religious-minded Lyell, who had warned him against confusing natural selection with the primary creational laws:

> One word more upon the Deification of Natural Selection: attributing so much weight to it does not exclude still more general laws, *i.e.* the ordering of the whole universe. I have said that Natural Selection is to the structure of organized beings what the human architect is to a building. The very existence of the human architect shows the existence of more general laws; but no one, in giving credit for a building to the human architect, thinks it necessary to refer to the laws by which man has appeared. No astronomer, in showing how the movements of planets are due to gravity, thinks it necessary to say that the law of gravity was designed that the planets should pursue the courses which they pursue. I cannot believe that there is a bit more interference by the Creator in the construction of each species than in the course of the planets. It is only owing to Paley and Co., I believe, that this more special interference is thought necessary with living bodies. . . . I demur also to your putting Huxley's "force and matter" in the same category with Natural Selection. The latter may, of course, be quite a false view; but surely it is not getting beyond our depth to first causes.[7]

This was an admirable statement of scientific caution in the face of philosophical issues. The only difficulty was that it led only to the negative conception of a noninterfering Deity, for whose causal operation in the universe no positive evidence was being supplied. Darwin was unable to find within the method of biology any reason for admitting some causal activity more basic than the laws of organic evolution and planetary formation. Especially after including man within the scope of evolutionary process, he had no ground in biology for regarding the more general laws as forces imparted to matter by God rather than as immanent patterns of activity without any transcendent reference, as Huxley was suggesting. And Darwin did not acknowledge any method other than the biological one for inquiring into the causal factors involved in the development of man and other living things. In the end, the only sure point was that Paley and Co. had been put out of business by his own explanations and that there were no evident reasons for pushing beyond his account. For the rest, Darwin simply confessed his inability at grasping metaphysical questions and so preserved a calm agnosticism about God.

Our present study of Darwin's gradual repudiation of the design argument suggests that the whole issue deserves some further historical and doctrinal investigation. For one thing, it would seem advisable to reserve the name "the design argument" for that definite sort of appeal to the order in the visible universe which was formulated historically within the framework of modern scientific mechanism and phenomenalism. Moreover, we must discriminate at least five major features in the argument as it was understood by Darwin and his associates, as well as by its defenders among orthodox minds. (1) It is a nonmetaphysical approach to the world and hence does not concern itself with that sort of finality which rests on a metaphysical analysis of action. (2) It is based directly and primarily on the maker-analogy as an independent source, instead of seeking its inferential strength in a causal study as the basis for a causally regulated analogy. (3) As it actually develops, the design argument depends upon the current state of scientific knowledge in the relevant areas. Hence it cannot aim at achieving more than a high probability which always remains open to future revision, in accord with the pattern of scientific research. (4) It sometimes supposes that there is an inverse relation between the limits of scientific knowledge and the extent of theistic assent. Every advance of science would then involve a correlative step of retreat on the part of a design-based theism. (5) Sometimes the proponents of the design argument add that their physico-theology constitutes the whole content of a valid natural theology. It is important to recognize that only the first three traits characterize the design argument in its main historical forms. The last two notes are found specially in the sources studied by Darwin, but they are removable without destroying its import. Unfortunately, Darwin himself does not weigh these various components and consider other theistic ways.

Commenting recently on this whole issue, the anthropologist Loren Eiseley has suggested that "Darwin did not destroy the argument from design. He destroyed only the watchmaker and the watch," that is, he presented a developmental view of nature which simply rendered obsolete Paley's metaphor about nature being a machine with a cosmic machinist as its tinkering maker.[8] But it was psychologically difficult for Darwin and especially for Huxley, who hardened and universalized the standpoint of evolutionary agnosticism, to slough off the watchmaker approach and still refrain from concluding that thereby all the empirically ascertainable avenues to God were cut off for the human mind. Huxley was fond of using the very terminology of Derham and Paley by referring to natural selection as a *vera causa*, as a real cause (and in a still more generalized form, as *the* most comprehensive, scientifically knowable cause), as the precise mode of causal efficiency in which the general agency of force and matter operates in the organic world. This real causal interpretation of evolutionary factors gave to time itself a limitless creative power for bringing about the emergence, modification, and indefinite divergence of all organic species. And when the causal power of evolution was linked to the universal cosmic forces, there would seem to be no need for supposing any more primary sort of causality to which the evolutionary and cosmic agencies themselves would remain subordinate and which would furnish the human mind with evidential grounds for accepting God's existence.

There were two aspects in Huxley's outlook, however, which considerably weakened this conclusion even for himself. He failed to examine critically the various meanings for "cause" and to determine the precise way in which the biological description of evolutionary process combined causal factors, in the biological sense, with other types of explanatory reasons. Furthermore, he remained unsure whether we do or can know anything about matter in its own reality. And since he conceived of evolutionary forces as the display of matter's causal power in the organic sphere, he could not supply any ultimate basis for actually ruling out a causal power more primary than that of the evolutionary factors. Hence there was a curious discrepancy between Huxley's public pronouncements on the ultimacy of evolution and his private admission that God may be operating in the universe as the hidden banker or cosmic chess player.[9]

The grand systematizer of evolutionary agnosticism was Herbert Spencer. The very low state of his reputation among present-day philosophers makes it difficult for us to realize the full extent of his influence during the latter half of the nineteenth century or his function as the point of departure for almost all subsequent philosophers of evolution. In his self-revealing essay on "The Filiation of Ideas," he traced the formation of his own developmental outlook to various sources in the pre-1859 period, thus reminding us that evolution was definitely in the air in the decades before Darwin and Alfred Wallace read their famous papers. Spencer acknowledged his debt to Schelling's typically Romantic philosophical view of life surging toward individual peaks, to Lyell's geological work on continuous development of the earth, to K. E. von Baer's embryological study of the trend from homogeneity to heterogeneity, and to some historical studies on the social differentiation and integration of peoples. Darwin only confirmed for Spencer what these earlier sources had already suggested on the evolutionary generalization that all kinds of motion tend from homogeneity to heterogeneity, from the undifferentiated to the differentiated state, and from disaggregation to close integration of parts.

Spencer tells us that the habit of selecting evidence for its value as illustrating this evolutionary pattern was strengthened in his mind by the need for some general conception to replace the outworn theory of special creation of the various forms of nonliving and living things.

In 1852 the belief in organic evolution had taken deep root, and had drawn to itself a large amount of evidence—evidence not derived from numerous special instances but derived from the general aspects of organic nature, and from the necessity of accepting the hypothesis of Evolution when the hypothesis of Special Creation has been rejected. . . . From this time onwards the evolutionary interpretation of things in general became habitual.[10]

It is noteworthy, however, that Spencer's rejection of the Derham-Paley position does not lead him to atheistic naturalism or to the thesis about the warfare of science and religion. Quite to the contrary, he concludes that science and religion can now be reconciled on the ground of their common recognition of the unknowable. They both admit that there is an absolute which transcends our ability to know or conceive, beyond the bare affirmation of its presence.

Underlying this interpretation is Spencer's own philosophical phenomenalism, which in some ways is more radical than that of Hamilton and Mill. Neither through scientific nor religious means can the human mind advance its range of knowledge beyond the sensible phenomena and their immanent laws. We can indeed ascertain the laws of order according to which the changes in the cosmos occur, but such a descriptive pattern "still leaves unexplained the *nature* and *origin* of them." [11] It is enough to know that phenomenal events and their immanent laws do have a nature and origin in order to conclude to the reality of the absolute, but we cannot advance a single step beyond this affirmation. All we can try to do is to apply to the unknowable our own subjective and symbolic conception of cause or power. But neither the scientist nor the religious mind can transcend the symbolic mode of signifying the unknowable absolute, and precisely in this joint disability to specify it any further lies the principle of their harmony. Thus Spencer regards his evolutionary agnosticism as the best means of reconciling science and religion in our age.

What still keeps Spencer's position intriguing is the way it combines agnosticism about the nature of the material world and God with a resolute systematizing of the human sciences and realms of experience. Within the phenomenal order, he is unlimitedly hopeful about the synthetic power of his evolutionary formula. It becomes a synthetic principle by moving beyond the biological procedures of assembling empirical facts, proposing inductive hypotheses, and supplying particular verifications for them. Evolution as a philosophy and not simply as a theory in biology or any other special scientific field depends upon the rule of giving a *deductive* interpretation to all inductively established positions.[12] Philosophical evolutionism rests upon this conversion of factual inductions and their attendant theories into necessary deductive consequences of the most universal phenomenal principles. Until this deduction is made, Darwinian evolutionary thought is regarded by Spencer as infraphilosophical.

Even the particular laws of evolution must be shown to be deductively related to the laws of motion and the supreme principle of the persistence of force. Spencer observes that the latter is not properly called the "conservation of force," since this might lead to illusory inferences to a conserver or some conserving act that would violate the phenomenal limits of human knowledge. The persistence of force is indeed the first deductive principle of the evolutionary system, but no ontological inferences can be drawn from it. In respect to the absolute, it is only the scientific way of making a symbolic reference to the unknowable something as being the powerful core of the universe.

Spencer was quite abstemious in his use of factual studies, being content with using a minimal amount of materials for suggesting an evolutionary pattern for some special area. His synthetic philosophical principles for biology, psychology, and sociology sought mainly to introduce a deductive rigor into these sciences by showing their necessary connection with his more general statement of the persistence of force, the laws of motion, and the formula for evolution. He made a peppery defense of this deductive procedure against Huxley by noting that biology and other sciences do not achieve their full standing within philosophical evolutionism until the deductive entailment is established. At the same time, he rendered his entire synthetic enterprise highly vulnerable to any attack concentrating on the concept of force. This was precisely the point singled out by Henri Bergson in his Collège de France lectures for 1904-05:

If one attributes here to the word "force" the meaning which the scientist gives to the word "energy," Spencer's conclusions must be greatly restricted. If, on the other hand, one takes the word in the broader meaning in which Spencer often seems to use it, the conclusions of this philosophy lose the basis which he thought to find for them in positive science.[13]

145

Bergson was suggesting that Spencer either had to sacrifice his grandiose systematic deduction of all areas of knowledge or else admit that it is lacking in scientific rigor. Taken in conjunction with the twentieth-century developments in the concept of energy, this criticism contributed toward the rapid erosion of Spencer's version of evolutionary agnosticism.

2. Evolution and Progress

There is another aspect of Spencer's philosophy which is still worth examining: its quite ambiguous support of the theory of continuous progress. All that his evolutionism can strictly guarantee from its deductive basis is the persistence of force, which means the persistence of relations among forces, together with the transformation and equivalence of forces in a Newtonian system. This accounts for the highly qualified manner in which he describes the evolutionary formula: "The re-distribution of the matter and of its retained motion, is from a relatively diffused, uniform, and indeterminate arrangement, to a relatively concentrated, multiform, and determinate arrangement." [14] The evolutionary trend is a relative one, because it is limited in principle by the equally basic movement of dissolution. The play of forces is a constant making and unmaking of the material order, with a probable tendency toward a total equilibrium of forces. As to whether we can state categorically that the cosmic process must terminate in a total extinction of all changes, Spencer maintains that this question concerns something ultimate and hence belongs in the realm of the unknowable. A universal quiescence is a possible outcome, but we cannot show it to be inescapably necessary. There is also an open possibility of indefinitely continuing the cycle of renewal and destruction, integration and disintegration, concentration and dispersion.

Spencer assures us that he himself leans toward the latter alternative. But he does so only as a matter of belief and reasonable inductive inference from organic and human development. The difficulty is that the hope for an indefinite alteration cannot be justified through any deductive argument from the persistence of force. According to Spencer's own methodology, therefore, his belief cannot acquire the standing of philosophical knowledge and cannot be regarded as a necessary consequence of evolutionism. There must be an element of strong natural faith behind any theory of progress which appeals to the evolutionary philosophy of Spencer for support.

Even if we do accept this view, however, the aid it gives to progress is only relative and temporary. Strictly speaking, what remains possible within the context of the Spencerian persistence of force is not evolution alone but the conjunct law of evolution-and-dissolution, the indefinite alteration of the processes of forming and dissolving. As a demurrer against the necessity of a universal heat-death, evolutionary agnosticism can only offer the possibility of an everlasting cycle of making and unmaking of all the structures involved in human experience of the world.

This is the point which Friedrich Nietzsche seeks to drive home with the hammer blows of his doctrine on the eternal return of the same state of affairs.[15] He contends that Spencer is too timid to acknowledge that cyclic alteration is not just a likelihood but the essential law of the universe. And Nietzsche suggests that the reason for the hesitation is found in the social and historical consequences of a thoroughgoing cyclism. Once we have tasted the Judaeo-Christian hope for an open-ended conception of time and history, we are reluctant to embrace the full consequences of evolutionism-and-dissolutionism and cannot summon the courage to engage in human affairs within this framework. For Nietzsche, the superman is by definition the mind which can lucidly accept the graven law of a cyclic return of everything to the same point and nevertheless work energetically within the present span of time.

Spencer and the so-called Social Darwinists in England and America might reply to Nietzsche that he has overstepped the limits of phenomenalism in treating cyclism as an essential law of ultimate reality. But even within their own context, they would have to concede that Spencer's favorite slogan about the survival of the fittest provides no strict guarantee of the endless improvement of the stock and especially of human society through competition. From the philosophical standpoint, evolutionary social meliorism has to be qualified by the distinction between a short-range and a long-range estimate. Within the brief era of modern science and industry, Spencer can point out that the prevailing trend is a gradualist evolution and slow spread of organized altruism. But he admits that this era belongs within an enormously broader time scale and is likely to lead to a dissolutional phase of human history. Taking this cosmic perspective, he finds it difficult to avoid the conclusion that social progress will inevitably be undone and the achievements of cultural integration dissolved. His social drive works in favor of short-range improvement but his synthetic principles do not yield any philosophical confirmation of the faith in long-range progress.

More recent evolutionary thought usually regards the developmental process as being unique and irreversible, although not always as progressive. This is often due to a resonance of Christian faith or of a natural faith in the significance of human history.[16] Another factor is the refusal of many biologists, anthropologists, sociologists, and interpreters of history to follow Spencer in seeking a deductive philosophical justification of their position. Thus they can avoid his quandary about whether or not to treat the irreversible and progressive view of time as a consoling parochialism holding good only within a limited reach in the biological and historical spans of time. Yet the consequence is that they do not share in Spencer's clarity about the noetic status of what he called the belief in progress as a beneficent necessity of the evolving cosmos. The contribution of Christian faith and of philosophically determinable evidence to this conviction has to be carefully weighed, if illusory interpretations of progress are to be discovered and eliminated.

As expressed in the *Descent of Man,* there are some unsettling features in Darwin's own theory which prevent any easy acceptance of automatic, universal progress.[17] Insofar as he accepts the uniformitarian (rather than the catastrophic) reading of the geological record, he is anticyclical and supports an open movement toward ever new forms of life. But he also criticizes a simplistic kind of progressionism which arranges all the forms of life in a single ladder of nature pointing climactically to man's perfection as the highest rung. The image of the ladder of nature does not necessarily involve a relation of descent among the arranged forms, whereas Darwin insists on the genetic descent of related organisms. Furthermore, his stress on the indefinite divergence of species demands a new metaphor, that of the continually branching tree of life, instead of the serial set of rungs along a single track.

These modifications have one further implication: Darwinism cannot enter into a simple alliance with the philosophical forms of the theory of progress popular during the eighteenth and nineteenth centuries. Both the physico-theologians and the Encyclopedists accept progress in the sense of a convergence of everything toward man and an indefinite perfectibility of man himself. For the Darwinian mind, however, man is one apex among many in nature, and he is an apex which is the genetic outcome of a development from simpler organisms. The latter do not merely point toward man and subserve his

148

needs: they give rise to the human organism along one of the lines of descent, without depreciating other lines and other peaks. The biological evidence alone does not furnish distinctive grounds for taking constant improvement to be the law of man's history. Other sources of evidence about man must also be consulted, and then there is the task of evaluating several reports and not simply of construing the idea of progress as the massive and inevitable conclusion of scientific studies.

The plural lines of descent also make it difficult to integrate the biological with the current philosophical meanings of development. When the Romantic mind or the Hegelian dialectician or the Comtean positivist declares that nature is undergoing development, he implies that this process is tightly organized according to rational laws and that it is ultimately unified in a convergent development toward man. But the Darwinian evolutionists specify that the evolutionary mechanism depends on chance variation, natural selection, and indefinite divergence of species. This view of the precise means of biological development need not be incompatible with every sort of belief in progress, but it does not specifically furnish confirmatory evidence for the reign of rationality and the convergence toward man's welfare upon which the prevailing philosophical conceptions of progress rested. The biological meaning for development cannot simply be equated with the philosophical sense elaborated by idealism and positivism, and hence a theory of man-centered progress is not an unavoidable corollary of biological evolution. The Social Darwinists clouded over this issue temporarily, but it was bound to reassert itself under less favorable social conditions and in a reflective analysis of the logic of Darwinian evolution.

Darwin himself concluded the *Origin of Species* with the hopeful picture of an indefinite progress on the part of all biological species, since they are not fixed in their present limits. But his recognition of the play of chance in nature and the interplay of complex nondirectional factors in the environment prevented him from giving unhesitant assent to progress as the intrinsic law of organisms and especially of human social life. In *The Descent of Man,* he did regard the progressive viewpoint as truer and more cheerful than that which centers on an original perfect state from which we have fallen, but he was aware of too many variable elements in human life to treat natural selection as a rigid law operating for social progress. The evolutionary tendency toward integration, complexity, and differentiation could not be interpreted as a constant improvement, unless one

149

identified such trends with the evolutionary phase in Spencer's cycle of change. Then, however, one would also have to admit that the downward trend of cosmic force would eventually prevail over temporary advances of man and other organisms in a counterdirection.

This was the point of Huxley's disenchanting remark, in his notable Romanes Lecture on evolution and ethics, that "the theory of evolution encourages no millennial anticipations." [18] Rather, it was at the non-millennial level or within the limited perspective of cultural history that there was some hope of forestalling for a while the completion of the full cosmic cycle of unmaking what natural selection and human art have made. Hence Huxley spelled out the condition under which evolutionary theory could be joined with a belief in progress: only if a temporary dualism were maintained between the state of nature in its plenary scope and the restricted order of human art. This involved a philosophical consideration and a decision which could not justify themselves on the ground of being an inevitable extension of the findings of biological evolution. Indeed, the naturalistic prejudice against any ultimately firm contrast between nature and man also operates against acceptance of long-run progress in the universe.

The thorough ambivalence of the relation between biological evolution and belief in progress explains why the sharp decline of the latter in the twentieth century has not undermined evolutionary thought among biologists. The crisis in theories of progress brings out the need for distinguishing clearly between biological development and the philosophical meanings for development in nature and society. And if there is indeed a millennial aspect to the acceptance of progress, its roots are to be sought partly in the Christian faith and its providential conception of all cosmic change and human history.[19] The act of accepting some sort of progress in time and human history is never a simple and univocal act, having the same meaning for all minds. The theme of progress is a complex locus today where scientific, philosophical, and religious elements are conjoined in many different ways by the individual mind. At least, a study of the nineteenty-century biological evolutionists shows that the coming of Darwinism did not relieve anyone of the responsibility to sift these various factors critically before making one's personal evaluation of the problem.

3. *Evolutionary Philosophy in America*

The relation of evolutionary thought to physico-theology, agnosticism, and the theory of progress was primarily the story of its effect upon philosophies already in being. In migrating to America, however, it played a germinal role in forming and directing some new scientifically oriented philosophies. During the speculative doldrums of the decade 1850-60, it would have required a hardy prophet to say that America was on the threshold of a philosophical renaissance which would control the course of thought for the next century. That this quickening did actually occur was due in large measure to the discussions aroused by the introduction of Darwin and Spencer to our soil. Their stimulus upon the philosophical minds maturing from 1860 to 1890 was a major contribution to the development of pragmatism in its several varieties.

Our concern is not with the American Social Darwinists and their apology for competitive individualism, since these men were singularly barren in new ideas and methods for philosophy.[20] But amid the gusts of economic and social propaganda, a few men were engaged quietly in examining the basis of evolution and its implications for philosophy. During the 1860's and 1870's a group of Harvard men, including Wright and Green, Peirce and James, Fiske and Holmes, met informally to discuss philosophical issues. Peirce liked to call them members of his Metaphysical Club, and in any case they were the seminal source of the pragmatic current of thought in America.[21] One of their major topics was evolution and the effect it would have upon the philosophical conception of man and knowledge and the universe. Historically considered, their approach to this nest of questions was unique in that they probed more fundamentally and critically into the philosophical meaning of evolution than did any other contemporary minds. And it can be added that the problematic character of evolutionism as a philosophical postulate was more vividly realized and objectively probed by these men than by their successors, many of whom tend to accord to it a dogmatic status which this pioneer group would scarcely countenance.

For our purposes, the key individuals are Chauncey Wright and Charles Peirce. Wright was affectionately called the boxing master of the group, since they all had to face the challenge of his bold analyses and his project of assessing Darwin and Spencer in the light

151

of Mill's logic of the sciences. His contribution lay precisely in the resolve not to play favorites with evolutionary speculation but to submit it to the ordinary canons of scientific method. Whereas Spencer, Haeckel, and lesser popularizers had uncritically used Darwin's theory to advance their own sprawling cosmological views, Wright recommended a reflective methodological study of evolutionary theory to determine its proper scope and its relation to philosophical topics. In carrying out this program, he made a devastating criticism of Spencer and succeeded in detaching the Harvard group from the synthetic philosophy long before it reached completion and full popular acceptance.

There are four main points in Wright's critical analysis of Spencer: the nature of principles, the meaning of force, the inductive use of examples, and the relation of scientific method and metaphysics.[22] (1) Spencer plunges directly into the work of grinding out philosophical principles for the several sciences, without stopping to inquire whether evolution or any other principle can have the same meaning in science and in philosophy. The working scientist regards a principle as an eye for looking beyond itself at some regularities discoverable among concrete events, but he does not regard a principle as an active component in the events themselves. From this standpoint, Spencer and other uncritical evolutionists mistake the tool for the handiwork. They disclaim metaphysics and yet they make their evolutionary principles function as constitutive causal agencies in natural process itself. Wright advises us to restrict the evolutionary principle to its explanatory role, without claiming any real causal significance for it, at least when we treat the principle as a scientific one.

Another trait of a scientific principle is its definite and revisable relation to what we can experience. Granted that it enjoys some relative stability and universality, still as a working scientific tool it never completely divests itself of its role as a leading question, as a scaffolding which will eventually give way after serving in some definite capacity. But Spencer treats the persistence of force and evolution as completely definitive, nonhypothetical principles whose deductive range reaches to the entire universe. His justification is that these principles express in abstract and generalized form the ultimate phenomenal truths about the process of things. Yet this supposes that a definitive understanding has already been reached in the major sciences, and hence that the only further need today is for principles which are summarizers of a complete and universal truth. Even within the framework of classical physics, however, Wright can point out that there are areas for fundamental research and hence principles in the more typically scientific sense of interrogators of nature or investigative leads for uncovering new aspects of nature.

Spencer never establishes in detail the transition from principles in this latter sense to his own philosophical notion of principles as abstract summarizers of a fixed totality of knowledge. In the scientific context, the evolutionary principle does not cease to be open to revision and deep modification of its import, regardless of the philosophical mansions built upon its meaning at some given stage of biological research. Wright does not dispute the need for abstract and broadly formulated principles in science, but he does insist that their purpose is rather to open our minds to new problems and observations of concrete events than to serve as deductive premises for a set of incorrigible truths about all events and relations in the cosmos.

(2) Spencer defends his distinctive philosophical use of the evolutionary principle on the ground that it is strictly deducible from the persistence of force. His further remark that "persistence" is preferable to "conservation," since the latter signifies a causal substrate or ultimate conserving source, rouses Wright's suspicion. Either Spencer does not grasp the Newtonian physical-system meaning for force or else he is using physical terms in an equivocal way in order to profit by the prestige of physics, but without assuming any of its methodological limitations. Anticipating Bergson's line of attack, Wright notes that in all his multivolumed enterprise Spencer fails to supply any extended account of physics itself, so that we may follow the steps in transforming the physical concepts of force, energy, and conservation into the deductive basis of the synthetic philosophy. Instead, he fuses many different meanings for "force" into a nebulous concept whose scientific grounding cannot be tested in any specific way.

To all the ideas which he [Spencer] adopts from science he adds a new sense, or rather a vagueness, so as to make them descriptive of as much as possible. . . . Out of mathematical formulas these terms lose their definiteness and their utility. They become corrupting and misleading ideas. They are none the less abstract, but they are less clear.[23]

The subsequent preoccupation of the pragmatists with finding ways of making our ideas functionally clear stems partly from a resolve to avoid such irremediable cloudiness. Wright's immediate conclusion here is that the first principle from which Spencer deduces his evolutionary law is hopelessly vague and hence cannot supply any scientific warrant for converting the biological notion of evolution into a full-blown philosophical evolutionism.

153

Spencer's law of evolution may be a consistent necessary consequence of his own notion of force, but there is no way to trace a scientific ancestry for the latter. Wright suggests that it may be an original expression of Spencer's subjective interests and aspirations toward system-building, but then its import is emotive and not scientific. Once the principles of evolution and persistence of force are wrenched from a definite context of predictive hypotheses, experimental situations, and mathematical formulas, they enter the realm of scientific unknowables. We should therefore be just as prudently agnostic about them in their philosophical use as Spencer is about the nature of the unknowable absolute.

(3) A defense of Spencer might be made by appealing to his inductive procedure of citing examples of evolution from many sciences. In reply, Wright notes that, with the exception of a careful report on von Baer's work in embryology, his examples are loose re-statements ranging from the nebular theory to the history of Roman laws. Spencer has a penchant for concentrating his inductive materials in such areas as the formation of the stars and the transition from the inorganic to the organic, areas where our present knowledge is most problematic and open to further revision. Furthermore, there is a decisive difference between the scientific effort of *universalizing* a position through deductive prediction and empirical verification and the Spencerian method of *generalizing* scientific data by means of noting loose similarities and then capping them into a law for the cosmos. The evolutionary law is the result of such a generalizing process. The references to increasing heterogeneity and integration evoke many analogies, but they do not permit of any determinate testing for validity. In this respect, the philosophical use of evolutionary analogies is just as loose as the watchmaker analogy of the outmoded physico-theologians.

Once more, then, Wright returns to the question of the source of the philosophical idea of evolutionary change. He grants that this idea exerts a powerful influence upon the contemporary mind and serves an effective unifying function. But in this highly generalized and analogical form, its source is to be found in the human mind's inclinations and dreams rather than in biological research. It is the outcome of transforming the limited Enlightenment belief in social progress into a universal belief in the progress of the whole universe. Using Mill's distinction between what we know by inductive belief and what we hope for through imagination, Wright assigns philosophical evolutionism to the latter point of origin. He attributes the powerful belief in evolutionism to the operation of "the moral and mythic instincts," to our human need for some kind of moral faith and mythopoeic imagery with which to interpret the universal fact of process in the world.[24] This doest not necessarily mean that the evolutionary outlook is illusory, but only that it is something other than a continuous expansion of the biological theory of evolution or a rigid deduction from some wider physical principle. The philosophical principle of evolution is not founded on the natural sciences but reflects the moral hope and esthetic imagery of man, when he seeks to deal with process as though it means universal progress.

Wright thinks that some sort of teleology is unavoidable for an effective belief in evolutionism. It need not be the kind which supposes that all events minister to human happiness. Evolutionism is teleological by the fact that it views all events as constituting a complete and intelligible order, operating under a few original and unchanging laws. "Teleology does not consist entirely of speculations having happy *dénouements,* save that the perfection of the end to which the progress tends is a happiness to the intellect that contemplates it in its evolution and beauty of orderliness." [25] Wright is no more antagonistic than Kant or Mill toward such teleology, as long as it openly acknowledges itself to be built upon moral faith rather than scientific knowledge of nature. But whereas Spencer would like to limit the play of hopeful imagination to his preference for the evolutionary part of the evolution-dissolution cycle, Wright extends the mythic factor to the very heart of the evolutionary law as a synthetic principle in philosophy.

(4) Underlying Wright's entire polemic is his aim of keeping modern science and philosophy distinct. In criticizing Spencer, he does not detract either from Darwin's own scientific work or from the need for philosophical inquiries. Yet he does stand for what he variously calls the *neutrality* of scientific method or the *nihilism* of modern science.[26] By these expressions he means that modern science is primarily a methodological discipline and that from its procedures and findings no consequences can be drawn for cosmology, metaphysics, ethics, and religion. Issues which belong properly in these fields cannot be given a definitive solution by appeal to biological evolution or any other scientific theory, no matter how far it is generalized.

As a scientific concept, evolution must be restricted to biology and some physiological aspects of psychology, along with the social growth of language and law. The claim for universal explanatory significance of evolutionism is not continuous with or supported by the biological position. The latter is too intimately bound up with the concrete data, problems, and hypothetical procedures of laboratory biology to permit its controlled transformation into a first principle of philosophy. And similarly, the leading concepts in physics are too closely specified by the mathematical formulas, predictive statements, and experimental stiuations in that area to furnish a deductive basis from which a philosophical law of evolution might be derived. This is the sense in which scientific thinking must preserve its neutrality in the face of all efforts to use its results for the resolution of philosophical issues. And if the philosopher derives the courage of his convictions only from invoking a scientific sanction for them, then Wright is ready to admit that science turns a nihilistic face toward such a project.

Owing to his grasp on the pluralism of scientific methods and the contextual meaning of scientific concepts, Wright remained skeptical toward the attempt of evolutionism to use biological theories as premises for metaphysical and moral inquiry. He granted the legitimacy of questions about God, duty, and a final end, but rejected the plan of answering them agnostically or otherwise through a philosophical generalization of scientific evidences and concepts. On this resolute neutrality of modern science, he appealed to Francis Bacon and might have added the testimony of Cardinal Newman. The last essay from his pen was a critique of "German Darwinism" or the attempt of Haeckel and others to metaphysicize the theories of evolutionary biology in favor of doctrinaire materialism and monism. In treating the scientific construct or realized abstraction "*as if* it had a meaning independently of the things which ought to determine the true limits and precision of its meaning," such philosophical exploiters of evolution really build their systems upon the fallacy of misplaced concreteness (to use Whitehead's phrase) rather than upon the facts and theories of biology.[27]

Wright is at his best when on the offensive against evolutionism rather than when engaged in constructive philosophical work. In philosophy, he accepts the consequences of strict phenomenalism concerning speculative issues and prefers to reformulate philosophical problems in terms of practical reason and moral belief. It is here that Peirce's handling of the evolutionary theme becomes significant, since he does attempt to draw some speculative philosophical significance from evolution without relaxing the stringency of scientific method. He cannot avoid a clash with Wright over this issue, since he proposes a philosophical treatment of evolution that will accord with the scientific method and yet avoid Spencer's loose-jointed use of force and differentiation.

As an opening wedge, Peirce suggests that there are two ways of taking the neutrality of science. The closed sense preferred by Wright is that the methods and concepts of science can in principle have no consequences bearing upon the nature of things. But this is a definitional closure of inquiry. It is not imposed from within by scientific method itself but is stipulated for it from without by acceptance of phenomenalism. The latter is a philosophical position and should not be allowed to dictate the basic scope of scientific inquiry. Wright is properly concerned to preserve the freedom of research, but this can done satisfactorily by the methodic refusal to settle inquiry by appeal to authority. The phenomenalist postulate is either an instance of interference by authority or else is an otiose view with which scientific intelligence can readily dispense. Inquiry can reflectively discover its own method and limits, without accepting interference from the prejudgment of phenomenalism or any other extrinsic authority.

Thus Peirce recommends a second or open meaning for the neutrality of science: It must conduct its inquiry without any interference from other sources and without any advance stipulation about the ways of being and the limits of knowing. Whether or not we can use the method and findings of science to obtain some knowledge of general structures and laws in nature must be left for the actual outcome of the effort to determine. Peirce holds that we can develop some metaphysical implications through the pragmaticist analysis of scientific procedures. And evolution is one of the cardinal points of departure for such an exploratory work.

Peirce often refers to the great upheaval in scientific thinking caused by Darwin.[28] This new influence is not only a cultural fact but also has a revolutionary philosophical significance. Darwin's ideas cannot be accommodated within the conventional British framework of empiricism and mechanistic determinism. The weakness of Spencer and other previous evolutionary philosophers lies precisely in failing to recognize that Darwin has brought about a major shift in our view of nature. Peirce pinpoints the precise locations where the evolutionary perspective calls for a radical criticism of the pre-Darwinian outlook in philosophy. As far as classical empiricism is concerned, evolution represents a challenge to its nominalism and its epistemological individualism. As for a mechanist philosophy, its determinism and reductive tendency must give way before the fresh insights of evolutionary thought.

In attacking the nominalist character of British empiricism, Peirce is sufficiently confident to state his case in the form of a dilemma that one must be either a nominalistic individualist or an evolutionist.[29] For if there is any summary statement of the evolutionary conception, it is that our universe is witnessing a growth in generality or the formed regularity of structures and functions. Genetic explanation is based upon factors of comparison and continuity among individuals in an organic group, showing that there is a real, effective foundation in natural things for general laws and relations. The evolutionary mode of inquiry is also incompatible with the epistemological bias of empiricism toward the isolated individual perceiver. On the contrary, evolutionary studies concentrate upon the individual-in-context, upon the organism already really related to its existent, active environment and the rest of the species, and not merely to its private impressions. Many classical puzzles of the empiricist theory of knowledge are bound to become artificial and irrelevant in a world which recognizes the reality of general laws and the open presence of mind to a real order of natural beings.

Even before the era of relativity theory and quantum mechanics, Peirce was using evolutionary considerations to criticize the deterministic basis of strict mechanism.[30] Together with Wright, he pointed out the significant use of the statistical notion of scientific law in Maxwell's theory of gases, in population and historical studies, and in Darwin's biological work. Evolutionary research was facilitated by taking a new view of laws of nature as being capable of formulation in terms of probability statements. Taken along with Darwin's stress on chance variation, this method indicated how thorough had to be the revision of the total determinism of events as pictured in the mechanist philosophies based on classical physics. Peirce maintained that scientific laws are regular, but with limits set on the exactness and universality of what they can predict. We have to recognize the presence of real contingency and the chance factor in natural process, as well as in our scientific means of explanation. Ours is a universe having the mixed condition of law-along-with-chance rather than a pure state of either complete determinism or utter chaos. A philosophy which formulates evolutionary laws without respecting these limitations is engaged in the hopeless task of pouring new wine into bottles that are already cracked open and discarded in biology.

The reductive tendency of philosophical mechanism is also brought under fire by Peirce. Once we become thoroughly imbued with the genetic approach of evolutionary thought, we also become dissatisfied

158

with the attempt to reduce all events to the uniformity of nature and to treat uniformity as an ultimate, inexplicable fact. The subjective counterpart of this reductionism is Hume's appeal to custom and the laws of association as ultimate and unanalyzable principles in the mental order. From an evolutionist standpoint, we may reasonably expect that the uniform aspects in nature also have a history, that they too have a genesis. The uniformity of nature is not an ultimate fact or a necessary logico-metaphysical principle, but an achievement which is still in process of being brought about.

If we take a fresh look at the world, instead of floating along on the tide of conventional mechanism, we are impressed that "everywhere the main fact is growth and increasing complexity." [31] The variety and diversity and constant growth of kinds of things reveal the presence of spontaneity at the heart of nature, as Darwin himself had suggested in his law of constant divergence of species. There is objective chance in the sense of variescence or the collective tendency to variableness. Peirce has his own doctrine of tychism or recognition of the inexpugnable chance factor in the universe, but he also warns against forgetting the inductive basis for the affirmation of chance and thus paying superstitious homage to it. Used in a critical way, however, the stress on spontaneity and chance as real ingredients in things helps us to see the developmental character of natural laws or the evolutionary tendency toward stable patterns of activity. Far from being a brute, unanalyzable postulate, the uniformity of nature is genetically intelligible as the drift toward law, the tendency of the universe to increase the habit of regular and generalized modes of action.

After using evolutionary ideas to undermine nominalism, empiricism, and mechanism, Peirce then employs them in constructing his own cosmogony and metaphysics. His evolutionary explanation

would suppose that in the beginning—infinitely remote—there was a chaos of unpersonalized feeling, which being without connection or regularity would properly be without existence. This feeling, sporting here and there in pure arbitrariness, would have started the germ of a generalizing tendency. Its other sportings would be evanescent, but this would have a growing virtue. Thus, the tendency to habit would be started; and from this with the other principles of evolution all the regularities of the universe would be evolved.[32]

This account is offered as a probable hypothesis requiring future verification, not as a demonstrative proof. One of Peirce's critics, Arthur O. Lovejoy, has objected that we never could verify the initial condition of pure spontaneity without introducing determinations into it, and that there would be no reasonable ground for expecting an initial condition of promiscuous diversity ever to develop a tendency to depart from purely random variations. But Peirce suggests that this evidence is not to be sought by dreaming oneself back to an evolutionary start but rather by analyzing the presently experienced variety, random tendency, and uniformity. And he describes the original indeterminate state not as a homogeneity but as a heterogeneity of indefinite specifiability, virtually involving in its dynamism two tendencies which we can actually see in our world: that toward novelty and that toward continuous formation of laws. The latter is a growing tendency, however, so that the laws and regularity now prevailing are themselves an evolutionary achievement.

Peirce is now prepared to give a thoroughly evolutionary definition of what the scientist calls a law of nature:

> So, then, I do not think a better definition of a *law of nature* can be given than this: it is a foreknowing generalization of observations. This said, the question is instantly started, How can the reason of a man attain such foreknowledge? How shall we answer? Must we not say that the fact that he can so attain proves that there is an energizing reasonableness that shapes phenomena in some sense, and that this same working reasonableness has molded the reason of man into something like its own image? [33]

This is a pregnant text for understanding the mind of Peirce and measuring the depth of his evolutionary way of thinking. He begins with a fact of scientific description: We do possess some knowledge that is inductive or observationally based, that involves a predictive factor, and that is held in a generalized form. In asking about the basis rendering this fact possible, he does not appeal to some permanent Kantian forms of the consciousness in general but rather to an evolutionary process of energizing and molding. Moreover, it is a growth in reasonableness, insofar as our world shows an increasing tendency to take on the characters of generality, continuity, and feasible form. They are the objective marks of law as a reasonableness energizing in the world, even though it is working under the limiting conditions of chance and contingency.

This growth of reasonableness is transpiring not only in the world but also in the human mind, to the extent that scientific inquiry is bringing it gradually more into responsive conformity with the living and developing pattern of generality in nature. Thus the evolution of law is a complex process occurring both in natural events and structures and in the scientifically progressing mind of man. The natural universe is just as thoroughly temporal and historical as is the

160

human world. Far from regarding his theory of the evolutionary beginning and the genesis of law in nature as a hindrance to theism, Peirce employs the harmony developing between the reasonableness of things and that of human inquiry as evidence of God's effective and providential presence in the universe.

All of the main doctrines in Peirce's philosophy have an evolutionary significance. It permeates his theory of method, doctrine of the categories, cosmology, scientific ethics, and even his account of the history of science. The common evolutionary ambience for all the parts of his philosophy can be indicated even in a brief description.

Thus in his theory of scientific method, Peirce stresses the role of hypothesis-forming or abduction. It has a spontaneous aspect corresponding to the spontaneity in developing nature. Yet responsible hypothesizing is never arbitrary but seeks to bear in a relevant way upon the data and problems at hand, as well as to submit itself to a continuing public verification by the scientific community. This abductive search after increasingly relevant and verified hypotheses is an instance of the growth of reasonableness on the part of the human inquirer, more specifically on the part of the scientific community as a whole. There is a growth of law as a firm and continuous pattern both in natural events and in scientific research, although contingency and revisibility remain in force in both areas. The reason why Peirce thinks that his remarks on the habit-taking tendency in nature do not constitute a mere extrapolation of psychology is that he finds a common evolutionary structure governing the logic of abduction and the course of natural events.

His theory of the three basic categories remains obscure unless there is some reference to its evolutionary import. It takes a triadic form, not because of the influence of Hegel but because of the predominance of the evolutionary model taken from biology and the analysis of scientific method. Every situation can be analyzed into its genetic source, its finalizing aim, and its continuous approach toward that end. This provides Peirce with his primary categories of an indeterminate possibility or undifferentiated feeling, a generality of final structure, and a mediating process of habit-taking which generates the directional movement from source toward a generalized goal.

The basic categorial scheme can then be used interpretatively in cosmology and ethics. Since Peirce defines the real in terms of the trend toward increased regularity and embodied or steadied generality, he regards the evolutionary flow quite literally as a continuous realizing of the natural world. This realization process can be given a categorial analysis. For the becoming of things must involve three cosmic traits: chance, the love and pursuit of generality, and the continuity of process between them.

Tychism or the doctrine on chance is an affirmation of the factor of spontaneity and contingency in all natural happening. Agapism or the doctrine on the love and pursuit of general structures defends the antinominalistic thesis that general factors are really present in nature and are constantly in course of being further actualized. And synechism or the doctrine on continuity seeks to explain the oriented character of the real as movement from the indeterminate to structured determinateness, from private feeling to publicly verified and commonly held knowledge. Peirce attaches these somewhat outlandish Greek names to his cosmological principles in order to signify a unique evolutionary standpoint which is reducible neither to the Hegelian dialectical triad nor to biological evolution apart from rigorous logical analysis of method.

He adds that agapism has a moral as well as a cosmic meaning, for it helps to define the purpose of human efforts. The pragmaticist or scientific philosopher must seek to embody generality or the network of regular and continuous patterns in his thought and action, corresponding to a similar tendency in nature. This is nothing less than saying that the well-disciplined mind finds its moral enthusiasm and direction in promoting evolution in the properly human sphere of mind, cultural response, and methodic control.

Accordingly, the pragmaticist does not make the *summum bonum* to consist in action, but makes it to consist in that process of evolution whereby the existent comes more and more to embody those generals which were just now said to be *destined*, which is what we strive to express in calling them *reasonable*. In its higher stages, evolution takes place more and more largely through self-control, and this gives the pragmaticist a sort of justification for making the rational purport to be general.[34]

This text contains a correction of the pragmatism of James precisely by interpreting the aim of evolution in function of increasing generality rather than action. By anticipation, it also criticizes that sort of existentialist stress which would divorce the existent from the reasonable and the general. As Peirce views the problem, to make such a divorce would be nothing less than to unmake the real and to reduce the existent to the purely possible, in a word, to strip man and the universe of their proper evolutionary tendency.

At the semicentennial celebration of Darwin's work held at Columbia University, John Dewey spoke on his influence upon philosophy. As we will show in the following chapter, this is one of Dewey's most personally intended papers, since he himself was born in 1859 and made the pilgrimage from idealism to instrumental naturalism under the growing pressure of Darwinian thought. Especially the suggestions of Darwin and Wallace concerning human emotional and intellectual development sapped his confidence in the doctrine of an immanent absolute spirit as the source and standard of human life. Dewey's initial idealism was unsettled also by the juxtaposition of "origin" and "species" in the very title of Darwin's masterwork. This meant that the essential and the fixed were giving way to the temporal and the fluid in the biological and human worlds, as well as in that of physics. For Dewey, the chief significance of Darwin was to justify a universal extension of the genetic viewpoint and thus to banish everywhere in nature the notion of a fixed ladder of being or hierarchy of forms.

But Dewey himself went on from the continuity and genetic descent of species established by evolutionary biology to urge that the process constitutes a self-sufficient whole of nature and excludes as meaningless the problem of the being and providential care of a God distinct from evolutionary nature. "Once admit that the sole verifiable or fruitful object of knowledge is the particular set of changes that generate the object of study together with the consequences that then flow from it, and no intelligible question can be asked about what, by assumption, lies outside." [35] This methodological restriction of meaningful issues to events in change was a philosophical addition made on Dewey's own responsibility to clear the way for his naturalistic theory of man and experience. This is clear from the weight he imparted to the operative phrase "the sole verifiable or fruitful object of knowledge." From Darwin's cautious agnosticism, he could not gather any such general and restrictive pronouncement about the object of knowledge, but only a description of what constitutes the business of the biologist.

Both Peirce and Dewey engage in methodological and metaphysical generalization on the theme of evolution. But in Peirce's case, it is made clearer that a distinctive philosophical analysis is being attempted and a new hypothesis being proposed for common testing. Dewey tends to consolidate his naturalistic interpretation with the biological meaning for evolution and evolutionary research, as though naturalism in philosophy is only a further chapter prolonged in the same line as the biological findings. Hence his account of Darwin's significance is more instructive as the story of how a new attitude

163

in philosophy is born in a Darwinian atmosphere than as the strict
logical defense of his contention that questions about God are meaningless today.

4. *Bergson and the Methodology of Evolutionism*

Among the more prominent twentieth-century thinkers who can be
regarded as philosophers of evolution are Samuel Alexander, Alfred
North Whitehead, and Henri Bergson. The theme emerges with purity
and dominance in the mind of Bergson, but in the other men it is
blended with many other considerations, especially those arising from
relativity theory and the search for a world of values. Here, we can
confine ourselves to a brief examination of some aspects in Bergson's
philosophical position. It remains closer to the biologist's approach
to nature and to the actual shifts in evolutionary theories, without
surrendering the human significance of the genesis of life.

We have already mentioned Bergson's criticism of the concept of
force in Spencer's system. As a beginner in philosophy, he thought
that Spencer was basically sound and needed only to be provided
with a more rigorous mathematico-mechanical notion of force. But to
his surprise, Bergson soon found that even this addition was insufficient
to close the gap between the Spencerian formula for change and
change as we experience it in its temporal reality.[36] And since time
is of the essence for every evolutionary theory, Bergson had to look
for another way of bringing a philosophy of evolution into conformity
with our temporal experience. His original contributions in philosophy arose from this need to provide a more adequate generalized
theory of evolution than any which was based on the notion of time
in classical mechanics. In his sensitivity toward the limitations of the
Newtonian outlook not so much on physical grounds as on those of
human experience, he resembled Peirce.

What is inadequate about the ordinary notion of time which is found
in most of the uncritical conceptions of evolution? The fact that it is
modeled after the concept of space, that it is only an echo of spatial
conditions. We tend to conceive of time as a series of point-instants
which stretch out homogeneously in a line, one discrete instant succeeding the other in a set groove, like raindrops rolling down a gutter.
Bergson does not maintain that this spatializing of time is false or
useless: it does serve the practical purpose of scientific prediction and
control. His criticism is directed against erecting this practical purpose

into the sole norm for our thinking about time. If we do so, we fail to respect the biologist's report on the inner spontaneity, continuity of action, and speciating divergence of temporal organisms. Above all, we fail to do justice to our own experience of temporal duration which refuses to conform with the spatial pattern of points on a pre-existent and fully determined linear course. Any notion of time which is in discrepancy with these approaches to temporal duration cannot be used in a reliable philosophy of evolution. The negative conclusion is that we will have to refrain from using the physicalized view of time in our description of evolutionary process.

Bergson thus involves himself in the recurrent problem of how to make a warranted generalization of evolutionary traits set forth in biological research. His answer is given in the methodological resolve to deal with evolution as far as possible within a humanly experience-able context and to resist explaining away the data of that experience in terms of anything else. The biological findings of Darwin and his successors do not arrange themselves automatically into a philosophical doctrine on the evolutionary nature of life. The only route for attaining a cosmic meaning of evolution is by close study of our human experience of duration, not because we fear dehumanization but because we can perhaps find the general nature of the evolutionary process as it is brought to conscious awareness in man.[37] For Bergson, it is not a question of anthropomorphizing evolution but rather of seizing it as an ongoing process in the region where it is most accessible to us: in our experience of the self as a spontaneous durational act. The details of Bergson's account, in *Creative Evolution,* of the branchings of the various evolutionary lines are ultimately not as important as his presentation of the *methodological* problem. Some of the more recent philosophical treatments of evolution seem to be more placidly inevitable than his, but this is often due to their way of gliding over the crucial point of how to develop the concepts of biological evolution into a reliable and illuminating philosophy of evolution.

Unlike most proponents of evolutionism, Bergson is uneasy about the procedure of interpreting the evolutionary process in terms of either classical or relativity physics.[38] He is unable to make the kind of synthesis which Alexander and Whitehead regard as inevitable between the evolutionary and the physical standpoints of our age. His difficulty stems not only from the problem of physicalized time but also from the nature of human experience as stipulated within the physical system. In Newtonian physics there is an absolute system of reference, and once the privileged observer is installed therein, it is indifferent to him whether other real observers exist and whether his own experience contains anything beyond the data relevant for the system itself. In relativity theory, the given real observer supposes that other frames of reference are occupied by other observers, but he does not have assurance of their actuality and his own interest does not extend beyond the requirements for space-time predictions.

But Bergson requires of the inductive basis for an evolutionary philosophy that it consist of the self-experience of several actual individuals, that it faithfully report these individuals' durational reality in its own being and not simply as a function of the space-time system, and that it seize upon the direction of life. Such conditions cannot be met by the abstraction called the physical observer but only by the concrete man in his reflective durational experience. Thus the Bergsonian intuition of duration is not intended as a flight from intelligence or from ordinary experience; it is the methodologically unavoidable instrument for gaining the sort of inductive data which can be generalized into an evolutionary philosophy.

What Bergson encounters in his interior exploration of lived duration is the vital impetus or the struggle of freedom moving in a spiritual direction toward God and against the eddies and obstacles of matter. This result has never appeared very convincing to biologists. In his Eddington Memorial Lecture, the pioneer geneticist R. A. Fisher rejects Bergson's vital impetus as a piece of mythological dualism which explains none of the particular evolutionary phenomena.[39] Bergson would have to admit that we cannot derive any statistical laws of gene mutation from his position, and that it does not provide guidance in setting up a biological experiment. However, he would probably add that its purpose is not to render the biologist's initiative superfluous but to state some general and yet concrete meaning for the life process.

His plane of approach can be appreciated by considering the twofold sense in which Fisher himself admits a valid meaning for "creative evolution." It signifies effective causation, along with the achieving of new and important results through the activities of living beings. The philosophical problems concern both the nature of the causation common to all living things and the meaning to be assigned to the judgment that a certain achievement is important. Bergson's suggestion is that our durational activity conveys a common meaning for evolutionary causation which is not reducible to statistical statement and spatial imagery. Furthermore, a philosophical signification for what is

166

important in evolutionary activity can be obtained by including a reference to our own maximal becoming in the direction of freedom and spiritual self-possession. This result is meager enough, but Bergson will insist that anyone who is searching for the philosophical meaning of evolution must at least proceed in this way for his answer.

Bergson was engaged neither in deducing the genetic theory of life nor in answering the questions of classical metaphysics. His chief concern was to determine how we can establish the wider implications of evolution. His approach through our experience of duration was inevitably psychological, so that he came to regard matter as sluggish imagery and to defend evolutionary progress by appeal to memory as a prolonging into the vital present. Within his own context, there are two further methodological questions which have to be formulated more clearly than he saw fit to do. Does biological evolution in fact contain any quite general metaphysical implications about the whole cosmic process and the full sweep of the nature of life? And if so, does our human experience of temporal duration and freedom lead to the core of the vital process or only to a special case, which is too narrow for such generalization? Philosophers of evolution answer the first question in the affirmative, but the sense is that here is a program to be tried out so that we can eventually test it by the results of particular efforts to reach the general meaning of evolution. This leads at once to the problem of method, and on this score Bergson presses hard for our taking reasonable advantage of our own reflective presence in the evolutionary field. Even after this is faithfully done, however, the difficulty remains of correlating the distinctively human meaning for vital operations with those which the biologists and other workers gather through their own methods.

5. *Three Idealistic Appraisals of Evolution*

Not all the young idealists followed Dewey supinely into disillusionment with their metaphysical position and eventual transformation of the main tenets of idealism. There were at least three types of idealistic response which involved no capitulation to naturalism but rather a vigorous effort to welcome Darwinism within the mansions of idealism. Royce's method was to engulf the whole evolutionary doctrine within the capacious arms of the absolute self. On behalf of a more personal idealism, Howison stressed the limits of evolutionary explanation in respect to the human self. And more recently, Harris has used the resources of the logic of science to reinstate an idealistic basis for the evolutionary view of things.

Josiah Royce testifies to the powerful challenge of evolution by devoting the entire second half of *The Spirit of Modern Philosophy* to this question. His first aim is to explain historically the eager acceptance and rapid application of Darwin's ideas. They could not have been so readily assimilated in the earlier periods of the rationalist static dualism of mind and body or the equally static skepticism of the empiricist mind, but only in the idealistic phase of modern philosophy. Schelling and Hegel have accustomed us to think of the spiritual absolute as being in constant development, to view nature as alive with this divine presence and process, and to approach all special problems in terms of the history of the subject in question. Thus idealism has tilled the soil for the enthusiastic welcome given to evolutionary views.

Royce is not blind to the defects in the view of nature found among the German idealists. No naturalistic critic speaks more bitingly than he about the grotesqueries of the Romantic and Hegelian philosophies of nature. But he locates their failure not in their metaphysical principles but in their inability to adhere rigorously by these principles in treating of empirical events. Granted that the source and subject of the orderly course of phenomenal objects is the infinite self or absolute spirit, it does not follow that our ideas under the conditions of human limitation are perfect enough to provide an a priori deductive basis for the study of nature. The mind of the idealistic philosopher is itself in process of growth: it requires a temporal process to discover the manifestations of the absolute self. Hence the well-disciplined idealist must accept the phenomena of nature as they come, forswearing any impatient schemes of anticipating their meaning by the manipulation of a symbolism or a dialectic.

Yet the idealist also possesses another perspective on nature, based on his confidence that

the Self is as truly present in evolution as he is in sin and ignorance. These are the World-Spirit's garments that we see him by . . . [but] only after a patient scientific scrutiny has revealed, as is the case with the doctrine of evolution, a vast unity in a long series of phenomena. . . . I rather delight in this craft whereby the Self thus hides its true nature in energetic nebulous masses and in flying meteors, pretends to be absent from the inorganic world, pretends to have descended from relatives of the anthropoid apes, pretends, in short, to be bounded in all sorts of nutshells.[40]

The very thoroughness and comprehensiveness of scientific evolutionary research raise the further question of the principle of unity for the whole series of living things. The Roycean reply is that all vital phenomena are the garments or manifestations of the one absolute self, which synthesizes them into a meaningful pattern for our investigation. There is even a certain playfulness or pretense in nature, insofar as the empirical forms do not immediately reveal the presence of the infinite self but seem to hide it. This provides a challenge not only for the scientist, who must find some proximate pattern of rationality, but also for the philosopher in his quest for a general interpretation of the life process.

Royce takes a clue from Peirce on how to use some scientific notions as aids toward reaching a satisfactory philosophical account of evolution.[41] There is a describable common tendency in nature and human affairs to form aggregates or statistically definable groups, to exert some natural selection at the group level, and to form habits which strengthen some older aggregates and engender some new ones. Behind the biological theory of evolution lies the logic of *aggregates*. The evolutionary law is that there is fecundity in whatever unites for orderly cooperation. Persons and bodies share in the evolutionary trend insofar as they join in promoting the welfare of a community, whether it be a spiritual or a physical one. The reason for the prevailing pattern of the logic of aggregates is that it is the common way in which the absolute spirit expresses itself in nature and man.

To clinch the idealistic interpretation of evolution, Royce adds that all aggregates are serial order-systems, which are types of cosmic selves. Their internal principle of unity is the effective presence of some ideal, which the individual members in the group or serial system are striving to realize. A self is simply a well-ordered series whose components are endeavoring to achieve a condition of activity and control through a continuum of evolutionary forms. Thus mountain ranges and biological species are cosmic selves having a different time span from each other and from the human individual self. Evolution is the pattern of interconnection and communication between these social order-systems, all of which are types of conscious processes of self-expression. Evolutionary law unifies all the aggregates on both a cosmic and an individual basis, thus enabling the absolute self to bring about the great community of material and spiritual agencies. The evolutionary law of self-representing aggregates is the means employed by the absolute to achieve continuity, similarity, and ultimately cooperative activity throughout natural and human history. Royce attaches to this interpretation of evolution the warning that it cannot be used deductively to establish or test the empirical theories in biology but only to give them a context of meaning and unity with the laws discovered for other order-systems in our universe.

While Royce was lecturing to his Boston and Cambridge audiences on how to incorporate evolution within the doctrine of the absolute, George Howison was building a case at the University of California for personal idealism against both evolutionary pragmatism and absolute idealism. He criticized the former position for its psychological use of evolution and its analysis of continuity in the universe. Instead of following Royce's absolutism of the infinite self, he found a basis in Kant and the inviolable human person from which to establish some limits for evolutionary thought.

Dewey had assumed that the a priori factor in knowledge is easily discredited by showing that our ideas and mental forms are the outcome of evolutionary process. Howison did not deny the legitimacy of a genetic description of thought, but he stressed the distinction between the psychological growth of a conception and its meaning and validity. The two latter questions are not settled simply by recounting the genesis of our thought. The evolutionary psychologizing of the forms of thought tends to confuse the feeling of being necessitated in our acts of mind with the perception of a necessary connection of meaning in the objects of thought.[42] One must also inquire about the general principles of thought which make it possible for us to have the associative bonds upon which a genetic psychology relies. Although he was lacking in the systematic range and penetration of Husserl, Howison took a similar stand against any attempt to convert an evolutionary description of the development of our thinking into a standard for judging its validity.

Another problem which he illuminates is the shift of meaning when we pass from the biological to the philosophical meaning of evolution. Biological evolution "means not only *logical* community, or resemblance for observation and thought, but also likeness due to descent and birth; due to a *physiological* community, through the process of reproduction."[43] But when we start speaking about evolution as a cosmic process, we have to weaken or eliminate the note of physiological community, in any definite biological and causal sense, and content ourselves with the thread of logical community. Howison grants that this is a perfectly legitimate act of the mind, but it has some consequences which pragmatic naturalism does not see. The generalized method of genetic and comparative research can be applied in all fields, but the success of its application does not warrant the inference that therefore all things are related solely by the immanent continuity and causal descent required for the naturalistic self-sufficient whole of being. The logical meaning for continuity of analysis cannot be made the premise for drawing a metaphysical conclusion about the real being and relatedness of the objects of analysis. The only way to do this is to coalesce the physiological and logical meanings for community, and such a coalescence empties out the biological theory from which we make our start.

The only thread of continuity between the different meanings for community and genetic descent is a logical one, a unity of congruous interpretative conceptions and not a naturalistic monism of real process. To attain a generalized evolutionism, we must not only make an extrapolation from paleontology and biology but also perform this act with the distinctive resources of the human mind. The life of the investigating human mind is one irreducible source for philosophical evolutionism. And against Royce, Howison defends the irreducibility of the individual intelligence of men to modes of an absolute self. Human minds do join cooperatively in the community of scientific research, but they remain personal centers and never become sheer manifestations of some overself. That they are not self-sufficient beings is seen from their receptivity in regard to sensation and their obligation under moral law, but this means that men stand open to the ideals and the activity of a personal God. Howison does not import evolutionary development into God, however, but confines it to the natural, nonpersonal world. Men are not related to the divine in the manner of evolutionary waves (as Samuel Alexander depicts the situation) but as finite persons to the personal, self-possessed being of God.

Howison's confining of evolution to nature as a nonpersonal realm depended in principle, however, upon the Kantian distinction between phenomena (the evolutionary events and laws in nature) and noumena (the personal, nonevolving being of man and God). Since this distinction is now widely challenged by analytic and naturalistic philosophies, more recent proponents of idealism are looking for approaches based more closely upon the logic of current science. This brings them much closer to Royce's plan of assimilating evolution to absolute idealism through a study of the implications of scientific concepts. This is the path followed by Errol Harris in his book *Nature, Mind, and Modern Science.*

A good portion of this work is devoted to showing that classical empiricism and logical positivism are dead ends, which cannot establish with rigor their principle for the verifiability of meaning.[44] Hence they cannot advance any a priori objections against the project of an idealistic interpretation of evolution on the ground that it is a meta-physical, and hence an intrinsically meaningless, enterprise. This easy solution founders on the fact that the operations of hypothesizing, relating, and classifying which belong to any scientific work, includ-ing the biological theory of evolution, involve much more than the registration of present sense contents. The establishing of connections between hypotheses and empirical data involves too many factors to permit logical positivism to maintain its criterion of empirical meaning as a definite bar against metaphysical studies of scientific concepts.

Thus Harris wants to reopen the idealistic examination of evolu-tion after the pause induced by the logical positivists and empiricists. Yet he refuses to accept Driesch's entelechy, since it is too vague, extrinsic, and dualistic to explain satisfactorily the traits of the organ-ism. Instead, he proposes that the concrete universal of Hegel can be reinterpreted as realizing itself in organic things and constituting their internal telic principle. Embryonic development is a dialectical type of process, wherein an undifferentiated potentiality is polarized with a specializing differentiation of parts, leading to a final synthesis of unity in diversity or an integrated complex whole, the organism. The only adequate philosophical analysis of the facts of integrative growth is furnished by the immanent concrete universal.

The modern scientific outlook and its evolutionary biology contain a fivefold set of implications for philosophy.[45] (1) Nature constitutes a single system in which there are no sharp breaks between matter, life, and mind. Harris remarks that, for absolute idealism, the primacy of mind is not based on a static dualism of mind and body but on the teleological principle that all roads of development lead eventually to mind as their supreme concretion. (2) Evolution is not only change but directional growth, not only efficient causation but final as well. Indeed, these types of causation tend to overlap and converge in such a way that events are adequately explained only through an evolu-tionary teleology. (3) We do not look for the telic completion of an evolutionary process in something isolated and apart from develop-ing nature but precisely in the climax of all organic wholes: the minded organism. Philosophically considered, mind or the final cause is immanently present in nature from the outset and exerts a con-trolling influence over all stages in the evolutionary movement. Evo-lution is progressive insofar as the immanent concrete universal constantly tends toward its realization in mind or the plenary instance of unity amid diversity.

(4) Because all of nature has mind as its dynamic internal prin-

172

ciple, the long-standing epistemological split between subject and object, mind and thing, is overcome. Man recognizes their ultimate identity when he experiences and reflects upon the outcome of evolution in his own mode of being, which is the natural world brought to conscious activity. The biologist's working conviction that the evolutionary process is intelligible and will yield definite results to research is thereby justified on the idealistic basis of the presence of mind or the rational principle in and as the forms of organic development. (5) Finally, a natural world whose evolution is a journey toward conscious mind cannot be a world deprived of value and real qualities, as the empiricist generalizers of Galilean mechanics presumed. Harris defends the actual presence of qualities and values in the evolving world as being more in harmony with the convictions of evolutionary theorists. Their appeal to survival value is not groundless, but it does require a justification and finds it in idealism. Survival value is only a preliminary way of stating that the valuable is that which promotes, remotely or proximately, the fuller realization of mind in nature and mind's active control over natural process.

Harris admits that these five points do not completely restore the metaphysics of absolute idealism. The implications drawn from evolutionary biology do not extend beyond the minded organism or mind in the human condition. Furthermore, the biological viewpoint does not establish the unitary convergence of all lines of evolution upon the human organism as the synthesizing telic principle of every evolutionary path. As supplementary evidence, then, Harris singles out the human mind's capacity to embrace the entire temporal flow of evolution in a reflective concept. Time's domain extends as far as bodies and animate processes, but then the temporal process gets comprehended as a whole and thus gets transcended by conscious mind. Yet our developing, fallible, finite minds do not achieve the full consciousness and perfect grasp of all phases of evolution as required by the unconditional telic actuality or concrete universal. "Consequently, the complete manifestation of the universal in a perfect mind is the inescapable presupposition of all science and all thought based upon the concept of evolution." [46] Without perhaps realizing it, therefore, the evolutionist is providing data whose ultimate significance requires acceptance of the absolute mind.

Harris adds that this is the real foundation for the ontological argument, which is now continuous with a thorough analysis of evolutionary findings. Yet, we must critically remark that evolutionary thought furnishes a support for the ontological argument *to* God only when the evolutionary course is viewed idealistically as the immanent development *of* the absolute mind itself. Hence this analysis of modern biology does not lead to God in the theistic sense, but rather to the developing absolute of a renovated Hegelian idealism. That is why Harris admits efficient causality only in order to fuse it completely with an immanent teleology and thus rule out any inference to a transcendent God by means of efficient cause.

Some obscurities continue to surround this renovation of dialectical absolutism. Harris does not show how the Hegelian notion of a scale of forms can be revised to mean a transformation of forms through descent or how there is any scientific warrant for maintaining a transformation from the minded organism to the absolute mind. He also leaves in the dark his crucial distinction between the temporal process of bodies and animate structures and what he calls the "timeless analytic-synthetic discursus" of self-conscious mind.[47] Temporality becomes only a preliminary manifestation of the concrete universal, whose true and abiding actuality is timeless. It is not sufficient to say that the reality of time is respected by treating timeless reflection as a terminal development. For in an absolute idealism, the timeless concrete universal is also the intimate principle and value standard which gives meaning and interior being to the temporal events as its own aspects or phases. We are left wondering whether temporal process can be anything more than a reflected play of graduated formal concepts, and hence whether the evolution studied by biologists is ever really dealt with in terms of the idealistic theory of an immanently developing timeless discursus.

6. *Julian Huxley's Evolutionary Humanism*

During the past generation, the most energetic champion of a philosophical humanism built upon Dawinism has been Sir Julian Huxley. He performed yeoman scientific service during the lean years when Darwin himself was in eclipse and when it required considerable staying power to defend natural selection. After the work of Fisher, Haldane, and Muller showed that the genetic mechanism could be related to the factors of adaptation and selection, Huxley took the lead in combining the new genetics with Darwinism to give the modified position now generally held. Huxley showed convincingly that Neo-Darwinism provides a unifying principle for all the sub-areas in biology and a fruitful guide for continuing research. In addition, he contended

174

that the evolutionary position can be expanded into a total philosophy for understanding the universe and guiding men in their valuational choices. Although his philosophical evolutionism did not receive the same wide allegiance among biologists, it was welcomed by many philosophical naturalists and humanists as scientific confirmation of their notion of self-sufficing nature and purely immanent values for man.

Huxley distinguishes formally between evolution as a mechanism of genetic and natural selection agencies and evolution as a process or the ongoing result of the operation of the agencies.[48] They are related not only descriptively but also causally: The selective-genetic mechanism is a real efficient cause and the process or course of evolutionary change is its real effect and product. Huxley thus takes the decisive step of treating the description of selective and adaptive situations and the mathematical analysis of gene factors as genuine causal statements, and indeed as the biological expression of evolutionary process or the sole causal agency in things. He does not argue this point but simply finds it just as customary as did his grandfather, Thomas Huxley, to speak about evolutionary principles as the true causes.

His next concern is to describe the evolutionary causes as being creative, mechanical, and progressive. Each of these qualifications is given a distinctive meaning in the Huxleyan context, although he offers his philosophical analysis as though it were the common heritage of all biologists.

"Creative" has the negative sense of excluding any more ultimate causal source outside of nature and the positive sense of producing real and basic results in nature. Julian Huxley moves far beyond the minimal agnostic position of Darwin and Thomas Huxley in his exclusion of God's causal activity. His purpose is ultimately the naturalistic ethical one of laying it down that "man must cease being afraid of his uniqueness, and must not continue to put off the responsibilities that are really his on to the shoulders of mythical gods or meta-physical absolutes." [49] On the positive side, Huxley seeks to establish a conjunction between the forces at work in the development of the inorganic universe and those in the living world. He speaks in a comprehensive way about a three-stage evolution from the nonliving to the living and to the human, but he does not make a detailed analysis of the common causal meaning underlying force in the physical system, biological agency, and cultural power.

As Huxley uses the term, "mechanical" serves mainly the negative function of removing any purpose or intelligent guidance from the

175

development of biological species. He stresses that the causal principles of evolution are blind and purposeless, without going into any further detail about the positive way in which evolutionary agencies are related to the mechanical principles in a system of physical change. Once he has eliminated the possibility of teleology as implying an intelligent agent distinct from nature, Huxley is quite generous in what he ascribes to evolutionary workings. They issue in real adaptations, apart from any purposive intending by a mind. In the Huxleyan universe, there are adaptations without purposes, final results without finality, directions without intelligent directing. And he intends this contrast to hold good in the real order in an unconditioned way, rather than to signify merely a methodological limitation placed upon the biological procedures.

As far as biologists are concerned, the creative and mechanical character of the evolutionary mechanism can be taken in a methodological sense which does not necessarily commit them to Huxley's metaphysical standpoint. But it is more difficult for them to give a similar purely procedural meaning to his third note of "progressiveness," and hence it is the most controversial one for them. He explains carefully that evolutionary progress is neither necessary nor universal and that it is not identical with all the results of natural selection.[50] It requires considerable selection of evidence and construction of a conceptual model before the meaning of a progressive evolutionary mechanism can be established. Despite the many instances of degeneration and stagnant equilibrium, there is the fact of dominant types appearing at various eras as improvements of living stocks. The criteria for determining such dominant types are their greater control over the changing environment and their increasing independence of action. Through these traits, they attain a broader biological efficiency than do other forms and thus they represent an evolutionary progress.

At this point, Huxley makes the transition from pre-human evolution to that of man.[51] Man is continuous with organic nature, since the same causal agencies of selection and mutation operate in producing the human organism. But Huxley also insists on man's uniqueness in respect to his particular genesis, his present mode of being, and especially his prospects for the future. Only the evolutionary line which actually did give rise to man could have done so, since it was the only one that could give rise to a form of life which is capable of true speech and conceptual thought. These are distinctive features of man's present mode of being, and on this score Huxley resists any efforts to whittle them down by comparative analysis or genetic psychology.

His chief reason for the nonreductive view of man's present capacities is to give evolutionary humanism a program and a hope for the future. Quite literally, he sees no future possibility of evolutionary progress except through man's agency. All other lines of descent have led into blind alleys, but man alone has found a substitute for genetic mutation. His intelligence permits him to transform biological into cultural progress, since he can retain, criticize, and heighten his social and individual experience. At the human level, then, progress must include not only the objective notes of biological efficiency but also some subjective notes of human value. Like Comte, Huxley adds a subjective criterion to the objective one, as soon as he comes to the human plane and turns his face to the future outlook. He also modifies the Darwinian metaphor of the branching tree of evolution to accommodate his own view that life will progress only through man, the growing edge.

Now it becomes clear why Huxley insisted on giving an ontological and antitheistic meaning to the general description of the evolutionary mechanism. His long-range aim was so to describe these general factors that they would furnish a causal pattern of a definite sort to serve as an objective basis and norm for human choice. God was ruled out not because of the biological facts and concepts but because of the desire to anticipate the question of human valuational choice, which must not be governed by any extranatural considerations. It was not Huxley the ornithologist and biological synthesizer but Huxley the naturalistic philosopher who specified the antitheistic meaning for the creative and mechanical aspects of the evolutionary agency. His naturalistic humanism is not merely continuous with his scientific views on evolution but transforms them into stages of a philosophical argument.

The criteria of evolutionary progress—control, independence, capacity for advance and, at the human level, capacity for increased experience—become the criteria for ethical action and religiousness, once we come to reflect on them and generalize them as the sole guides for human decision. By responding deeply to the task of advancing the evolutionary line in terms of intensified human experience of individuals and social groups, we can enjoy all the values of moral and religious experience without calling upon any absolute. The standards of ethical choice are relative to the given stage of the evolutionary process, but they also have a certain permanence as long as the human type persists and can reflect on this process. "The ultimate guarantees for

177

the correctness of our labels of rightness and wrongness are to be sought for among the facts of evolutionary direction." [52] This is the decisive sense in which Huxley's philosophical preoccupations tend to transform all of his scientific descriptions of evolutionary mechanism and its general notes. He makes them furnish a basis for restricting humanistic religion to a feeling of awe and a practical commitment to the evolutionary forces immanent in nature, the individual self, and society. Hence although Huxley agrees explicitly with Father Teilhard de Chardin on our obligation to promote convergent cooperation among men rather than divergent competition, he denies that any future phase of evolutionary transcendence can lead men to the presence of God.

Huxley's evolutionary humanism has become the focal point for some interesting critical discussion of evolutionism from various standpoints. The geneticist Theodosius Dobzhansky is skeptical about drawing our ethical criteria from his science: The evolutionary and the eternal perspectives on human life are distinct and unreducible one to the other. He presents two objections against making an ethical use of evolutionary findings. On the factual side, there are many trends at work within the several species, including man. To define the direction of evolution as the one which promotes the traits which Huxley regards as progressive depends upon making a selection among actual tendencies and then defining directionality of evolution in these privileged terms. This is not only a highly selective and constructural procedure but also leads to the second point of showing why we ought to take our duty from the results of such selection. Given man's freedom, he can call evolutionary directional progress into question as a norm for his choice. Merely the repetition that this is Huxley's constructed meaning for progress does not answer the question of why we should be obliged morally to take the progressive path at all.

The question cannot be stilled by a form of cosmic intimidation about how the forces in the world are moving, since we make our moral choices on distinctively human grounds and not simply on descriptive translations of the prevailing forces in biological evolution. "Human acts and aspirations may be morally right or morally wrong, regardless of whether they assist the evolutionary process to proceed in the direction in which it has been going, or whether they assist it in any direction at all." [53] Evolutionary considerations are sometimes too vague and sometimes simply irrelevant to the task of determining our moral obligation and ordering of values in the concrete situation of moral choice.

The zoologist Paul Moody concludes his recent study of evolution with a personal acceptance of God as the source of natural laws of life and the goal of evolutionary process. Looking at all the blind alleys, retrogressions, and random actions involved in the course of evolution, he asks: "May not they in themselves form part of the pattern? Why should we assume that the laws of the universe, including those of evolution, must be so organized as to reach a goal by what seems to our human minds the most direct route?" [54] His point is not that there is no pattern or route to discern, but that it has to be studied comprehensively in its own actual contours, rather than measured abstractly and selectively by some particular conception of economy of mechanical action. As Peirce noted, there is a logical pattern for the interplay of chance and law and for the gradual growth of the latter under conditions of contingency. God's purposive intelligence can achieve the gradual emergence of a many-leveled cosmos through this evolutionary polarity, rendering questionable the divorcement which Huxley proposes between adaptation and purpose, selective progress and a theistic context for the whole account of evolution.

Philosophers of science have started to study the trend among Neo-Darwinians to erase the distinction between a descriptive and a causally explanatory concept. Marjorie Grene suggests that correlations based on statistical trends in population groups do not themselves constitute, and only indirectly indicate, some of the real causal factors present in living nature. Hence such data do not justify the philosophical inference drawn by Huxley and American evolutionist, George Simpson, that the selective-genetic mechanism is the total and exclusive cause of the biological changes observed in evolutionary process. What we today refer to as the selective-genetic mechanism is a complex concept, containing a direct element of causal agency in generation along with some considerable interpretation of population facts by the inquiring mind. This combination of real causal factors and descriptive instruments of probable explanation cannot be regarded as a massive flow of uniform causal power, and still less can it be appealed to philosophically as being simply the biological expression of an all-sufficient causal principle of cosmic evolution. When genetical selection is treated in a descriptive way as a tool of explanation bearing some reference to causal agency but not simply equated with a purposeless mechanical cause, it loses none of its mathematical rigor or its biological usefulness in developing the explanations proper to this discipline. It only ceases to support Simpson's and Huxley's philosophical exclusion of God as the ultimate intelligent cause and goal of nature. We can expect that genetics will eventually follow the example of quantum physics in reflecting upon the meaning and limitations of its causal language, without regarding physical types of explanation as its own model.

Grene admits that if the meaning of the term "scientific" is confined to the mechanical prototype, then the Neo-Darwinian stress upon the genetic-selective mechanism has the advantage of being logically simple and automatic. But in additon to logical simplicity and automatism, every evolutionary theory must also be measured by its adequacy in admitting all the factors which are required in our actual explanatory efforts. In this respect, the Huxley position proves to be reductionist and hence to be lacking in explanatory range.

Where concepts of more than one logical level are necessary to the interpretation of a set of phenomena, we ought not to pretend to be operating on one level only. In the context of evolution where we in fact acknowledge novel operational principles, we should not pretend that nothing is there but the conditions without which (admittedly) they could not operate. The sum total of necessary conditions for the coming into being of an individual, a species, a phylum or of life itself are not logically or historically identical *with* the individual, or species, or phylum, or life itself. . . . I suggest, therefore, that instead of Ockham's razor we might adopt as a test of theories of evolution the opposite principle: that entities, or more generally perhaps aspects of reality—for principles of organization are not entities, though they do define entities—should not be *subtracted* beyond what is honest.[55]

This inverse criterion is specially pertinent when it is a question of transmuting present biological theory into philosophical evolutionism as a naturalistic account of the genesis of the universe.

In his analytic study of the philosophical uses of scientific thinking, Stephen Toulmin uses Huxley's evolutionary naturalism as a case history in the transition from scientific explanation to scientifically oriented myth. The passage is made whenever a selected biological order is treated as the Sovereign Order of Nature and thus proposed as the ethical norm for men. In the past, the Aristotelian scale of nature was so used, and at present the evolutionary tree of life is serving the same pupose. The mythic use of evolution by Spencer was noted long ago by Chauncey Wright. For his part, Toulmin specifies two criteria for recognizing when a scientific concept is being mythologized.[56] The concept must be used in an extended sense rather than in its straight scientific meaning, and the extension must be made for motives other than the explanatory aims of the science in question. When these conditions are fulfilled, disputes that may arise in regard to the full-blown myth cannot be settled by having recourse to the usual scientific procedures, even though the myth itself may continue to thrive upon the achievements of the scientific substrate.

Huxley's appeal to evolutionary progress as an ethical and religious principle displays these two traits. In his usage, "evolution" is the evocative term for a highly selective and complex conceptual artefact. Biological selection is linked up vaguely at one end with physico-chemical events in the inorganic world, and at the other end it is made continuous with the moral and religious aims of human society. The resulting cosmic image includes far more than the theory of natural selection and genetic mutation, so that critical discussion of its scope and use cannot reach a conclusion solely by reference to the data and procedures in biology. Evolutionary process now assumes the mythic status of the Sovereign Order of Nature and, as such, provides a standard and sanction for our moral choices and religious aspirations. Huxley's complex constructural account of evolution is intended not as a testable scientific hypothesis but rather as a stabilizing, controlling, and consoling image of the world for the use of naturalistic humanists. As distinct from the scientific notion of evolution based on genetics and paleontology, this evolutionary myth functions as a means of securing cosmic backing for the transition from *is* to *ought,* from impersonal survival-value of the stock to convergent value as the moral good and duty of man. To use Dewey's language, the mythic imagery of evolution serves to underwrite the naturalistic version of the quest for certainty in human values.

In his major treatise on *The Sources of Value,* S. C. Pepper reopens the question of the ethical significance of survival value and its relation to the rest of the human value system. He criticizes the tooth-and-claw version of survival, since modern biological research brings out the importance of cooperation and interdependence of the various species and their individual members. He also rejects Julian Huxley's notion of continuous evolutionary progress as the norm for determining ethical values and obligations. Pepper observes that, on this score, Huxley does not enjoy the full support of Simpson and other leading evolutionists. We can discover various modes of adaptation within some definite zone of life and then determine the dominant form within that situation. But there are many zones of life, some of them unrelated in time and biological competition and some of them existing contemporaneously and yet with little or no competiton. We cannot significantly grade as lower and higher the dominant forms in these different life zones, since their dominance refers to their mode of adaptation within their own life situation and not to a succession of forms passing from one such zone to another. There is no continuous march of evolutionary progress from one dominant form to another, culminating at last in man.

In short, there are as many dynamically sanctioned lines of biological progress as there are life zones within which adaptation is going on through natural selection. But there is no dynamically sanctioned line of progress across life zones, and consequently none for the course of evolutionary history as a whole.[57]

In view of this evolutionary pluralism, a carefully constructed evolutionary theory will not attempt to provide a cosmic sanction for the features which have enabled man to survive, and will not erect them into a value standard on the basis of their being identical with some universal norm of evolutionary progress.

Pepper's critique is significant on several counts. For one thing, it suggests that the relation between evolutionary theory and the notion of cosmic progress is just as problematic today as in the time of Spencer. Hence it counsels the ethician and value philosopher against taking the easy road of invoking progress as a basis for moral judgments. A second point is that Pepper returns to a position much closer to that of Darwin himself, both in stressing the plural lines of evolutionary adaptation and in looking for the value significance of survival directly in the operation of natural selection in human life, rather than in any essential link between natural selection and some schema of progress. He also credits Darwin with seeing that the precise way in which natural selection operates most effectively in the region of man is through his intelligence and moral conscience. Cultural evolution is not discontinuous with biological evolution, since they are both present in human development and both furnish modes of operation for securing the survival of the human species. Pepper does not reduce purposive values simply to that of survival, but he does maintain that in any situation of ultimate decision the latter must be dominant. His conclusion is that natural selection in its cultural and social form is the ultimate sanction for all human values and obligations. Where he differs from Huxley is in taking the selective process as an ultimate evaluative process in itself, without need for any further sanction in a structure of continuous cosmic progress.

7. Evolution, Evolutionism, and Philosophy

The outcome of this study of the impact of Darwin and evolutionary theories upon philosophy can be briefly stated. Perhaps the most striking point is the variety of philosophic responses that have been evoked by the evolutionary findings in biology. The scientific data and theories do not necessarily generate by their own weight any one single conclusion in the philosophical order or support one favored general interpretation of the universe. This is where an analysis of the consequences of evolution for philosophy proper must be carefully distinguished from a psychological and cultural description in terms of the history of ideas. The latter approach is valuable for underlining certain pervasive, concrete traits in our contemporary outlook which are either derived from evolutionary thought or greatly strengthened by it. For instance, we are now accustomed to a vastly enlarged time scale and to a view of time itself as a struggling, creative, irreversible process bringing forth ever novel forms of life. We take a genetic and historical approach to everything, looking for the meaning and the possibilities of things in their path of growth and the seed of novelty they contain. Man's kinship with the organic world is recognized, his thoroughly temporal and historical mode of reality is being explored, and the feeling is abroad that he stands at the threshold of a new mode of life. These convictions belong to our evolutionary atmosphere as a matter of daily respiration. Nevertheless, they remain fundamentally neutral as far as the major philosophical issues are concerned. The common stock of evolutionary ideas is open to diverse and conflicting philosophical interpretations. The idealist and the naturalist, the phenomenologist and the realistic theist, are all fully aware of the descriptive notes in the evolutionary climate, but the cultural facts themselves are not decisive for settling the principal differences among these philosophers.

This does not mean that evolutionary research is irrelevant for philosophy but only that its contribution has to be estimated in every instance through the proper canons of philosophical inquiry and cannot be automatically registered. We have seen this to be the case in the two problems of physico-theology and progress. A careful historical description and philosophical evaluation are required to determine the precise grounds of conflict between the Derham-Paley argument from design and the biological position of Darwin. A further analysis is needed to find out whether or not the untenability of Paley's watch argument entails the abandoning of all natural theology and hence leads to agnosticism as an unavoidable standpoint. Again, the question of whether there is any sort of progress in the universe and human history is not completely decided on biological and physical grounds, although they may rule out certain lines of argument or show that other views are more likely. There is still the problem of whether a philosophical conception can be found to account for random, retrogressive, and cyclic instances.

Among philosophers of evolution, the persistent problem has been that of making the transition from the scientific data and hypotheses about evolution to a philosophical evolutionism. This is a question of methodology which does not get resolved simply by watching what the scientific contributors to evolutionary theory do. For many of them do not enlarge their work to include a philosophical significance, and those who do follow this path are employing some additional instruments of philosophical generalization which are precisely what still require identification, analysis, and evaluation. We have noticed some divergent ways in which men conceive the right method for generalizing evolutionary thought. Wright claims that there is no speculatively valid method available; Peirce looks for it in a logic of the growth of law or reasonableness; Dewey finds it in converting the scientific mode of description into a naturalistic logic and ontology; Harris appeals to the idealistic notion of immanent mind; Bergson plunges into interior awareness of temporal duration.

One useful result of taking a synoptic historical view of these positions is that it furnishes a strong reminder of the persistent difficulties surrounding evolutionism as a philosophical claim. Anyone sharing the climate of evolution in its scientific and cultural aspects finds it difficult to retain a vivid sense of the problematic character of evolutionary discussion, when it begins to supply general answers about the origin of the universe, the nature of causal relations and what they exclude, and the basis of moral obligation and religious search. Yet it is illusory to think that one can move continuously and without any further instruments from genetics and paleontology into these other areas. The value of a critically used methodology is to dispel this illusion by distinguishing the scientific aspects of evolution from philosophical evolutionism and requiring the latter to face explicitly the task of reflecting upon and testing the bases in method and evidence for a generalized interpretation of evolution.

To recognize a mythic element in much contemporary speculation on evolution is not to pass any judgment on the intrinsic soundness of that speculation. It is intended only to clarify from another perspective the point that the incorporation of scientific findings and theories about evolution into a general view of the universe and human destiny requires more justification than a loose restatement of the scientific findings and theories themselves. Largely under the pressure of the evolu-

184

tionary mode of thinking in all fields, we have lost confidence in the Newtonian model of the world machine and yet have not been able to live familiarly with any of the newer physical accounts, some of which discourage any efforts at visualization of the mathematical theory. Yet men insistently require some concrete symbols and analogies expressing the significance of the universe and human history to them. And since in a scientific age this demand gets focused upon the resources of the sciences, the tendency is to built the imagery from a basis in the more concrete evolutionary sciences. Thus one of the cultural functions of evolutionary speculation today is to grope toward a humanly satisfying, as well as approximately correct, image of the developing universe and man's role in it.

The functions of philosophy, however, are never exhaustively described in terms of present cultural needs. Philosophy is here to make us critically aware of both the validity and the limitations of the evidence, the complex reference of scientific theories to the natural world as well as to the mind's constructural operations, and the mythic fusion on the side of the human subject, all of which are cooperating in trying to provide an evolutionary image for our age. Because of its deliberately critical and reflective standpoint, philosophy cannot merely submit to the impact of evolutionary thought and serve as a component in the process of forming an evolutionary outlook. It must continue to assess, restrict, and revise this process, as well as hold before our view other ways of looking at the world and forming our patterns of conduct. Philosophies which remain loyal to their methodological and critical tasks are never fully integrated with the reigning world-image, evolutionary or otherwise, but retain a certain salutary distance which keeps us responsive to the rigorous demands of inquiry and always open to new ways of reaching evidence.

The need to make a personal appraisal of the scientific sources on evolution stands out plainly in a comparison between Julian Huxley and Father Pierre Teilhard de Chardin, S.J. Teilhard's work is becoming increasingly known to scientists and theologians, but as yet it has not influenced the philosophers of evolution very deeply.[58] Both Huxley and Teilhard are working from roughly the same evidence, although the latter stresses his own field of paleontology and human development. Each approaches the task of finding the general significance of evolution not only with the resources of his scientific training but also with those of his philosophy and his faith—faith in self-contained nature in the one instance and faith in the revealing God in the other. They agree upon the convergent and cooperative character of evolutionary

185

forces at the human level, as well as that man embodies a distinctive living reality, what Teilhard calls the noösphere within the encompassing biosphere. Furthermore, both inquirers maintain that present-day man is not the final stage in the evolutionary process but that still higher modes of living lie open for realization by human social agencies.

Yet they disagree sharply about the kind of reality which lies beyond the evolutionary threshold or "point omega" toward which human history is moving. For Huxley, this next level can be characterized at least negatively as involving no reality which transcends the totality of evolving nature itself. Teilhard, on the other hand, describes the evolutionary convergence as leading man into the presence of God as the personal, energic source of all life, immanent in and also personally distinct from natural process. Thus Teilhard arrives at a spiritual and theistic conception of evolution. But he does so with the aid of some arguments which are largely philosophical in significance.

In terms of the present survey, we can orient Teilhard's position with respect to some of the main philosophical tendencies. He agrees with the idealists, especially Harris and personalism, that we should reinterpret the emergence of mind from matter in a finalistic way. It does not mean that mind is reducible to its organic basis but rather that "spirit is cosmically more important than matter, more valuable, more powerful, more final." [59] Thus a teleological approach can be taken, in which the emergence of spirit is a token of its unique reality and dominating importance. Yet Teilhard does not lessen the naturalistic insistence that the emergence of a new level of reality with man required a slight organic transformation. The point is that by means of this organic change there is introduced into the universe a new factor, so that it is now possible to reflect upon the nature of evolution and to control its future course.

On the methodological issue of finding in man's distinctive consciousness a means of access to the general nature and finalizing import of evolutionary process, Teilhard remains close to Bergson and even to Huxley. "If man is nothing else than evolution become conscious of itself, man, then, in order to be true to himself and to the universe, has to push forward individually and socially, the spiritual progress of nature." The reality of progress and the irreversibility of the growth toward spiritual reality are not left ambiguous by Teilhard, who accepts them at the same time that he rejects any facile optimism about automatic improvement. We have to work hard as persons and

186

social groups to maintain human existence and achieve any advance. By contrast with naturalistic humanism, however, Teilhard combines a stress upon man's natural origin and transforming capacities with a wholehearted religious acceptance of God. Ours is a gradually awakening universe, and what we are awakening to is the common summons of all forms of life and especially man's spiritual reality to a convergent sharing in the life of the personal God. Thus for post-Darwinian man, the meaning of mechanism is transformed to integrate it with teleology and the effective presence of God in the course of evolutionary striving.

In the deadlock between Huxley and Teilhard over an ultimate interpretation of evolution, we can observe how the scientific sources of evidence do not entirely determine the structure of an evolutionary philosophy. Especially in the case of the persistent problem of the relation between descriptive and causal elements in our concept of the agencies in evolutionary change, a broadened and reflective philosophical analysis of the scientific findings and language is unavoidable. Even when the contribution of the various components is discriminated, there remains the further issue of how biological causation is related to a cosmic evolutionary process, and whether the evolutionary causal explanations are the only ones required to account for our universe in causal terms. Thus the questions of *generalization and causality* in evolutionary theory tend to make a juncture, indicating for the philosopher that they constitute the core of any present-day study of evolutionism.

The philosopher's duty is to make a careful scrutiny of all the contributing factors in our contemporary evolutionary outlooks. This involves a study of the natural world of real organisms and their processes, the scientific constructs and theories, the controlling world-imagery, the naturalistic or theistic working faiths, and the philosophical methods and concepts being used. In addition, however, the philosophical inquirer must bring to bear some other human resources which may not figure immediately as components in some prevailing evolutionary position. He is under obligation to make his own direct philosophical analysis of the experienced world of natural change and to make this the basis for his evaluation of the evolutionary philosophies. And he has to consult what is suggested about the nature of temporal process and history, the structure of human experience and the ways to God, by philosophies not so directly implicated in the biological work of Darwin and his successors as are the philosophical positions considered here. This is a complex task. But to become aware of the need for it and of the futility of expecting any pre-packaged solution of evolutionary difficulties is the first step toward getting it done. In the problem of evolution as well as everywhere else in the philosophy of nature, our philosophical judgment must be disciplined to rest ultimately upon our personal study and evaluation of the whole tissue of relevant sources open to man.

CHAPTER 8

HOW DEWEY BECAME A NATURALIST

A GOOD way to gain access to John Dewey's mind is to focus attention upon some master theme in his philosophy. One topic which animates his work from beginning to end is the question of nature and naturalism. Under one aspect or another, this general problem is close to the center of discussion in every phase of his development. It certainly permeates all the writings of his last thirty years of active work. Indeed, the naturalism of this last period, during which he became a public figure, is so massive and dominant that it seems to resist a careful analytic and genetic study. We tend to give the term "naturalism" a vague and conventional meaning when applied to Dewey, as though the emotion of approval or hostility evoked by its use is self-explanatory and settles the issue. The fact is, however, that his position on nature and naturalism does have a definite structure and a definite history which are open to investigation. The purpose of the present chapter is to follow the genesis of his views on this question during the crucial formative years from 1884 to 1909. The conception of nature gradually forged during this quarter-century span became one of the permanent bases of his philosophy and served to determine the sense in which it was a naturalistic philosophy. Dewey's subsequent elaborations of naturalism built upon this foundation by expanding its themes and by dealing aggressively with obstacles to its full acceptance in our society.

1. *Nature as the Irritant against Idealism*

Schopenhauer once remarked that no great work is done in philosophy unless the individual thinker is goaded into it by some deeply troubling issue, which he cannot soothe over and forget. In Dewey's philosophical development, the role of creative irritant was played by the problem of nature.[1] He was attracted to it almost from the outset and, for a while, thought that he could provide a neat idealistic solution to difficulties arising in this area. After trying to carry out an idealistic interpretation of nature, he found the results too unsatisfactory to avoid making a radical revision of some basic points and thus moving beyond idealism to a distinctive philosophy which could do more justice to the views on nature then coming to the fore. The record of Dewey's preoccupation with this matter is found in the articles published during his years at Michigan and Minnesota (1884-1894). They show that the theme of nature antedated his naturalism itself and that his reflections upon it furnished some of the prime considerations eventually compelling him to make the journey from idealism to naturalism.

What strikes us at once in Dewey's initial publications is their confidence that the idealist can take full account of the current findings in biology and psychology, the sciences of nature then making the most rapid and revolutionary advances. Idealism is especially recommended as providing the best philosophical integration for the work being done on reflex action, evolutionary theory, and empirical description of consciousness. Far from excusing the notoriously weak Hegelian philosophy of nature as being an unimportant part of the system, Dewey seeks to improve idealism precisely at this point so that it can become adequate to the scientific findings about natural reality.

He analyzes Wundt's research on reflex action, for instance, in order to show that it brings out pertinent evidence against the Cartesian view of mind, without lending any real support to materialism.[2] Reflex action is a basic nervous activity which involves purposive adaptation and hence a teleological category which cannot be reduced simply to physical causation. In studying its significance, we move from the purely physical description to a recognition of mind as being immanent in physical operations. Dewey is already interested in adjustment as a mediating concept both for showing the immanence of purposive mind and for guarding against a simple reduction to physical conditions. The adjusting function is one way in which a goal-seeking mind or spirit realizes its own purposes through the means of the bodily organism.

Thus a test case was made of the explanatory power of idealism to show the presence of telic mind in that area of nature studied by physiological psychology. That is why Dewey's later functional explanation of the reflex arc, without making any use of the theory of purposive spirit, assumed such decisive philosophical importance for him. To be able to dispense with the idealistic account of mind in this significant region in the study of nature suggested to him that idealism is irrelevant to the actual world that holds our interest.

Even in his original idealistic interpretation of reflex action, however, Dewey established two traits about the philosophical study of nature which became part of his permanent doctrine. That the critical thinker should be on his guard against a panoramic or picture-thinking approach to problems raised by experience, was the first point made. Thus he should not look for an easy set of pictures for visualizing the mind-body question, but should seek reflectively after the interpretative principles which can account for the scientifically describable condition of man. And on the broader scale, Dewey observed that his "object is not to get into the inside of nature and behold with mortal eyes what is going on there, but the less ambitious one of inquiring what principles must be used in order to give meaning to the facts of the case." [3] In the inquiry into nature, we should be skeptical about theories based upon the claim to have intuitive access to the workings of nature and about theories relying upon pictorial explanation. Dewey's constant stress upon treating philosophy mainly as a method rather than a content sprang from his adherence to this rule. He always remained suspicious of "inside stories" about the real structure of nature, even though he himself did not always resist claiming to be on the inside of the only proper method for inquiring into the natural world.

That the facts turned up in the course of Darwin's research radically modify our conception of nature and, in turn, require a rethinking of philosophy, was Dewey's second conclusion. Neither the philosophical Darwinism of Spencer nor the older idealism seemed to him adequate for interpreting the evidences of biological evolution. He criticized Spencer for basing his synthesis upon the picture of age-long accidental changes, since this was a panoramic approach offering no specific account of the presence of intelligence and active adaptation. Spencer either glossed over the problem of intelligence and purpose by the vagueness of his universal formulas or else introduced a covert element of purposiveness into nature as a whole, as the price paid for making a mechanistic account of some particular instances. Even during Dewey's idealistic period, however, he readily admitted that German and British idealism could not meet the challenge of evolution without undergoing some incisive modifications. It is important to remark that Dewey's criticism of idealism began as an *internal reconstruction*, while he was still its firm adherent. That is why he did not have to cross too wide a gulf or leave behind all his key notions when at last he did move on to naturalism. Furthermore, it is significant that he felt the need to modify idealism precisely in the face of psychological and biological findings about man within the context of nature.

His problem was to accommodate these findings without permitting them to have the decisive word in determining the real status of nature and man. Dewey's initial solution was to redefine the method of experience and the psychological standpoint, so that they would fit into the idealistic context.[4] To adopt the *psychological method* in philosophy means to confine all questions about the reality of things to the manner in which they present themselves in experience. But experience itself refers to the relations which arise within consciousness as a wider whole; the experimental method supposes that consciousness is the only inclusive standard for being and knowing. All philosophically significant existence is relative to consciousness, and even our individual consciousness is relative to the universal consciousness. When we say that consciousness is the philosophical absolute in method and reality, however, we are referring neither to an isolated individual consciousness nor to a separated universal one. The decisive word rests with absolute mind or consciousness, taken precisely as a concrete synthesis of the individual and the universal components.

Dewey expected that this reformulation of idealism would enable him to meet the argument of evolutionary realism. The latter position included every effort to explain consciousness genetically as being intrinsically dependent upon prior physiological states and ultimately upon a scientifically described evolutionary process, which precedes individual minds and is their causal source. Dewey criticized this explanation with counterarguments which at first seemed incontrovertible to him. The evolutionary approach applies only to your mind and mine, *i.e.*, to the individual aspects of consciousness. But these individual modes, together with all their objective correlates on the side of the evolving organism, are only abstractions made from the concrete totality of absolute mind or consciousness in which the full reality of experience resides. Furthermore, our very ability to devise an evolutionary theory about individual consciousness is testimony that the latter can transcend itself and its biological context. It moves beyond its immediate antecedents by recognizing its synthesis with universal consciousness, and hence its capacity for studying experience as a totality, within which the course of biological evolution is a particular strand of explanation.

Dewey's final objection against evolutionary realism is in the sphere of methodology. Philosophical issues cannot be settled either by an independent logic or by a philosophy of nature founded upon the empirical sciences as its fundamental source of control. From the viewpoint of Dewey's version of psychological idealism, logic and philosophy of nature must be regarded as abstractions made within the context of the organic totality of individual-and-universal consciousness. Logic treats of the formal structure of thought found within this whole, whereas philosophy of nature deals with its material side or objective content. These approaches are valid abstractions, insofar as they respect the controlling reality of spirit or the totality of self-consciousness. But if they subordinate this reality to a supposedly autonomous standard, such as the laws of formal logic or the evolutionary theory of natural selection, then they become vicious abstractions and violate the method and order of philosophy.

This is the high point in the early Dewey's defense of a revised idealism and its claim to deal adequately with the sciences of nature and the philosophy of nature. In attempting to make the defense more detailed and pointed, however, he begins to encounter the difficulties which will eventually require him to abandon his psychological idealism. For instance, he agrees with Hegel's empirical critics that no dialectical passage can be made from logic to philosophy of nature.[5] We must start with facts rather than logical categories, and hence we must move from nature to the logical sphere rather than try to follow the reverse path. In granting a relative primacy to the domain of nature, Dewey already comes dangerously close to conceding that we make our unconditioned start with nature as factually experienced and analyzed by the empirical sciences.

Furthermore, in order to distinguish clearly between his own psychological idealism and Hegel's logic of the absolute idea, he must describe nature as the realm of fact and existent relations. Although he does try to save idealism by measuring the factual and concrete traits of nature by the standard of the totality of consciousness, Dewey cannot quiet the suggestion that this reference of natural fact, existence, and relation to another standard is just a further instance of vicious abstraction or of trying to impose a set of logical categories on nature. The question becomes increasingly more pertinent as to whether experience is correlated primarily with the idealistic postulate of universal consciousness or with natural existents, including our ordinary conscious acts and organic states.

Under pressure from such considerations, Dewey begins to hesitate whether to regard philosophy of nature simply as an abstractive application of a philosophical method grounded in the consciousness-postulate, or as a reflective synthesis of the working procedures of the empirical sciences. He concedes that the former position would weaken the philosophical significance of the actual methods used in the sciences of nature. Yet he also recognizes that the latter alternative would affect much more than the philosophy of nature. It would open the way for specifying the general meaning of experience and philosophical method in terms of a natural reality given fundamentally through the empirical sciences and not through an idealistic conception of the totality of consciousness. An unqualified and fully concrete start would then have to be made with nature as directly experienced by man and with the actual procedures of the sciences of nature.

We can conclude this section on how the problem of nature functioned as an irritant against Dewey's initial adherence to idealism by noting four weaknesses in his reply to evolutionary realism.

1. Dewey's argument on the abstract character of the genetic approach to man simply supposed that the concrete is identical with the idealistic description of consciousness. But this was the point at issue and could not simply be assumed. In practice, Dewey found himself using the term "concrete fact" in a thoroughly ambiguous way. Sometimes it signified the idealistic norm of "conscious experience in its totality," whereas in other uses it was a descriptive term for the particular elements given in our ordinary acquaintance with, and scientific account of, natural existents and relations. The trouble with the former usage was that, on Dewey's own admission, philosophy "can deal with this absolute self-consciousness only so far as it has partially and interruptedly realised itself in man." [6] Under these unavoidable human conditions, the totality of spirit does not enjoy the status of a founding and specifying fact for the philosophy of nature, but is a dialectical construction measured by some facts of human experience of natural things.

2. One such fact is our ability to work out an evolutionary theory of the minded organism of man. This testifies to our capacity to reflect on evidence and follow out its implications, even in cases which involve our own history. But the analytic and inferential operations required for elaborating a theory about man's genesis do not force us to suppose

194

any merger or synthetic union between individual and universal consciousness, as the idealistic doctrine of absolute spirit argues. Evolutionary theories about man do rest upon the cooperative work of many researchers over the generations, and yet a decisive difference persists between the idealistic notion of consciousness as a whole and the community of scientific researchers. The latter never gets totalized and transcended into some absolute self-consciousness, because the community of investigation remains open-ended and resists hypostasization. There is an interesting resemblance here between Dewey and Edith Stein, since they both refuse to concede that the social group becomes a complete reflective entity or totality.

3. As a consequence, Dewey found it impossible to remove the obscurity from the venerable idealistic term "synthesis," even in reference to the relation of individual and universal consciousness. Granted his rejection of an autonomous logic, he could not clarify its meaning merely by means of the dialectical theory of logic. And on the experiential plane, it could be replaced by describing the interdependence between philosophy of nature on the one hand and the complexus of our ordinary acquaintance with natural events and the scientific ways of analysis on the other, without making use of the postulate of universal consciousness at all. Indeed, Dewey was beginning to suspect that this interdependence which we can experience is only disrupted by trying to refer all the components in it to the idealist standard of absolute self-consciousness. Here was also the root of the unremitting hostility he later displayed toward any form of dualism involving a transcendent factor. He came to view every type of transcendence after the model of this idealistic totality which is disruptive of the actual relations holding between human experience, nature, and scientific inquiry.

4. One special form of dualism which plagued him from the start was that between time and eternity. He recognized the distinctively temporal character of all natural events and human acts. Now idealism would require him to treat nature and everyday man as a manifestation of self-consciousness, to locate their true reality only in their organic containment within the eternal totality of mind, and thus to conclude that their "manifestation is an act not occuring in time, but eternally completed in the nature of the Absolute, and that it occurs only 'partially' and 'interruptedly' *through* (not in) time, in a being like man." [7] On this reckoning, acceptance of the eternal would sap the temporal order of its intrinsic significance and initiative. Yet the weight of ordinary experience and scientific research favored the view that

the natural world in its temporal aspect is real and valuable in its own mode of acting.

Thus Dewey felt himself confronted with the choice of either preserving the integrity of nature as a temporal course or reducing it to the instrumental role of a manifestation of an eternal consciousness. That is why he soon came to understand the temporal character of nature as involving the exclusion of any claim for eternity. He generalized the idealistic account of time and eternity to cover every way of relating them, and hence he looked upon every defense of the eternal as containing an attack upon the intrinsic worth of nature in its temporal traits. The polemical note in Dewey's stress on time became a permanent aspect of his naturalism.

All these problems pointed unavoidably to one negative conclusion for Dewey. He could not make a fruitful study of nature and man within an idealistic framework. Whatever idealistic elements might survive in his later thought, he could not permit them to reassemble into the central thesis that the really real consists in an all-enveloping eternal totality of consciousness or absolute spirit. He therefore forged a way of philosophizing which rests upon the direct polarity between nature and experience and scientific method.

2. *Critique of Ethical and Religious Conceptions of Nature*

To appreciate the actual direction which his search for a more adequate philosophy of nature and man took, we must now consider certain difficulties uncovered by Dewey in the area of ethics and religion during the 1884-1894 period. We will choose two prominent topics: his attack on Spencer's way of founding ethics and his treatment of the Christian message. In both instances, we will find that his criticism turns around the meaning of natural reality and that the result is a permanent contribution to his growing naturalism. This difference will also be observed, however, that whereas in the case of Spencer he is treating of a popular philosophy to which he is not personally committed, his reflections on Christianity do concern his own religious position during these formative years. In the case of both idealism and religion, some factors survive in his later philosophy, albeit in a transformed way and as dominated by a new organizing principle concerning nature and man's role in it.

Even during his college days in Vermont, Dewey was interested in the striking contrast between Kant and Spencer on the foundation of ethics.[8] Kant built his ethics around a sharp dualism of the moral agent and the natural world, whereas Spencer relied upon a close unification of them. This raised the question whether nature inhibits the moral life, until man finds some autonomous footing apart from it, or whether nature furnishes the very impetus and laws for our moral life. Thus in the formulation of the ethical problem familiar to him, Dewey was accustomed to regard one's view of nature as being highly relevant to one's account of the ethical order.

It seemed to him that the Kantian dualism between moral man and determined nature was rapidly becoming untenable in the wake of current scientific findings. Biology, laboratory psychology, and the social sciences were bringing man wholly within the domain of nature as the inclusive subject of scientific investigation. To use Dewey's own metaphor, the arms of scientifically articulated nature were reaching out to engulf man in his entirety. Hence if the ethical order depended upon retaining the Kantian contrast, then it was doomed to be undermined by every advance in the scientific study of man.

At this point, Spencer held out the possibility of renovating moral life precisely by incorporating it within the general process of nature. As he formulated them, the evolutionary laws themselves contain an ethical implication and hence permit an ethical foundation within the context of scientifically described nature, rather than in opposition to it. The Spencerian evolutionary thinker would have the basic assurance that human life is not anarchic but regulated by natural laws which our intelligence can discover. Moreover, he would be able to establish that evolutionary laws specify man's ethical aim to be the development of the cooperative spirit of the social organism rather than the self-centered individual. Again, evolutionary science would bring out the powerful sanction of conscience as embodying the sifted results of social experience. And it would lend the full force of the order of nature to such virtues as honesty and courage, since it would present them as objectively dictated means for attaining the evolutionary goal of the human social organism.

In describing Dewey's attitude toward Spencer, we must distinguish between the general and quite indeterminate proposal to develop ethics within the context of nature and the specific way in which Spencer tried to make a natural justification of ethical judgments. On the more general issue, Dewey modified his position in accordance with his shift from an idealistic ordering of nature itself to absolute spirit to his later centering of ethical values within the natural world. Nevertheless, it is significant that neither in his idealistic phase nor

197

in his full-fledged naturalism did he accept Spencer's precise method for justifying moral values on the basis of the evolutionary laws of nature. His reluctance on this score is important for understanding his view of nature as well as his ethical standpoint. The reasons advanced during his idealistic period for not following Spencer reveal some of his enduring conceptions of nature. They also generate some difficulties which eventually force him to seek for a better philosophical foundation of the theory of nature than idealism can provide. Thus a study of Dewey's moral critique can be as rewarding for us as was the analysis of Wright's and Peirce's methodological criticism of Spencer.

In the writings now being analyzed, Dewey sets forth three major objections against the Spencerian doctrine that the physical categories underlying the theory of evolution can also determine the moral ideal for man.

1. It is doubtful that any direct induction can be made from the evolutionary traits established by biologists to the moral ideal of social cooperation. If we were to mold our conduct in conformity with Darwin's description of natural selection, for instance, we would have to support an incessant rivalry and unequal sharing in goods rather than the pattern of mutual help and equal opportunity of access to values. Competition and social divergence would be our graven law. Although evolution stresses the common origin for all human life, it does not follow on physical and biological grounds alone that men therefore must have a community of interest which is moral in kind. It is fallacious to argue that "because there is a physical community of origin there *must* be an ethical community of end." [9] Organisms develop out of the common pool of life precisely by conflict and by reference to a survival goal in which they do *not* all equally share.

One interesting feature about this argument is that it appeals over the head of Spencer to the working biologist's notion of evolutionary traits. Whatever Spencer may deduce from his own statement of general evolutionary laws, Dewey finds it more informative to study the biological account. We can get a more reliable conclusion about whether or not to found ethics upon the evolutionary account of nature by examining what a Darwin actually regards as the mechanism of natural selection than by following a Spencer's elaborate deduction from physical laws. Although this is an effective tactic against Spencer, it raises in Dewey's mind the question of the larger consistency in his own practice. His own appeal to the universal consciousness is just as remote from the biological reports as is Spencer's invoking of the law of the persistence of force. Hence he is faced with the task of attending to his own counsel that one should first develop the theory of nature in close reliance upon actual scientific procedures, and then consider how an ethical doctrine can be elaborated.

2. Dewey also remarks on the ambiguity surrounding Spencer's talk about the goal or end toward which evolution is moving. It can mean either a factual last term and outcome in some future situation or else a present ideal energizing our ongoing action. Even if the universe has an end in the sense of an outcome to a phase of drift, this does not supply man with a moral end for controlling his present decisions. The goal of evolutionary nature is not an ethical one, in the sense that it aims specially at the personal and social fulfillment of man. If we take the cosmic drift as our sole moral basis, we will treat man only as a passing phase and instrument in the universal change. Our moral need is not satisfied by values and ends which are merely set for man as a part of the cosmic scene. Moral ends must be present in man in such a way as to respect his distinctive nature as a self-realizing agent.

Once more, we may notice that Dewey is in possession of an aspect of his view of nature which will survive his passage beyond idealism and will help to characterize his naturalism. Nature is basically characterized by its constant change and factual existence in space and time. The natural process has phases and outcomes, but they cannot be construed as determining the moral goals and scale of values for man. We have already seen the relevance of this point in dealing with the notion of progress in Spencer and Julian Huxley. Whatever the patterns we may discern in the cosmic process, it remains morally neutral and cannot provide us with a ready-made basis of values. We cannot just read off the moral goals of man from the making and unmaking which transpire in nature, since their moral relevance comes from their bearing upon man as an agent responsible for his own development. Hence we have to beware of reading our own moralizing interpretations into nature and then appealing to a purely objective cosmic sanction for them. Spencer's justification of ethics makes man into a passive recipient of values and deprives moral ends of their specific reference to the interests and needs of man.

Yet in the course of working out this criticism, Dewey finds it difficult not to apply it forcibly to his own idealism. The idealistic position on individual and universal consciousness permits him to hold that moral values are present in man, but not that they also have their source from human activities and interests. From the idealistic standpoint, man is a self-realizing agent only in the sense of manifesting his truer self or the universal consciousness present in him. Whereas Spencer

199

reads his own moral proclivities into natural process, idealism reads into it the aims of absolute spirit. In both cases, nature is asked to provide more of a guide and sanction for moral ideals than it is fitted to yield, and man in the concrete is given less responsibility for shaping his values than he is able and eager to take. The solution toward which this situation points is to achieve some direct bond between man and nature, so that moral values can arise from this relationship rather than from an extrinsic legislation.

3. Finally, Dewey questions whether there are indeed any ends in nature, when it is considered by itself alone.

Nature has no end, no aim, no purpose. There is change only, not advance toward a goal. . . . We utterly deny that the physical world, as physical, has any end; that nature, as natural, can give birth to an ideal.[10]

Teleology finds no place in physical explanation, and hence no analysis of physical categories and the evolutionary laws founded on them can furnish a moral ideal or end for human conduct. Once we are in possession of a moral ideal, then the scientific study of nature is very helpful for discovering the conditions retarding and aiding its realization. But we should not confuse the seed of moral life with the soil where it is planted and grows.

This last text brings out one major tension in Dewey's early program of accommodating nature and its scientific explanation to the ideaistic presuppositions. What he denies is that there are ends and ideals in nature taken precisely "as physical," "as natural." But the argumentation he uses to support this denial is still based on the idealistic notion that a knowledge of ends depends on our conceiving the universe as a whole. Clearly enough, such knowledge is not supplied by the natural sciences and can come only from the theory of absolute spirit. To treat nature as natural means, then, to regard it apart from reference to the absolute consciousness which supposedly sets the general purpose and meaning for natural process. Yet Dewey is starting to realize that it is possible to forego all claims to understand the total cosmic purpose and still to have some knowledge of ends, considered in a particular and plural way. This can be done if we take into account the interests and aims of men as we find them, not as they are explained within idealism. Particular ends and ideals are established by men in their dealings with nature and with each other. If we restrict ourselves to this humanly derived significance for moral ends, then we can recognize their presence in the natural world without having to read them into natural process from a deductive premise taken either in Spencer's evolutionary formula or in the idealistic absolute.

Nature has no inherently inscribed values and ends. Dewey adheres to this as a reliable statement and includes it in his later naturalism. But the fact that ends do arise in our human experience leads him to revise his original idealistic interpretation of the statement that nature, as natural, cannot give rise to an ideal or an end. Nature does give birth to the kind of being which envisions ideals and establishes ends for action. What makes moral purposes meaningful is not the relating of nature to a universal consciousness, but the relating of it to men in their concrete existence and planning activities.

But before exploring how values, ends, and norms arise from the direct relation and intercourse of nature and man in society, Dewey must face the further objection that the Christian conception of things requires us to relate man only indirectly to nature and to orient his intellectual and moral interests basically away from it. This is the reason why Dewey cannot avoid treating of a Christian conception of nature. His handling of this theme is not a superfluous work but an essential strand in his gradually developing conception of nature. His growth toward naturalism is bound up with his achieving a critical, but by no means entirely negative, position toward what he takes to be the Christian view of the man-and-nature relationship.

The prevalent idea in Dewey's religious conferences at Michigan is that we must distinguish between the essential Christian idea and the hardened conventions of institutional Christianity.[11] The former is not only distinct from the latter, but is now engaged in the historical act of disengaging itself from the institutional forms. This contrast is the forerunner of Dewey's later distinction between the religious attitude and particular religions. For our purpose, however, the significant point is that the antithesis originated in his early search for a direct highway between man and nature. He felt that institutional Christianity had erected a barrier between them, forbidden any direct relations, and routed all their traffic to the absolute as their only legitimate point of meeting.

Here is the philosophical source of Dewey's antipathy toward the Christian tradition, an antipathy which is so puzzling to those who are familiar with the humanistic resources of Christian thought. He customarily interprets the distinctions between the spiritual and the worldly, the eternal and the temporal, the hereafter and the here-and-now, as dualisms in a pejorative sense. They express a separative movement on the part of institutional Christianity to withdraw man

201

as much as possible from natural concerns, to insulate him from any fresh experience and challenge of natural events, and to concede meaning to the latter only as imperfect images of a spiritual purpose. On this basis, Dewey concludes that every affirmation of the transcendent and the supernatural entails a separatism and a depreciation of earthly life. He hardens his equation between the transcendent and the antinatural into a permanent pattern of thought, ruling out beforehand any possibility of revision in the light of examining various ways in which the above distinctions are intended. The pressure behind his polemical stiffness concerning the dualisms of institutional Christianity is his concern to open up and maintain a direct route for man's activities in the natural world.

Yet it is noteworthy that Dewey does not regard the Christian idea itself as antinatural. Instead, he argues that this idea was never properly realized by the dualistic forms of traditional Christianity and that it is now actively seeking for a more adequate means of expression. The Christian idea never was a specialized religious truth but was a first approach to the naturalistic meaning of human experience. The core truth

was propounded as the realization of the meaning of experience, as the working truth which all experience bases itself upon and carries within itself. This truth was that man is an expression or an organ of the Reality of the universe. That, as such organ, he participates in truth, and through the completeness of his access to ultimate truth, is free, there being no essential barriers to his action either in his relation to the world or in his relations to his fellowmen.[12]

The last phrase in this text expresses what Dewey deems to be the really salvageable element in the Christian idea. For even in this vague form, it allies the Christian principle with the general naturalistic effort to remove the barriers preventing a direct intercourse between individual man, the natural world, and human society. If we want to identify the concrete ways in which the Christian idea is now acting to overcome these obstacles for fulfilling the meaning of experience, Dewey bids us to consider "the development of science, the conquest of nature through the application of this science in invention and industry, and its application to the activities of men in determining their relations to one another and the resulting forms of social organization."[13] These are the contemporary bearers of the Christian idea, its ways of realization in the modern world.

In offering this interpretation, Dewey explicitly acknowledges that he is engaged in a task of reconstruction.[14] Thus one of his earliest

developments of the basic theme that the work of philosophy consists
in critical reconstruction occurs in connection with the religious conception of man and nature. The essential Christian idea must be reconstructed, in order to eliminate any reference of man to an order
of being and value that transcends nature. Religious energies have to
be radically reorientated toward the experiential whole of nature
and man, lest they be drained off from the primary work of the understanding and control of nature and the improvement of human social
relations. In seeking to find an acceptable core in the Christian outlook
rather than remove it entirely, Dewey remains closer to Hegel and
Comte than to Nietzsche and the scientific materialists. Yet in the
course of naturalizing the Christian idea, he also discovers himself to
be reconstructing his own earlier psychological idealism. The primary
meaning for the totality of experience is not found in the polarity
of individual and universal consciousness but rather in the polarity
between human actions and the natural world. Reconstruction of the
Christian message about experience and man's place in the universe
is thus one of the major paths in Dewey's journey from idealism to
naturalism.

The vagueness still clinging to even the reconstructed religious outlook can be removed by specifying the more adequate instruments for
actualizing it under today's conditions. We can identify these working
forms in accordance with the axiom that, if the Christian idea is at all
revelatory, then it must actually reveal truths and continue to do so
in our own historical age. Dewey remarks that the most effective and
constant sources of increment of knowledge and practical control today
are the scientific method and its applications in technology and democratic process. They constitute the real incarnation of the Christian
idea for contemporary man. "Revelation means effective discovery,
the actual ascertaining or guaranteeing to man of the truth of his life
and the reality of the Universe." [15] Measured by this criterion, the
religious spirit must now place its entire hope in the scientific method's
exploration of the ways of natural process, as well as in the democratic
means for enriching the human community. The only valid standing
henceforth for the religious attitude is as an encouraging symbol of the
ongoing relations which science and democracy are striving to achieve
between men in society and the natural order. The functions of revelation are to be wholly secularized and embodied in scientific and democratic activities.

Dewey patiently undertakes even the particular work of making an
exegesis of Biblical passages and common Christian notions about the

kingdom of God and the truth which liberates man. His purpose is to show that they can be translated, without remainder, into the context of man and nature as the only kingdom within human reach. The truth which makes man free is the recognition that we can realize our potentialities only within the environment of natural needs and opportunities. The repetition of the word "only" at this point is intended to underline the significant fact that Dewey's teaching on the sole cognitive competence of the scientific method is the other side of the theme which reformulates the Christian idea. He cannot be sure that the reconstruction of the latter is definitive until he assigns all the reliable sources of knowledge and disciplined power to scientific method and democratic procedures.

It is because science represents a method of truth to which, so far as we can discover, no limits whatsoever can be put, that it is necessary for the church to reconstruct its doctrines of revelation and inspiration, and for the individual to reconstruct, within his own religious life, his conception of what spiritual truth is and the nature of its authority over him. Science has made real to us, and is found to make still more real, the actual incarnation of truth in human experience and the need for giving heed to it. . . . [In conformity with the Christian outlook] it is assumed, however unconsciously, that all truth which is worth while, all truth which promises to be of practical avail in the direction of man's life, may be gotten at by scientific method.[16]

Thus Dewey is transferring from institutional Christianity to his own reconstructed idea of Christian truth and hence to the naturalistic position the absolute confidence in a revealing source of truth and practical control. Only, this source is now to be understood not as the transcendent God and not as the idealistic absolute spirit but as the effective presence of scientific method and its organization of environment and society. Paradoxically enough, then, Dewey helps to consolidate his methodological and metaphysical claims about the scientific method and the natural field of experienceable reality by means of his reconstruction of the Christian idea. It lends a certain absoluteness to his naturalism and a sense of exclusive dedication to the good for man which might otherwise not characterize it.

Deweyan naturalism does not treat science and democracy purely as descriptive principles of method. They are more properly regarded as normative counterprinciples against inserting any third domain of reality or method of investigation between the complex, dynamic whole composed of inquiring man and nature as a visible process of inter-change with man. These principles function as assurances both against diverting human plans and moral ideals away from the symbiosis of man and nature and in favor of devoting our energies and hopes completely and solely to the study, control, and enjoyment of this relationship.

3. *Evolution Seals the Circle*

Our purpose in the remainder of this chapter is to examine the essays which Dewey composed between 1897 and 1909 and published in 1910 under the title of *The Influence of Darwin on Philosophy*. Together with his book on experimental logic, these essays were the main philosophical fruit of his Chicago professorship and his first years at Columbia University. They were concerned with one serious residual problem from his previous critique of idealistic and religious conceptions of nature. The outcome of that critique could plausibly be interpreted as being nothing more than the substitution of the new dualism of man and nature for the older ones under fire. Such a dualism might open the way once more for ordering our experience toward a principle of unity located in the transcendent God or the absolute consciousness of idealism. Dewey found it necessary to seal in the mutual relations of man and nature in such a manner as to prevent any real reference of inquiry and desire beyond the man-and-nature complexus. He found a way of doing this by making his own reconstruction of Darwin's import for philosophy, and thus by challenging Spencer's claim to provide *the* philosophical system of evolutionism. With this reinterpretation, Dewey came into firm possession of the chief components in his conception of nature. His naturalism was well established in its main lines by 1909, and thereafter it was only necessary to work out in fuller detail its various aspects and extend them into the particular facets of human experience.

A. *The substitutional method used in naturalistic reconstruction.* One striking result of Dewey's study of Darwin is his resolve to model his theory of philosophical reconstruction after the evolutionary reconstruction of biology. The pattern of progress which holds good in biology must also be the pattern of progress in philosophy. This means that unserviceable doctrines are to be replaced by experimentally more adequate ones just as inexorably and definitively in philosophy as in the physical and biological sciences. It would be just as senseless to worry about antiquated philosophical problems as about the concepts of pre-evolutionary biology. Hence the philosopher must reconstruct his discipline by a deliberate use of the two-phase method of elimination and substitution.

The method of philosophical reconstruction, as carried on in the naturalistic spirit, has an eliminative aspect which simply removes as meaningless in an evolutionary age certain of the long-standing disputes. The example used by Dewey shows that he wants to be even more rigorous in philosophy than Darwin had dared to be. Darwin confessed in the autobiographical statement already quoted by us that his mind wavered between attributing the order of the universe ultimately to chance or to a designing intelligence. Dewey comments that there are two ways of taking this hesitation. Either the question is a genuine issue which is too difficult for our minds to encompass or else it is a meaningless difficulty from which we must try to extricate ourselves entirely. Now philosophy is learning not to claim for itself any distinctive method or data, but to work out the general implications of the method and data furnished by the sciences, especially biology. Hence in our age of evolutionary science, "philosophy forswears inquiry after absolute origins and finalities in order to explore specific values and the specific conditions that generate them." [17] This forswearing implies that the whole question about the ultimate principle of order in nature is a meaningless one. We are bound to reject both sides of the Darwinian alternative and to hold that the issue itself must be dropped from philosophy. To reconstruct the philosophy of nature means to unburden our minds of the very problems which do not hold out the prospect of being settled within an immanent and particularized evolutionary mode of inquiry.

From this standpoint, Dewey's naturalism is nothing more than that set of questions about nature and human experience thereof which survives the process of elimination according to these scientific canons. In later years, he registered strong disapproval of the way that logical positivism used a physicalistic standard to outlaw many problems as meaningless. But his own naturalism owed its genesis to a similar elimination of what he judged to be meaningless according to the pattern of biological inquiry and evolutionary interests.

An effective reconstruction must be substitutional as well as eliminative. In outlawing questions about ultimate origins and goals, it must replace them positively by a concern for specific lines of growth and particular ends of activity. There is a psychological and even a therapeutic aspect to Dewey's description of the substitutional method. To philosophize in the naturalistic manner means to undergo a process of healing and growth, to mend the wounds occurred in eliminating past concepts and then to spurt ahead in developing the new ones which fit an evolutionary view of nature. As far as traditional points of dispute are concerned, "we do not solve them: we get over them. Old questions are solved by disappearing, evaporating, while new questions corresponding to the changed attitude of endeavor and preference take their place." [18] Darwin's *Origin of Species* is the greatest dissolvent of philosophical issues in the precise sense that it redirects our main interests and renders the previous scene in philosophy simply archaic and unproblematic for us.

Dewey's thinking on the question of philosophical diversity and progress is wholly dominated by the biological metaphor and by a consequent psychologizing of the task for the naturalistic critic. He conceives of philosophical progress as transpiring through a linear series, in which one position totally supplants another, after the fashion of scientific theories. The philosophical issues and ideas of the past become vestigial and useless, so that they atrophy and eventually disappear when the course of scientific research directs our interests elsewhere. The traditional habits of mind may persist temporarily, and then the naturalistic critic must trace out their particular origins, their past responsiveness to the situation, and their present condition as outmoded illusions. He must treat the states of mind which persist in reopening the old problems in the same way that the psychologist deals with reports about the converging Zöllner lines.

Dewey relies on a convictional shift generated by new scientific interests, as well as on a psychologizing of recalcitrant positions, to deal with the diversity among philosophers and the recurrence of philosophical issues. But this is scarcely sufficient to take account of the actual ways in which philosophers proceed. They explore issues not by any linear displacement but by a societal continuance of the basic modes of interpretation. Their concern is directed to the questions which persist under many kinds of cultural, scientific, and psychological conditions. These questions do not conveniently become meaningless and disappear, when one philosopher chooses to appeal to a generalization of evolutionary thought as a solvent. Moreover, the metaphor of a vestigial survival of outmoded problems and theories leads Dewey to rely indulgently upon the same panoramic mode of thinking which he had previously criticized with vigor in Spencer's case.

B. *Naturalistic pathos against the transcendental.* Dewey was aware that his substitutional method, considered only as a theoretical recommendation, could not secure the total disengagement of minds from the doctrinal positions and attitudes of the past. As he phrased it, evolutionary thought and the naturalism stemming from it are not merely an additional law but a complete about-face.[19] They involve a withdrawal of respect for ultimate explanations, fixed structures, and universal purposes, so that men can concentrate upon nature in its particular phases, its fluent qualities, and its capacity for limited aims and satisfactions. And to bring about this reversal, a practical act is required in addition to a theoretical critique. Hence Dewey found it necessary to surround his version of the inquiry into nature and human experience with a new affective atmosphere, which would encourage a permanent practical adherence to it. Naturalistic reconstruction would thus have to reach into our emotions and concrete valuations as well as our theoretical principles.

As an instrument for arousing a new naturalistic pathos, Dewey began using the term "transcendental" with a strongly polemical ring in his writings after about 1894. As he had employed it in his idealistic period, it had signified only the method of relating objects and a knowledge of objects to their context and ultimate foundation in the doctrine of absolute mind or consciousness. But now he began to use it to mean that, in this process of tracing out the basic presuppositions of objectivity, there is also involved an active denigrating of empirical objects and states of mind. They lose their intrinsic significance and worth in the degree that they are given an underpinning in universal consciousness. Indeed, the transcendental type of thinker enjoys derogating them for the greater glory of God or the greater expansion of the absolute. In painting this somewhat horrendous portrait of the transcendental mind, Dewey was not so far removed from Marx's and Nietzsche's call for loyalty to the earth by abandoning belief in an absolute which is distinct from man and nature.

To the reply that the transcendental standpoint does eventually establish the importance of finite things and the natural sciences, Dewey makes a quick and scornful retort. The transcendental vindication comes in the form of a wholesale engulfing. In the order of knowledge, it amounts to a praise of truth-at-large and of the universal presence of conscious mind. But it fails to supply us with any definite recommendations for resolving the particular problems of life or for improving the scientific methods which do face these problems specifically at their own level. And in the moral order, the transcendentally oriented mind is prone to give blanket approval to all existing conditions as being justified expressions of the absolute. The only practical advice we get is not to worry about anything, since the absolute consciousness has eternally healed and rectified all situations.[20] But nothing is forthcoming as to how we can go about manifesting this happy state in terms of our empirical situation.

The case for naturalism receives practical and emotional support from this pathos against the transcendental outlook. That outlook encourages a vague and sterile mentality, which remains unable to analyze our actual problems or improve our daily lot. Instead of beguiling ourselves with wholesale talk about the absolute mode of reality, Dewey advises us to concentrate upon the specific instruments of inquiry and policy for bettering our control over nature and our social living. The pathos against a world-fleeing transcendentalism is thus converted into a positive ethos of scientific study and cultivation of naturally available values. We are prepared to withdraw all interest from a search after the absolute, if for no other reason than that such a search may entail a dangerous diverting of human skills away from the responsibilities of our world. It is precisely at this point where naturalism as a philosophical doctrine moves beyond ordinary respect for nature and human society. It contends that this respect cannot be wholehearted and effective until we treat the question of the absolute as theoretically meaningless and practically disastrous for man.

One notable feature of this theory of the transcendental must be criticized. Dewey expands its range customarily to include not only the idealistic notion of absolute mind, from which he was reacting, but also every theistic affirmation of a transcendent God. He does not justify in detail this extended usage, but blurs together the idealistic absolute and the God of personal theism. It then becomes impossible for us to respect the proper distinctions and to make a precise test of the soundness of Dewey's argument in any particular case of a philosophy which he may regard as transcendental. This procedure defeats the ends of inquiry, since it prevents any controlled analysis of the position in question or any pointed comparison of its view of natural reality with the naturalistic view. Although Dewey is satirical about a wholesale defense of absolute truth and goodness, he himself makes a wholesale use of his theory of the transcendental to include many sorts of non-naturalistic positions. The unsettled philosophical question concerns whether the undesirable consequences for scientific work and practical control follow with necessity from every theory to which he attaches the label of transcendental. No answer can be given while we allow the question to remain in Dewey's formulation, which is not so much a precise articulation of the connections as a blanket assertion that they must exist in every case where the real is not identified with nature and the human activities it sustains.

C. *The example of Darwin.* It was not until after he had worked out his capacious meaning for the transcendental that Dewey was in a good position to complete his naturalistic interpretation of Darwin and thus effect a passage from biological evolution to evolutionism as a philosophical doctrine. There is a revealing contrast between Freud and Dewey in respect to their way of including Darwin in the modern intellectual movement. Freud takes what we may call a *stigmatic* approach to modern science. He regard the Copernican revolution, Darwinian evolution, and his own exploration of the unconscious as so many successive wounds inflicted upon Western man's pride of place, origin, and rational control. For his part, Dewey prefers to give a *liberational* meaning to the growth of modern science.[21] He views the movement from classical physics to evolutionary biology to his own experimental logic as so many moments in the healing of Western man from transcendental preoccupations and the freeing of him for a greater appreciation of his active role in nature. They are successive stages in a gradual extension of scientific method from the physical world to the sphere of life and finally to man's intellectual and moral activities. With each step, the opportunities for understanding, control, and satisfaction increase.

There is an internal relation between the three moments in the expansion of the scientific way, however, such that, until Darwin made his contribution, it was not yet possible for a fully developed philosophical naturalism to appear. Hence it was vital for Dewey's purposes to make a reconstructive appraisal of Darwin's work, in order to present it as the penultimate discovery paving the road for his own philosophical position. Only after Darwin had overcome the reluctance to submit living things to the general procedures in science did it become feasible to bring human reality thoroughly within the range of these same procedures. And only after the psychological and social sciences had made a good start in naturalizing man as an object of scientific investigation was the situation ripe for making Dewey's own philosophical attack on the transcendental attitude and his generalization about nature and man. In bringing man within the scope of his evolutionary explanation, Darwin was also providing philosophy with sufficient evidence for sealing the circle of natural being and limiting our cognitive and valuational interests to human operations within the natural domain.

Taken in this reconstructive way, then, the figure of Darwin is used as part of the argument favoring the acceptance of naturalism. In anticipation of Julian Huxley, Dewey burdens the Darwinian treatment of the species problem and the genesis of mind with definite philosophical consequences of a naturalistic sort. On these two scores, he seeks to invest his own position with scientific and historical inevitability and to show that other philosophies belong to a pre-evolutionary outlook, which can no longer seriously hold our assent.

Since Darwin's greatest advance was made in revising the biological notion of species, Dewey presented the whole metaphysics of theism and transcendental idealism as being essentially dependent upon the now outmoded Greek view of biological species. His argument was that only the acceptance of species as a fixed form which progressively realizes its own preordained end lends strength to the metaphysical assertion of the superior reality of a fixed order of essences and ends, which can be known only through a special rational insight.

These inferences were extended to nature: (*a*) She does nothing in vain; but all for an ulterior purpose. (*b*) Within natural sensible events there is therefore contained a spiritual causal force, which as spiritual escapes perception, but is apprehended by an enlightened reason. (*c*) The manifestation of this principle brings about a subordination of matter and sense to its own realization, and this ultimate fulfilment is the goal of nature and of man.[22]

But this whole fabric for interpreting nature, Dewey contends, is only an extrapolation on a grand scale of a biological theory of species which Darwin has swept away. His evolutionary research shows that species have a definite temporal origin, that their structure is subject to constant modification, that chance variation rather than purposive planning accounts for their successful adaptations, and that they are wholly subject to a history and death within nature and apart from any further reference beyond it.

The consequences of evolutionary research for one's philosophical conception of nature can be spelled out in definite opposition to the three inferences mentioned above. First, there is not a sufficient basis in the events we can study for concluding that nature itself is purposive. The random variations are too pervasive for us to think that the entire natural process is planned by an intelligent agent working out its own ends. Ends do play a part in human affairs, but then we can see that in their origin and import they are purely natural, immanent, and plural. Next, the so-called laws of evolution are not transcripts of some hidden spiritual force but are convenient summaries of trends made for the convenience of our reading and controlling of natural events.[23] We can learn to remain satisfied with a study of natural being just as it displays itself to our perception, scientific analysis, and practical planning. And finally, the worth of our analytic and planning activities comes from their direct relevance to nature and human affairs, not from their serving any further purpose or realizing any transcendent plan. Nature and man find their continuing fulfilment in the experience and values which arise from their interrelated activities, without any subordination to a God or an absolute center of consciousness.

The work of Darwin and subsequent evolutionists in making a genetic study of man and especially the human mind is also used by Dewey to strengthen the case for philosophical naturalism. The inclusion of man within the evolutionary process helps Dewey to resolve two prominent issues. One of these is the idealistic argument he himself had previously used to the effect that the evolutionary origin of individual minds is reconcilable with the subordination of nature as a whole to absolute mind. The striking feature about all the evolutionary sciences of man is that they uncover strong positive reasons for involving the human mind in the evolutionary sweep, and yet find no good reasons for adding that nature and man are real only as realizing the purpose of cosmic mind. All the weight of the evidence points toward an evolutionary account of human reality, but it leaves quite unsupported any transcendental reference of man and nature to an eternal purposive consciousness.

Another major question affected decisively by an evolutionary explanation of man is the kind of relation holding between nature and man. Dewey is specially concerned about this implication, since it enables him at last to avoid the charge of dualism without obliterating what is distinctive about man. Nature and man are not coeval, independent entities. Man comes to be through an evolutionary growth of nature, and it is within the totality of nature that he develops his intelligence and pursues his goals. Once we agree to take the human mind only as we experience it in its natural being, then we must admit it to be an evolutionary outcome, an active principle arising within nature and finding there its whole sphere of inquiry and values. There is something distinctive about our intelligence, not by reason of its being an expression of some absolute mind but by reason of the properly human activities in which it consists. Distinctive modes of being develop within natural process, but to recognize them is not to open a door for the kind of dualism which will reinstate some transcendental principle.

In his highly concentrated 1909 dialogue on nature and its good, Dewey completes the revision of his previous opinion that nature cannot give rise to moral ideals and values. He remains opposed to the excessively moralizing view of nature advanced by idealism and by Spencer, but he is now able to offer a positive naturalistic account of intelligence and value. Nature cannot be said to care for values until it produces an intelligence which can select and fight for what it prefers.

Not, then, when Nature produces health or efficiency or complexity does Nature exhibit regard for value, but only when it produces a living organism that has settled preferences and endeavors. The mere happening of complexity, health, adjustment, is all that Nature effects, as rightly called accident as purpose. But when Nature produces an intelligence—ah, then, indeed Nature has achieved something. Not, however, because this intelligence impartially pictures the nature which has produced it, but because in human consciousness Nature becomes genuinely partial. Because in consciousness an end is preferred, is selected for maintenance, and because intelligence pictures not a world just as it is *in toto*, but images forth the conditions and obstacles of the continued maintenance of the selected good.[24]

This text tells heavily against Spencer's notion that the laws of nature directly intend a moral aim and dictate to our passive intelligence what its values and goals must be. Nature is mindless and purposeless until it brings the minded organism of man into being. But then we can define human intelligence adequately as the function of holding particular ends in view and working selectively with the naturally available means for realizing these chosen ends or goods. There is no need to invoke either a moralizing nature or a universal consciousness to explain mind and value.

From this point onward in Dewey's own philosophy, he feels that naturalism is securely based against both the transcendental types of philosophy and reductive materialism. His attention is devoted henceforth to working out the detailed applications of his naturalistic position, especially the new theory of experience and value which it implies. His investigations after 1909 are consciously carried on within the already established outlines of a philosophy which maintains that humanly meaningful reality is found solely in the dynamic relations between inquiring and valuing man and the rest of nature.

4. Nature and Naturalism

One question remains outstanding as a result of this study of the genesis of Dewey's naturalism. Are his findings about *nature* indistinguishably one with his *philosophical naturalism?* That they do not strictly coincide is clear enough from a comparison between a few of the components in his conception of nature and some of his philosophical arguments.

We have already considered how Dewey's early reflections on nature served as an irritant provoking some new ideas. On the main points of provocation, however, Dewey's movement away from idealism need not have been directed toward naturalism. A realistic approach to nature is also on guard against the illusions of panoramic thinking and the claims to get into the inside of nature. Theistic realism is more concerned with getting at adequate principles of explanation for the experienced facts than with seeking an intuitive vision of the whole of nature. And it regards the experienced facts as having an intelligibility and integrity of their own which cannot be disrupted by being referred to the concept of total consciousness. The temporal, spatial, and changing character of the natural world expresses its own reality, and that reality cannot be revoked or rendered illusory by being related to anything else. Recognition that the natural world is a spatial and temporal process, having meaning and worth precisely in these modes of being, is not confined to naturalism. Liberating itself decisively from the idealism-naturalism alternative, a realistic view of the personal creative God encourages us to respect and enrich the natural ways of existing, knowing, and valuing.

Dewey's critique of some prevailing ethical and religious conceptions of nature contains some sound features, which are not reserved exclusively for a naturalistic philosophy. A realistic theism also holds that man does not simply read off his moral values from the book of nature, as though he were passively related to the natural world. Valuating and determining our moral goals are distinctively human acts: they do not occur in isolation from the rest of nature, but they do require human intelligence and interest in order to come into being. Nevertheless, there need be no incompatibility between using our intelligence and funded experience in determining the aims of action and also searching after God as our ultimate good. The defense of particular ends of human action is not bound up with a rejection of God, although it does require a stubborn insistence on man's own responsibility in making his selections and realizing them.

Dewey moves away from a descriptive examination of the traits of natural being and toward a philosophical naturalism in his treatment of Christianity and the transcendental. Yet just here his inquiry becomes unsatisfactory, because of its very restricted historical basis of induction for studying the ideals and institutions of Christianity. His stylized objection that institutional Christianity prevents the direct communication of man and nature does not survive the test of comparison with actual Christian views of the natural world. In the Christian tradition as everywhere else, there is a pluralism of attitudes toward nature. The function of the discriminating mind is not to lump them together but to examine each one separately on the question of the relation between Christian values and natural ones. This is a safer and fairer procedure than Dewey's methodic dualism between the institutions and the idea of Christianity, since it avoids the arbitrariness of his descriptions.

As for his theory about the transcendental, it is better as a weapon of persuasion than as a tool of analysis. By coalescing many sorts of idealism and theism under the heading of a transcendental doctrine, Dewey does not overcome them so much as he prevents the patient study of how various forms of idealism and theism consider the domain of nature. It cannot be said of them all that they denigrate the natural objects of experience or that they ask us to choose between particular scientific procedures and the truth about the ultimate principle of natural reality. For advancing the inquiry into nature in our own day, it seems advisable to refrain from posing the question of God and nature in terms of a transcendental metaphysics versus anti-transcendentalism, since this alternative is too vague for rigorous treatment.

Furthermore, the appeal to Darwin's example has to be evaluated critically as an instance of the substitutional-reconstructive method, as it transforms the historical materials. One thing which stands out clearly from our previous chapter on how the different philosophies have interpreted Darwinian evolution is the variety of inferences drawn from it. There is a definite gap between biological theories of evolution and philosophical forms of evolutionism. The work of Darwin and his scientific successors does not have a one-way univocal meaning for philosophy and does not lead automatically to a naturalistic view of evolving nature. Dewey's conviction that it does is the consequence of his own prior philosophical commitment, as the following text shows.

> The conception of evolution is no more and no less the discovery of a general law of life than it is the generalization of all scientific method. . . . Philosophy must go to school to the sciences; must have *no* data save such as it receives at their hands; and be hospitable to *no* method of inquiry and reflection not akin to those in daily use among the sciences.[25]

The theory of biological evolution does not itself provide the generalization of all scientific method, for this is a philosophical interpretation

215

which Dewey makes in the course of reconstructing the significance of evolutionary thought. Similarly, the two negative exclusions which he emphasizes flow from his fundamental naturalism; they are not inevitably entailed by our going to school to the sciences. We can be faithful to a direct experiential acquaintance with nature and to a careful study of what evolutionary science and other disciplines say about the natural world, without having to stipulate that there are no data and no methods other than those furnished by the sciences. If it is precisely a question of the degree of kinship between scientific methods and those used in philosophy, then the likeness is determined more by the range of our questioning and the findings responsive to it than by Dewey's prior negative norms. The latter are not imposed as conditions for doing good scientific work, and hence need not be prescribed for philosophies of nature which attend to the scientific account of things.

A particular instance in which Dewey tries to draw more out of the scientific achievement than it can yield is provided by his treatment of the species problem. What he calls the Hegelian bacillus in his blood is dominant in his effort to make every metaphysical doctrine on the essential structure, finality, and order of things dependent upon the Greek view of biological species. The importance of this notion is undeniable, especially in Aristotle's philosophy. But it is too narrow a pivot whereby to summarize and overcome all these metaphysical positions. They involve some non-biological meanings for species, and they rest on some direct inspection of the ways of nature which is not uncritically determined by the biological metaphor. The results of evolutionary research certainly require some deep modifications in philosophies which remain responsive to scientific findings and theories, but the process of modifying and enlarging one's philosophy is not the same as submitting to a naturalistic substitution.

Dewey's thought is admirably sensitive to many aspects of natural existence. He keeps us alive to the process and novelty of natural events, to the tireless creativity of nature, to the integrity of its spatial and temporal traits, and to the unity which man establishes with the rest of natural reality through his inquiring and valuing activities. The meaningfulness of nature within the perspective of human experience and scientific methods is his insistent theme and his great contribution to philosophy.[26] We can honor our debt to him in these respects without embracing his philosophical naturalism. The gap remains between Dewey's defense of the human significance of nature

216

and the naturalistic principle that we should confine our inquiries, values, and ends to the man-and-nature totality.

Behind Dewey's attempt to solidify the analysis of nature and his philosophical naturalism lies his uneasiness about introducing gradations into the natural world. The danger is that the hierarchical view of natural things is apt to slight those aspects of natural being which are regarded as inferior or less perfect in the scale of nature. This concern on Dewey's part is historically well founded in instances where such ranking of things does often lead to a depreciation and neglect of whole areas of the natural world. However, the historical examples cannot be converted into the necessary law in philosophy that evaluative ranking is incompatible with an open interest in all the configurations of natural reality.

Every metaphysician who admits an experiential basis for his studies will hold that there is a double sense in which everything he encounters is on the same footing with the rest of the experienced world. For one thing, all the events and traits which we do discover through direct analysis of our experience have the common note of being factors in that experience. As such, each factor has a claim to be included in the descriptive study of nature and to receive a careful inspection from the investigator. Moreover, there is no moment in a metaphysical inquiry when anyone is validly dispensed from consulting these experiential deliverances and accounting for them in his generalized theory. The metaphysician is always bound to show some basis in his direct acquaintance with the natural world for the inferences he makes, and thus to show the experiential relevance of every step in his inferential work and the adequacy of his theory for explaining the experienced things. In these two senses, the theistic realist insists as strongly as does the philosophical naturalist upon the all-of-a-pieceness of the natural world. The realistic study of nature aims at respecting the capacious variety of our world and giving honest consideration to every event and aspect of our human experience of natural reality.

Yet in his metaphysical masterwork, *Experience and Nature* (1925), Dewey himself came to acknowledge that our intellectual humility before natural events is not the sole determining note of a valid metaphysics. Our respect for natural reality is shown not only in our receptive openness but also in our continual work of selection, inference, and evaluation.[27] To determine the generic traits of existence, the metaphysician must make comparisons between different regions in his experience and between the methods and findings of different sciences. Moreover, the philosopher has to explore the traits thus ascertained for their interconnectedness, their varying kinds and degrees of generality, and their practical consequences of many sorts for man. The thorough philosophical study of nature rests on these operations, which involve a selective study and a valuational discrimination among the many forms of natural being. There has to be a certain systematizing of the results and a well founded designation of what is higher and lower, less perfect and more perfect, among the natural realities attained through reflective and inferential study of our experience.

There is no good reason for maintaining that these functions are valid for a naturalistic philosophy and invalid for any other philosophical approach to nature. For such functions are the common lot of every study of nature which admits both a basis in our ordinary experience and the need for analytic, inferential, and evaluative inspection of that basis. From the fact that realistic theism acknowledges the existence of God and the presence in nature of many kinds and values among things, therefore, one cannot draw the necessary conclusion that this philosophy is incompatible with a strong respect for the natural world. Each individual instance of philosophical inference and evaluation has to be studied on its own ground. The natural world is not "simply there" for any philosopher. Natural events and traits are there in their connectedness and separation, their more or less complex structure, their various kinds of relevance for human action. Every philosophy dealing with nature must take account of these features, if it intends to base itself upon the evidence and the problems furnished by our experience of the natural world.

Fidelity to all aspects of nature involves an ordering and evaluation which in principle need not be confined to distinctions drawn within some sealed circle of man-in-nature. Thus a real gap persists between Dewey's recognition of certain traits in nature and his further claim that their recognition can only be protected by adopting his standpoint of enclosure within philosophical naturalism.

Once this gap is clearly recognized, it should exert an influence upon one's way of evaluating Dewey's mature philosophy. When we speak about his conception of nature, we are referring to a compound position, the two main elements of which are not bound together by any necessary link and hence do not have the same implications for criticism. One element consists of those traits in our human experience of the natural world which Dewey shares in common with realism. This part of his compound conception of nature accounts for his dissatisfaction with idealism and expresses the common realistic criticism of the idealistic view of nature and our way of knowing it. But there is no strict entailment leading from this position to Dewey's distinctive naturalism, where nature and knowable reality are made equivalent. The common realistic factors in his conception of nature tell against idealism, but they are not in solidarity with his closed naturalism which excludes God from the scope of human knowledge and religious search. In making a consistent evaluation of his mature philosophy, then, one can agree with Dewey about the inadequacy of the idealistic theory of nature and also indicate the failure of his own naturalism to remove God from the range of our philosophical inquiry and human desire.

CHAPTER 9

HUMANISTIC NATURALISM
IN MARX AND DEWEY

The strength of modern naturalism lies in its effort to bring into a single perspective the humanistic and the scientific components in our civilization. It seeks to integrate man so closely with the natural world that henceforth naturalism cannot be anything except humanistic. And conversely, it seeks to make the natural process so relevant for understanding and improving human existence that henceforth humanism cannot be anything except naturalistic. In this proposed marriage between the naturalistic and the humanistic motifs consists much of the attractiveness of contemporary naturalism. The intent of the present chapter is to scrutinize this humanistic naturalism as furnishing one of the compelling paths in philosophy today.

Such an analysis must be carried out in three steps. There are two leading forms taken by humanistic naturalism in our time: Marxism and the experimentalism of Dewey. Hence the first two tasks in working out our theme consist in making a precise internal study of the Marxist type of humanism and then the Deweyan type. Only after each one is considered in its own shape will we be in a position to compare them. Our final task will be to make this comparison, both in order to bring out the common basis in humanistic naturalism for Marx and Dewey and also to determine the main points of difference which separate them. In examining these two forms of humanistic naturalism, however, it is well to bear in mind that they are not only theoretical positions but also powerful tendencies in the practical social world. They are both philosophies and powers. Moreover, in both respects, the Marxist and Deweyan conceptions of man are opposed to any kind of humanism which is integrated with a theistic philosophy. Thus there is a significant comparison to make between naturalistic humanism and

220

theistic humanism on all the major points of doctrinal and practical interest.

1. *Marxian Humanism*

We are so accustomed to viewing Karl Marx primarily as the analyst and critic of European capitalist economy that we find it difficult to discern any humanistic implications in his work. But his detailed investigations of economic problems must be replaced in the wider setting of his constant preoccupation with man and nature. Something of this broader context of his thought can be detected in the pages of the *Communist Manifesto*, when that document is read as a sustained protest against the inhumanity of men toward men. The ruthless exploitation of child labor, the steady undermining of family relations, the degrading conditions of industrial employment, the profanation of art by business—these unwholesome features of nineteenth-century industrial society aroused Marx's wrath because they violated his definite conception concerning the ideal development of human existence. The basis of his denunciation of capitalism was not a vague, philanthropic sentiment and not even a residual stirring of the spirit of the Jewish prophets, with whom he is often compared. Rather, his mind was being guided by a highly developed theory of man's place in the cosmos. Hence to appreciate the germinal source of both his revolutionary pronouncements and his laborious economic research, we must probe into the philosophical background acquired during the decade just prior to the issuance of the *Communist Manifesto* in 1848.

It is to the pre-1848 Marx that both pro-Soviet and anti-Soviet Marxian humanists appeal for their guiding principles.[1] Critics who base their analysis of Marxist humanism mainly upon the writings of Engels and Lenin often find their arguments shunted aside as being irrelevant to the main body of doctrine, which is solidly based upon Marx's early thoughts about man. The Marx of these early years was primarily a speculative thinker. His work at the University of Berlin had centered around jurisprudence and philosophy, with the aim of preparing him for a post as a professor of philosophy. He was disappointed in this ambition because of his disagreements with the more conservative followers of Hegel who then controlled German academic life. Away from the university centers, however, Marx succeeded in hammering out the basic conception of human nature which was to underlie all his later activities and publications. He never underrated

221

the need for providing a philosophical foundation for the revolutionary work of the communist movement. Lenin and other later Marxists continued the tradition of giving their followers a careful intellectual formation in the meaning of man and his world. This training is distinct from the practical instruction in propaganda, sabotage, and revolution, which contains the technique for realizing the aims of Marxist humanism.

The contemporary Marxist outlook is characterized by its anti-theistic and anti-religious postulates. They can properly be called postulates, since they constitute a part of the primal, unquestioned equipment of the Marxist mind. The problems of God and religion are not examined impartially and with a resolve to accept whatever the inquiry reveals. On the contrary, all discussion in this area is governed by the prior decision to eliminate belief in God and religious worship as positively harmful to man. In particular instances a policy decision may call for temporary tolerance, but always with the understanding that a change of circumstances will permit the main work of eliminating the religious attitude to continue.

In order to grasp the grounds of this hostility, Marx's own atheistic position must be examined.[2] He was utterly convinced of the antagonism between human welfare, on the one side, and belief in God and the observance of religious worship on the other. The epithets which he applied most frequently to his many foes were: "religious minds" and "crypto-believers in God." This attitude stems from his uncritical acceptance of the typical Hegelian thesis that the *God* of Christian religion is only one subordinate way of viewing the *Absolute* of Hegel's own philosophy. Once this identification is made between the Christian God and the Hegelian Absolute, theism is saddled with all the special difficulties attendant on Hegel's philosophical system. The most crucial one concerns the relation between the Absolute and the relative or finite modes, which is the Hegelian substitute for the Christian problem of creator and creature. Whereas creator and creature are utterly distinct ways of being, the Hegelian relative modes are only aspects of the Absolute. This means that the finite things of our experience are unreal and faulty, insofar as they fail to express the whole nature of the absolute. Only to the extent that finite things constitute a phase in the development of the Absolute itself, can they claim any actual perfection and a rightful place in the universe. Hegel claimed that the inner essence of any finite thing turns out to be nothing more than an aspect of the developing being of the Absolute itself.

What Marx did was to substitute the definite term "man," in places where Hegel spoke indefinitely about "finite, relative thing." Once having made this substitution, he had no difficulty in demonstrating that Hegel's theory of the Absolute is antihumanistic in tenor. It poses a serious threat to the integrity of human nature, since this theory acknowledges no intrinsic perfection in man himself and the world around him. The Absolute constitutes an invasion upon man's distinctive way of existing and acting, since it deprives him of a proper significance and value of his own. Marx added that, since the Hegelian Absolute is nothing other than the fullest expression of the traditional God, the antithesis between human integrity and the Absolute extends to God as well. Thus Marx's charge that belief in God is antihumanistic had its basis in his criticism of the Hegelian doctrine on the Absolute. Although later Marxists are not so close to the original controversy between Hegelians of the left and right wings, they continue to pose the question of God in the same way as Marx did. It is a mark of Marxian orthodoxy that this issue may not be re-examined in a fresh way, apart from the very special historical conditions that prevailed during Marx's own early years.

Marx regarded the religious attitude as something wider than belief in God, although he treated the latter as the supreme instance of religious belief. In defining the nature of religion, he followed the lead of another left-wing Hegelian, Ludwig Feuerbach, who tried to explain the religious attitude in terms of the fundamental Hegelian notion of alienation or estrangement.[3] In practical life, the alienating process means that man sets up a dichotomy between the realm of things as they are and as they ought to be. But instead of treating both members of this contrast as poles within his own nature, man tends to identify himself exclusively with the factual order of what is and to set apart from himself the ideal order of what ought to be. Thus, he becomes alienated or estranged from his own better nature. He treats the latter as a separate realm of its own, existing independently of himself. This gives birth to belief in some transcendent reality, toward which man is supposed to owe special duties. The religious attitude consists in a subordination of the empirical, everyday human being to some distant ideal that has been given an autonomous status. The illusory character of religion consists in forgetting that the ideal norm originated from human nature itself and acquired its transcendent position solely through the activity of man's self-estrangement.

Marx enthusiastically adopted Feuerbach's account of religion, without considering whether it would be valid apart from the dialectical machinery and special categories of Hegelian philosophy. He was so convinced that Feuerbach had said the last word about the genesis of religious belief that he invariably grew impatient with those of his colleagues who devoted their energies to inquiring into the nature of religion, since their activities implied that the definitive explanation had not yet been discovered.

He admitted, however, that something more precise could be added concerning *why* men allowed themselves to become involved in the alienating process. Marx found the motive for this idealization to lie in the wretched social and economic conditions of modern capitalist society. Hence he described the religious attitude as nothing more than an unconscious protest against the cruel world of fact and a projection of an ideal arrangement into the illusory beyond. Religion is the sigh of oppressed spirits, burdened down by the ills of industrial capitalism. This opiate conception of religion has been strictly adhered to by subsequent Marxists, who also accept the systematic consequences that flow from conceiving religion in this way. Of course, Marx also asserts that religion is fostered as a conservative force by those who seek to preserve the social and economic establishment.

Marx established a strict parallel between religion and private property, rejecting both on his humanistic grounds. Both are the consequence of the process of human self-alienation: religion in the theoretical sphere, and private property in the practical.[4] In both instances, man robs himself of his own dignity by paying homage to something supposed to be greater than himself, whether it be God or the power of economic laws. And in both cases the cure is the same: remove the oppressive material conditions that drive men into this self-estrangement, and then the objects of religious and capitalistic belief will automatically crumble to the earth. When the impetus to flee from the actual world is eliminated, allegiance to religion and private property will disappear. Marx confidently predicted the disappearance of the tendency toward self-alienation (and hence the disappearance of theoretical and practical products of this activity) after the inception of communist society. Whatever the nuances of emphasis or the practical requirements of interim policy, Marxist humanism continues to be qualified negatively by a lively conviction that God, religion, and private property will be jointly wiped out, once the communist organization of the social economy is achieved.

The humanistic motive for this orientation of the Marxist mind needs to be underlined. If the above descriptions of belief in God and religion are accepted, then it follows that human nature must be liberated from notions which only deplete and degrade it. Every form of self-estrangement empties man of his reality and proper dignity: hence Marx is careful to associate God and religion with this self-emptying operation. He warns that they represent a flight from the real world and an evasion of man's secular responsibilities. Instead of draining away our energies in the cult of transcendent or supernatural beings, a constructive humanism proposes to expose the purely human origins of the objects of religious belief. Once they are effectively uncovered, man will be ready to devote himself wholeheartedly to the cultivation of his own powers and the control of nature.

On the positive side, what is the "real" condition of man, as Marx outlines it? [5] The constructive aim of his humanism can be described succinctly as an overcoming of the separations generated by the process of self-estrangement. Man must be reconciled to himself by learning to surmount the false dualisms he himself has called forth. There are three major schisms which Marx proposes to heal: (1) between man and nature, (2) between man and his work, (3) between individual men and society. These three antitheses are closely inter-related: hence the solutions for reducing them converge in a common method and doctrine. Marx's humanism is the synthesis which results from his concerted endeavor to achieve this threefold unification.

1. Marx once said that the criticism of religion is the basis of all other criticism. By this, he meant that when men become disillusioned about the reality of something transcendent, they come to discover the truth about the world here below. For Marx, the truth about our world is that it is to be taken as the sole reality and the sole locus of human values. Having cut off man's religious bond with the transcendent, he transferred all the strength of a religious attachment to man himself and his world. Marx's humanism is founded upon a belief in the total immanence and self-sufficiency of finite being. His scale of humanistic values is similarly determined by the assumption that human goals are completely limited to the self-founded world of our experience, and that values are self-created by man in his natural environment.

The ordination of man to an exclusively this-worldly end brings out the thoroughly naturalistic character of Marxian humanism. This means both that there is neither a God nor a supernatural realm of grace from which man may expect any aid, and that man is in every respect a part of the autonomous whole of nature. Despite his denial of the supernatural, however, Marx does not rule out differences between natural beings themselves, as long as the principles of difference do not exceed the scope of the material world. He admits that there is something distinctive about man, since he is capable of self-conscious activities and can make his own powers and operations the object of his reflection. Man has a distinctive sort of reality, not as being outside of nature but as being a reflective agent within nature. Against the idealistic tendency to treat the external world as merely an exteriorized form of thought, however, Marx stressed the dependence of human self-reflection upon the material world. The latter is also the ultimate object toward which our creative efforts must be directed.

Marxist humanism defends the strict complementarity between nature and man. Man is dependent upon nature and must adapt himself to its conditions. Yet in the process of adaptation, he discovers that he can exert some control over nature; he can adapt it, in some measure, to his own purposes. Hence there is a mutual relation of conformity and cooperation between the conscious human agent and the rest of nature. The immanent whole of finite being consists in neither factor taken by itself, but only in their dynamic union. *Reality,* for Marx, signifies the interaction between man and nature. Anything that tries to move beyond this man-nature plenum is branded as a "transcendent illusion." Any attempt to reduce the one element to the other or to withdraw one element from its exclusive ordination to the other is labelled a "vicious abstraction." The only humane and realistic attitude is one based upon the concrete and indissoluble synthesis of man and nature, in a single closed circle of reality.

2. Nevertheless, the perfect union of man and nature is not an achieved fact to which no further contribution need be made. Marx was just as convinced as Hegel that the essential character of the real is its need for development from a primitive to a well-articulated condition. Our human powers must be employed intelligently and energetically if we are to acquire any determinate perfections. Moreover, our activities must be directed toward material nature in order to obtain fruitful results and escape from purely subjective dreams. The operation by which we use our abilities in the cultivation of nature and the development of our own essence is labor.[6] It is the conscious act by which man seeks to gain progressive control over nature and to satisfy his own needs.

Marx reacted vigorously against the extreme idealistic view of man as a disembodied spirit, whose only proper activity consists in speculative thinking. In order to show that theory without practice is barren and deceptive, he paid special attention to the fact that man is a corporal being, subject to urgent bodily needs. Whereas these bodily needs were a scandal to idealism, Marx made them the crux of his own humanism. For they can be satisfied only through work that embodies human purposes in some material medium. The dignity of human labor consists not only in its ministration to bodily needs but also in its role as the main agent for the development of man's mental and moral constitution. Whatever the perfections of human character and culture, they are ultimately traceable to our labor upon the material world. Marx exalts labor into a literally creative force, the fruitful principle of all human values. Thus, he deliberately replaces the idealistic mystique of speculative thinking with his own activistic mystique of human labor. Through its mediation, the union of man and nature is brought to perfection. In working upon nature, man simultaneously expresses a rational pattern in nature and reveals his own developing essence to himself. Labor shapes nature to human purposes, thereby building up man's own intrinsic structure.

It is a far cry, however, from this lyrical view of labor to the harsh actualities of the laboring man's lot in capitalist society. Under the existing system, Marx pointed out, the worker is separated from the product of his labor. Whereas matter is ennobled by human labor, man himself is degraded and impoverished. The more he works, the more the dehumanizing process of capitalist production overcomes him. Marx attributed this alienation of the worker from the fruits of his toil to private property, whose final form he identified polemically with the capitalist regime of the early part of his century. This identification enabled him to argue that, just as the theoretical union between man and nature depends upon the abolition of religion and belief in God, so their practical union depends upon the abolition of private property. In this way, the negative and positive aspects of Marxist humanism are inseparable; the one cannot stand in independence of the other.

In the ideal communistic society, labor provides the dynamic connecting link between man and nature. For, under optimum conditions, nature becomes wholly responsive to human needs and desires, while conversely man becomes reconciled to a this-worldly destiny in his purely natural environment. Nature is humanized in the precise proportion that man is naturalized. This brings to light the utopian motif behind Marxian scientific socialism. The hope is that when the forces and relations of production are sufficiently transformed by social revolution, labor will cease to be an instrument of exploitation and enslavement. It will become the sure means of realizing Marx's paramount ideal, the perfect union of man and nature. He refers to this

227

final condition indifferently as a naturalistic humanism and a humanistic naturalism. Although he distinguishes this goal of human history from Hegel's notion of a fully articulated system of absolute thought, Marx is equally sure that history does have a definite goal and that human development is subject to an immanent, necessary law, leading to this consummation of our endeavors.

3. So far, Marx's analyses have dealt with man, rather than with men. But modern economic and social history witnesses to a separation of one individual from another, as well as a separation of man from nature and his work.[7] The social character of human existence needs to be justified just as much as its foundation in nature and labor. The tendency of empiricism is to reduce everything to the individual human perceiver, who becomes the subjective measure of reality. This fits in with the capitalist policy of treating men as separate wares and cost units of production. Men are thus separated from each other, both at the theoretical level and in the practical world.

Marx proposed to remedy both types of division, because they threaten to destroy the social essence of man. In his doctrine on labor, he found a way of achieving a double refutation. Perception and other phases of knowledge are not independent processes. They have no self-contained, purely speculative significance. Knowledge is essentially a pragmatic activity: it is ordained to practice and to the fulfillment of human bodily needs. These needs are satisfied only through labor, and consequently the knowing process always bears an intrinsic ordination to the material world. Since this connection is a common feature for all individuals and since their point of reference is the common material world, the separation of one individual perceiver from another can be removed in the theoretical order. Similarly, the practical sphere of production is dominated by the requirements of labor. Now, labor is basically a social task, a testimony to the social character of human nature. Hence, Marx considers as antihumanistic any economic arrangement that violates the social unity of the human race by setting men in competition with each other, instead of encouraging peaceful cooperation among workers.

Marxian social humanism stands at the opposite pole from individualism, which it regards as an abstract way of viewing man. Because work is cooperative activity, it manifests the concrete essence of man as being social or collective. Only social man is really human. Marx intends this statement to be understood as literally as possible. On numerous occasions, he remarks that the "really human man" is found only in the social organism, since only in the collectivity of work is the condition of human conformity with, and control over, nature fully realized. Work molds individuals into being not just men (abstract individuals) but man (the concrete social whole). Whereas Hegel referred to the Absolute as the concrete universal reality, Marx reserved this privileged designation for the community of workers organized into the social collectivity. Here alone is the true character of human reality achieved in its fullness.

In recapitulation, Marxist humanism is centered around three factors: nature, work, and the social organism. These three notes have a definite metaphysical significance, since in defining man's genuine condition, they also define the only reality acknowledged by the Marxian mind. Furthermore, these three factors must be taken together, rather than in isolation from each other. For instance, it is not enough to maintain indeterminately that the sealed globe of man-in-nature constitutes the totality of being. Marxism wants to establish the specific way in which man is related to the rest of material nature: primarily, through the bond of labor, which provides an objective standard for both his states of knowledge and his cultural products. It also seeks to make it clear that empirical, individual men find their adequate human essence only by sharing in the collective work of society, which alone embodies humanity as a distinctive mode of natural being. When all these conditions are jointly realized, then Marxist man can be regarded as attaining social freedom, the only sort of freedom and value. Only the *collectivity-of-workers-in-relation-to-nature* is genuinely free, since only here are the necessary laws of human nature fully developed.

This three-pronged humanism can readily be restated in terms of dialectical and historical materialism, which is the more familiar form of Marxist doctrine. The secret of the attracting power of dialectical, historical materialism lies in its correlation with Marxist humanism. This humanistic orientation of the doctrine has motivated men to make great sacrifices for its spread and practical realization.

Marx himself was never too happy about the term "materialism." [8] It did serve as a handy club to wield against the idealists, who tried in vain to reduce the world to a mode of thought and man to a center of speculation. The term was also useful to convey Marx's denial of God and any immaterial reality in man. But "materialism" had an embarrassing connotation, too, since it seemed to league Marxism with the so-called scientific materialism of the Enlightenment and the nineteenth-century. Marx had two objections against the latter school: it supported economic individualism and it regarded matter as something intrinsically low and static. If matter is low and static, then it cannot account for the human world of agencies and qualitative values. Hence Marx recommended a broad and dynamic conception of matter which is indistinguishable from the totality of nature itself. By definition, then, anything that is discoverable in nature has an origin in matter. Man is wholly the product of matter, in the sense that he is a completely natural being and owes his makeup to natural forces. By equating matter and nature, Marx gave to the former a capacious but vague meaning. His successors have been obliged to alternate between trying to find some precise significance for matter and yet trying to include within its scope all the objects of human experience.

Marx's materialism is dialectical, since his naturalism embraces within itself the dualism between what is and what ought to be.[9] If all the cleavages and conflicting principles of life are systematically included within the field of nature, then nature or the material world is subject to the law of development among opposites. Hegel called this law a dialectical one, since the extremes clash with each other and also combine to produce new forms of being. Although Marx rejected the Hegelian view that the laws of dialectic express the nature of the Absolute, he did place the dialectical development at the heart of matter, so that the latter might have a dynamic principle. Since he made matter dynamic in a dialectical way, he was committed to the general principle that all genuine advances spring out of a contradiction between opposing forces.

In humanistic language, the dialectical tension is found primarily in the relation between man, as a worker, and nature as the field of his labor. The main area of dialectical conflict is located in the social economy, which comprises the forces and relations of production instituted between man and nature as well as between man and man. The process of humanizing nature and naturalizing man is the supreme instance of a dialectical transaction. Its mainspring is human labor, which is therefore the key to all human progress. This is the reason why Marx claims that the changing relations of productive forces constitute the radical and ultimate determinant of human cultural institutions and history. "In the final analysis," the structure of the economic forces and relations determines all human beliefs and institutions, provided that the analysis rests upon the Marxian humanistic premise that man's labor or economic production is his most characteristic activity.

Finally, the historical aspect of dialectical materialism has a humanistic significance.[10] Man's labor is the motive force of history, on condition that the relation between labor and the natural environment is preserved. Now, since labor manifests the human essence as something social, the Marxian interpretation of history is based upon social classes, rather than upon individual agents. And because historical change must conform with the dialectical law of clashing opposites, Marx has a priori assurance that history is constituted not only by social classes, but more precisely by the conflicts between these classes. Thus, the revolutionary approach to history is not merely an induction from history or a propaganda device; essentially, it is a requirement for the dialectical development of the new humanism.

The outstanding question is: When will history reveal to men at large the Marxian truth that only social man is truly human man? The answer is given, not in chronological terms, but in function of the revolutionary view of history. If all great historical changes are the consequence of dialectical oppositions among men in respect to their economic relations, then the culminating upheaval leading to communist society will have its prelude in the greatest conceivable contrast between opposing social classes. This is found in the antagonism between the capitalist owners and the dispossessed proletariat. The latter class is the farthest removed from the idyllic picture Marx has painted of the true essence of work and social man. Precisely because the proletariat is so utterly dehumanized under capitalism, it generates dialectically within itself sufficient creative force to carry through the supreme social revolution. This involves the passage from a world of class warfare to a world of classless social humanism. Class man is only fragmentary man, whereas classless man is integrally human man. When the worldwide revolution of the proletariat is consummated, class-ridden man will have overcome his alienations and fragmentations. The verdict of history is to be, at the same time, the vindication of the truth of Marxist humanism.

This provides us with a clue to a disconcerting trait about Marxist humanism. It seems to oscillate indecisively between excessive pessimism and excessive optimism about man and his capacities. Actually, these extremes are deliberately regulated by the underlying theory of the historical dialectic of revolutions. The latter demands that all creative advances arise from class warfare and that the ultimate revolution (leading to the definitive and worldwide introduction of communist classless society) be the outcome of a clash between the exclusive possessors of productive means and a class that is totally dispossessed. It is to the interest of this doctrine of social revolution, then, that all working men be aggregated to the proletariat, and that this class be depicted as being not only completely deprived of productive ownership but also totally bereft of humane values.

Hence Marx is under a systematic necessity to extend the condition of the proletariat as much as possible and to describe its lot as an utter dehumanization. His purpose is not to spread gloom and resentment, but primarily to produce the precise favorable conditions for the total overthrow of oppression and the arrival of communist humanism. The revolutionary technique of a deliberate worsening of social conditions is dictated not so much by hard hearted cynicism as by a burning faith in the necessary laws of the social dialectic. This vision of Marxist humanism animates the revolutionary work of bringing class warfare to its ultimate pitch, where it overcomes itself in securing the advent of thoroughly socialized man.

2. *Dewey's Experimentalist Humanism*

The transition from strict Marxism to the experimentalism of the average American naturalist introduces us to quite a different intellectual atmosphere. One prominent difference is the lack of any sacred scripture comparable to the writings of Marx and Engels. It is impossible to fix upon any basic text upon which all experimentalists agree as a minimal platform for their position. Hence it is risky to try to give any generalizations that will hold good for the entire group. The most that can be done is to describe some fairly representative trends, to which there are admittedly a good many exceptions. In fact, the cultivation of a hardly pluralism of beliefs—up to a certain point—is a hallmark of the experimentalist mind, which is not so insistent upon doctrinal uniformity as is its Marxist counterpart. But at least it is possible to determine with some accuracy the boundary line, beyond which one ceases to be an experimentalist in good standing.

What may be called the native mood of naturalistic humanism in America was best expressed in the writings of John Dewey. He came closest to providing a basic rallying point for the several varieties of experimentalist naturalism. As he embodied it, the experimentalist mood consists partly in a repudiation of theistic values and partly in a prudent appeal to scientific method. The former aspect provides the moving emotional inspiration for a this-worldly heroism, whereas the latter conveys a sense of the reasonableness and inevitability of the experimentalist standpoint. The combination is irresistible for many generous people who are spiritually adrift and who hope that science can provide authoritative guidance and sure methods. Instead of treating Dewey's thought genetically, as we did in the previous chapter, our present aim is to examine his mature naturalistic conception of man and to make the comparison with Marx.

Nature is the all-encompassing whole, to which our entire allegiance is owed. There is no God beyond the natural order and no human immortality, reaching beyond the temporal end of our existence. To seek after God or to regulate one's conduct by a supposed divine law is worse than illusion: it is an attitude which is treasonous to one's manhood and nature itself.[11] Only he who cannot bear the full truth of man's predicament in the natural world will turn to God and a divine law for guidance and strength. Dewey regards the repudiation of any reality beyond nature as the touchstone of authentic experimentalist humanism. Whoever fails to pass this test is guilty of "a failure of nerve" and hence must call upon supernatural help.

Those with sufficient manly fortitude must learn to work out their destiny solely within the context of nature and with nothing more than the resources of human nature. We should not imagine that nature as a whole entertains any bias in man's favor, since it is not regulated by any divine providential purpose. We have to carve out our own opportunities for the good life, with the sole help of the scientific method. It enables us to secure progressively more control over nature and to organize human society for the wider satisfaction of our various needs. Human values are completely our own creation. They admit of many degrees, but they can make no valid pretense of surpassing their natural origin and direction. Human activities can transform nature, but they cannot transcend it.

This naturalistic creed is more definite in its negations than in its affirmations. Negatively, it characterizes itself as being antidualistic and antireductionist. Experimentalist humanism seeks to remove all the dualisms that govern our traditional thinking, especially the twofold contrast erected between nature and the supernatural and between nature and man. In order to justify this policy, the theistic *distinction* between God and nature is interpreted to mean an *antagonism*, in which the reality of the one or the other is jeopardized. Hence experimentalists consider it impossible to accept both the eternal and the temporal, both the unchanging and the changing. They warn that admission of the reality of the eternal would empty out all significance from the temporal order, and that belief in an immutable being is incompatible with full acceptance of our world of change.

233

American naturalists concur with Nietzsche's aphorism that he who remains loyal to the earth is sworn enemy to the transcendent God. The dualism between the natural and the supernatural is removed by the simple expedient of denying the possibility of harmony between the two realms and eliminating the latter.

The second sort of dualism placed under attack is that between man and nature, mind and body. Again it is by way of reaction against an unacceptable doctrine that experimentalist humanism specifies its own position. The dualistic views of man propounded by Descartes and Kant are regarded as the "traditional" ones. What Descartes says about the relation of mind and body the experimentalists have taken to be a continuation of the medieval teaching on soul and matter, despite historical research into the basic differences. Experimentalists rebel against viewing the body as a mere prison-house for the soul and against locating the essence of the self in man's mind alone. This Cartesian depreciation of bodily values in favor of a purely mentalistic or spiritualistic conception of man does not square with our experience. Man is a single whole in which there are no deep chasms separating mind and body. Instead of seeking a non-Cartesian way of explaining the distinction between the intellectual and material principles in man, however, experimentalism holds that an immaterial principle is totally irreconcilable with the unity of human nature. If something must be sacrificed, let it be the immaterial principle rather than the unitary nature of man.

Another dualism which naturalistic experimentalism criticizes is the Kantian one between knowledge and faith. Kant had rigorously limited the sphere of knowledge to the content of the mathematical and physical sciences. Since these sciences deal only with objects existing in the world of space and time, Kant was also obliged to confine strict knowledge to the field of spatial and temporal objects. Hence, he had to devise some other form of cognition, in order to take account of our acquaintance with our own freedom and immortality, as well as the reality of God. Kant concluded that man can reach God and can grasp himself as a free agent and immortal being only through faith, not through knowledge. By faith he did not mean adhesion to a revealed truth, but only a kind of cognitive acquaintance that does not employ the scientific method and contents.

This distinction is intolerable to American naturalism for two reasons. First, it supposes that there are realities other than the world of space and time, i.e., real modes of being that are not thoroughly contained within material nature. In the second place, it supposes that the scientific method is not in principle coextensive with the cognizable real order and that, therefore, there are some reaches of real being that are cognitively accessible only to some non-scientific method. For experimentalism, on the contrary, whatever is real is natural, both in the sense of not being supernatural and in the sense of being available in principle only to scientific knowledge. Since nature is ultimately defined by experimentalist thinkers in terms of what falls within the scope of the scientific method, they must defend at all costs the sole reliability of one method and one type of knowledge.

At this juncture, however, experimentalists realize that they are apt to run into absurdities, if they press their antidualistic campaign to the point of denying the evident variety and qualitative differences among things and values. Hence they try to counterbalance the monism of nature and scientific method by the principle of antireductionism. This means that the discovery of causes and conditions for some fact of experience does not entail the reduction of the given fact to the evolutionary level of its causes and conditions. Like Marxism, experimentalist humanism is opposed to old-fashioned materialism, which claimed that the higher phases of human experience are "nothing but" matter in motion. Dewey's experimentalism proclaims its hospitality toward new evolutionary emergents, new qualitative developments in nature and human experience—but with the proviso that this recognition of fuller modes of being does not entitle one to infer the existence of God or an immaterial principle in man.[12] For such an inference would break the biological continuity of life and would place some modes of being beyond the competence of scientific inquiry to ascertain and study. Experimentalism seeks to reconcile both the antireductionist thesis that new values are not simply resolvable into their components and elements and the antidualistic thesis that God and the immortal soul of man violate the unity of nature and scientific method.

Within the experimentalist perspective, man is studied both as an individual and as a social being. From the former standpoint, he is analyzed by concepts that adhere to the basic pattern set by biology, whereas in his social aspects he is treated according to sociological procedures (which themselves have a remote biological origin). The predominance of biology and sociology as tools of scientific inquiry into human nature is a legacy from both Darwinian evolutionism and Comte's positivism, just as the monism of nature and method is a legacy from Hegel's idealism. The effect of this twofold approach is that experimentalism can treat of man, the biological and social unit, without ever coming to grips with man precisely as a person.[13] The methodological commitments of experimentalism lead it to propound a humanism minus the human person.

Dewey's biological interpretation of knowledge contains a double advantage for his view of man. First, it strengthens the plan of treating the knowing process in much the same way as any vital interchange between an organism and its environment. This favors the evolutionary theory that human consciousness developed from animal instinct. At the same time the biological approach to knowledge does underline the vital character of cognition and does encourage a realistic account of the process. Although experimentalist humanism leans toward the idealistic side in respect to the totality of nature, it also recognizes that man is influenced by the real forces existing in the natural environment and that knowing involves an assimilation of data received from the material world. Secondly, the biological pattern of knowledge emphasizes the initiative of the knower, who does not remain entirely passive in the reception of data. There is a vital adaptation of the materials of knowledge to the needs of the knower, just as any organism shapes its materials toward the preservation and improvement of its own condition. In this respect, William James' comparison between the adaptive functions of the organism and the process of cognition has exerted great influence upon the experimentalist conception of the human individual. Because a parallel can be established, experimentalist humanism concludes that no special soul or immaterial principle is needed to account for human cognition.

Although pragmatism as a strict theory of truth is no longer widely held, the pragmatic emphasis upon discernible empirical consequences is retained by experimentalism. It regards man the knower as involved essentially in a process of adjustment to his environment and as employing knowledge as a practical means of satisfying his needs and desires. Dewey's general polemic against the eternal aspects of being carries over into a criticism of what he calls the "spectator" attitude toward knowledge.[14] He fears that a purely speculative concern for eternal objects will lead to a depreciation of knowledge of practical and temporal affairs and will paralyze the vital response on the part of the knower. Some of Dewey's followers have given a very liberal interpretation to the "observable consequences" that must follow from reliable knowledge, in order to make room for theoretical discoveries. But experimentalist humanism remains basically activistic: it distrusts the contemplative life for man. Contemplation must be formally subordinated to action or it loses all standing in the experi-

236

mentalist scale of values. This antagonism toward untrammeled contemplation follows from the naturalistic foundation of the experimentalist outlook. For the human operation of contemplating tends to break through the carefully sealed borders of nature, in search of God's eternal life. It makes a claim to reach not merely some permanent aspect of nature but the eternal being of God, and this claim cannot be tested by the scientific method, as naturalistically conceived. It is also extremely difficult to justify contemplation on any social grounds, given the experimentalist dedication of society to an exclusively this-worldly set of goods.

The sociological treatment of human knowledge and action is a further mark of experimentalist humanism. Man is viewed both as an organism in relation to the natural environment and as a member of the social whole. Our outlook is determined not only by influences received from the material world, but also by intercourse with the community of men. The process of practical adjustment has in view both a technical control of nature and a social control of men, the latter being based upon mutual understanding. Hence the practical consequences of knowledge bear an even more important relation to the community of men than to the natural environment. Dewey expresses this primacy of the social relationship by affirming that the cultural matrix of knowing and acting is more decisive than the biological matrix. For it is primarily as members of the social group that we think and act. Our human values are measured by their aptitude to promote the social integration of individuals and dynamic satisfaction of their needs.

Although belief in God is regarded as a dangerous drain on social energies, there is a place for religious feeling within the experimentalist conception of society. Experimentalist humanism is antitheistic but not unqualifiedly antireligious. Dewey distinguishes sharply between religions and religiousness, criticizing the former and offering his own interpretation of the latter. The religions comprise the various Churches and creeds, which accept a God distinct from nature and which preach a supernatural way of salvation. To the extent that these extra-natural factors are emphasized and made the determinants of personal conduct and public policy, there is no room for the churches in secular society. The experimentalist tendency is not merely to eliminate all the churches from political life, but also to reduce their effectiveness as extra-natural agencies in private life. Institutional religion serves no legitimate function, unless it agrees to become orientated in a completely naturalistic direction and hence to serve as one

237

subordinate instrument of social integration. Religious feeling, on the other hand, is the sense of dedication to a social ideal. It is the attitude of regarding the welfare of the experimentalist community as the highest human good and of devoting all one's strength to its betterment. The utterness of one's dedication to the common welfare is the only valid religious meaning for the absolute.[15] Even then, it must be kept in mind that social needs and means of satisfaction are subject to constant modification and development.

Any other significance attached to the religious spirit is treated by Dewey as an antisocial illusion, since it diverts interest and endeavor away from the natural world of temporal values. This is the systematic import behind the currently popular, pejorative use of the term "divisive." Whereas differences of opinion within the context of naturalism are respected as a healthy pluralism and tradition of dissent, any differences that radically challenge the naturalistic postulate itself and its social consequences are treated as socially dangerous. A religion is socially divisive, insofar as it gives practical credence to a divine law and attempts to mold personal and social conduct in conformity with norms that look beyond the closed sphere of temporal society in its natural setting.

A radical clash is also inescapable between a theistic and a naturalistic view of moral law and the moral purposes of society, since naturalism does not admit that moral reason shares in any way the perfection of divine wisdom and law. Hence naturalistic experimentalism is perhaps more keenly aware than theism of the hopelessness of trying to reach agreement on the basis of natural law and the dictates of natural reason. For it realizes that the theoretical dispute about the status of nature has its practical counterpart in a dispute concerning natural morality and the moral exercise of reason. The divisive effect of theistic humanism is unavoidable, wherever the experimentalist view of society and law prevails as the standard. Whereas theists believe that the word of God cleaves in a salutary way, experimentalists deem conduct based upon the word of God to be inimical to the best interests of society. Yet if "divisiveness" were understood to mean a challenge to the adequacy of experimentalist humanism, rather than a threat to social institutions and order, the term would be used with much more accuracy and much less persuasive effect than is customary in current social and political discussions.

Naturalistic experimentalism denies that moral concepts can be based upon any permanent, essential traits and relations in man. Men are subject to fundamental changes, both as individuals and as members of the social group. Moral judgments can be framed only with respect to specific and developing situations, so that we should not look for any universal norms of conduct. The evolutionary character of morality fits in with the experimentalist contention that our values are determined by their consequences. Since the consequences of human action for the individual and society depend upon the flux of circumstances, we must refrain from according any absolute and permanent significance to our moral values.

Experimentalist humanism looks for a new basis of moral obligation apart from any foundation in the divine nature and divine sanction. Some experimentalists remove obligation entirely from the sphere of knowledge and equate it with an intensely experienced feeling. When a man says that he must perform a certain action, he is expressing a feeling of compulsion which has its origin in some psychological or semantic association connected with his proposed plan. Another explanation comes close to what Kant would call a technical or pragmatic imperative, envisaging the useful relation between an action and a goal. An individual may choose a certain value as being supremely important for him. In relation to this chosen value, certain actions leading to it will now assume the aspect of necessary means to the end. If he wants to attain that specific value, then he is obliged to use these definite means to acquire it. But, experimentalist thinkers quickly point out, there is no telling what an individual or a society may chose as its paramount value. One man's end may be another man's means, or it may be treated as a means by the same individual, in other circumstances. Man is confronted with no fixed and eternal ends. Hence there are no universally valid standards of moral obligation. They are entirely relative to his choice, with the latter determined by the available, ever-evolving conditions of his nature and environment.

Although naturalistic humanism foregoes any unconditionally ultimate ends and duties, it does suggest that social adequacy provides a working criterion for individual and social choice.[16] Those individual acts and social measures are morally good, which tend to promote the wider distribution of the values underlying the naturalistic outlook. Julian Huxley agrees with Dewey in accepting this minimal criterion. The freedom of secular intelligence to pursue its inquiries, unhampered by opposing philosophies and institutions, is one such social good. The constant broadening of opportunities for education, work and cultural experience constitutes another steady goal. Experimentalist man faces toward the future, much more than toward the past. His destiny lies wholly in his own hands, so that he need not seek support from history or benevolent nature. Cooperative, democratic effort in shaping social agencies in conformity with scientific inquiries provides him with his chief hope. Law is a pragmatic instrument for satisfying the needs of all groups joined in the wider community. Law expresses the resolves of social intelligence to keep pace with these changing needs and with the new techniques supplied by science for meeting them.

3. *The Common Fund of Humanistic Naturalism*

A comparison between the humanisms of Marx and Dewey brings out some significant similarities and differences which are helpful in charting the present course for a theistic humanism. It also suggests certain methods to be followed in dealing with these philosophies.

Taken by itself, the term "humanism" is a relatively neutral word conveying only a minimum of definite meaning. It has been used at various periods of history to designate standpoints that are often in direct contradiction to each other. The term has no inherent eulogistic significance and should be employed, at the outset of a discussion, in a purely descriptive way. Descriptively speaking, a doctrine is humanistic insofar as it concerns itself largely with the problem of man's nature and destiny and accords to man some prominence and dignity, within the total view of the universe. This would exclude a small number of explanations in which man's cosmic status is insignificant, but it would apply to most of the important Western philosophies.

This minimal meaning deliberately refrains from specifying how the nature of man is regarded or what principle is used to defend his dignity. Such a descriptive minimum can cope, therefore, with the familiar situation in which two conflicting systems accuse each other of being antihumanistic. They may both be humanisms, in the broadest preliminary sense of being preoccupied with the question of human nature and its values. But they may disagree violently with each other concerning man's distinctive constitution and his relation to the cosmos. It is at this second or explanatory level that the clashes become meaningful. From the standpoint of his own account of man's nature, one thinker may then regard another explanation as being fundamentally antihumanistic. This supposes, however, that a certain doc-

240

trinal standard is now being used to evaluate various ways of viewing the human condition.

We have already noted that our age is characterized by the co-presence of several counter-humanisms. Marxism, Deweyan experimentalism, and realistic theism all fulfill the first or descriptive meaning of humanism, because they are all centrally concerned with our human destiny. In the second or explanatory sense of humanism, they exhibit differences of various kinds. Hence, the theistic doctrine on man is bound to be charged with antihumanistic implications from the doctrinal standpoints of Marxism and Dewey's experimentalism. This indictment settles nothing about the adequacy of the theistic view of man, however, but merely registers differences in the respective ways of explaining human nature and its dignity. Consequently, the effort must continually be made to get behind the term "humanism" to the metaphysical and methodological issues really at stake. One must work back patiently from the descriptive to the doctrinal sense of the word. Only after the opposing positions concerning the structure of being and the method of knowledge are examined, are we in a position to supply cogent reasons for regarding the theistic doctrine on man as the most adequate form of humanism. Once the various humanisms are qualified in meaningful ways and given a metaphysical evaluation, purely rhetorical and self-laudatory use of the term "humanism" can be avoided.

A second procedural rule for the comparative study of humanisms brings further clarification to a confused situation. Theistic realists are bound by a two-fold positive commitment: to maintain intact the theistic truth about man and to acknowledge and appropriate sound anthropological insights, regardless of where they originate. All of our critical activities should be regulated by these two positive aims, lest our examination of other doctrines degenerate into nagging faultfinding or blind, total negation. The execution of these aims is specified in large measure, however, by the character of the doctrine under examination, so that the concrete evaluations made by theistic humanism will differ from case to case. Perhaps the most important question to ask is whether the doctrine in question has been formulated in a systematic way or has been left in a more or less unorganized condition. In the latter case, it may be more difficult to gain a precise understanding of the total position, but it will be easier to detect and incorporate elements that are compatible with the theistic conception of man. Where the doctrine is highly systematized, just the opposite set of conditions prevails: to understand the view will be fairly easy, but to sort out the wheat from the chaff will be quite difficult.

An historical example of the unsystematic approach to man is the movement called Renaissance humanism. Actually, one should refer to the Renaissance humanisms, since each thinker had his own distinctive explanation. The Renaissance humanists were men of apt quotation and pithy saying rather than patient builders of massive systems. On the contrary, Marxism and (to a lesser degree) Dewey's experimentalism show a concern for systematic development and organization of doctrines. This makes the task of grasping their teaching an easier one, but it renders the work of criticism proportionately more difficult. For we are not confronted with single observations that can be readily detached and weighed for their own sake, but rather with an organic unity in which each particular proposition is intimately bound up with a whole network of closely related propositions. Patience is needed to estimate justly the worth of each assertion about the nature of man and his world.

One method of handling this situation is to ask, in proper order, the following four questions. What is the underlying central principle that orders and unifies all the other doctrines? What is the meaning of some single doctrine, considered precisely in its organic relation to the animating principle of the entire system? Does this particular doctrine have any significance and any factual basis, even apart from its incorporation into the given system? If so, can that separable meaning and its factual basis be included within the context of a theistic humanism? If such questions are asked as a matter of regular policy, when the varieties of humanism are under consideration, then a constructive and discriminating approach can be developed to the problem of competing humanisms.

The first above-mentioned question can be posed in regard to both the Marxist and the Deweyan brands of humanism. A paradoxical situation is encountered when one inquires about the fundamental principle organizing these systems. There is, indeed, one rock-bottom conviction held in common by the two philosophies. And yet each gives its own characteristic interpretation of this common premise and employs it in a distinctive systematic way. The methods of explaining and applying the common foundation differ in several respects, so that Marxist and experimentalist humanisms sometimes run a common course and sometimes diverge in considerable degree. Both the basis of agreement and the points of difference must be firmly held in view, if we are to understand these two humanisms accurately.

Marx and Dewey shape their conceptions of man in the light of one basic common affirmation: nature is the self-sufficing totality of being, of which man and the rest of the material world are component parts. This is the dogma of naturalism, which is the common doctrinal fund shared by both Marxism and experimentalism. Both are varieties of naturalistic humanism, which excludes God and an immortal soul and concentrates the whole of reality in self-founded nature. Marx explicitly defines his teaching on man as a naturalistic humanism or humanistic naturalism. Dewey also accepts naturalism and its equivalence between being and nature. Since both systems base the dignity of man upon the naturalistic postulate, they manifest a common pathos or way of expressing the feel-for-the-human. On the stipulation that human dignity rests on a courageous recognition of the independence and sufficiency of nature, God appears to be an intruder from without, and any religious bond with Him is subversive of the proper human order. Antitheism and antisupernaturalism are counted as the sure marks of genuine humanism. If there is any help for man, it cannot be summoned from beyond the sphere of natural being.

A common naturalistic parentage leads both Marx and Dewey to oppose dualisms of every sort. They even regard the distinction between man and nature as a loose mode of speech, unless it be explicitly pointed out that this is a distinction between a part and the whole within which the part is included. They contend that to say that man and *the rest of* nature constitute the plenum of real being being means that man is real only insofar as he is treated as a part of nature. Furthermore, man is a part of nature not because he is one kind of being among others commonly created by God, but because he is a member of the autonomous realm of natural being. The dualism between mind and body also comes under the common fire of experimentalist and Marxist humanism. Although the immediate point of departure for their criticism is dissatisfaction with modern dualistic views of man, the full sweep of their negations includes every theory of a distinctive immaterial principle in human nature. Both forms of naturalism are hard pressed to establish the precise basis of difference between themselves and what they scornfully call old-fashioned materialism. They advocate a dynamic, qualitative conception of matter, equipping it with sufficient capacities to bring forth all the varieties of objects of our experience. But this subtilization of matter empties it of all distinctive meaning and renders it simply the equivalent of being and nature. Marxism and experimentalist naturalism jointly subscribe to the irremediably trivial proposition that matter (i.e., being) brings forth whatever is (i.e., has being).

The converse side of this opposition to dualisms in being is an opposition to dualisms in method and knowledge. If man is in every respect bound to nature and of one kind with all other material things, then the same method must embrace the study of man and the rest of nature. There cannot be one method employed in the so-called natural sciences and a different one reserved for the so-called humane disciplines. All departments of knowledge have a naturalistic basis, in that they commonly study natural events by means of a single method. Marxism and Dewey's experimentalism agree in calling this single method of gaining reliable knowledge "the scientific method." Admittedly, they do not derive this monism of method from any one of the existing sciences, since the latter do not include any claim of omnicompetence for the investigation of all modes of being. Rather, there is a philosophical source for the monism of method in naturalism. The postulate about a single method is a correlate of the metaphysical postulate about the unity and self-sufficiency of nature. It is employed by both varieties of naturalism for polemical purposes, even more than for the construction of a positive system. Appeal to scientific method is intended as a foil for the stubborn obscurantism of non-naturalistic humanists, who are depicted as futilely resisting the inevitable extension of empirical reason to all areas of human experience.

Once this generic unanimity concerning nature and scientific method is sufficiently emphasized, however, the specific differences between the Marxist and Deweyan versions of humanistic naturalism must also be recognized, even at the level of first principles. The main divergence is seen in their respective attitudes toward the empirical sciences. The basic Marxist convictions about human nature are not founded upon the empirical sciences, but upon the Hegelian dialectic. Friedrich Engels, it is true, tried to dress up Marxism in the garments of empirical science by furnishing empirical confirmation of the Marxist theories about nature, property, the family, and the state. The grotesque character of some of his arguments foreshadowed the present Soviet manner of drawing philosophical lessons from the sciences. Marxism sometimes tries to make strategic use of scientific materials, but it does not draw its strength and guidance from such sources. American experimentalist humanism, on the contrary, does show fundamental respect for the temper and findings of practicing scientists. It retains a close continuity with the biological and social sciences, although its link with mathematical physics is rather tenuous. The program of broadening the generalizations of the natural sciences is carried out more faithfully by experimentalism than by Marxism.

This principal difference can be stated as a contrast between a dialectical and a non-dialectical conception of man-in-nature. In closing the gap between what is and what ought to be, Marx inscribed the law of what ought to be at the heart of nature itself. For him, the entire material world is impregnated with an immanent and necessitating dialectic. The dialectical law of nature is purposive or directed toward an end; human history is similarly regulated by the march of the dialectic toward its consummation. Marx specified that end in both cosmological and sociological terms. From the latter standpoint, the dialectic of human history is orientated toward the classless, communist society. But this goal is bound up with the cosmic reconciliation between man and nature, since neither the productive relations nor the system of cultural beliefs and institutions will be sufficiently transformed to permit the appearance of worldwide communism, until man and nature are thoroughly integrated. Both the universe as a whole and human society are moving forward together, under the impetus of the dialectic, toward the assured plenary realization of naturalistic humanism.

For Marxism, the scientific method refers primarily to an understanding of the dialectic and the techniques for its advancement. There are serious speculative difficulties concerning the way to reconcile human initiative and dialectical necessity, but they do not stand in the way of an enthusiastic, practical adherence to the Marxist conception of history and class struggle. The Marxist mind is fully confident that the injustices of modern industrial society can be overcome, since these forms of dehumanization are dialectically required to generate, and give way before, the humanism of communist society. Both natural process and history are on the side of this new humanism.

Since he regards himself as the heir of the entire dialectical development, Marxist man has a lively sense of his historical mission and redemptive function. The new birth of nature and humanity depends upon his own efforts to realize the dialectical development, as it converges toward its final term. In one sense, truly human history does not begin until the oppositions characterizing a class-ridden society are removed. Marxist man looks upon the ages preceding the communist organization of the world as pre-history, but a pre-history leading inexorably to the full historical realization of naturalistic humanism in communist society. The only obligation he acknowledges is that of assuring the imminent triumph of the Marxist conception of social man which will usher in the genuinely historical and humane epoch of human existence.

Dewey's experimentalist man is satisfied, on the contrary, with a somewhat bleaker and more modest prospect. He repudiates the Marxist notion that nature is on man's side, that there is some purposeful dialectic operative in nature for man's special benefit. He regards this as a lingering superstition due to Marx's failure to banish entirely the Hegelian theory of a cosmic dialectical law. For the experimentalist mind, a thorough-going naturalism requires man not only to refuse any supernatural assistance but also to refrain from reading any humane intentions into the rest of nature. The supreme expression of Promethean defiance is given by experimentalist man, who asks nothing of God and asks of nature only the chance to carve out his own domain of social life on earth.

Despite this secular asceticism, however, there are both cosmic and social grounds for entertaining a moderate optimism about man's predicament. What the laws of dialectic mean to Marxist man, the trend of evolution means to experimentalist man. The doctrine of man's total derivation from biological antecedents undermines the traditional basis for human dignity, but it also brings with it a confident feeling that the upward surge of life will continue to improve the lot of the human species. Once more, the positions of Dewey and Julian Huxley are remarkably similar. If nature is not friendly toward man, at least he can claim intimate kinship with the universal stream of life and can hope that the evolutionary process will enable him to control his environment and satisfy his needs.

In the social sphere, experimentalist naturalism is even more optimistic and provides a subdued equivalent of the messianic aspects of Marxist naturalism. Although Dewey's experimentalism lacks the grand design of dialectical, historical materialism, it finds in social intelligence its own providential principle. Man may never have been a sinner, but he has certainly conducted himself in ways that are unintelligent and antisocial. Experimentalist humanism appeals to cooperative inquiry as the sure means for saving our civilization from the mortal effects of social stupidity and perversity. Education and social planning are the main instruments of progress, because they enable the scientific method to form individual minds and organize social forces in a reasonable (i.e., naturalistic) way. There must be constant revaluation of policies in the light of new empirical materials and problems: this is the essence of social and political democracy.

Despite the setback of wars and totalitarianism, experimentalist humanism believes in social progress based upon evolutionary trends and rational inquiry. But it specifies that the rational inquiry in question must satisfy two conditions: it must be conducted along naturalistic lines, without being influenced by belief in God, immortality, and a divine law; it must also be social in method and orientation, rather than centered upon the needs of the isolated individual. Once these requirements are met, experimentalist man is confident in the ability of social intelligence to guide society along paths that will increasingly fulfill the legitimate aspirations of man.

In summary, then, Marxism and Deweyan experimentalism share a common generic foundation in humanistic naturalism. They agree upon the broadest definition of reality and the univocity of scientific method. Yet each constitutes a specifically different formulation of the naturalistic principle, depending upon acceptance or rejection of the laws of dialectical development. Balanced criticism of the Marxist and experimentalist views of man should reckon both with the first-level or generic agreement and with the second level or specific difference, in respect to naturalism. To dwell exclusively upon the former would detract from the accuracy and honesty of a critique; to accentuate only the latter would render a critique harmfully shortsighted and parochial.

The second and third questions previously formulated concern the way in which the central principle of naturalism affects the Marxist and experimentalist treatment of special issues, and whether these issues have a minimal meaning and factual basis, even apart from the naturalistic interpretation. These two questions belong together and should always be asked together. Moreover, the two elements of each question, *minimal meaning* and *factual basis,* must be jointly considered. If their proper unity is not resolutely preserved, non-naturalistic humanism becomes hopelessly entangled in a network of polemical objections. The offensive strategy of both Marxism and experimentalism is directed precisely toward forcing theistic humanists to pose these questions at separate times and places.

If the strategy of separation works, then the theistic humanist finds himself caught in an unenviable dilemma: (a) Should he approach a humanistic theme only insofar as it has been stamped with the mark of the naturalistic principle and incorporated into the naturalistic system, he is bound to stress his opposition. In that case, the naturalist

247

will concentrate discussion upon the factual basis and extra-systematic meaning, in order to convey the impression that realistic theism is opposed to these latter aspects as such and hence is essentially an antihumanist position. (b) The opposite procedure is followed, should the unwary theist agree to separate discussion of the factual descriptions and minimal meanings. While he is acknowledging the weight of the empirical evidence concerning the human condition, his naturalistic colleague is locating the results within the framework of his own system. The theistic humanist now appears to be lending support to the Marxist or experimentalist outlook as such.

The first alternative represents the "hard" side of naturalistic controversy, while the second one represents the "soft" side. The former is exemplified in any one of Dewey's frequent homilies on the Greek and medieval devaluation of man and the finite world; the latter is the governing rule behind the Marxist policies of the extended hand and the common front. Since both alternatives involve a misrepresentation of theistic humanism, it is worth the effort to refuse to separate the two questions of fact and interpretation, even though it makes the discussion somewhat cumbersome.

An example or two from our previous descriptions of Marxism and Dewey's experimentalism will illustrate the problem. Both schools protest against the Cartesian dualism of man and nature, mind and body. They are able to appeal to undeniable facts of ordinary experience. Nature is not a pure geometrical machine, stripped of real qualities and intrinsic causal agencies, as the Cartesian philosophy maintains. Similarly, mind and body are not two opposed substances which interact in some inexplicable way. The intimacy between our organic and mental states testifies to the composite unity of the one human self. These deliverances of our experience are not to be gainsaid; they testify to the soundness of the naturalistic rejection of Cartesian dualism. But these facts are no monopoly of naturalism and do nothing to strengthen the positive case for a naturalistic humanism. They merely indicate that rejection of excessive dualism is a condition that must be fulfilled by *any* humanism which respects the integral unity of man's nature. Hence, acceptance of the facts about human unity and the qualitative and causal aspects of nature is no presumption in favor of naturalism. There is no empirical basis for narrowing down the alternative to the Cartesian versus the naturalistic conception of man's nature.

Another capital instance of the hiatus between fact and systematic interpretation is presented by the Marxist treatment of labor. Marx

248

submitted a brilliant and acute report on the status of the worker in nineteenth-century industrial capitalism. He coupled a sensitive understanding of the workingman's plight with a vivid awareness of the perfecting and ennobling effect that work should have upon men. His remark about the degradation of men in the same factory where materials are perfected is a keen observation and agrees with the humanistic criticism made by realistic theism on the question of work. We are still confronted with the problem of how to counter the disintegrating effects of machine production and assembly-line specialization. Although some of Marx's ideas about the interchange of occupations bordered on the fantastic, he did have a firm grip upon the principle that work should develop rather than narrow the worker, and that it should be a source of joy and creative satisfaction to him and not a painful servitude, from which he escapes into the bliss of canned recreation. Marx also caught a glimpse of the redemptive function of human labor, in both its cosmic and its social significance.

These facts and meanings must be recognized by any humanism that wishes to function in our time. But their acceptance does not necessarily entail adoption of the Hegelian-Marxian concept of alienation as their systematic interpretative principle. Indeed, there are positive indications that Marx's use of the concept of alienation led him to distort the factual basis itself and to overlook historical developments that were in the making. His description of the proletariat as the class in which labor is totally divorced from control of its product and from all humanizing influences falls within his own category of vicious abstractions and ideological myths. For it does not take into account the real social power acquired by labor unions in our society and the new forms of property. The identification of private property with the capitalist regime is another frozen judgment dictated by the requirements of the dialectic, rather than by a direct continuing analysis of human affairs. If workingmen need not be destined for a proletariat class and if private property need not be confined to capitalism, then the Marxian antagonism between work and private property expresses no historical necessity and furnishes no norm of true humanism.

One further example of the need to discuss fact and systematic explanation together is furnished by the manner in which American naturalism applies evolution to morality and law. Dewey's experimentalism does its best to set up an antithesis between what it calls the temporalistic and the eternalistic views of man. It does so by treating separately the questions of fact and interpretation. From anthropology and other sciences, it draws some rich and arresting materials illustrative of the growth of moral and legal concepts. This evidence shows in detail how specific rules of morality and law develop in conformity with changing physical, cultural, and political circumstances. The inference is then drawn that because our moral and legal views are subject to growth and are affected by particular circumstances, therefore there can be no permanent and universal aspect in ethics and jurisprudence. Unfortunately, some theistic moralists are led by their opposition to this inference to deny or minimize the historical and developmental side of moral doctrine. This lack of discrimination then lends credence to the naturalistic contention that anyone who accepts the ordination of man toward the eternal life of God must be hostile to the temporal factors in human moral existence. But, according to the main tradition of theistic moral philosophy, the permanence of some universal moral principles is not only compatible with historical growth in moral insight, but positively demands a scrupulous concern for the variable and particular features of human life. The naturalistic interpretation of moral variability should not deflect us from a steady recognition of the empirical materials that require progressive incorporation into the body of theistic humanism today.

Finally, a lesson can be learned from a jocose remark, attributed to some American experimentalist humanists. "Modern philosophy—thank goodness, it is over with!" This saying implies that humanistic naturalism alone is in full accord with contemporary scientific method and that other doctrines on man are outmoded positions. From a more critical viewpoint, however, it yields another meaning: naturalists are immoderately relieved when their type of humanism ceases to be examined on historical grounds. It is not difficult to see why the historical approach to naturalistic humanism is not encouraged.

As far as Marxian naturalism is concerned, the iron clad necessity of its criticism of God and religion, as well as its verdicts on historical development, depends upon its adoption and adaptation of the Hegelian dialectic. Historical study of the relations between Hegel and Marx raises the question of the legitimacy of the latter's generalization of the particular philosophical situation prevailing in his own youth. When God and religion, nature and man, labor and property, are considered in the light of the various interpretations and institutional forms actually developed in human history, then the particular analysis made by Marxism loses its claim to be comprehensive and inevitable.

Much the same consequence follows when we view Dewey's humanistic naturalism in its historical context. The point of our last chapter was precisely to furnish some of the historical grounds for concluding that, in making his passage from idealism to naturalism, Dewey remained faithful in many decisive ways to his Hegelian heritage and retained far greater continuity than is sometimes supposed with the idealistic postulate of a single basic method of knowing nature and defining reality or natural being. We can apply here our previous twofold distinction between evolution and philosophical evolutionism, the study of nature and philosophical naturalism, as historically based evidence that Dewey's humanistic naturalism is not generated in solidarity with twentieth-century science but rests on a special philosophical interpretation.

In the two forms studied here, humanistic naturalism provides an attractive and powerful conception of modern man and his social destiny. But it is not the unavoidable position which must be shared by anyone who participates fully in the methods and opportunities of the physical and social sciences today. Not only does philosophical naturalism rest upon some unspoken premises which it fails to clarify and validate, but it also remains a partial interpretation of the human condition. Perhaps that is why existentialism has earned the right to be considered by contemporary minds. For it emphasizes just those aspects of personal integrity and personally based freedom which naturalism tends to glide over as being unimportant. Any constructive work done by realistic theism in the coming years on the meaning of man will have to rest upon a close understanding and patient evaluation of both the existentialist and the naturalist aspects of our integral human reality.

PART
THREE

THEISTIC REALISM

CHAPTER 10

THE PROBLEM OF A
PERENNIAL PHILOSOPHY

PHILOSOPHERS are a disputatious breed of men, but at least they all agree that the unexamined life is not worth living. Philosophical inquiry is a persistent effort to push back the region of unexamined convictions and prejudices ever farther, so that the work of critical sifting and testing may continue in an unimpeded way. This task is an unending one, and provides a measure for the worth of our speculative efforts. The more resolutely we face the issues raised by honest inquiry, the more intimately do we share in the spirit of philosophy.

At least among theistic philosophers, there is one notion which exerts wide influence today and yet which still lingers in the shade of unexamined opinions. This is the notion of a perennial philosophy. The emotional resonances of this ideal reach quite deeply into our souls, and yet we seldom bother to inspect its precise meaning and test its philosophical value. It may be worth while, then, to submit the idea of a perennial philosophy to sustained analysis, so that we can make an intelligent appraisal of the problems it entails. I propose to attempt this task in three stages. The first step will be to give a rapid review of some current Scholastic views on the subject. Next, considerably more attention will be paid to the non-Scholastic contributions to this issue than is usually the case. Finally, some critical evaluation will be made of the different conceptions of a perennial philosophy. The outcome will be to show that this notion is a thoroughly problematic one and, at the present time, belongs properly among the disputed questions confronting philosophers of every school.

1. *Some Scholastic Opinions on Perennial Philosophy*

It requires very little delving beneath the surface of verbal agreements to discover a wide variety of conflicting views about the nature of a perennial philosophy, even within what we can vaguely call Scholastic circles. Perhaps the most common use of the term is simply as a synonym for Scholastic philosophy in general. When "perennial philosophy" and "Scholasticism" are used interchangeably, the assumption is made that there is such a thing as a unified Scholastic philosophy. This latter position was maintained by Maurice De Wulf. At the end of his pioneering work, *History of Mediaeval Philosophy,* De Wulf included a synthetic study on what he called the common Scholastic patrimony left to us by the medievals.[1] Despite the doctrinal divergencies among the great thirteenth-century thinkers, he ascribed to them a tendency toward convergence at the higher plane of a community of basic doctrines. He instanced the widespread agreement concerning the nature and divisions of philosophy, as well as its distinction from theology, the reality of the finite individual and its real distinction from God, an objective and realistic view of the principles of knowledge and metaphysics, the demonstrability of God's existence, the freedom of human choice and the incorruptibility of the human soul. This fund of homogeneous doctrine serves as the common bond among Scholastics in medieval and modern times, and hence provides some definite content for the notion of a perennial philosophy.

De Wulf himself noted, however, that this Scholastic patrimony was largely dissipated by the developments in late medieval philosophy. Furthermore, he observed that, even during the high Middle Ages, the unity of thought was largely shaped by such extraphilosophical forces as a uniform feudal society, a common belief in the truths of Christianity, and a joint preoccupation with the social and spiritual consequences of the newly introduced body of Aristotle's writings. Both the internal conflicts and the pressure of social and theological motives became of central importance in the researches of Étienne Gilson. He focused attention upon the radically different conceptions of philosophy and philosophical demonstration which are to be found in Bonaventure and Aquinas, Scotus and Ockham. According to his findings, the strictly philosophical agreements among medieval thinkers are less significant and less extensive than their disagreements. Gilson traced the tendency toward uniformity mainly to the unity of the Christian faith, whereas he viewed the divergencies as springing

256

forth from properly philosophical sources. Hence he regarded the idea of a common Scholastic patrimony as a schematic construct, which wrings out most of the historical content from the rich diversity of medieval thought. The principles held in common take on quite different meanings, when they are incorporated into different concrete contexts of philosophical speculation. And agreement about the conclusions should not blind us to the contrasting methods by which these conclusions are arrived at, on the part of different thinkers. Both principles and conclusions must eventually be reset within the distinctive and irreducibly different bodies of medieval thought, which we discover in the actual texts. Gilson therefore substituted the notion of a Christian philosophy for that of a common Scholastic patrimony as a way of looking at the medieval period as a unity.

One could have calculated beforehand, perhaps, the effect which this difference of opinion between De Wulf and Gilson would have upon the concept of a perennial philosophy. Granting the presence of deep cleavages in the medieval thought, two courses lay open for anyone trying to stabilize the meaning of this concept. Either the differences could be regarded as irreducible or else an attempt could be made to bridge the gap and achieve a certain reconciliation. If the former alternative were accepted, then the norm of truth for a perennial philosophy could lie only in some one philosophy. This was the stand taken by certain Thomists and Scotists and Ockhamists, with regard to their respective masters. The other alternative led to a doctrine on the polar relation among all the varieties of medieval thought, so that the content of a perennial philosophy could be located in the interplay between the doctrines of the leading schools.

Because of the great practical influence of Thomism, the view that the perennial philosophy is equivalent to the philosophy of St. Thomas requires special attention. This identification was not made by the most eminent contemporary Thomists, but it had its appeal for certain minds, especially for those who were congenitally incapable of giving a sympathetic hearing to the problems and findings of other masters. According to this view, all previous philosophies serve merely as preparations, positive or negative, for the advent of Thomas, whereas later ones are useful mainly as foils for bringing out the truth of his doctrines. The totality of philosophical truth is found completely embodied in the Thomistic synthesis. It is the perennial philosophy, in the sense that it sets forth the answers to all our philosophical problems, once for all time. This is a caricature of the spirit of St. Thomas himself, but it does represent a widespread attitude on the part of those who are more anxious to have ready answers than to reason in a philosophical way.

It was inevitable that a reaction should set in against this summary settlement of the problem of a perennial philosophy. A solution was sought that would avoid the skeptical consequences of a mutual cancellation between the several forms of Scholastic thought, each of which might defend the complete and exclusive truth of its own position. A middle way was proposed by Father Przywara and is now being developed dialectically by some writers in Europe and America.[2] For convenience, we may refer to their standpoint as that of a philosophical *pluralism-in-principle*, to distinguish it from the *factual plurality* which will be discussed in the final chapter. It has a definite bearing upon the question of a perennial philosophy.

The key notions of philosophical pluralism-in-principle are polarity and analogy. One way to familiarize ourselves with this special meaning of polarity is to recall the traditional Catholic attitude toward the various religious orders and congregations. No single one of them claims a monopoly upon the religious life, and yet each of them cultivates a distinctive path toward holiness. It is only in the totality of these mutually helpful ways of life that we find an adequate expression of the religious state of Christian piety and action. By extending this theological consideration into the sphere of natural speculation, the view is reached that complete philosophical truth is not an exclusive possession of any one thinker or school. It shines forth only in the polar field of mutual relations established between the various positions. Their relationship is not of mutual contradiction and exclusion but rather of mutual supplementing and inclusion. What one school lacks, is supplied by another, so that from their dynamic interchange the life of the perennial philosophy draws its nourishment. It is the resultant synthesis of the positive elements in all the various schools, brought to polar convergence in a totality that welcomes and flourishes upon diversities.

In order to preserve unity amid the diversity, philosophical pluralism-in-principle regards the unity of a perennial philosophy as an analogical one. Use is made of the traditional image of the light of divine truth, which is one and undivided in God's mind, but which becomes progressively fragmentated and dispersed as it moves down the orders of angelic intelligence and into the human zone. Each type of philosophical mind embodies one facet of the brilliance of divine truth, but it is a law of finite intelligence that each separate philosoph-

258

ical system is a partial (and to that extent, one-sided) representation of the total verity. From the standpoint of any particular perspective on the whole, of course, its own deliverances may seem to be complete and to be contradictorily related to other philosophical positions. But philosophical pluralism-in-principle seeks to embrace all particular perspectives in a polar unity of tension. Hence it claims that the several forms of Scholasticism do not actually contradict each other, but stand rather in the relation of complementarity.

There is an analogical unity of meaning among the various doctrinal systems, a unity which is precisely fitted to admit legitimate differences in the presentation of the one common body of truth. The latter is refracted in analogically similar ways in the different schools. Pluralism-in-principle makes a reflexive use of the notion of analogy, applying it not only to direct predications about being but also to diverse philosophical doctrines about our predications concerning being. Even those theistic standpoints that reject the theory of the analogical predication of being, would presumably be embraced within this analogical topology of philosophical systems.

This version of pluralism is concerned primarily with differences among the various Christian theistic systems, all of which admit at least a certain broad set of conclusions. It recognizes that there is irreconcilable opposition at least between this set of conclusions and philosophies which deny the existence of God, the immateriality of the soul, freedom of human choice, and other basic truths. Nevertheless, a historical study of theistic philosophies themselves in the medieval and modern periods shows that, even among theists, there are irreducible differences concerning the import of these truths, the proper way of demonstrating them, and their necessary relation to certain systematic principles which may themselves stand in contradictory opposition from one system to another.

2. The Modern Debate on Perennial Philosophy

In order to appreciate the full sweep of the contemporary problem of a perennial philosophy, we must extend our survey beyond the ambit of Scholasticism. There are three relevant contributions to the question which deserve a hearing. Brief mention will first be made of a Christian view which does not take its point of departure in the atmosphere of medieval and modern Scholastic thought. Then, attention will be paid to several non-Scholastic and non-Christian conceptions of a per-

259

ennial philosophy. Finally, notice will be taken of the contention that, no matter how it be understood, a perennial philosophy is neither a valid nor a desirable goal for the contemporary mind to strive toward.

What has been rather loosely termed the Christian spiritualist tradition in philosophy claims several prominent adherents in France and Italy. One of the major theses of Maurice Blondel and Michele Sciacca is that it would be a fatal foreshortening of the historical perspective to forget the independent stream of Augustinian thought or to cut off the development of Christian philosophy with the Scholastic systems of the sixteenth century. Whereas the Scholastic mind adopted a policy of separatism during most of the modern centuries, Christian spiritualism claims continuity with one of the main formative influences within modern philosophy itself. There are persistent, identifiable elements of the Augustinian outlook in the writings of Descartes and Malebranche, Pascal and Maine de Biran, Rosmini and Gratry. Hence the notion of a perennial philosophy must be widened to include these thinkers, who accentuated the plight of the individual in the temporal world, his free ordination toward God, and the crucial role of Christian faith in the interpretation and direction of human life.

In a special way, the philosophers of spirit call for a readjustment of the requirement of a fundamental realism. They want a modern view of cognition which will accommodate the philosophical method of interiority, in the specifically nonsensuous form it has taken since the Cartesian critique of sense perception and the sensible world. Precisely how even an analogical unity of doctrine can be maintained between a realism founded upon sense perception and this way of interiority remains one of the outstanding problems facing the advocates of philosophical pluralism-in-principle.

In addition to Scholastic and other Christian thinkers, however, there are many other minds attracted toward the ideal of a perennial philosophy. Among the existentialists, for instance, this issue is one of the few considerations that would recommend making a division along national lines. Neither Sartre nor Marcel has displayed a consuming interest in the history of philosophical traditions, and neither one has developed a theory about a perennial philosophy. In Germany, however, quite the contrary situation prevails. We have noted that both Jaspers and Heidegger have devoted long reflections to the meaning of philosophical history and the structure of a perennial philosophy. In certain respects, these two existentialists have given contemporary expression to the classical positions taken by Kant and Hegel on precisely these issues.

Kant, who was the teacher and friend of Herder, was by no means devoid of interest in the problems of history and philosophical diversity. In the seldom noticed concluding chapter of the *Critique of Pure Reason* entitled "The History of Pure Reason," he recognized a certain historical continuity in the development of reason and certain recurrent patterns of metaphysical speculation.[3] He brought out a threefold polarity, underlying all previous philosophical investigations and relating them significantly to his own critical method.

1. With respect to the object of knowledge, Kant distinguished between the sensualist and the intellectualist tendencies, using the Epicureans and Plato as classical examples. The question here concerns whether the objects of intellectual knowledge have only a logical value, as the sensualists maintain, or whether they give some real access to a supersensible realm of being. Kant himself suggested that the truth lies in the polarity between the two views, each of which is valid within a certain sphere. Our intellectual concepts have only a logical value, as far as knowledge in the strict sense is concerned; but they have a real import in the order of faith. Hence, from the higher standpoint of the critique of reason, there is not a contradiction but a complementarity between the sensualist and immaterialist doctrines. The purpose of the Kantian distinction between the phenomenal and noumenal aspects is to effect a dynamic reconciliation not only of abstract antinomies but also of these opposing historical tendencies in philosophy. Here I am summarizing, and making no judgment on the Kantian position.

2. In examining the question of the origin of our purely rational knowledge, Kant discerned two perennial types of solution: the empiricist and the rationalist, the Aristotelian and the Platonic. In modern times, this inevitable division of opinion is illustrated in the controversy between Locke and Leibniz. Kant regarded his own critical position as a synthesis of both experience and reason, and hence as a means of rescuing the sound features in both empiricism and rationalism. In its critical function, reason is an impartial arbiter, which removes the contradictions and restores harmony within the intellectual community.

3. Finally, the human mind tends inevitably toward a bifurcation on the problem of method. A few thinkers pretend to employ our natural powers philosophically without benefit of any method, but the majority admits the need for methodic thinking. The main difference

springs from the way in which a scientific method is to be used: a Wolff favors a dogmatic procedure, whereas a Hume prefers the skeptical approach. As usual, Kant recommended his own critical standpoint as a way of reconciling the permanent tensions of the human mind concerning the use of method. Whenever he surveyed the progress of metaphysics, he distinguished between three stages. The first is a purely dogmatic employment of reason; the second is a skeptical reaction to the dogmatic method; the third is the critical resolution of this issue, by combining an initial skepticism about the scope of knowledge with a terminal dogmatism, based on a firm use of the distinction between knowledge and belief. Through his perennialist synthesis, Kant hoped to satisfy the age-long desires of reason, without overlooking the limitations placed upon cognition by our human situation.

Karl Jaspers has developed these Kantian suggestions into an explicit doctrine on a perennial philosophy.[4] He agrees with Gabriel Marcel that science differs from philosophy in respect to development. Science makes a linear progress from one problem to the next, replacing previously accepted solutions with new ones, in endless succession. But philosophy is an enduring contemplation of the same mystery of being, toward which the thinkers of all ages make their permanently valid contributions. Hence philosophy is essentially a perennial process and is not subject to the law of temporal displacement. But precisely because philosophical inquiry is directed toward God, the one encompassing reality, it can never express the absolute truth in any single system or in a completely universal way. By the very nature of our finite minds, there must be a plurality of limited manifestations of philosophical truth. Philosophy in its essence is one, but in its actual human developments, it subsists in and through a multiplicity of particular expressions.

Jaspers assures us that in this inevitable disproportion between the ideal of the one human philosophy and the plurality of its partial realizations, we can discover that the idea of a perennial philosophy is not a constitutive, but a regulative one. It guides the thought of each individual thinker, but it never incarnates itself completely as the internal principle of any one system. We are encouraged by our vocation toward achieving a perennial philosophy, but we must also recognize the need for a company of diverse approximations toward it. A perennial philosophy reserves for itself the right to manifest itself only in the clashes between several doctrinal positions.

Renewed interest in the philosophy of Hegel has provided another one of the main spurs toward contemporary speculation about a perennial philosophy. The basic notions of polarity and dialectical unity-in-tension were Hegel's principal tools in solving doctrinal problems and in explaining the historical development of philosophy. It was axiomatic with him (according to his introductory lecture on the history of philosophy) that any contemporary philosophy is the result of the continuous labor of all the centuries. Nothing is lost in the course of philosophical development down the ages, since the various particular systems are fragmentary and complementary expressions of the unity of the absolute spirit itself.

Hegel's main problem was to determine the nature of this unity. He openly criticized what seemed to him to be the naive inference that, because truth is ultimately one, therefore only one particular philosophy is true and all others contradict its truth. This inference would hold only if the unity of truth were something abstract and static. Instead, philosophical truth is something concrete, dynamic, and intrinsically animated by a dialectical polarity between opposing views. Truth comes into our possession only when we grasp all the various philosophical standpoints to our bosom, and master their creative tensions. Only when they are synthesized in a dialectical unity, do the fragmentary outlooks give birth to truth as an organic totality. The adequate philosophical truth lies only in the whole, composed of all the apparently irreconcilable positions constituting the long history of philosophy. Philosophy has a concrete historical unity, grounded in a progressive reconciliation of all the partial insights that come into the minds of men.

Martin Heidegger resembles Karl Marx in his ironical and dramatic relation to Hegel. Both thinkers are very eager to grant Hegel's contention that his own philosophy of absolute spirit is the culmination and hospitable synthesis of all previous historical developments. But they concede this point only in order to lend deeper historical significance to their own respective criticisms of the Hegelian philosophy. Quite frequently Marx congratulates Hegel upon bringing the different modes of speculative thought to a climactic unity. He then suggests that we pass over from the speculative order to a practical control of man and nature—a transition that can only be made by overturning the entire tradition of the primacy of spirit, in favor of a new view of the dynamic self-sufficiency of matter. The notion of a perennial philosophy is merely a convenient means for summarizing the primacy of the spirit, and hence for assuring Marx that his inversion affects all philosophical systems of the past.

263

For his part, Heidegger agrees that the several varieties of metaphysical thinking constitute an organic, polarized approach to the nature of the things-that-are.[5] But a study of the modes of the concrete things-that-are is distinguished in principle from a genuine ontology or doctrine on being as such. Heidegger admits the operation of a comprehensive perennial philosophy in the history of metaphysics, but he tries to make capital out of its very comprehensiveness or polar inclusion of many viewpoints. These philosophical approaches neatly mesh together and supplement each other, only because they all share the common trait of mistaking a study of the things-that-are for a study of being in its own meaning. Because of this confusion, perennial philosophy is quite literally foundationless. It concentrates upon harmonizing a plurality of doctrines rather than upon inspecting the truth of being, at first hand.

Heidegger does not repudiate a perennial philosophy or seek to "invert" it in a Marxian way, but he does seek to "underwrite" it, i.e., to provide a basis that is lacking in the entire perennial tradition of metaphysics. He illustrates a twofold attitude toward a perennial philosophy: first, to regard the perennial mentality as itself only a limited approach, needing its proper complement in turn, and second, to remain unconvinced about whether a successful harmonization of opposing doctrines is in any way relevant for settling the question of the truth of being.

Interest in the nature of a perennial philosophy is by no means confined to European philosophers. In twentieth-century America, one of the most ardent defenders of a version of perennial philosophy has been Wilbur Urban.[6] Like Jaspers, he warns that our philosophical wellsprings will dry up unless we retain our openness to the great philosophical tradition. And again like Jaspers and Whitehead, he views this tradition chiefly as a development of the problems and concepts suggested by Plato. But whereas Jaspers describes the modern phase of a perennial philosophy as a synthesis of Kant's theory of knowledge and Nietzsche's experience of nihilism, Urban locates it primarily in the orthodox line of the Neo-Kantian idealism of values. The medievals tried to reconcile Plato and Aristotle, and Kant tried to combine rationalism and empiricism. Urban claims that the present-day task of a perennial philosophy is to transcend the extremes of idealism and realism, to find a higher synthesis within which to reconcile the parties in the modern epistemological dispute.

This perennialist attempt to go beyond both idealism and realism rests upon the conviction that these oppositions in the philosophical

264

sphere are not permanently unyielding. With patience and sympathy, we seem to be told, a way can be found to provide a peaceful settlement on the basis of mutual aid. Conflicts appear to be insurmountable only because they are regarded from the limited and inescapably one-sided perspective of one of the interested parties. A sublation of opposing theories is required, in order to transcend their shortcomings and appropriate the fruitful insights contained in each position. Instead of seeking this ground of harmony in the Hegelian doctrine of a developing absolute spirit, however, Urban retains the Kantian distinction between the intelligible and the sensible world. The natural metaphysic of the human mind impels us to seek after an intelligible and transcendent causal ground for the world of experience and scientific laws. The reality of the soul, the world as such, and God, is the perennial affirmation of philosophers. But a careful study of the perennial tradition also shows that it supports the primacy of the good over the realm of being and knowing. Hence both a realism of being and an idealism of knowing must be transcended, although preserved, in a comprehensive idealism of value. The polarity between a realism of sense experience and an idealism of intelligible structures can only be made fruitful within the broader context of a metaphysic of values. The primacy of value-acknowledgments and axiology is the watermark of Urban's version of a perennial philosophy, since it provides the only adequate basis for reconciliation of epistemological and metaphysical extremes.

One more Western contribution to this theme may be mentioned. In summarizing his life work, the Swiss philosopher, Paul Häberlin, has chosen as the title of the final statement of his thought: *Philosophia Perennis*.[7] In justification of this choice, he remarks that all instances of genuine philosophizing share in the spirit of the one, perennial philosophy. In its essential impulse, philosophy is a will-to-knowledge. It seeks to grasp the unconditioned truth about being, the cosmos, and the human situation by means of an unconditioned and nonempirical insight. Because the philosophical insight is unconditioned and purely a priori, philosophy is distinguished from both traditional dogmatism (which makes truth depend upon belief in a particular revelation) and scientistic empiricism (which seeks to give philosophy an empirical basis). Häberlin resembles Jaspers in his opposition to scientism and any dogmatic alliance between reason and a nonphilosophical kind of faith. Both thinkers deny that a perennial philosophy should permit Christian faith to exert any vital influence upon the question of truth. When a revealed deposit of faith is used as any sort

265

of norm, positive or negative, the truth is no longer being grasped through a purely rational insight and hence is not constructive of a perennial philosophy. Christian philosophy does not genuinely constitute the perennialist outlook.

Although Häberlin orients philosophy toward an a priori apprehension of unconditioned truth, he admits that every particular philosophical system is a conditioned one. The pure essence of philosophizing is realized only through limited examples, which he calls configurations or *Gestalten* in both the Hegelian and the psychological senses. Each configuration expresses one motif in the symphony of philosophical insight. Only when all the themes are dialectically orchestrated, can we hear the full-toned message of philosophical truth. Philosophical progress does not consist in replacing one limited utterance by another, but in the deliberate program of orchestrating all the individual efforts in the interests of the whole. Among the major configurations of philosophic insight, Häberlin lists the philosophies of Parmenides and Heraclitus, Plato and Aristotle, Augustine and Aquinas (in their nondogmatic aspects), Descartes and Leibniz, Kant and Hegel, Fechner, Wundt and Fischer (in their nonempiricist aspects), Schopenhauer and the contemporary existentialists.

This impressive roll call makes perennial philosophy practically equivalent to all the forms of Western philosophy. Nevertheless, there are some persistent efforts being made today to widen its scope even more, so as to include the Eastern philosophies as well. In the concluding chapter of his survey of Eastern and Western philosophy, the eminent Indian thinker and statesman, Sarvepalli Radhakrishnan, makes an eloquent plea for a perennial philosophy conceived on a world-wide scale.[8] For, a comparative study of human intellectual history shows that philosophy recognizes no national, cultural, or religious frontiers. Although the different systems of thought are conditioned by temporal circumstances, there is a universal and abiding core of method and doctrine.

Radhakrishnan experiences no difficulty, for instance, in establishing a detailed *rapprochement* between the Upanishads of India and European existentialism. Both movements are concerned with the nature of man, treated not merely as a natural object of scientific investigation but also as a conscious center of freedom. They exhibit a common, perennial awareness of man's plight, at the moment when he becomes aware of eternal horizons beyond nature, and yet is in anguished dread about his ability to make the flight of transcendence. "Lead me from the unreal to the real: lead me from darkness to light. Lead me from death to immortality." This cry for divine help is sounded in the Upanishads, but it is re-echoed in all the epochs of history. Radhakrishnan quotes Plotinus, Augustine, and the Koran as witnesses to the central human intuition that man can find fulfillment of his aspirations only in a union with God. Every doctrinal effort is an elaboration upon this theme, a one-sided attempt to express it within a special historical situation. The world-wide perennial philosophy appears in many garments, yet through them all it displays but one inner spirit: the nisus of man's transcendence toward God.

In our own country a similar tendency to broaden the basis for a perennial philosophy is found in Filmer Northrop and Aldous Huxley.[9] The former relies mainly on the techniques of philosophical and sociological analysis, whereas the latter makes an informal religious and mystical appeal. Northrop erects a sharp contrast between the intuitive-esthetic mind of the East and the analytic-rational traits of Western thought. Huxley is less doctrinaire, and is more hopeful about finding common currents of thought, especially of a mystico-religious sort, in both traditions. Both men agree that a balanced perennialist outlook should include the best qualities of Eastern and Western philosophies, and Huxley explicitly characterizes such a synthesis as a perennial philosophy. But the arduous work of making a detailed, historical comparison between the metaphysical developments of East and West has scarcely started.

This canvass of contemporary views about a perennial philosophy cannot afford to ignore the vigorous dissenting opinions entered by naturalism and logical positivism. Both schools are hostile toward any variety of perennial philosophy, and firmly refuse to be incorporated within the inviting polar field. We are already prepared to expect that John Dewey's naturalistic criticism of the perennialist thesis can be traced to his general opposition to anything that smacks of the eternal and the permanent. In the degree that the proponents of a perennial philosophy seek to escape from relativism and historicism by affirming a central body of enduring, absolute truths, they come under the censure of his naturalism. Dewey questions the reality of any such permanent set of philosophical truths and adds that, even if such truths could be ascertained, they would carry no special weight simply in virtue of their perennial character. The claim to be in possession of a perennial set of doctrines arouses no warm glow of assent in the naturalist mind. For the latter associates this claim with an extreme conservative attitude and a refusal to commit oneself fully to the provisional nature of scientific inquiry.

As for logical positivism, it goes to the heart of the matter when it points out the dependence of the notion of a perennial philosophy upon the validity of metaphysics. If the possibility of metaphysics is merely assumed by the advocates of a perennial philosophy, then the entire discussion constitutes a huge begging of the issue. Logical positivism is perfectly indifferent about whether a single metaphysics be accepted, or whether the truth be sought in a polar tension between several metaphysical systems. In either case, the same skeptical question applies: With what right does the human mind make metaphysical statements, which transcend the conditions of empirical verification and yet pretend to refer meaningfully to the order of real things? According to the logical positivist, no amount of perennialist reconciliation between different metaphysical positions is sufficient to establish the meaningfulness and real reference of metaphysical inference as such. This criticism remains acute, even after the general decline of logical positivism.

3. *A Restricted Theory of Perennial Philosophy*

After taking stock of the present status of the question, a final task remains. My purpose in the concluding section is to try to determine the worth and proper function of the concept of a perennial philosophy. A number of significant points have been uncovered in the course of the previous survey. With their aid, it may be possible to establish a sound footing in this region, where everything seems to turn into quicksand.

Perhaps the most obvious finding is the indeterminate and polyvalent character of the term "perennial philosophy." Whether the various meanings assigned to it can themselves form an analogical unity or whether we are in the presence of some genuinely irreducible and contradictory usages, is one of the outstanding questions raised by our survey. The term is open to a very wide range of determinate meanings, no one of which appears to have pre-emptory right to be treated as the only legitimate one. No definite information is conveyed by speaking about *the* perennial philosophy without further qualification, since one cannot point to any actual philosophy or group of philosophies which embody all the traits assigned under this term. In actual practice, there are as many notions of perennial philosophy as there are perennialist thinkers recommending their own general principles of unification for metaphysical doctrines. Hence it might be advisable to discipline our language in this respect, so that we come to speak about a perennial philosophy, qualified in this or that particular way.

Because of this factually pluralistic situation among the versions of a perennial philosophy, this concept is neither self-explanatory nor self-validating. Explanations must be furnished, for instance, concerning the historical range of the perspective which serves as a basis of unification. One must specify whether the perennial philosophy in question is organized around all the Western attempts to synthesize the Platonic and Aristotelian trends in philosophy, or whether it is confined to the medieval and Scholastic systems of metaphysics, or whether it has mainly in view the modern opposition between empiricism and rationalism, or whether it seeks to include the whole range of Eastern and Western speculation. Furthermore, the precise reason for choosing one's special perspective has to be indicated. Sometimes appeal is made to a historical sort of unity, as when one defines the content of a perennial philosophy in terms of the common Scholastic patrimony of the high medieval period, as described by De Wulf. This basis is philosophically inconclusive, however, since other temporal unities can be chosen.

On the other hand, a purely doctrinal ground for determining the significance of a perennial philosophy can be advanced. Such is the case with Jaspers' conception, since his definition of philosophizing as a search after transcendence or the encompassing reality settles at once the way in which he will describe the abiding concern of human intelligence, throughout its history. Yet this doctrinal reason for a perennial unity of philosophies finds itself in competition with other views of the human mind, which are also capable of providing a remarkable unification of the various philosophical positions.

Once a definite meaning has been assigned to a perennial philosophy, the work of testing this particular conception must be undertaken. For, however careful the description of one's meaning for a perennial philosophy, there is still need for validation of this determinate meaning. There are two major reasons why its truth is never self-evident. One of these concerns the broad, indeterminate criteria for a perennial philosophy, while the other concerns the more determinate and particular use of the same criteria.

1. In a general way, an appeal can be made to the endurance and the inclusiveness of a designated historical tradition or doctrinal complexus. Yet neither one of these notes is a guarantee of the truth of the tradition or doctrinal polarity in question. Although naturalism

is mistaken about regarding the temporal and eternal aspects of being as mutually exclusive, it does make a reasonable case against using the term "perennial" or "enduring" in an inherently eulogistic way. In human intellectual history, fundamental metaphysical errors are just as persistent and indestructible as are the ways of truth. This is one sphere where time does not necessarily vindicate the correct position, even in the long run. The enduring character of certain conceptions of being is highly significant, indeed, but this trait is not decisive by itself.

Nor is it sufficient to point out the inclusive nature of one's notion of a perennial philosophy. Here, one must be careful to avoid an ambiguity concerning the type of inclusiveness at stake. For a philosophy can be comprehensive, either in the sense of embracing a variety of *systems about* reality or in the sense of embracing a wide sweep of *real traits of* experience. The former sort of inclusiveness does not necessarily entail the latter: the fact that many systems are combined in a unity of polar tension does not establish the fact that this unity also provides a plenary explanation of the real. Conversely, a philosophy can try to include all the factors in our experience of being, without attempting to integrate several systems of metaphysics. Philosophical adequacy does require that an explanation pass the test of experienced reality but not that of systems. Because of this distinction between showing that one's principles account for the various aspects of being and showing that one's position harmonizes several explanations about being, the note of systematic inclusiveness is not decisive for determining the philosophical truth of a perennial philosophy.

2. The second major obstacle against taking the idea of a perennial philosophy as an independent, self-warranting criterion stems from the first one. It arises when the broad notes of perenniality and inclusiveness are rendered more determinate, in support of one or another particular version of a perennial philosophy. When the reasons for the enduring character of a tradition are specified, a conflict develops between the divergent explanations. What Urban deems to be the natural metaphysic of the human mind does not coincide with Hegel's or Przywara's conceptions of this natural metaphysic. The differences are radical ones. They cannot be overcome merely by making readjustments in one's theory of polar reconciliation, since they concern the very principles upon which such a theory is built. The doctrines of Urban, Hegel, and Przywara are deprived of their distinctive structure and intellectual sting, when they are watered down to the status of

270

complementary opposites in some over-arching polar unity of analogical meaning. At some point in one's defense of a perennial philosophy, one must make a direct examination of man's relation to being. What may be called an *extraperennialist* discussion about the nature of the real and of our knowledge of it is unavoidable when the question of philosophical truth is at stake. Otherwise, each one of the several proponents of a perennial philosophy will be working on the illusory assumption that his own view of the human mind's natural and enduring metaphysic is acceptable, by definition, to all the others.

A similar forcing of the inquiry back to the terrain of being, from the terrain of systems about being, occurs also in the more particular explanations of inclusiveness. This is clearly seen in a comparison between the various temporal spans which serve as an inductive basis for harmonizing the different philosophies. Unless the investigator is willing to let the discussion remain in the region of cultural history and the history of ideas, he cannot be content with stating that a particular theory of polar opposites accounts for all medieval systems or all the forms of patristic thought. For an equally successful synthesis of the various modern standpoints can also be made. This raises the question of the philosophical relevance, today, of even the most comprehensive interweaving of the doctrinal views of another era. Northrop made this challenge when he asked whether the medieval systems need be given serious consideration in a post-Ptolemaic and even post-Newtonian period. This objection is not unanswerable, but the most cogent answer does not consist in pointing to the inclusiveness and eirenic intent of one's synthesis of various patristic and medieval writers. More than this is demanded by those who take another measure for a perennial philosophy. Somewhere in the discussion, one must accept the responsibility of dealing directly with the epistemological and metaphysical problems raised by modern scientific methods and philosophies. This cannot be done by appealing to the enduring and comprehensive nature of one's own systematic reconciliations, but only by a personal confrontation with the ways of being and knowing in relation to the scientific methods.

Every convincing effort at constructing a perennial philosophy involves some independent, extraperennialist principles for rooting out the deadwood and retaining only the living stems of thought. This need for independent inquiry into the nature of the real is verified in the case of the first great modern proponent of a *philosophia perennis*. Leibniz strove to continue the medieval work of reconciling Plato and Aristotle and to reintroduce some Scholastic concepts into the mainstream of modern thought.[10] On both counts, however, he recognized that something over and above the intention of reconciling apparent extremes is required, if one's perennial philosophy is to be accepted as theoretically sound. Even the principle of harmony recommended itself to his mind first of all upon logical and metaphysical grounds. Its primary reference was to the plenitude of being, the connection between perfection and unity-amid-multiplicity, and the ordination of God's will toward perfection. Only because it proved its independent worth in logic and metaphysics did Leibniz feel warranted in applying the principle of harmony in a reflexive way to the conflicting systems of thought. When he praised the Scholastic notions of entelechy, substantial form, finality, and exemplar idea, he was nevertheless quite careful to interpret them in strict accord with *his own* leading metaphysical principles. His own personal vision of the real dictated his interpretation of both Plato and Aristotle, as well as governed his selection and explanation of Scholastic ideas. Although he always gave a prominent place in his mind to the goal of achieving intellectual harmony and social peace, he founded his harmonizing efforts upon his direct inspection of logical principles and the structure of the universe.

In several versions of a perennial philosophy, demonstrative arguments are offered for locating the complete truth only within the dynamic field of tension between many philosophical standpoints. Thus, Jaspers says that no particular doctrinal system can claim to be the one philosophy, since every human mind is finite and yet the aim of philosophizing is to grasp the unconditioned One. Not only is there a disproportion in kind between the human mind and ultimate being, but the mind comes to know about ultimate being through an interpretation of the objects of experience. Given Kant's premise that the world of experience is purely phenomenal, the objects of empirical and scientific knowledge do not give any certain and unequivocal information about the being of the unconditioned One. Hence there are bound to be conflicting readings of the metaphysical implications of the phenomenal world. Philosophers cannot avoid giving divergent interpretations to empirical objects and defending different ways of deciphering the riddle of the phenomenal universe. Philosophical awareness, says Jaspers, rests on a resolute inclusion of all the conflicting reports, together with an act of resignation to their basic failure to seize upon the mystery of being as an encompassing whole.

The Hegelian position on this question is even more rigorously worked out. Individual minds are finite manifestations of the absolute

272

mind. Consequently, no single philosophical system can adequately express the absolute truth. The truth is found only in the organic whole or polar unity, constituted by the interworking of all the finite philosophical standpoints. Hegel adds the further thesis that there cannot possibly be any unyielding contradictions among philosophical positions. This follows from his dialectical and metaphysical view that a portion of the activity and insight of the absolute spirit is embodied in every thesis, every antithesis, and every partial synthesis. Whatever the oppositions at the finite level, there is an internal conspiracy on the part of all conflicting doctrines to rejoin in the organic unity of the absolute spirit and its complete truth. All antinomies can be overcome in principle, since the drive of philosophy is toward developing a perfectly concrete, organic totality out of the partial insights and fragmentary truths of finite philosophical systems.[11]

Now, a problem arises in the case of any philosophy that refuses to accept the Kantian postulate of the phenomenal character of the objects of experience and scientific knowledge, or the Hegelian postulate of an immanent absolute mind and dialectical totality of being. It does not seem possible for such a philosophy either to make a strict demonstration or even to care to make a strict demonstration of the two following propositions: philosophical truth can be found only in the polar interplay of several different philosophies; and all oppositions among philosophies are essentially reducible to complementary relations and exclude contradictory doctrinal positions.

With regard to the first proposition, there is a notable difference between showing that philosophical truth *can only* be found in the unity of polar tensions between systems, and showing that it *is often* found or expressed in that way. The former states a condition that must hold good in principle and in right, whereas the latter merely describes a factual situation of contingent occurrence. From a factual description of how various historical outlooks sometimes supplement each other and make joint contributions to the total report on the real, no stringent inference can be drawn concerning the necessity of locating philosophical truth in a philosophical pluralism-in-principle. In this respect extreme caution must be taken, lest we become the victims of our own metaphors. We naturally speak about families of minds and classify each type, as the biologist would classify the specimens taken on a field trip. We tend to picture the white radiance of eternal light as being stained and dispersed, as it passes through the filter of various finite minds. The philosophical life is visualized as an orchestral symphony, in which each system or doctrinal configuration carries a limited share of the music of absolute truth.

These images help us to remain personally sensitive to the nuanced differences of temporal situation, the available evidence at any period, and the differences in temperament and conceptual tools arising among philosophers of various historical origins. But their vividness and psychological usefulness should not be mistaken for any sort of demonstration about the nature and location of truth or the structure of philosophy. For these images do not deal with the speculative operations and truth in their proper nature as intentional relations, but treat them as things that can be likened to other things in the visible world. Such metaphors cannot settle the question of the precise nature of the unity proper to philosophy, since they cannot convey the unitive function exercised by the philosopher's judgmental grasp upon the principles of being and knowing. Some further difficulties entailed by the metaphor of related poles will be discussed in connection with Husserl's phenomenology of philosophies.

A factual plurality cannot be converted validly into an argument favoring a philosophical pluralism-in-principle. The unity of wisdom toward which metaphysical principles impel us—amid all the sharp and tragic differences of human history—is that of a common sharing in the same immaterial perfection of truth, a common affirmation of the same intentional meaning of being. However diverse our personal, historical, and intellectual backgrounds may be, we are all fitted to acknowledge being as existent under sensible conditions. Each of us shares individually in the intellectual light, precisely so that our many judgmental acts may affirm the same act of being. The unity of philosophy is rooted immediately in this joint reference toward being as that which has the act of existing, rather than in the second-level relations among systems concerning being. Acknowledgment of being and its principles unites our philosophical judgments, not after the fashion of the perennialist orchestration, but through a common recognition of the same grounds of evidence and resolution for all our inferences.[12]

In analyzing the second proposition, we must respect another basic distinction. It is one thing to claim that there cannot be *any* irreducible oppositions among philosophers, and quite another thing to hold that *many* apparent contradictions turn out to be relations of contrariety and complementarity. The latter thesis is a commonplace of both practical life and intellectual inquiries in every field. But it conveys no necessary rule that all philosophical differences must be regarded as

274

noncontradictory and reducible to a complementary relation within a polar field. Apart from the dialectical theory of absolute idealism, no necessary reasons are forthcoming for sublating all oppositions and treating them as partial expressions of a single whole or truth. A nonidealistic version of a perennial philosophy cannot settle disputes by claiming, in principle, that the conflicting views cannot contradict each other and must find a place within the total framework. It is prevented from arguing with necessity in this way, both with respect to the particular field of its own systems and with respect to those systems which have not yet been harmonized. For instance, the standpoint of philosophical pluralism-in-principle has no strictly cogent grounds for claiming that the various theistic systems involve no irreconcilable differences and can all be reduced to analogical variations on a common doctrinal unity. Still less is it able to pronounce anything in principle about what the relation between theistic and non-theistic systems will turn out to be.

If there is no unconditional necessity on this score, then the notion of a perennial philosophy furnishes no basic directions about how to deal with philosophical differences. We may reasonably expect that many conflicts will manifest themselves, under patient analysis, to be of a reconcilable sort. But this practical rule does not enable us to settle any particular controversy, merely by showing how a mutual adaptation of positions is possible. That such an adaptation may be due only to a verbal harmony or to a watering down of the different positions, remains an open possibility. Quite apart from the desire to harmonize the various positions with each other, a direct examination of the question on its own merits and with respect to the actual situation in being is unavoidable. Philosophers are still able to contradict each other genuinely and definitively; they can still utter a yea, yea and a nay, nay, which do not turn out to be complementary poles of the one complex truth.[13] For polarity comes after the fact of our knowledge of being: it does not specify in a primary way how this knowledge must be found in human intellects.

The purpose of my critique of current views of a perennial philosophy is not to discard this notion as being utterly worthless, but only to deprive it of the role of criterion and ultimate determinant of philosophical truth. Once it has been removed from this function, it can perform some constructive and even indispensable services. For when a perennial philosophy is no longer asked to provide the fundamental criterion for dealing with philosophical differences, we are no longer faced with the artificial alternative of either accepting one philosophy alone and entirely closing our minds to all other ones, or else striving to find the truth only in the tensions among the several philosophies. We can both wholeheartedly accept the metaphysical principles of one philosophy and also have a constant concern and historical sympathy for the persistent problems and explanations found in other philosophies. The purpose of a perennial philosophy is, then, to keep our intellectual horizons always open and receptive to the experience of men and the findings of fellow philosophers throughout the ages. It also provides a means for making one's metaphysical principles operate and grow within the context of the actual process of human inquiry. The recognition of a factual plurality of philosophies makes us receptive of new truths, as long as it does not rigidify itself into a pluralism-in-principle.

Contemporary Thomists stand in special need of the liaison work and the fruitful challenges provided by such a conception of a perennial philosophy. They agree, for the most part, that Thomism is not supposed to be a closed and immutable system, incapable of further development and unable to profit by a careful study of other ways of viewing the universe. But they are nevertheless ill at ease in the hurly-burly world of competing philosophies and jostling traditions. The Thomists know that they should not retreat to their own quiet preserve, and yet they often lack a definite program and adequate set of tools for remaining within the intellectual community and sharing in the give-and-take of the philosophical life. They would like to take part in the joint enterprise, and yet they see no way to do so without endangering truths that are supremely important.

In such a predicament, Thomists can make advantageous use of the idea of a perennial philosophy. Most theistic exponents of this idea remind us that God, in His providence, does not abandon any individual thinker or historical movement in philosophy. Some kernel of truth is lodged in every philosophical standpoint. No matter how unpromising or hostile it may be, it is likely to contain some valuable insight. This is a true but purely formal statement, however, since it provides no means of determining precisely what aspect of any given system is a sound one. And the import of the previous critical analysis is that reconcilability with one's conception of a perennial philosophy cannot, as such, provide the required norm for ascertaining the element of truth.

But a perennial philosophy can serve the ends of truth in another, even though subordinate and indirect, way. Instead of standing for some one particular historical movement or synthesis of doctrinal sys-

276

tems, it can signify an attitude or frame of mind on the part of one who has seen for himself the truth of the metaphysical bases of a theistic realism. It can signify the personal attitude of openness and the resolve to attend sympathetically to other views on the nature of the real. To accept the burden of a perennial philosophy means, in this context, to commit oneself to the unending work of clarifying the precise relationship between the metaphysics of being as existent and the other approaches of men to the mystery of being. It means the willingness to continue growing in one's insight into the structure and act of being, and to do so precisely with whatever help can be furnished by the wider community of philosophers.

In this purely instrumental function, a perennial philosophy builds upon a factual plurality, but not upon a pluralism-in-principle. Conceived in this way, a perennial philosophy operates at a descriptive or phenomenological plane. It is the effective point of insertion of one's metaphysical doctrine into the general current of philosophizing, since it provides an exact description of the efforts of thinkers to determine the nature of being and the nature of the science of being. Such a perennial philosophy is neither pure philosophical speculation nor the ordinary history of philosophy. Rather, it is the effective bridge between the two, so that a realistic metaphysics can show its abiding relevance for the problems of the human mind, and so that the determinate historical positions can stand out clearly as containing challenges and guidance for the further development of this metaphysical doctrine.

To think in the spirit of a perennial philosophy is to view the historical materials from a comparative standpoint. It focuses attention upon the enduring problems and methods that recur, in various ways, throughout the history of philosophy. Another office of such a perennial philosophy is to probe into the psychological, cultural, and other contingent factors affecting the concrete developments in philosophy, especially in their bearing upon the problem of doctrinal differences. But it does this without pretending to make any ultimate pronouncements about the nature of philosophical differences or any settlement of this or that area of differences. The final speculative evaluation rests with the philosopher himself, whose intellect is directly responsive to the act and structure of being, as well as to the intellectual and sensuous conditions under which man grasps being. The discipline of an attitude of perennial philosophy will quicken his perception of how other minds approach being. But he will not derive his touchstone for treating philosophical differences from any supposed conditions for constructing an independent perennial philosophy as an autonomous body of truth. Irreducible oppositions in doctrine are bound to remain, and they can only be dealt with by returning directly to our sources in experience and to the judgments and inferences relevant to these sources.

Perennial philosophy, so understood, is an aspect of methodology rather than of doctrinal content. There are several conceptions of perennial philosophy, because there are different ways of adapting this method to different doctrinal principles and historical traditions. It is not a speculative premise from which any conclusions follow about the nature of being and the content of metaphysics. But, it is an important tool for metaphysics, taken in its contingent and historical aspects.

Even in the history of philosophy, however, the notion of a perennial philosophy cannot properly serve as a doctrinal norm for dealing with the various philosophies. The restricted instrumental theory of a perennial philosophy which I propose here is therefore opposed to the thesis of Johannes Hirschberger and some historians of philosophy that there is a common Western perennial philosophy, embracing the greatest minds and furnishing us with a norm of judgment for weighing all the systems of thought and particular doctrines.[14] This ideal is too grandiose and embracing to find its realization in any human philosophy. When it is used to guide one's historical thinking, it leads to a vague and unlikely amalgamation of ideas drawn from Plato and Aristotle, Augustine and Aquinas, Leibniz and perhaps Hegel, without having proper regard for the systematic context and method which actually specify the meaning of those ideas in these different philosophies. This is too stiff a penalty to pay for using the notion of a perennial philosophy in a normative way.

In conclusion, the only safe use of the concept of a perennial philosophy is as a methodic instrument, rigorously subject to the following five restrictions. (1) There are some permanent and widely recurrent problems found throughout the history of philosophy. Thus there are some perennial problems, and to come to an awareness of them is part of the process of developing philosophical acumen. (2) Furthermore, there are some basic truths which the human mind has grasped under many different circumstances and which remain valid for the various ages. They constitute a core of perennial truths, whether in the form of particular propositions or principles concerning being and thought. (3) Such perennial problems and true propositions and principles enable us to establish a sort of continuity of relevance among

278

the different philosophies. But the continuity is precisely that of a problematic and basic-propositional sort. This is enough to provide an intelligible context for our study of the history of philosophy. But it is not enough to warrant the conclusion that there is some definite perennial philosophy, to which we can make a controlled reference and appeal in evaluating various doctrines. For there is a real distance between admitting the historical presence of some perennial problems and truths and maintaining that they constitute a perennial philosophy, in the determinate sense of having its own method, context of interpretation of evidence, and unified meaning for the judgments and inferences bearing systematically on the specific issues in human speculation.

(4) The abidingly true propositions can be used as a separate test of the particular conclusions reached by philosophers. But this sort of testing on the basis of some perennially true propositions does not suppose that these propositions are functioning precisely within the context of some determinate philosophy, arrived at in a human philosophical way. Hence the philosophers and theologians who have recourse to such perennially true statements and principles can validly do so, without strengthening the claim that there is a perennial philosophy in any further, determinate sense. (5) There is no ascertainable meaning for a perennial philosophy over and above the reference to some permanent problems and some permanently true propositions. For, the latter do not comprise a distinctive body of thought developed and organized in a philosophical order, through its own method and interpretation of evidence. Hence it is inadvisable to move from a minimal, instrumental meaning for perennial philosophy to a maximal, doctrinally normative meaning. A theistic realism which is developing according to the human manner, order, and sources of evidence will make good use of the restricted meaning of perennial philosophy, as designating certain persistent problems and truths, and will try to avoid making an overclaim about some one perennial philosophy embracing the best insights of all positions.

CHAPTER 11

TOWARD A PHILOSOPHICALLY
ORDERED THOMISM

THE IMPACT of Maritain and Gilson upon the intellectual life of Christians in America is deep and widely ramified. It is difficult to conceive of the precise shape which our present philosophizing would be taking, had we not been affected so basically by their work. As far as Gilson is concerned, his long-range educational influence will probably be exerted primarily through his *History of Christian Philosophy in the Middle Ages* and *The Christian Philosophy of St. Thomas Aquinas.* These books expertly distill for us the main points of his contribution: an awareness of the historical method and its many uses in philosophy, particular researches throughout the history of philosophy but especially in the great medieval thinkers, doctrinal teaching on the meaning of being as existent and on the existential judgment, and historical generalization concerning the persistent current of essentialism in contrast with the Thomistic philosophy of being and its recognition of the existential act.

The proper office of a philosopher is not exhausted, however, in enshrining his past results in compact and striking form. He also has the task of proposing further problems which lie at the very frontier of knowledge, questions which are themselves unsettled and which therefore demand of the rest of us some independent thinking. This is the function of raising new issues, reformulating old ones in arresting ways, and thus arousing some new responses from others. It is in this spirit that an attempt is made here to advance the line of philosophical discussion on one point of major concern for Christian philosophers and the philosophical community at large.

The question itself is clearly formulated by Gilson in a footnote which must be transcribed here in full, since it provides the major text for analysis.

Some [who] profess to reconstruct St. Thomas's teaching in the philosophical order proceeding from things to God rather than in the theological order proceeding from God to things fail to take into consideration the difficulties of such an undertaking. In point of fact, not one of them does so. Those of them who honestly try, either substitute the philosophy of Aristotle for that of St. Thomas, or else, as is happening in our own days, flatly contradict the philosophy which they pretend to teach. To summarize what could not be proved without long and tedious developments, let us say that: *one does* [not] *miraculously find the theology of Thomas Aquinas at the end of the philosophy of Aristotle.* To isolate his philosophy from his theology is to present the philosophical thought of St. Thomas in an arrangement demanded by a philosophy in which everything is "considered by natural reason without the light of faith." (Descartes, *Principes,* Preface, ed. Adam-Tannery, IX, 4, i. 19-21 and 5, i. 13-18.) In brief, it is to present a *philosophia ad mentem sancti Thomae* as though it were a *philosophia ad mentem Cartesii.* To discuss the consequences would carry us into the field of dogmatic philosophy which does not concern us here.[1]

Side one of this proposed alternative in philosophy is that the authentic reconstruction of Thomistic philosophy must develop in accord with the theological order of going from God to things. Side two of the alternative states that those who attempt to follow the philosophical order of going from things to God will lapse into one or the other non-Thomistic position: Aristotelian essentialism or Cartesian post-Christian naturalism. These latter two subdivisions can be taken either as historical descriptions or as pure positions. There is still a good deal of historical research and discussion going on in the field of Aristotle's notion of being and Descartes' view of philosophy and faith. But these historical names can also be treated as designating the theoretical standpoints of an essentialism of substantial form and a naturalism of reverting to a situation where faith is irrelevant for philosophy, whatever the historical complications in the actual teachings of Aristotle and Descartes.

This alternative is a dire one for those who may want to philosophize as Christians and Thomists, who cannot conceive of themselves as doing so according to the theological order, and who nevertheless seek to avoid the predicted theoretical consequences of following another order of inference. In such a situation, some people may regard it as advisable to abandon work altogether in the philosophical field. Another course is to re-examine both sides of the proposed alternative. The issue is a complicated one which has exercised

Christian minds throughout history and which has been a central preoccupation of Gilson's entire life. Hence it would be presumptuous to attempt a resolution of the whole matter. Without being able to provide a definitive treatment, it is nevertheless possible to clarify a few of the chief difficulties insofar as they present themselves within this context. Some light can be thrown on the issue by considering the problem of Christian philosophy in a few of Gilson's previous works, by studying some features in the immediate context of his book on Aquinas, and by making two independent suggestions. There will be the positive point that several ways are open to us for philosophizing in a Christian and Thomistic spirit, and the negative point that we should not regard Malebranche and Pascal as our exemplars for realizing a modern Christian philosophy.

1. *The Question of a Christian Philosophy*

As far as present-day discussion about Christian philosophy is concerned, the date of 1930 can roughly be assigned as a crucial one. For by this time Émile Bréhier had issued the sections of his famous history of philosophy which covered the ancient and medieval periods.[2] Writing from a rationalist standpoint, he reported that he could find no significant historical content for the term "Christian philosophy." The medievals had received the hard core of Greek philosophy and modified it in various extrinsic ways, according to apologetic needs. But as far as the main thrust of philosophical work was concerned, it was not deeply modified in direction and depth by the Christian faith.

The immediate response to this challenge was undertaken by three Christian philosophers: Blondel, Maritain, and Gilson. At that period, Blondel had not yet elaborated his main system on being, thought, and action. His reply was interpreted mainly as an effort to keep the religious sphere entirely free from commerce with objective conceptual philosophy, and hence as an indirect support of Bréhier's thesis. In his later writings he sought to bring out another way of philosophizing and hence a way of conceiving the positive relation between faith and philosophy. For him, a Christian philosophy is centered on a reflective study of the symbiotic relation between the natural dynamism of our being and activities toward God and the supernatural directing of our life toward a final sharing in divine life which is not yet achieved.

Maritain's contribution was contained in his lucid and compact *Essay on Christian Philosophy.* There, he proposed a crucial distinction between the nature and the state of philosophy. Considered in its nature or its own constitution according to a distinctive method, principles, and object of knowledge, philosophy is and remains a natural, rational discipline. In the concrete order of its state or human development, however, philosophy is deeply affected by the life of faith.[3] It receives objective help when revelation focuses it more strongly upon certain natural truths, and when revelation suggests new problems and new reaches of study that were previously overlooked. And on the subjective side, Christian faith helps to strengthen the philosophic bent of mind and sustain it in the pursuit of truths about God and man. In view of these aids to the mind of the philosopher, there is such a thing as a Christian state of philosophy. Nevertheless, the philosopher has the responsibility of making his own proper use of these aids, scrutinizing the objects in their nature, and making valid demonstrations according to the philosophical order of ascending from experience. Even after he introduced certain qualifications concerning an adequately considered moral philosophy, Maritain was careful to observe recently about speculative philosophy that, "in its own realm it does not have to borrow anything from theology."[4] Metaphysics directly considers the natural content of reality, whatever the objective and subjective help it receives from faith in making the investigation.

Before concentrating upon Gilson's treatment, it may be remarked that the articles and books devoted to this question proliferated at a rapid rate during the nineteen-thirties. The various professional bibliographies were laden down with titles, so that it became difficult even to summarize the many twists and turns of the controversy. Since the question was not a purely philosophical one, it involved various theologies with their different theories about the relation between nature and grace, reason and faith. The experience of philosophers was that one rapidly reached a point of diminishing philosophical returns, once the broad distinction was made by Maritain and the historical description furnished by Gilson. The term "Christian philosophy" became almost unusable, because of the difficulty in giving it a commonly accepted determinate content. Yet the use of this name in both of Gilson's above-mentioned books indicates his effort to arrive at a specific meaning, especially for a Thomistic Christian philosophy.

At the outset of his trail-breaking Gifford Lectures, *The Spirit of Mediaeval Philosophy,* Gilson asks two central questions. The first is whether philosophy remains essentially unchanged in its passage from the Greek world to the Christian world of medieval thought. His reply constitutes the substance of that decisive presentation of the medieval mind. The medievals clearly distinguished God as the personal transcendent being, the creator of a world from nothing, the free source of being and governance for finite things. There was a deepening of the Greek and Hebrew conceptions of man, bringing out the reality of the person, the integrity of free choice, and the search for a final condition transcending earthly satisfactions. This is a historically traceable development, and the new impetus given to reason in matters philosophical is also traceable to the presence of Hebrew-Christian revelation. The findings of these Gifford Lectures, together with Gilson's specialized works on the major thinkers, mark a definitive achievement. Scholars of whatever philosophical position now recognize the historical reality of Christian philosophy, in the sense of these definite developments. They see that the great medieval thinkers were theologians, that some of them carried on a philosophical work, but that they did so within the context of revelation and theology.

This acknowledged result is not presently in question, apart from noting that it need not entail for Christian philosophers today the alternative under consideration. This can be seen in the response to the second main question of these lectures. Gilson asks whether the modern philosophers from Descartes to Kant and beyond would have speculated in the same way, had there been no Christian medieval period. To show that this period was no mere interlude during which nothing philosophically important happened to the Greek heritage, he stresses the creator-God of Descartes, the concern of Malebranche for divine power and glory, Leibniz's defense of personal providence, and Kant's interest in freedom, immortality, and a personal God in the practical order. Without making Christian philosophers out of these men, the presence of such themes indicates the vast transformation undergone by philosophy during its middle span of history.

If pure philosophy took any of its ideas from Christian revelation, if anything of the Bible and the Gospel has passed into metaphysics, if, in short, it is inconceivable that the systems of Descartes, Malebranche and Leibniz would be what in fact they are had they been altogether withdrawn from Christian influence, then it becomes highly probable that since the influence of Christianity on philosophy was a reality, the concept of Christian philosophy is not without a real meaning.[5]

This view of modern philosophy is expanded in Gilson's later books, especially *The Unity of Philosophical Experience*. What is noteworthy about it for the present question, however, is that the reality of a Christian philosophy is broadly based upon the passage of influential ideas into metaphysics. It is not the defining note of a Christian philosophy that the suggestions it takes from revelation are developed by it solely according to a theological order of reasoning. Whether this note is indispensable at least for a Christian Thomistic philosophy is a further question, one that concerned Gilson most acutely during the next years.

To clinch the argument of *The Spirit of Mediaeval Philosophy*, the alternative was framed that either metaphysics will continue, and along with it the beneficial influence of Christian revelation, or else metaphysics and theology will succumb to Comte's law of being replaced by the positivist state of mind. That some other intellectual possibilities still remained open, however, was soon made apparent by the Protestant reception of the concept of a Christian philosophy. Protestant scholars argued that, just as we cannot act as though the Christian middle ages did not exist for philosophy, so we cannot lay aside the irreversible, permeating fact of the Reformation. Either one must state specifically that one means a Catholic type of Christian philosophy or else one must explore the Reformed views of faith and reason, especially Calvin's call for the restoration of a Christian philosophy. Gilson accepted this invitation in his book on *Christianity and Philosophy*, the revised English edition of which appeared on the eve of World War II.

Here, he takes as a thesis that the essential domain of Christian philosophy is coextensive with the field of natural theology.[6] It reaches into the rest of philosophy accidentally, insofar as almost the whole of philosophy is ordered to the knowledge of divine things. On this basis, the essential requirement of a Christian philosophy is missing from the classical theologies of Luther and Calvin, as well as from many modern Protestant theologians. Although they do not eliminate nature, they do deny its supernaturally religious efficacity, as well as the human mind's natural ability to develop a speculative philosophy of God. Since Gilson's book was published, there has been considerable discussion particularly among Calvinist theologians about various valid meanings for natural theology. But they do not reach as far as granting the capacity of our natural reason to demonstrate the truth of natural theology from the evidence furnished by the world. Hence they do not satisfy the criterion Gilson uses in this book for determining a Christian philosophy.

More recently, Michael Foster and Herman Dooyeweerd have posed the problem of a Protestant Christian philosophy in a somewhat

285

different light.[7] They propose to admit the existence of a Christian philosophy wherever a factor of Christian faith is present fundamentally in a philosophical doctrine, whether or not it treats directly of God. Their test case is the conviction of scientists and modern philosophers that our universe is intelligible. They trace the source of the conviction in the intelligibility of the universe to the Christian faith in an intelligent creator-God. Even though the domain of philosophy is narrowed down to what Kant calls a *Weltweisheit* or wisdom of the world, it involves a founding act of faith and hence has a Christian dimension. Two questions raised by this argument are whether the belief in question is the specifically Christian act of faith, and whether there are other positions on the knowability of specific objects enabling contemporary scientists to avoid a universal postulate.

During the war years, Gilson was engaged in the meditative revision of his view of St. Thomas and hence also in laying the basis of the law of essentialism in the history of philosophy. Aristotle had done the best he could without even knowing about the existence of a supernatural revelation, and hence his position was different from that of the modern naturalizers. But the hard historical fact was that it required St. Thomas' reflection on the Vulgate text of *Exodus* to arrive at the truth of God as the subsistent act of existing itself. In close solidarity with this insight was his appreciation of being and the existential act, as well as the perfection of knowledge in the existential judgment. Here was the heart of Thomistic philosophy as a distinctive doctrine, and it lay deeply imbedded within the context of his Christian faith. By striking contrast, the modern Thomistic manualists had pretended to treat of philosophy apart from any influence of faith, and as a consequence had become an isolated and ineffective enclave in the modern world. The remedy lay both in recalling the true condition of the philosophy of St. Thomas and in furthering the restoration of Christian philosophy called for in the *Aeterni Patris* of Leo XIII.

This program was joined in Gilson's mind, however, with an historical generalization about the essentialist character of non-Thomistic philosophies. He found traces of essentialism not only in the modern naturalists but also in the other medieval theologians, despite the influence of the Christian faith upon the latter group. His problem concerned the respective relations between the law of essentialism and the presence of faith in determining the philosophical standpoints of the medieval theologians. Another issue concerned whether St. Thomas could be taken as a norm for the most authentic sort of Christian philosophy. The very uniqueness of his metaphysics of being as existent tended to isolate him effectively from the rest of the history of philosophy on the crucial points for a Christian philosophy. The relation between Aquinas' philosophical acumen, Christian faith, and historical role in Christian philosophy thus came to the fore in Gilson's revision of his book on the Common Doctor.

2. *St. Thomas and Christian Philosophy*

Two cardinal doctrines in *The Christian Philosophy of St. Thomas Aquinas* concern the concept of the revealable and the ground for distinguishing philosophy and theology. Certain natural truths bear closely upon our salvation, since they have a bearing upon the act of faith and the ordination of man to his real last end. They can be revealed and some of them are actually revealed, although they do not thereby become strict articles of faith. It is from the perspective of the revealable that Gilson's magisterial study is written.

He places two significant qualifications upon his approach to St. Thomas.

We are not maintaining that St. Thomas identified the two notions of "revealable" and "philosophy," nor do we claim that the philosophy of St. Thomas cannot be legitimately examined from another point of view. But we beg leave to examine it under the aspect which St. Thomas himself claims to have examined it, that of the Christian Doctor, because it is for having envisaged metaphysics under this definite aspect, that his genius has renovated it.[8]

There is no perfect identity between philosophy and that which can be revealed. This is clear enough in the case of the Greek and Arabian thinkers, who deserve the name of philosophers even when they remain unaware of Christian revelation and hence do not receive its special guidance. It is also implied in the case of contemporary non-Christian philosophers, whom Gilson customarily addresses as "our philosophical colleagues." Indeed, he ordinarily reserves this name for such philosophers, thus enforcing in practice his point that Thomists should follow the theological order or cease to call themselves Thomistic philosophers. Even in the case of St. Thomas, however, he grants that there is a small number of works in which the philosophical method is followed, including the use of the philosophical order. This is the case at least with the commentaries on Aristotle and some of the *Opuscula*, although even here the theological influence is by no means absent.

Hence there are admittedly some important philosophical aspects of the mind of Aquinas which cannot be thoroughly understood, if one studies his philosophy exclusively in terms of the revealable.

That is why Gilson makes the second careful qualifying remark that he is not denying the legitimacy of taking another approach to the philosophy of Aquinas, one that is not regulated by the exigencies of the revealable. His own purpose is to explore Thomistic thought from the latter standpoint, and the results strongly justify this method of treatment. Yet something is to be gained also from following the other legitimate way of viewing Thomistic thought, which can be done without denying the importance of Gilson's approach in terms of the revealable. Both viewpoints help to cast light on the sources, and need not be treated as mutually antagonistic methods. It is important to ascertain how St. Thomas *examines* his teaching in function of his office as a theologian, but it is also important to study the way in which he philosophically *grounds* and develops the teaching so that it can be philosophically sound doctrine, worthy of a theological use and presentation. Both functions concern his work as a Christian Doctor. There are risks connected with both approaches, since they both require interpretation on the part of the modern student of St. Thomas.

Gilson next makes use of the Thomistic way of distinguishing between philosophy and theology.[9] The first basis of difference is in their principles of demonstration. Whereas philosophy argues from the essence of things and their proper causes, theology argues from God's revealed word or considerations of divine power and glory. Secondly, the two disciplines differ in the order of demonstration: philosophy starts from sensible finite things and moves toward a knowledge of God through inference, whereas theology begins with God and considers created things only subsequently and in relation to God. Which one of these bases of difference is indispensable for maintaining the difference in kind between philosophy and theology which persists even when they are in agreement and close organic unity? Gilson replies that the specific difference between the two sciences is based upon their different principles of demonstration. In the case of the philosophy of St. Thomas, considered in terms of the revealable, however, the theological order is followed even in regard to naturally attainable truths. As far as his main philosophical positions are concerned (those concerning God, the production of the world, and man's nature and destiny), St. Thomas uses the principles of philosophical demonstration but presents truths according to the order of theological demonstration. Here is Gilson's precise meaning for the distinctively Thomistic sort of Christian philosophy.

With the help of the key concepts of the revealable and the theological order of reasoning, Gilson is now ready to show what they entail for his historical exposition of the philosophy of Aquinas.

If we consider the philosophy of St. Thomas under the aspect of the revealable, its resulting theological order brings it immediately to grips with the problem of the existence of God. This problem itself supposes some preliminary understanding of the meaning of the term "existence," that is, a definition of what is meant by the verbs "to be" or "to exist." St. Thomas himself seems to have been aware of the urgency of this problem since one of his first works is the treatise *On Being and Essence*.[10]

The first sentence in this text is accurately phrased and delicately nuanced. Not from every viewpoint, but precisely when considered under this aspect of the revealable, the philosophy of St. Thomas is organized according to the theological order. From this standpoint, the first problem it confronts is that of the truth about God's existence. The closest one can get to treating philosophy according to the theological order is to say that it starts immediately with the problem of whether God exists.

But although this is a kind of theological beginning, as far as philosophical thought is concerned there is an entire sub-basement of prior questions. They can be briefly indicated under the rubric of ascertaining the meaning of existence and the existential judgment. But in fact, they include the basic analysis of the being of finite sensible things and of our knowledge of them. As far as a theological order of presentation of philosophical doctrine is concerned, this analysis can be presupposed. But it has to be made somewhere, not purely in terms of presenting a doctrine already in one's possession but in terms of establishing the validity of the meaning itself. Hence the urgency of the problem for St. Thomas and his efforts to make the required metaphysical investigation, even within an overarching theological disposition of topics. Because he is a Christian Doctor with a difference, one who recognizes the irreducible nature of philosophical methods, data, and demonstrations, he does not confine his philosophy to the revealable aspect and to the theological ordering. He also considers directly the finite sensible sources of evidence, and to some extent works out the meaning of being and of existential knowledge from the starting point which these sources furnish.

In effect, this means that the immediate beginning dictated by the theological order of reasoning is not the unqualified beginning of the philosophical work of Aquinas. This order is acceptable for philosophy on the supposition that the individual mind which is developing the theologically ordered body of knowledge has examined the evidence supporting the conception of being and knowing involved in the doctrine. This examination of evidence from finite sources was not carried out in complete systematic form and literary embodiment by St. Thomas. But the presence of the need in principle to do so and of certain actual instances of reasoning in the philosophical order, as distinct from an overall theological plan, is testified by Gilson's own arrangement of chapters. He does not begin immediately with a chapter on God's existence but with one on existence and reality.[11] This opening chapter summarizes the major metaphysical doctrines on act and potency, the co-principles of being, and the existential judgment. Its position at the initial point in Gilson's own exposition of Thomistic philosophy indicates the work done by Aquinas not only in terms of philosophical principles of demonstration but also in terms of a philosophical order of reasoning. Even within the movement of thought characteristic of St. Thomas' major theological writings, there are instances of issues handled according to the philosophical order imposed by finite things and natural evidence. The philosophical order is never simply replaced by a theological order of reasoning in philosophical matters, since philosophical demonstration carries with it an order regulated by the finite source from which our human minds derive knowledge of the natures and proximate causes of things.

The persistence of the philosophical order of reasoning even in the highest reaches of St. Thomas' philosophizing is problematically recognized by Gilson at the close of his chapter on God as the act of being.

Is it St. Thomas the theologian who, reading in *Exodus* the identity of essence and existence in God, taught St. Thomas the philosopher the distinction between essence and existence in creatures? Or is it St. Thomas the philosopher who, pushing his analysis of the metaphysical structure of the concrete even as far as the distinction between essence and existence, taught St. Thomas the theologian that *He Who Is* in *Exodus* means the *Act-of-Being?* St. Thomas himself as a philosopher thought of these two propositions as the two sides of one and the same metaphysical thesis. And from the day he understood them, he always thought of them as being in Holy Scripture.[12]

The problem here is not to discuss the various textual readings of this enigmatic passage in *Exodus*. The historical originality of St. Thomas' interpretation of the Vulgate rendering of *Exodus* is well established by Gilson. From this historical fact it does not follow, however, either that St. Thomas thought the metaphysical thesis about the distinction between essence and existence to be contained in Holy Scripture

290

or that every authentic Christian Thomism must exclusively use the theological order of reasoning concerning the sublime truth about the being of God. As Gilson allows, it remains a thorny question of determining precisely how Aquinas did come to understand these truths.

3. A Path for Contemporary Thomism

We are now in a position to return to the original text of Gilson, stating the alternative for Christian philosophers in the Thomistic tradition. The position which I am taking is that side one of the alternative is not unavoidable, since Thomism as a philosophy of the revealable is not the only legitimate way of interpreting and developing the philosophical doctrines of St. Thomas. And side two is not the inevitable consequence of criticizing the Gilsonian conception of the Christian philosophy of Aquinas, since these standpoints of essentialism and naturalism do not impose themselves with necessity. There are five considerations which lead me to the conclusion that the proposed alternative need not be accepted by those who are trying to philosophize today as Christians and Thomists.

(a) *Philosophical reconstruction.* For all of us, it is indeed a question of reconstructing Thomism and not of becoming shadow-reproductions of St. Thomas. There are various kinds of reconstruction, depending upon the aim of the individual mind. The chief modes are those of the historian, the theologian, and the philosopher. Gilson's work belongs mainly in the field of historical reconstruction, without excluding the other concerns. Its definitive result is to locate the philosophy of Aquinas within its actual context of Christian faith and theological speculation. Given this historical finding, it will not be possible for us to imagine that his philosophy was elaborated entirely apart from revelation and the ordering of theological science. There is also a distinctive way in which the contemporary theologian can recover the mind of Aquinas. One hallmark of a Christian philosophy is to recognize the urgency of formal theological studies in this area. Finally, there is the philosophical work of reconstruction. It cannot go on in ignorance of the findings made by the historian and the theologian, and yet it remains a distinct task.

The purpose of philosophical reconstruction is to deal directly with the great problems of natural human speculation, to seek out the founding evidence and meaning relevant to the issues, and thus to attain some demonstrated, verified truths. When this work is done in a Christian and Thomistic spirit, it will remain open to the revealed doctrine bearing on the case and will use the tested metaphysical positions of St. Thomas in the course of further work. One need not proceed by laying down that there is only one valid way of doing a philosophical reconstruction of Thomism. The basic need today is that many minds should work out—each in his own way—the detailed reconstruction according to the philosophical order.

The general basis for this approach is present in the Thomistic theory of the sciences, and there is the persistent influence of philosophically ordered truths throughout his thought. Although the development of Thomistic philosophy under this aspect is different from the approach in terms of the revealable, it does not contradict this latter aspect but develops the other historically grounded directions of Thomistic philosophic reasoning. This type of philosophic reconstruction of Thomism is done on one's own responsibility, but with a twofold concern for respecting the leads given by Aquinas himself and the actual state of the question.

(b) *Historical laws.* The work of philosophizing is never totally governed by the laws discovered by the historian of philosophy. These laws of the historian are inductive inferences from past cases. They may be significantly widespread and recurrent enough to warrant the name of pure positions, but there always remains a certain gap between these pure positions and the concrete standpoint being taken by some present philosopher. The pure positions indicate broad trends, extreme standpoints, ideal courses of dialectic, reductive bases of argument. Yet a discrepancy is bound to remain between them and the living mind which is aware of them. The laws of the history of philosophy are not real causal agencies in the intellectual order: they do not exert a determining influence under their own power, such that the person philosophizing cannot break through their pattern.[18] Alternatives based on historical generalizations do not confront us strictly with ironclad dilemmas, but rather with lessons from which we can profit while yet retaining our own path of thought.

Such is the case with the argument that unless the theological order is followed, the Thomist will land in metaphysical essentialism or naturalism. The two subdivisions of side two of this alternative can be regarded as difficulties or extremes that should be avoided. They are warnings well taken, but they do not represent unavoidable consequences. There is no systematic exigency compelling a philosophically ordered Thomism to terminate in a metaphysics of substantial form and a philosophy cut off from all influence of faith, although it is well to keep these pitfalls clearly before the mind. Not to follow the theological order of reasoning does not mean to turn away from the evidence of the act of existing of sensible beings, and neither does it mean to close off one's mind to the objective and subjective aids of revelation. The evidence of existing finite things and the suggestions of faith remain in full force for the Thomistic philosopher who seeks to build up his propositions according to the philosophical order. Hence he need not submit to Gilson's law of substituting the Aristotelian or Cartesian pure positions for Thomistic philosophy.

(c) *"The Philosopher."* Our problem concerns not only the objective order of reasoning but also the standpoint of the minds doing the philosophizing, since it involves the state of philosophy and the attitude taken toward various sources of evidence. There is no univocal meaning for "the philosopher," since it is realized differently under different historical conditions. A Thomist who follows the philosophical order today does not automatically align himself with Siger of Brabant and the medieval Arts-Faculty men on such issues as the authority of Aristotle, the split between demonstrated conclusions and truths, and the real end of man. These positions are the consequence of separating faith and philosophical inquiry, rather than simply of following the philosophical order in one's inquiry. The latter is a method for working out the implications of finite sensible things, but it does not stipulate that our study of these things must be wholly unaffected by what faith teaches about them.

When the name of Descartes is introduced into the alternative, however, the discussion is brought irrevocably into the modern world. This reinforces the fact that we are concerned with a personal work of reconstruction being done by contemporary philosophers. The Thomists in question are not only in the modern age, but in it in a post-Cartesian way. Thanks to historical studies by Gilson and others, they are informed about the position of Descartes on faith and reason and about its consequences in philosophy. No historical dialectic forces them to substitute the pure Cartesian position on the self and on faith for the Thomistic view of the starting point and real context of philosophy. The development of a philosophical rather than a theological order of reasoning in philosophy does not entail the attempt to construct a philosophy entirely without reference to the light of faith. All it requires is that the philosopher, while remaining steadily open to all sources of instruction concerning things, will examine the facts of finite being on their own evidence and develop his philosophical propositions from this starting point, as far as the formal con-

293

stitution of the science is concerned. There is no methodic resolution to treat the doctrine of faith provisionally or put it out of play until the system is completed.

In this respect, there is also a difference between a contemporary philosophically ordered Thomism and the Thomism of the manual writers during modern centuries. For one thing, these authors did not possess the controls afforded by the historical method with reference to St. Thomas and the modern philosophers in Descartes' wake. In many cases, the philosophy manuals were composed as strategic preludes to a theology course inevitably shaping up on the horizon. They were related to theology by way of not mentioning it and yet preparing for it, sometimes through the use of current rationalistic methods and doctrines. This is a quite different enterprise from the effort of contemporary Thomists to make a positive development of philosophy according to its own order and data, with the aid of the metaphysical doctrines of St. Thomas, and for the sake of ascertaining the philosophical truth. The latter aim does not exclude the ultimate ordering of philosophical knowledge in terms of finality to the knowledge of God in the beatific vision, but this ordering is not the same as a preadapting of one's philosophical reasoning to eventual theological use or a casting of it in the order of thought proper to theology. Yet extreme caution is needed in discussing the manuals of Thomistic philosophy published in the modern era, since so little is known as yet about the complex details of their history and achievement.

Gilson proposes the admirable definition that "Christian philosophy is a philosophy which, though formally distinguishing the two orders, considers Christian Revelation to be an indispensable guide to truth," a guiding star for the philosopher in his inquiries.[14] The Christian philosopher seeks to take advantage of every source of truth and instruction that can aid him in his proper work. He realizes that his philosophical studies will be carried out more perfectly by remaining constantly attentive to what faith assures him about God and the world. For the sake of being a better philosopher, his mind maintains a permanent alertness and responsiveness to the content of revelation, on those points which are relevant for his sphere of investigation. To this general requirement for the Christian philosopher it is not necessary to add the further specification that the Thomist must philosophize according to the theological order. When we acknowledge the indispensable guidance and influence of revelation upon our philosophizing, we do not thereby specify anything about what order must be followed in connecting the philosophically established propositions among themselves. This is a further issue, which is not predetermined by the living influence of one's faith.

That influence does not do the philosopher's work for him. It does not relieve him of the responsibility of consulting other sources and of seeing for himself how the matter stands. Along with revelation, the Christian philosopher will still have to consult the teachings of other philosophers and competent workers in the different fields. And above all, he cannot forego a direct consultation of things within range of his experience and inference.

Whatever guidance he receives from the various sources, his task as a philosopher is to base his philosophical assent to propositions upon the evidence as he himself grasps it in direct experience or demonstrative reasoning. The formal constitution of his philosophical science depends upon this establishment of the required evidence for philosophical assent. Using all the guidance available to man, he must rigorously respect the requirements of his own work. The principles of demonstration constituting philosophical science are the being and natures of things and the proximate causes, to the extent that they actually come within the range of the philosopher's mind and meet the tests set for direct confirmation and demonstrative inference. The influence of revelation does not make the Christian philosopher less scrupulous, but more so, in conforming to the requirements for the philosophical acceptance of propositions as true.

(d) *From sensible beings to God.* The sources of evidence which determine the ground of assent and the range of demonstration in philosophy also impose an order of reasoning to be followed. In developing a theistic realism, we make a start with finite and composed beings in the sensible world. In the case of metaphysical inquiry, the movement of inference is from these beings to the truth that God exists and is distinct from the world. In the case of a philosophy of man, the inference proceeds from a study of his operations to his powers and composite nature. This order of reasoning refers to the objective connection of implication between the propositions variously established in the inferential work of developing a philosophical science. It does not specify in any exclusive way the sources employed by the philosophic mind in its examination of sensible things and their demonstrable implications. How the particular inquirer makes his start in studying sensible things is left open to various determinations, depending upon the aids he uses in searching after significant data and problems. The Christian philosopher does not leave out his faith when he constructs a philosophical science whose propositions are grounded by way of implication upon some basic metaphysical propositions concerning sensible things.

One characteristic of St. Thomas is his readiness to use the philosophical sources of evidence and order of reasoning, where they are appropriate within the general theological movement of his teaching. This is the case with his remarks on the philosophical demonstration that God exists, with his basic positions on the knowledge of existential act and substance, with his metaphysical analysis of the principles of being and change in finite things, and with particular questions concerning the powers and nature of man. He does not bring all of these themes together into a comprehensive work, developed according to the philosophical order. And he does not carry through the investigation of these issues in the full depth and detail required by this ordering of knowledge. But St. Thomas does provide instructive and fundamental examples of how to proceed in accordance with philosophical principles and order, as much as concerns his function as a Christian Doctor who accepts the difference in kind between philosophy and theology. He also indicates that there is no radical incompatibility between a philosophical assent to propositions on the ground of the evidence furnished by experience or demonstration, an investigation of questions proceeding in a philosophical movement of inference, and a directing of all such philosophical knowledge to the ultimate vision of God, in the order of finality.

With this guidance, it seems to me that contemporary thinkers can develop a philosophy that is Christian and Thomist, without being organized according to the theological order. For this philosophical reconstruction of Thomism, there is no complete and fully executed plan furnished by St. Thomas himself. But there is his central conception of the nature of philosophical demonstration and assent, the example of his significant particular investigations, and his broad plan of proceeding from sensible beings to God. How the reasoning is to be carried out in detail with regard to the main subjects of study depends upon variable factors in any case, so that the Thomist philosopher is always left with his own risk. He can assume the risk in a responsible way, however, with the help of an exact historical study of St. Thomas, a competent use of all the other available sources for examining our world and its implications, and an informed awareness of the present philosophical situation. This way of philosophizing is independently faithful to the mind of St. Thomas, without involving any dialectical reduction to a naturalist and essentialist philosophy.

The only negative suggestion which I would propose is that a contemporary Thomism should not and could not take its guidance from Malebranche and Pascal on how to be a Christian philosophy.[15] There is sufficient definiteness about St. Thomas' teaching on the philosophical order of reasoning to hold that it does proceed from sensible things to God. In the case of Malebranche, however, the existence of the external world and the existence of God are assented to only in virtue of faith in the content of revelation. Pascal also relies upon faith for the only certain source of knowledge of God's existence. For them, faith not only impels a man to search out the philosophical basis of this truth but supplies the basis itself, in the form of the only compelling evidence that God exists.

To acknowledge openly that one is a Christian and that revelation provides us with significant truths is not sufficient, by itself, to constitute one a Christian philosopher. The question about the principles and order of philosophical demonstration must then be settled in a determinate way. And the responses given by Malebranche and Pascal to this question indicate that they assign to reasons drawn from revelation the decisive role of determining their assent to the basic propositions in philosophy. That is also why they tend to deprive sensible things of positive metaphysical significance at the outset of the philosophical inquiry, a point of philosophical order which they share with Descartes. But it is precisely a mark of the Thomistic position that sensible beings must serve as the foundation for a natural and philosophical demonstration of the truth that God exists, and that they do not have to wait for a prior certification from God in order to serve this minimal function. This is the most radical sense in which St. Thomas maintains a philosophical order of reasoning even within his theological context.

It is important to add that the philosophical order of reasoning from sensible things to God refers to the *primary* movement of inference required in the order of discovery of some important truths in metaphysics. It does not preclude the further movement of explanatory analysis and development of the truths acquired in this way. On the contrary, the philosophical ordering of demonstration demands an eventual return of the investigation to sensible things once more, but viewed this time in the light of the truths established through advancing causal inference to the study of the first causal being, God. Since this is definitely a *return* movement and not the initial path followed in the order of knowing, it remains distinct from any theologically ordered type of philosophy. But the order of philosophical demonstration does vindicate the importance not only of arriving at the truth about the existence of God, the first cause of finite beings, but also of employing that truth for the purpose of a further elucidation and perfection of our knowledge of finite beings.

The conscience of the philosopher obliges him to keep these two phases of the philosophical investigation distinct, to maintain the proper order of knowing in which we go first of all from sensible things to God, and then to cultivate in its full philosophical range the judgmental reconsideration of sensible beings and the human philosophical sciences within the perspective afforded by the previously established truth about God as the primary cause of beings. Yet this latter phase cannot be confused with adopting the theological order in one's philosophy.

(e) *A contemporary need.* Along with the intrinsic constitution of philosophy and the guidance of St. Thomas, there is also the relevant concern about our contemporary situation in philosophy. One of the present needs in our day and country is certainly that the Christian philosopher frankly and explicitly bring out all the conditions under which he is doing his study, including the influence of his faith. In his discussion of this matter with others, he can also ask that they become reflectively aware of whether or not their positions on revelation have a positive or a negative bearing upon their own manner of philosophizing. As far as the philosophical issues themselves are concerned, however, the outcome will depend upon the strength of the evidence itself insofar as it is made available for public inspection and testing, whatever the aids employed to find and analyze it. Every working philosopher today must eventually appeal to the common standards for determining what is a philosophically well-established proposition and a philosophically well-structured connection among a group of such propositions. Respect for this appeal does not automatically guarantee complete philosophical agreement, but it does supply the soundest basis in the long run for discussions among philosophers leading to some measure of common understanding and sharing of truth.

Moreover, unless the inquiry follows the philosophical order throughout the long process of analysis and inference, it is not likely to be accepted today as an instance of philosophically relevant reasoning. Hence both for the sake of perfecting philosophical truth itself and for engaging effectively in philosophical discussion under contemporary conditions, it is essential that contemporary Thomists use it and use it in full depth and thoroughness. A Thomism that is both reflectively Christian and developed according to the font of evidence and order of demonstration proper to philosophy has the inner resources for doing some effective work in the present intellectual world. Theistic realism is not a mere restatement of Thomism, but it can incorporate the resources of philosophical Thomism only on condition that the latter achieve a profound grasp of its own nature as a philosophical teaching, responsible for developing itself according to the content and order of commonly available human evidence.

CHAPTER 12

LEO XIII AND THE PHILOSOPHICAL
APPROACH TO MODERNITY

WHEN a Christian philosopher sets out to deal with the encyclicals and other relevant materials of Leo XIII pertaining to his own discipline, he does not presume to invade the theologian's domain or to render the latter's professional office superfluous. But the documents in question do bear upon the work and the ideals of the philosopher, so that to this extent he is being specially addressed and must render back his own kind of response. This is not an easy task, and neither is it one that has already been accomplished so thoroughly that further investigation is unnecessary. There is a strenuously demanding quality about all of Leo's writings, since they combine a finely balanced literary form with an intense compression and precision of thought. They present a real challenge to the philosopher who is willing to read them carefully and take instruction from them, even though his approach does not exhaust their significance. What he can attempt is to relate the papal teaching as closely as possible to his own experience of philosophical thinking and its concrete conditions. In this way he can hope to capture at least some aspects of Leo's abiding significance for those whose vocation it is to respond both to the life of Christian faith and the intrinsic requirements of philosophy.

There are many facets in Pope Leo's relationship with philosophy. We are familiar with what his successor, Pope Pius XI, did not hesitate to call his greatest service to the Church and civil society, namely, the strong impetus which Leo gave to the renewal of Christian philosophy, mainly in its Thomistic form, but with due regard for the doctrines of the Fathers and the other Schoolmen. This is the main theme of *Aeterni Patris,* the key encyclical which has served since 1879 as the guiding stimulus toward recovering the sources of Christian philosophical ideas.[1] But Pope Leo's encouragement of this vast work of historical investigation does not exhaust his significance for philosophical studies. Both in *Aeterni Patris* itself and in most other Leonine pronouncements bearing upon philosophy there is another intention, closely related with that of restoration but nevertheless sufficiently distinct from it to permit a separate analysis. This is the theme of making a proper appraisal of modern philosophy, determining the philosophical relevance of the advances made in the modern arts and sciences, and thereby enriching the whole body of Christian philosophical wisdom. This other concern of Leo did not escape the attention of his successors, particularly Pius XII, so that it can be said to define the most authentic Catholic position on the study of modern and contemporary tendencies in philosophy.

It is this latter side of Pope Leo's mind which we intend to examine here and to link up with the more familiar aspects of his attitude on philosophy. We will try to bring out how the study of modern philosophy is bound up intimately with three major Leonine teachings: on the best way in which the Christian can philosophize, on the method for recapturing the wisdom of St. Thomas, and on the policy of continuous building rather than destroying in philosophical discussions. Combining these three themes, we will then be in a position to see that Leo XIII is pre-eminently the Pope of *the open tradition in philosophy,* which joins a firm rooting in our Christian philosophical heritage with a critical yet generous response to modern thought.

1. *The Best Way of Philosophizing*

To discover why Leo included the study of modern philosophy in most of his general counsels on philosophical matters, we have to keep in mind the conception of philosophy underlying his teaching. His attitude toward the philosophical enterprise as a whole helped to determine his remarks on how a Christian thinker should relate himself to postmedieval philosophies. This connection has to be made clear.

One characteristic note running through all of Pope Leo's treatments of philosophy is that the Church has a stake in the issue and hence has the right to speak with authority about at least some aspects of philosophy. In maintaining that there is a real basis for this relationship, he establishes his continuity with the views of Pope Pius IX. Some of Leo's contemporaries were puzzled by his remark about wanting people to understand and be reconciled to his predecessor's *Syllabus of Errors,* but on many crucial matters this is indeed the case. It is likely that, as the Bishop of Perugia, he had been influential in urging Pius IX to draw up the 1864 *Syllabus* and in suggesting some of the doctrines to be condemned. Prominent in the official list are two closely related propositions taken from a previous letter of Pius IX to the Archbishop of Munich. Among the errors of rationalism are these two statements: "Philosophy is to be treated without taking any account of supernatural revelation," and therefore "the Church not only ought never to pass judgment on philosophy, but ought to tolerate the errors of philosophy, leaving it to correct itself." [2] A cognate proposition holds that, whereas the philosopher as an individual ought to submit to Church authority, philosophy itself cannot and should never do so. These propositions are the speculative counterparts of other ones which advocate the total separation of the Church from all the vital interests of modern man in social and religious affairs. Hence their net effect is to recommend the isolation of the Church from all of our living concerns, both in the order of ideas and in practical life.

To appreciate why Leo XIII regarded his position as being essentially one with that of his immediate predecessor, we have to watch him develop the positive conception of philosophy with respect to which the above condemned propositions are shown to be untenable. At the very outset of *Aeterni Patris,* he touches the core of the issue by noting some hard facts about man which we cannot ignore or legislate away. Since the Christian faith involves an act of the understanding and an intellectually determinate content, its relation to our minds is concretely affected by what we think. Not only what we think in an informal way but also the formal elements contained in the arts and sciences, especially in philosophy, exert a deep influence over the integrity of faith as entertained by the minds of living men. Under the actual conditions of human existence, our integrity of faith tends to be either safeguarded or else corrupted by our philosophical convictions. A man who accepts the philosophical notion that God is a projective compensatory myth, that all our actions are determined by impersonal natural laws, and that our little life is wholly snuffed out at bodily death, is apt to be ill-disposed for accepting or remaining loyal to the Christian faith. Furthermore, the influence of philosophical ideas is practical as well as speculative and, within the practical order, spills out far beyond one's individual conduct to the whole shape and direction of public life.

On the wide and observable social repercussions of philosophical doctrines, Leo speaks incisively and out of the fullness of his own varied experiences.

Whoso turns his attention to the bitter strifes of these days and seeks a reason for the troubles that vex public and private life must come to the conclusion that a fruitful cause of the evils which now afflict, as well as those which threaten, us lies in this: that false conclusions concerning divine and human things, which originated in the schools of philosophy, have now crept into all the orders of the State, and have been accepted by the common consent of the masses.[3]

On the basis of our present forms of social knowledge and our experience of the domestic effects of naturalism and the international effects of communist ideas, we have good grounds for reaffirming this connection as a very potent one. Little wonder, then, that Leo's great social encyclicals are distinguished by their persistent care to analyze the philosophical principles which help to shape modern social life, and which have to be critically revised in order to open up new possibilities.

Leo grants that there are major areas in philosophical discussion which do not have a traceable bond with issues of faith and morals, and hence where the Church cannot and should not make any authoritative pronouncements affecting the field of speculation. Yet the fact that there are other large areas where such a link is present between philosophical ideas and the attitudes of men toward revelation and moral law means that the Church cannot remain entirely indifferent to such ideas. That is why the total separatism mentioned in the 1864 Syllabus is both unrealistic for the Christian mind and undiscerning from the philosophical standpoint.

Let us now consider the sense in which doctrinaire separation is at once unrealistic and undiscerning. It is unrealistic, once we grant that philosophy has a very important set of human functions to perform. Both Leo XIII and Pius XII correlate the Church's concern about some aspects of philosophy with their high conception of the office and power of philosophical thought. Operating at its peak, philosophy can bring out and safeguard the natural evidence supporting our confidence in the human mind and its ability to reach some real truths concerning God, human reality, and moral law.[4] One's philosophical position on these issues profoundly affects one's growth as an intellectual inquirer, a man of faith, and a shaping agent in the moral community of men. Leo's favorite image for expressing the function of philosophy is that of the bridge. Philosophical activity provides the bridge for joining together our secular concerns and our religious beliefs, our intellectual interests and the practical arts of life. Because of this unifying work within its own sphere, philosophy does actually affect the relation of men to the practical organizing of society and the order of grace.

Were it not for this rather exalted notion of the philosopher's vocation, the problem of a sound philosophy capable of working effectively in the modern world would not be nearly so acute in Leo's estimation. And were it not for this same conception, his interpretation of philosophy would be much less relevant for our own intellectual climate than in point of fact it is. We can feel the sting behind his contention that any lower evaluation of philosophical work is undiscerning, when we compare the functions specified by him with some current opinions on the job of the philosopher.

Outside of the naturalists and Marxists, the phenomenologists and existentialists, it is presently fashionable for philosophers to disclaim any burning interest in the grand problems of human destiny and any definite responsibility for the practical consequences of their theoretical analyses. Making a careful analysis of the linguistic and conceptual structures would presumably exhaust the philosopher's task, and would leave him professionally unaccountable for how people may use the results in deciding what to believe and how to act as individuals and groups. But historical experience shows that this disavowal does not tell the whole story, and that it cannot sustain itself over a long period and with respect to all the main issues. Usually, the policy of abstention from inquiring beyond the language system or the conceptual structure contains an implicit assumption about the range of the human mind and about the accessibility of human nature, the moral law, and the truth about God to our human intelligence. When this latent element is eventually brought to open statement, it usually does affect the concrete moral attitudes of men toward these matters.

Another provocative aspect of Pope Leo's general conception of philosophy comes in view when we pay careful attention to the language he customarily uses to describe it. It is quite noticeable that he often prefers to speak about "philosophizing" rather than "philosophy," especially when there is question of the optimum functions and the relationship with faith. This preference for the verbal form is not accidental, and neither is it merely an adornment of style. It is a significant, deliberately chosen usage which recurs in many different contexts. Leo likes to speak about the *ratio philosophandi* and the *forma philosophandi*, the *optima ratio philosophandi* and the *optima forma philosophandi*.[5] He secures several advantages in thus approaching philosophy as an operation having a form and a pattern. This usage helps to undercut the proposition in the 1864 *Syllabus* which advocates a divorcement between the philosopher as an individual agent and his philosophy taken as a separate entity, molded by purely impersonal laws. Leo suggests, on the one hand, that philosophy lives and flourishes as a habit and mode of activity in the individual human mind and, on the other, that the activity itself is of a reasonable sort which respects the intelligible structures of things. Philosophizing constitutes this conjunction between the personal activity of living minds and the reasonable pattern of beings, and only in such a meeting does philosophy achieve its perfection as a human discipline.

To show the essential modernity as well as traditional character of Leo's thought on this issue, we do not have to attempt any strained comparison with the elaboration of the theme of philosophizing in Dewey, Husserl, Jaspers, and other twentieth-century thinkers.[6] It is sufficient to note that the Pope is responding to some definite intellectual needs of our age and also is responding to them precisely in the manner appropriate for the chief teacher in the Church. His conception of effective philosophizing as a union between the living intelligence and the patterns of being points out the way of overcoming that gaping estrangement of mind from nature and God which underlies our psychic and social disorders. When we engage in philosophical work, we should retain a basic openness both to the significance of things within our experience and to the initiative of the revealing God. Once we learn to place the accent upon philosophizing, we will be disinclined to regard philosophy any longer as a closed universe in which there are no pathways leading from the linguistic or analytic scheme to the significance of natural things and the traces of God which they bear.

Speaking not as a philosopher but as the supreme teacher of revealed truth to whom the religious renewal of all things human is a prime concern, Leo XIII compresses into a pregnant sentence his view of the best way to philosophize: "Those, therefore, who to the study of philosophy unite obedience to the Christian faith, are philosophizing in the best possible way; for the splendor of the divine truths, received into the mind, helps the understanding, and not only detracts in nowise from its dignity, but adds greatly to its nobility, keenness, and stability."[7] In a word, the Christian mind's mode of philosophizing offers the best prospects of obtaining humanly valuable results, provided that it is careful to unite professional competence of the highest order with a meditative grasp of the truths of faith.

Leo's teaching on this score is sharply critical of the widespread modern assumption that one can best philosophize by keeping the mind isolated from any sort of influence of religious faith. This premise has been the working law for philosophers who have come in the wake of Machiavelli and Bruno, Descartes and Locke. The Pope is well aware, however, of the depth of his challenge and its connection with considerations joining philosophy to a wider context of thought. He often associates the estrangement between faith and philosophical activity with his broader theme about the historical stages in the dismemberment of human intelligence.[8] The sixteenth-century revolt took a decisive step by contrasting the sphere of Christian faith with all our secular interests, among which was counted the whole human interest in philosophy. This contrast between the domains of faith and philosophical reason was solidified and extended systematically by the key modern philosophers to the point where one's religious faith came to be regarded as an alien intruder and as a hindrance to speculative work. But Leo XIII makes the bold suggestion that the time has now come to review critically this conventional assumption and to move ahead to a more positive and fruitful conception of the influence which one's assent to revealed truth can have upon philosophical inquiry, provided that the professional standpoint is also operative.

Throughout this discussion, the Pope shows much more concern about the philosopher's general attitude than about this or that particular idea he may entertain. Here perhaps is the ultimate reason prompting Leo XIII to emphasize the theme of philosophizing. The root of the matter reaches down to the philosopher's personal conviction about how he ought to do his work and what constitutes an aid or a hindrance to it. A transformation in our view of how best to philosophize is the most reliable path for achieving a radical improvement both in the intellectual sphere and in the political and social order, insofar as the latter reflects the philosophical separation between religious and philosophical truths. The Christian philosopher cannot cut himself off from a direct and careful study of modern philosophical ideas, since such an attitude of separatism would be only compounding that mutual estrangement between Christian faith and human inquiry which Leo seeks to overcome on both sides.

Both in the text just quoted and in other crucial places, the Pope is quite careful in designating the component factors in the best way of philosophizing. He speaks not simply about Christian faith but about obedience or service to the Christian faith: *obsequium fidei christianae;* and similarly, he refers not simply to philosophy but to the study of philosophy: *studium philosophiae.* This language underlines once more the cardinal role of the living human mind in achieving a genuine restoration of Christian philosophy. The latter cannot spring into being through decree, through curricular shifts, or through descriptive praise from the outside. Although these conditions may help to provide an atmosphere in which Christian philosophizing can go on, that activity itself has to grow out of the mind's own acts and habits of studying philosophy and serving the truths of faith.

Provided that there is no methodological withdrawal of philosophical intelligence from the influence of faith, Leo XIII and Pius XI regard it as only just that a Christian philosopher should adhere carefully to the method, principles, and arguments proper to his own discipline.[9] Philosophy must inquire into those truths which can be shown from a close study of natural things, and hence it has an order and a set of tasks distinctively its own. The Christian philosopher enjoys the guiding and illuminating influence of his faith, and he shows in practice its consonance with the truths established from his philosophical investigation of nature. His responsiveness to the truths of faith helps him to stabilize, sharpen, and ennoble within its own order the philosophical inquiry which seeks to move from a strenuous analysis of natural things and human reality to their bond with God. The relation of friendship and fidelity to distinct offices which Pope Leo envisages between faith and philosophical intelligence can only lead to the enrichment of the Christian philosophical life within the modern context.

In outlining the main functions for the Christian philosopher today, the Pope usually specifies three areas of work. One task is to reread and revivify the wisdom of the ancient Greek and Roman sources. Another is to feed upon and develop the Christian wisdom slowly elaborated by the Fathers and Scholastic doctors, especially St. Thomas. And finally, one must make a careful study of the fruits of modern research in the physical, psychological, social, and historical fields, especially for the relevant light they may cast on philosophical issues. We should not be surprised to find this latter duty assigned to the Christian philosopher. There is a sharply practical note in all the papal teachings during the past eighty years on the subject of Christian philosophy.[10] Its practical growth and influence can occur only within the actual conditions of modern thought as well as modern social circumstances. The Christian philosopher must preserve his roots in the great sources of the past, but he has to carry on his own work within the field defined by the modern centuries of inquiry and discovery.

This three-fold function has become embodied in the curriculum requirements of Catholic universities and seminaries, but at the level of advanced original work it is not always realized even now that such an integration constitutes the best way of philosophizing on a long-term basis.

2. *The Wisdom of St. Thomas and Modern Problems*

One reason for Pope Leo's admiration of St. Thomas is that the latter made an adequate preparation for approaching the questions prominent in his own day. The Common Doctor set the example of making a comprehensive and continuing study of his intellectual heritage and reorganizing the materials under firm principles of order and future growth. In turn, our own personal reading of St. Thomas should be a liberating experience in the sense of inducing us to examine the intellectual riches of the ancient and medieval worlds, providing us with some lasting truths of being which still have a yield to give, and inviting us to do some creative work of critical evaluation and assimilation within our own philosophical environment. Here we must confine our attention to one aspect in recent papal recommendations of the study of St. Thomas, namely, that it should lead us eventually to make an internal and constructive study of the scientific and philosophical evidences and difficulties developed since the Middle Ages.

No one was better aware of the need for this new dimension of awareness on the part of Thomists themselves than was Leo XIII. During the full generation preceding *Aeterni Patris* he was a keen observer and promoter of the Italian developments leading up to the full revival of Thomistic doctrine. As the Bishop of Perugia, he took definite measures to have this doctrine taught in his seminary and to have it discussed and developed with respect to modern ideas, during the sessions of his Academy of St. Thomas. Through the wide contacts of his brother, Cardinal Joseph Pecci, he continued throughout his lifetime to keep abreast of the men and writings in the Thomistic field. Through this fund of first-hand information about the state of Thomistic studies, he acquired a deep conviction that at least one condition for the full restoration and growth of the Christian philosophy of St. Thomas lay in securing a profound and sustained engagement of that philosophy with all the tendencies in modern philosophy and science. Moreover, the Pope held that it was essential for the Thomists of today to realize just how far they were already involved in modern problems and methods, with the aim of getting a better grasp on the authentic doctrine of Aquinas and also of making a more reflective and adequate approach to the issues of our age in philosophy.

It is only by keeping in mind this broad experience of Leo XIII with respect to the quality and predicament of Thomism in his own day that we can understand why *Aeterni Patris* calls for the restoration, not precisely of Thomism, but of "the widom of St. Thomas"—*Sapientia Sancti Thomae*. These words do not have a purely eulogistic sense but convey a normative and critical meaning. Their intent is to urge us both to study the writings of St. Thomas himself without remaining content with the Thomistic manuals and schools, and also to take due account of later advances in human knowledge so that what we accept from St. Thomas are the permanently sound and wise foundations.

On the need for making a direct reading of St. Thomas the controlling factor in forming our conception of his teaching, the results of historical research have fully confirmed Pope Leo's caution. Our historical work is putting us in a better position for comparing Aquinas with the leading Thomists of Leo XIII's day. In connection with many specific issues in methodology, metaphysics, theory of knowledge, and social ethics, we can see how deeply these Thomists were already involved in modern philosophy. Men such as Sanseverino and Taparelli, Liberatore and Kleutgen, were originally grounded in an eclectic position combining some Scholastic elements with Cartesian, Lockean, and Wolffian borrowings.[11] When such writers made a shift toward the medieval sources after the social upheavals of 1848, they did not simply slough off their eclectic modern background. Nor did they feel that they could do so and still fulfill their responsibility to students in their own generation. Even after the turning point of 1879, many Thomistic manuals continued to employ the modern rationalist framework in terminology, statement of principles, division and organization of materials, and mode of inference.

We cannot treat these pioneers in a patronizing or satirical fashion, for they responded as promptly and completely to their intellectual challenge as it was possible for men in that transitional time to do. But Leo XIII had the further responsibility of promoting the long-range welfare of Christian philosophy, and this he saw to consist in a double policy. One side of it was to encourage an accurate and exhaustive study of the sources of Christian philosophy such as would live up to the high critical and historical standards of our time. Even in asking researchers to return to the genuine sources of Thomism

309

in the writings of the Common Doctor himself, the Pope was inviting a revolutionary approach to the sources of Christian thought which would meet the requirements of rigor in our historical references in philosophy. His general conviction that careful historical studies can only advance the cause of truth found particular application here in his encouragement of exact research into the mind of St. Thomas and the other doctors.

The second part of the Leonine policy in this matter was to direct that there be a conscientious and sustained comparison made between St. Thomas and the modern leaders in philosophy and the relevant sciences. The Pope did not disapprove of the fact that Thomists in his day were concerned about modern philosophical problems and were trying their best to deal with them. His point of criticism was that many men who called themselves Thomists were nevertheless lacking in a precise textual and contextual understanding of both the thought of St. Thomas and the thought of modern philosophers. To have an unsteady and non-rigorous grasp upon both poles of the comparison was an invitation to confusion and easy criticism. This was a dangerous condition for the instrinsic development of Christian philosophy, as well as for all the educational activities and practical policies dependent upon this philosophy. Perhaps the peculiar genius of Leo XIII in this area lay in his ability to distinguish clearly between the historical work in St. Thomas and other doctors and the careful investigation of modern philosophical and scientific theories, and yet to insist on the need for both tasks as being related phases in the Christian mode of philosophizing at its best. He did not conceive of the restoration of the philosophy of St. Thomas as a flight from the modern scene, but rather as a process of recovering the sound origins and foundation which will enable us to philosophize more effectively and stably within our present field of resources and problems.

The word "wisdom" was also employed in an evaluative way in the program of restoring and rethinking the teaching of St. Thomas. Leo XIII made this unmistakably evident in a paragraph toward the end of *Aeterni Patris* where he looked forward to the practical use and influence of the doctrine he was recommending.

While, therefore, we hold that every word of wisdom, every useful thing by whomsoever discovered or planned, ought to be received with a willing and grateful mind, We exhort you, venerable brethren, in all earnestness to restore the golden wisdom of St. Thomas, and to spread it far and wide for the defense and beauty of the Catholic faith, for the good of society, and for the advantage of all the sciences. The wisdom of St. Thomas, We say; for if anything is taken up with too great subtlety by the Scholastic doctors, or too carelessly stated—if there be anything that ill agrees with the discoveries of a later age, or, in a word, improbable in whatever way—it does not enter Our mind to propose that for imitation to Our age.[12]

In the Pope's mind, then, even the success of revitalizing the philosophical and theological doctrines of Aquinas was indissolubly bound up with a careful critical weighing of it in the light of modern findings, so that we could be sure that we would be building upon what is genuinely wise and tested in his thought. Restoration of the wisdom of St. Thomas is to be a discriminating task involving our speculative judgment as well as our historical recall, and involving that speculative judgment precisely as being well informed about the subsequent work done in modern philosophy and science.

To underline the importance of Leo's statement and to insure its force even during the confusing period of Modernist activities, Pope St. Pius X incorporated the above text in full into the 1907 encyclical *Pascendi*. He added that the truth of his predecessor's position is obvious and does not need insisting upon. However, we can now see that the Modernists themselves were instances of overhasty apologists, who had not followed Leo's counsel of making a detailed and patient study of both the great Christian sources and the background in modern philosophy and the sciences for the issues they sought to resolve so rapidly.

The finely balanced text of Leo which we have just given will repay a closer examination from our center of interest in philosophy. It concerns three aspects of philosophical wisdom. The first is the fact that the seeds of wisdom have been widely scattered under God's providence. Corresponding to this fact is the attitude it demands in us of remaining open to and grateful for any ray of illumination we can find, without being predisposed against the source and context in which it may actually be imbedded. We do not have the right or the power of predetermining where the words of wisdom are to be found, but we do have the duty to remain on the alert for them and to cultivate a prudent frame of mind for recognizing and incorporating them, whether they have been spoken by the ancient Greeks or by the modern authors. Secondly, Leo directs our study specially to St. Thomas as providing a unification of many scattered themes of philosophical and theological truth broached elsewhere, and as forming the mind with principles for continuing the search after philosophical wisdom.

But along with the fact of fragmented pieces of wisdom and the counsel to base oneself upon the principles in Aquinas, the Pope asks us to consider a third facet of wisdom under its human, philosophical form: this wisdom must continue to do its work in the world, to profit by the findings of the human mind in modern history, and thus to grow and perfect itself even in our own era. This open-ended character of philosophical wisdom is specially important in Leo's view, since without it a Christian philosophy cannot perform its proper functions of defending the faith, consolidating and ordering the sciences, and enlightening our social decisions. The sciences do not stand still, and society does not freeze itself into a single mold forever. Moreover, the new forms they take, the new methods they use, the new problems they uncover—all these factors are *philosophically* significant and hence affect the sound development and presentation of Christian philosophical wisdom. That wisdom cannot rightly be proposed for imitation in our own age unless it shows that it has assimilated the findings of our age, tussled with its problems, in their explicit philosophical form, and thus proved itself in fact as well as profession to be a mature philosophical wisdom in and for our time.

In making this last point as concrete as possible, without pretending to do the philosopher's work for him, Pope Leo mentions four specific ways in which we must become critical of our heritage and willing to add to the store of wisdom. Here he extends his view to the body of doctrines received from all the Scholastic doctors, without confining the analysis to St. Thomas. He asks workers in the field of philosophy to make good use of their modernity by being on guard against excessive subtlety, carelessness, conflict with sound modern discoveries, and improbabilities of any sort. These four avenues for improvement are not carelessly chosen, since they can be correlated with some of the constructive trends in modern philosophy with which Kleutgen and other advisers of Leo XIII were quite familiar. We will make an independent reflection upon this fourfold caution, since it may prove helpful to us even today, when the intellectual situation has changed so vastly in some respects.

(a) One of the strongest forces aiding the early growth of modern philosophy in the time of Bacon and Descartes was the revulsion people experienced when they tried to enter into discussion with the representatives of Scholasticism. The Scholastics gave the strong impression of being more interested in perpetuating their school disputes and in outrivaling each other in subtle distinctions and terminology than in reaching the truth and conveying it to men. Hence the moderns took drastic measures in simplifying their approach and in seeking to make a fresh start closer to what we can all experience. Whatever their particular failures, they did teach the lesson that in the modern period a philosophy cannot long survive unless it pares down on the subtleties and develops in an intelligible, straightforward, relatively public fashion. We do not want to lose this lesson, even now that we have entered an age of analysis which sometimes outbids the older Scholasticism for its involuted discussions. One of the marks of identity and attraction on the part of a Christian philosophy today should be its sense of primary concern for the significance of being as it manifests itself in the human persons and things of our ordinary experience.

(b) Even a well-substantiated body of wisdom can fail to win the mind's assent, if it is presented in a careless way or if it fails to take full advantage of modern means of attaining rigor of proof and statement. One great modern objection against the late medievals was that they were being subtle to no good purpose. We now know through the resources of symbolic logic that some of these medievals were striving, somewhat cumbersomely, to attain to a new exactness of thought. But this was the case mostly in the logical treatises, and even there the mathematical means were not available for a more economical expression of their ideal of precision. In large areas of natural philosophy, even in areas touching on man and God, however, subtlety of expression was combined with considerable carelessness in the description of evidence, the analysis of structures, and the proof of implications. This is always a fateful sort of combination, since it can easily convince the reader that truth is not seriously being sought and that it is not likely to be found in the direction indicated by the careless thinkers.

The modern stress upon methodology, analytic techniques, and symbolic logic has led to the acceptance of a high standard of rigor in philosophical thinking. Every advantage should be taken of these instruments. But as Husserl once pointed out, this still leaves unsettled the question of the pluralism of modes of rigorous investigation and hence the question of which type of rigor is best suited to a particular line of study. The Christian philosopher must be concerned to show that he respects the general requirements of rigor, and also that he is employing that sort of rigorous method which is best adapted to his kind of inquiry.

(c) That the discoveries of the modern age do have a significance for the Christian philosopher and do impose on him the obligation to revise his positions against any ill-considered disagreements, is

313

one of Pope Leo's strongest convictions. It underlies his repeated affirmation that the Church is not opposed to genuine intellectual progress, in the sense of the human effort at obtaining always a better understanding of our own nature and capacities and always more efficient means of controlling our world.[18] This is not a piece of fatuous optimism, since the recognition of a slow elaboration of methods and insights is combined by Pope Leo with the acknowledgment that they bring in their wake a whole new set of problems to be considered. Apart from a few exceptions among Scholastics who took the restoration of Christian philosophy to mean a simple repetition of previous ideas, most of the nineteenth-century Christian philosophers were quite sensitive to the philosophical difficulties raised by modern views of method and knowledge, by Newtonian physics, and by the infant sciences of laboratory psychology and psychiatry. Leo characterized the advances made in the sciences of nature and man as being so many sparks coming from the Creator and bearing witness to the dignity of our human vocation. But the sparks of new understanding embodied in the work of various kinds of modern scientists and artists are relevant for the philosopher's own interpretation of the natural and human universe. We cannot simply juxtapose an historical form of Thomism and the latest scientific teachings, since there are many philosophical implications in the sciences which are variously interpreted by philosophers today.

The ultimate unity of all truths in their divine source should not have a lulling effect upon our minds. Instead, this conviction should operate in two ways to prevent a complacent quiescence of intellectual outlook. For one thing, it means that the steady advances made in the other sciences and the arts do have some bearing upon philosophy: growth in one part of the body of truth tends to affect the other parts and to require a careful review and often an advance in philosophical insight itself. In the second place, the perfect harmony and unity of various kinds of knowledge are assured from God's standpoint, but have to be worked out in actual steps by our human minds. We can draw comfort and encouragement from accepting the ultimate unity of all truths in God, but the encouragement is intended to sustain us in a difficult human task rather than to dispense us from actually carrying it out. We have to traverse the long and sometimes rocky path between the plural condition of knowledges at our human level of vision and their ultimate unification, which for us always remains radically in the status of a continuing program of work still to be undertaken.

That process is one of growth on the basis of solid foundations, so that the permanent truths of Christian philosophy remain fully operative throughout the work of assessing and assimilating relevant findings from the physical and psychological, social and methodological, sciences of our day. Only it is necessary to keep these principles in working order and to display their critical and assimilative power in the detailed cases of difficulty. Precisely how this continuous relating of philosophy to modern discoveries should go on does not belong within the province of Pope Leo to specify, since he is not teaching as a philosopher. But he does regard it as part of his religious office to remind philosophers that it must go on as an indispensable phase in the restoration of Christian philosophy, in its Thomistic form as well as any other form.

(d) All of these previous notes of counsel add up to the warning to avoid any semblance of improbability in the program of restoring, enriching, and spreading our Christian philosophical wisdom. Not to avoid it would be doing an injustice to St. Augustine, St. Thomas, and the other great men in this tradition, and it would also be placing an unnecessary hindrance in the way of a ready acceptance on the part of our contemporaries. Here we are touching upon the springs of assent and upon the subjective conditions required for a firm adherence to philosophical truths. One of the great lines of modern exploration reaches into the domain of the human subject and his interiority. Philosophers are keenly interested in this domain, both as a way of access to human reality and as a means for understanding why some ideas win our ready assent and others leave us doubtful or indifferent.

A philosophy displays the look of improbability about it when it fails to establish meaningful links with the problems of greatest concern to a particular age, or when it ignores the sources of evidence and method made available in that age. When it fails in these two ways, it also *disconnects* itself from the framework of positions which are taken seriously as relevant interpretations and aids for the reflective minds of the time. It then appears to be a philosophy belonging to another era, an antiquated set of doctrines which have seen their day and which can no longer have a real claim upon our interest and assent. In such a situation it is not enough to maintain that truths are permanently valid for every age of man. This is indeed the case, but those who are not already convinced of its correctness are not likely to be moved by the mere assertion itself. The relevance of the doctrines has to be shown in actual instances, where they come to

315

grips with current problems and prove in action their capacity to illuminate, to criticize, and to grow. If one remains content with a general affirmation of lasting truths and then refrains from making those truths visibly operative within the intellectual context of our time, one is responsible for the air of improbability and remoteness surrounding so many presentations of Christian philosophies. One of the aspects in the restoration of this tradition is the restoring of it to a real, functional role within the range of teachings which the modern mind regards as urgently significant and worthy of acceptance. It is this problem of achieving philosophical relevance which links the topics of a perennial philosophy and a philosophically ordered Thomism with the questions raised by Pope Leo.

The precept of avoiding the appearance of unlikelihood and of earning the right to be treated as a challenging, pertinently true body of philosophical wisdom is consonant with Leo XIII's stress upon the Christian way of philosophizing. So that this philosophizing may be more widely shared, it must be related closely with all the other areas where our contemporary evidence and concerns lie. This synthesis between well-tested doctrines and respect for the peculiar concrete conditions affecting modern man's assent to the doctrines helps to explain Cardinal Newman's enthusiastic reception of *Aeterni Patris*. Although he could not claim to be a Thomist, he did see a likeness between his conception of how philosophy should be carried on today and the recommendations made by Leo XIII on the spirit of Christian philosophizing in the modern world. In a letter drafted to congratulate the Pope upon the occasion of the encyclical, he observed firmly that creative Christian work of an intellectual sort "should be grafted on the Catholic tradition of philosophy, and should not start from a novel and simply original tradition." [14] In his own way the English Cardinal was striving to achieve a living balance between the wisdom of the classical philosophers and Christian doctors and the concrete way of philosophizing which can address and move our contemporary intelligence.

It is noteworthy that Pope Leo, in turn, should have included his counsel about philosophizing within the modern context in his encyclical asking for the restoration of the wisdom of St. Thomas. He continued to join these themes in the later practical acts which carried out his intention. In his letters concerning the Roman Academy of St. Thomas Aquinas, the establishment of the chair of Thomistic philosophy and the school of philosophy at Louvain, and the founding of the

Catholic University of America, Pope Leo asked that responsible scholars undertake the twofold labor of studying St. Thomas in his own writings and comparing his doctrine with the teachings of ancient and modern philosophers.[15] He specified that the comparison be made not only to show in actual detail the basic integrity of the Thomistic position but also to enrich the general body of wisdom. We should expect to find some new teachings which bear the marks of industry, knowledge, and wisdom, and we should be quick to praise and incorporate whatever stands up under critical scrutiny. This same generous and constructive spirit in philosophical work was reaffirmed in *Humani Generis,* when Pius XII remarked that the study of modern and contemporary philosophies is not simply a cataloguing of errors but also a mining of sound nuggets, and hence an instrument for the internal perfecting of Christian philosophy itself.

We can now appreciate the striking covergence which has been gradually made between our first theme of philosophizing in the best way and our second theme of studying the modern thinkers. The Pope's basic advice is that our philosophizing should combine a permanent fidelity to the traditional sources of wisdom with a reflective study of the new paths in human scientific and philosophical knowledge. His pithy phrase, "strengthen and complete the old by aid of the new," [16] furnishes the guiding motto for those who are trying to work effectively as Christian philosophers under present intellectual conditions.

3. *Completing the Old by Aid of the New*

The Leonine ideal for the contemporary Christian philosopher is, then, that he should build upon the tested heritage of doctrines rather than reject the foundation and destroy the continuity in philosophical thought. He should strive to complete the old by the aid of the new, while carefully avoiding the two extremes of standing still with a napkin-wrapped treasure or eliminating the solid work of the past. The precise way in which this organic growth is to be accomplished is properly left to the Christian philosophers themselves. There is leeway for legitimate differences among them, for specialized interests leading in many diverse directions, and even for errors which must be expected in new work and for which they have to develop the methods of detecting and correcting. The responsibility for the actual state of Christian philosophizing at a given time lies squarely with the men whose professional vocation leads them to devote their lives to this work.

In this final section, it may be useful to ask whether Pope Leo's counsel and direction have started to yield any definite fruit in our century, always bearing in mind that progress in philosophy is never sensationally rapid. Although it would be invidious to pretend to make any definitive selection, the people whom we will mention are generally recognized as having done competent work lying chiefly in the modern field, and having done it in the spirit of building upon their Christian philosophical heritage.

The decisive breakthrough was the handiwork of Cardinal Mercier at Louvain.[17] Even his insistence upon teaching some philosophy courses in the vernacular helped to bring the Scholastic mind within closer hailing distance of modern philosophers and their distinctive problems. For it gradually forced the men in the field to rethink the older doctrines in modern terms, to take account of new evidence on the perennial issues, and thus to engage in the kind of restoration of Christian philosophy which Pope Leo had in mind. Mercier's own study of psychological findings and the new field of psychiatry helped to open up one avenue to a deepening grasp of man and his life of affections, desires, and imagery. And it was Mercier's example in taking Descartes and the problem of knowledge seriously which gave the lead to the intense epistemological investigations of the first four decades of our century.

Many early efforts in this field were hampered by a faulty knowledge of the critical problem, as it was formulated by Kant. One of Father Maréchal's major services was to provide us with a precise historical understanding of the Kantian system. Furthermore, he tried to make the Kantian problem more accessible by linking it up with the centuries-long speculation of Greek, medieval, and early modern thinkers on the nature of knowledge, its relation with the real, and the basis for metaphysics.[18] By rethinking some Thomistic sentences on the relation of being and action, the dynamic nature of knowledge, and the basic search of man for God, Maréchal provided a powerful example of what it means to use one's philosophical heritage in an original way to meet the problems of modern criticism. His psychological studies of mysticism show this same exploratory spirit. In his wake, there has been a re-examination of the implications of physical science, along with a renewed study of the role of love in constituting the human person and leading him to God.

For a better grasp of the general history of modern philosophy, we are indebted to the studies of Monsignor Olgiati and Father Copleston.[19] The former has brought out how difficult it is to make any comprehensive generalization about the modern thinkers. He has worked out a minimal interpretation of the various modern movements around the principle of phenomenalism. By calling attention to the scientific line which stems from Galileo and the empiricist line from Hobbes and Locke to the positivists, he has helped to overcome a tendency of Catholic authors to emphasize only the rationalists. In his works on Descartes and Berkeley, Olgiati shows in detail the fundamental phenomenalist assumptions held in common by rationalists and empiricists. From Copleston's writings, we learn to connect the modern thinkers with their predecessors through the presence of recurrent problems. Perhaps even more helpful is the example he gives of dealing with analytic philosophy in its own terms and with full command of its techniques. He is doing a cautious, professional work of reviving the central metaphysical questions within the analytic context and only so far as that context permits.

Jacques Maritain's arresting quality springs from his sensitivity to what is specifically new in our world, as combined with his fidelity to St. Thomas and some commentators.[20] This cross-graining of old and new underlies his approach to natural philosophy and modern science. He sees no need to sacrifice the essential points in either standpoint, provided that we recognize them to be distinct types of knowledge. He refuses to reduce the modern scientific analysis to an already anticipated subdivision of the Aristotelian philosophy of nature, just as he finds no good grounds for eliminating that philosophy itself in the line of ontological explanation. To observe Maritain's mind working on the testimony of the French poets or on the data of social scientists is to learn how a philosopher proceeds at the very frontier of research. There, the modern esthetic and social discoveries of the human spirit retain their freshness, without being cut off from all relationship with the Thomistic metaphysics of knowledge and theory of society.

Many younger Catholics today are engaged in studying the existentialisms of Marcel and Heidegger, as well as the phenomenological movement from Husserl to his German and French descendants. For many young people, this experience induces an intellectual crisis. They become so keenly aware of the significance of existentialist and phenomenological concepts for penetrating into the perceptual, ontological, and historical dimensions of man that they sometimes wonder whether such concepts and techniques must not simply replace the older doctrines.[21] There is no easy solution here, any more than there is in the question of how to reconcile recent analytic theories with metaphysical inferences. But that a patient wrestling with this complex issue is better than a simplistic choice of only one side is the import of Edith Stein's life work. Our previous examination of her phenomenology showed that, in philosophy, she never achieved the close integration of things which marked her religious life. Yet she did embody that precious virtue of the modern Christian philosopher: *stabilitas*. For hers was the method of tenaciously confronting the traditional positions with new methods of description and argument and then, in turn, submitting the newer problems to analysis in the light of the permanent principles of act and potency. She spelled out for our instruction the meaning of a lifelong, unevasive inquiry into the problem of Christian philosophizing in a phenomenological milieu.

It is appropriate for to bring our study to a close with two texts taken from *Aeterni Patris*. The first is a piece of salutary advice from Leo XIII addressed to those Christian philosophers whose main work lies in the modern field.

We have no intention of discountenancing the learned and able men who bring their industry and erudition, and, what is more, the wealth of new discoveries, to the service of philosophy; for, of course, We understand that this tends to the development of learning. But one should be very careful lest all of his chief labor be exhausted in these pursuits and in mere erudition.[22]

All our research stands rightly in an instrumental relationship with the chief task of the philosopher which is to achieve true acts of judging concerning the natural things in the world, the being of man, and our common rootedness in God. The philosopher has to work constantly to bring his erudition to bear on questions, and to stay alert to all the findings of the human spirit in his own age, as well as the past. Yet these are ministerial functions, not the ends of his activity. They minister to his most characteristic act for which he is personally and chiefly responsible, namely, the act of true judging about beings and especially about God, wherein wisdom lies. The second text is a quotation from Scripture itself which Pope Leo offers us as a final encouragement in our labors:

If any of you want wisdom, let him ask of God, who giveth to all men abundantly, and upbraideth not: and it shall be given him.[23]

Today, as well as in the former ages, the Christian philosopher is impelled both by his faith and by the ultimate reaches of his philosophical inquiry to ask for this wisdom from God Himself and to remain confident that it will be given him in proper measure and manner.

320

CHAPTER 13

ANALYTIC PHILOSOPHY AND
DEMONSTRATIVE THEISM

IN THIS chapter on analytic philosophy and the following one on
Husserl, my aim is to show in two specific areas of contemporary discussion how crucial the question of the human mode and order of
philosophizing actually becomes. It is not primarily a matter of adjusting theistic realism to a special situation or of strengthening its American cultural influence through the use of current styles of thought and
language. Rather, the problem facing the philosophical theist is to
achieve for himself a properly philosophical kind of knowledge about
God through a reflective study of our human experience of existing
natural beings. The basic purpose of discussing the starting point and
ground of philosophical inference with the analytic and phenomenological thinkers is to bring out some conditions required for making
an inference to God in a philosophically elaborated manner. In these
two chapters, the movement of inquiry goes back from the analytic
school's treatment of discourse about God to the need for some causal
warrant in experience for making statements in philosophy about
God, and then from Husserl's phenomenological conception of human
experience to a realistic consideration of it as the foundation for a
metaphysics of natural beings and their bond with God.

There is a direct relationship between analytic philosophy and realistic theism, insofar as the former is beginning to pay positive attention to statements made about God and religion. The question arises
at once as to whether the analytic work done so far in the area of
theistic discourse has come to grips with realistic theism. There have
been some interesting analytic explanations and criticisms of what
men do in their philosophical and religious talk about God. Our problem is to consider whether the analysts have obtained an accurate

321

understanding of the intention and pattern of discourse about God which are governed by the approach of a realistic theism, claiming as it does to have some demonstrative propositions about God. Since the realistic foundation for philosophically demonstrative knowledge concerning God lies in a causal inference from sensible things to the truth of some statements about God as the first cause, the question concerns whether the analytic treatments of theistic discourse have taken precise account of those statements about God which rest upon causal analysis and inference, regarded as the backing for the claim to have some demonstrative knowledge of the truth of some statements about God. Our study is limited to analytic work that is already done and published. This does not close off the possibility of new developments in other directions, and yet it does give us an understanding of the actual situation today.

For our purposes, there are four major issues which call for investigation. The first is to determine whether logical positivism and naturalism are at all relevant to the present analytic studies in theism or whether this background is a distant episode in the past. A second task is to examine the explicit statements of the analytic theists concerning how they regard the problem of our knowledge of God's existence. As a third theme, we will consider the way in which the specific question of the falsifiability of theistic statements is handled, since this may illuminate the relation between realistic theism and analytic philosophy. Finally, we must look at the defense which many believing analysts are making of theistic language on the ground of its displaying an appropriate oddness.

1. *The Active Residue of Logical Positivism*

At least in respect to the philosophy of God, the passage from logical positivism to conceptual analysis is more of a reshuffling than a revolution. There is a strong element of continuity in respect to the always crucial case of whether or not to admit any inferential knowledge of God into good philosophical standing. This question is still being given an answer belonging well within the tradition of logical positivism and naturalism, despite the remarkable flowering of analytic investigations into the language of religion and the belief in God. The advance which has been made is to recognize that in this field of meanings and linguistic forms there is a rich opportunity for applying the analytic techniques and even for modifying them in some important ways to meet some new conditions. However, most of the discussion does go on within the broad context of admitting that in philosophy we do not have, and more than likely cannot obtain, any demonstrative knowledge about God. Once this common premise is granted, there is still plenty of room left for uncovering the various kinds of cognitive and noncognitive meanings imbedded in our theistic and religious discourse. But the context does qualify and deeply affect the significance of the work that is accomplished. It is not simply a matter of analyzing meanings about God and religious convictions but of analyzing them in the admitted absence of any way of demonstration or demonstrative kind of knowledge about God. It is difficult to find instances where the analytic inquiry is regarded as a long-range preparation for founding or recovering such demonstrative knowledge, even the desirability of which is often challenged.

When we look for the grounds upon which analytic writers accept this broad position, we are referred back at least implicitly to the limits placed upon the knowledge-claim by phenomenalism. Equivalently, this means that we must still reckon with the core of A. J. Ayer's position. Hence it does not seem correct to maintain that there is no point any longer in making antediluvian researches into what Ayer once held about a natural theology.[1] What he once thought on this score still has a dominant influence not only over his own present views but also over the general attitude of analytic thinkers who have moved beyond him in so many other respects. This is an instance of selective continuity between positivism and analysis and even of a certain static element in these philosophies. Although the principle of verifiability has been notably shrunk for other purposes, it is still regarded as quite workable for barring any proposed claims to demonstrate propositions concerning God from an experiential point of departure. Even where the younger analytic writers are making attempts to renovate metaphysics in some sense, the proposed sense does not ordinarily include any plans for rehabilitating demonstrative inferences bearing on the existence of God.

The 1949 debate between Ayer and Fr. Copleston illustrates the former's willingness to adapt the principle of verifiability to his more recent empirical analysis of ordinary and scientific language.[2] At least, he regards the principle as still retaining sufficient negative relevance to disqualify that particular function of metaphysical thinking which would aim at obtaining a demonstrative knowledge of the transcendent being of God. Throughout the back-and-forth play of the argument, Ayer's chief point against any metaphysical knowledge of

God is that he does not understand what one can do with the ideas involved or how one does any explaining with the theistic proofs. He is perfectly willing to admit a verifiable meaning for causality, necessity, and even the name "God" (as standing for certain human experiences). But if they are supposed to serve a function other than working in a formal system or supporting the deduction of some observable consequence, he confesses that he does not understand what their use and meaning can be. If a theory about God and religion claims to do no more than elucidate our human experiences and beliefs in terms of their observable consequences in this world, then Ayer grants that it is performing a definite work and has some empirically relevant meaning. But as soon as theistic reasoning claims to bring our intelligence to a demonstrated knowledge of the supra-empirical being of God, it ceases to be doing a job within the range of understandable explanations and hence Ayer denies that it is an explanation.

Our present task is not to examine Copleston's counter-suggestion that we should not set an a priori limit upon the valid ways in which the conclusion of an inference can establish its relevance for experienced things, even though this is a fruitful lead. Instead, we have to underline the fact that Ayer is here engaged in restating his principle of verifiability to suit the new climate of analytic philosophy. He has sufficient confidence in its fundamental phenomenalistic power of limitation to continue to employ it at least in this area where a metaphysics tries to furnish inferential knowledge of some truths about God. What J. O. Urmson calls the overused slogans of recent analysis ("Don't ask for the meaning, ask for the use," and "Every statement has its own logic") are being accommodated within Ayer's reformulation of his criticism of a natural theology, taken as an effort to supply demonstrative knowledge of the truth of some statements about God. That is why he stresses the absence of any statable function for theistic discourse when it tries to lead us to the transcendent reality of God. If the distinctive function of this sort of discourse evaporates, then it does no good to ask about the use of the language in respect to what the philosopher of God claims to be doing. Ayer's readiness today to include introspection and private human states within the logic of experience enables phenomenalism to be perfectly hospitable to religious experiences, without conceding a whit about there being a definite cognitive basis for making the theistic inference. And he wants to know whether such an inference does involve any distinctive logic of the type that would yield a demonstrative knowledge. The analytic

324

slogans do not clear the path toward showing the way to some demonstrative knowledge about the transcendent God.

In asking these questions, Ayer is posing a real challenge for those analytic philosophers who are trying to refashion their instruments so as to include theism and religious belief within their positive scope. He does not crudely dismiss their efforts as being concerned only with emotive meaning, since he now admits that a study of theistic and religious usage can cast light on some aspects of human experience. But the knowledge concerns nothing more than man and his many attitudes, however much we may use the ideas of theism and show that religious statements are responding to a logic of their own. The slogans resolve nothing concerning the precise claims for reaching demonstrative knowledge about God through metaphysical means. Hence Ayer invites theistic analysts either to remain satisfied with making a purely immanent description of the language forms for the human situation or else to back up the additional claim that there is an understandable way of knowledge which yields us truths about the somehow understandable reality of God.

If we now look at that group of analytic philosophers attacking every knowledge-claim about God, we find that the strength of their reasoning depends either directly upon Ayer or upon the phenomenalism underlying his own critical standpoint. John Hospers' *An Introduction to Philosophical Analysis* provides a good example, both because it reflects classroom practice and because it is a clear and detailed presentation. In many other problems, he uses analytic techniques and distinctions which move beyond Ayer and logical positivism. But Hospers becomes sharply conservative on the subject of God. Here he hews closely to the tradition worked out by Hume and Ayer. After admitting the difficulty of finding an acceptable general formulation for the verifiability principle, especially on its empirical side, he nevertheless maintains that a weak form of it is still enough to rule out a metaphysical approach which aims to go beyond human religious experience in the direction of demonstrated knowledge about God. And if the theist discards metaphysical demonstration for empirical suasions, then Hospers is ready with all of Hume's familiar objections against inferences to God from design, utility, religious aspiration, and miracles. It is in this sense that his stand is highly conservative in the empiricist pattern of response: it raises the question of how far analytic philosophy can move beyond Hume and Ayer in the direction of a philosophy of God.

One particular point in Hospers' critique helps to sharpen the issue

325

for theistic analysts. After discussing the causal principle and the meaning of a timeless being, he concludes: "However a timeless God (or any timeless entity) might be related to the temporal universe, the relation could hardly be a *causal* one, for the causal relation is a relation among temporal events." [3] This objection echoes the line of argument used by Ayer. Its significance for our inquiry consists in forcing the analytic thinker to deal explicitly with causality, not merely in the sense of calling God a cause but in the more pregnant sense of using causal inference to justify saying anything about God on the part of the human mind.

One path open for the theist is to work out a meaning for causality that is not confined entirely to intratemporal relations among events and then to work out some causally based demonstrations concerning God. The other way is to forego the causal basis entirely as a means of showing the foundation of our philosophical predications about God. If the first path were followed, then it would require the philosopher to do something more than analyze the meanings intended in religious discourse and in our ordinary talk about God, although such analysis might be useful at some stage in the discussion. And if the latter route were followed, it would require the theistic analyst to state explicitly that he is not employing causal inference to show the real foundation of his statements about God and to give them a causally demonstrative status. In this case, he would also be led to state that the metaphysics he may want to defend does not lead to a causal demonstration of any statements about God. Even though he may explore the logic of statements about God that use a causal vocabulary, their truth rests on religious belief that God is first cause. It would be beneficial to have such consequences spelled out, now that some analytic thinkers are engaged in studying the pattern of the language of religious belief and are speculating about the possibility of some kind of metaphysics.

Just how important it is to determine whether or not one can appeal to causal considerations in interpreting and justifying theistic discourse comes out in the account of God made by Jason Xenakis and in the accompanying remarks by other men. [4] Xenakis makes a bold appeal to the orthodoxy of Ayer's earliest book, as though challenging the analytic theists to show why its position should not be retained at least in respect to knowledge of God. He proposes that we include "God" as an emotive word signifying only the relation of being worshipped. The entire language system built around "God" can then be treated as a disguised psychological language of value-words indicating the act of holding in worship, although deceptively set forth as a set of object-words referring to an independent reality apart from our human worshipping acts. On this reckoning, the whole language concerning a personal transcendent God rests on a misleading reification of relations whose entire meaning is really restricted to the human attitude of holding in reverence. In effect, Xenakis is suggesting that theistic discourse is reducible without remainder to religious discourse and that the latter is the language expressive of human acts of giving worship. This is the place for drawing the line against the common tendency to slip so easily from saying that every statement has its own logic into saying that the logical rules of usage for statements must be accepted as valid, as they stand. Theistic discourse may have a logical intent of its own, but analysis shows that the only reality-claim which such language can validly make is coextensive with the reference of religious language to states of human experience.

The commentators on the Xenakis paper were agreed that it represented a return to logical positivism, but they offered different reasons against accepting such a return. John Wisdom—whose essay on "Gods" gave the original impetus to the problem of linguistic theism—suggests the relevance of the distinction between reporting the presence in oneself or others of a worshipful feeling toward something and defending the appropriateness of this feeling in some particular case. This distinction indicates a hunch that something more may be involved here than a description of a psychological operation of worshipping. For this operation is selectively used. It is often claimed to be reserved for some reality which is deemed to be worthy of receiving man's response of worship.

Wisdom does not provide directions on how to go about setting up a criterion of appropriateness, but Virgil Aldrich and Philip Wheelwright point out that some element other than psychic factuality is involved. On Xenakis' own admission, the worshipping act is like other valuing acts insofar as it concerns some quality or power presumed to be present in the term of the worship. The psychological act is not identical in every respect with the object meant by that act. We cannot offhand reduce the meaning of God to the fact of someone worshipping, since the act-and-object distinction refers the act to some object which is being worshipped. This distinction is not peculiarly the instrument of phenomenological research but is a common feature of our experience which the analytic thinker can also employ. The only way to refer the meaning of God automatically back to a valuational aspect conferred by the psychological subject is by a rigid acceptance of the cognitive-emotive division of terms. But Aldrich and Wheelwright note that analytic research has brought out a use of value-terms which is neither scientifically descriptive nor emotive nor psychologistic. Our ordinary references to God simply bypass the rigid dichotomy used in the Xenakis argument.

This countercriticism suggests that the residue of logical empiricism need not be passively accepted in a discussion of religious and theistic language, since the findings in other areas of analytic research may require some radical revisions in the original positivist explanation. For instance, the distinction between act and object, together with the presence of logical patterns not conforming to the ready distinction between cognitive, emotive, and psychological terms, has a definite bearing upon the problem of God. By themselves, it is true, they do not resolve the question forthwith in favor of the reality of God as persisting even apart from our worshipful attitudes. They are too general to be able to resolve the issue, since we still must ask whether the object intended exists as a distinct reality and indeed precisely as the transcendent personal God of theism. But at least such considerations keep the matter open for further inquiry. We are not entitled to write off the research of the analytic theists as a foregone futility, although neither are we warranted in conceding their conclusions simply on the general grounds that something can be said in favor of some sort of distinction between act and object. It is now time to examine some specific attempts being made to overcome the residual positivism which still shapes the views of many analytic thinkers on the question of God.

2. *Knowledge of God's Existence*

One striking feature about that portion of analytic research being devoted to the language and conceptual structure of theism and religious belief is its preoccupation with issues connected with basic epistemology. A much greater portion of analytic theism is concerned with general issues of human knowledge than holds good for analytic work in other fields. This emphasis seems to reflect two traits of the analytic theists: their greater sensitivity to the implicit phenomenalism regulating so much of the discussion, and their hope that in the long run more can be drawn from the analysis than is usually regarded as likely. There is an expectation that analysis of religious and theistic statements will remove the bar in principle against granting any human cognitive acquaintance with God. The linguistic materials used for the study are usually drawn from three sources: statements of the Christian religious belief in God, statements of the natural nonphilosophical mind about God, and statements found in works on natural theology. However, the use of these three sources does not imply that they are being treated in the same way. The question of a diversity of religious credal statements, Christian and non-Christian, is customarily laid aside with the remark that the massive actual source of most Western discourse about God is found in the Christian tradition and in that tradition as stated in the main Patristic symbols of faith. The precise relation obtaining between the Christian statements about God and those which are assigned to our natural approach to God is not precisely determined beforehand, and is envisaged differently from one analytic theist to another. Where they do tend to agree is in making a joint defense of the concepts and language forms employed in stating Christian belief and natural theism, while refusing to vindicate any natural theology as a distinct science claiming to have a demonstrative inferential backing for its statements about God. Statements drawn from treatises on natural theology are often used in a constructive way, not in order to defend the claim of demonstrative knowledge but in order to have more formal illustrations of the expression of natural theism and to expand the Christian formulas. Such an aim governs the symposium of *New Essays in Philosophical Theology* and other recent analytic studies in the language of theism and religion.

This tendency to dissociate the analysis of Christian and natural theistic statements about God from a context of demonstrative knowledge is visible in the discussions centering around the problem of God's existence. For the most part, the aim of theistic analysis is not to help us clarify what we mean and what we do when we make demonstration of the truth of certain propositions about God. Rather, it is to show that the meaning and cogency of our theistic discourse do not depend upon efforts to make such demonstration and can stand in independence of all discussion of these efforts. This dissociative aim is apparent even in the critical attempt of J. N. Findlay to show that God's existence can be disproved, as well as in the comments his paper provoked.[5] The heart of Findlay's difficulty is not that the inference to God does not proceed with necessity but that we cannot both accept Kant's view of there being no necessary facts of existence and also hold that God necessarily exists. His ontological disproof concerns the impossibility of uniting the notes of existence and necessity in our concept of the divine nature, rather than the character of proposed demonstrative inferences to the truth that God exists.

Similarly, his critics confine their replies to showing that the connection between the necessary and the nonexistential holds for some propositions but not for the being itself of God. They do not try to vindicate the inference itself which leads our mind to the truth about God's being. Indeed, A. C. A. Rainer maintains that our assertion about God's necessary existence is itself always contingent and is (probably) verifiable through analysis of moral and mystical experience and the test of total coherence. Proof and disproof of statements about God's existence are involved here only in terms of a discussion of the terminal propositions which we can frame about God's nature. There is no treatment of proof in the sense of a demonstrative philosophical inference establishing the truth that God exists.

In a very few cases, the reluctance to deal with proof in the latter sense is due to acceptance of Ayer's original contention that utterances about God are emotive expressions and not statements of fact having existential import. But the more typical position is that theistic statements, especially in their Christian form, do intend to assert something about the character of reality and about the real being of God. Such statements are metaphysical, not in the specific sense of belonging within a science which obtains some demonstrated truths, but in the vaguer meaning of designating some reality which is not itself directly verifiable in the sense experience proportionate to physical science. The metaphysical quality of theistic statements is thus taken to signify the supersensuous reality of their object rather than the mode of the cognitive basis upon which they may rest. Hence most theistic analysts are ready to defend the meaningfulness and existential cognitive reference of statements about God, without feeling obliged to show that their validity rests on a demonstrative philosophical inference. This latter consideration is divorced from their description of what the theistic mind is doing and what sort of logic it is obeying. Once the divorcement is obtained, it becomes possible to reinstate natural theology in the sense of a domain of meaningful, cognitive-existential assertions about God, without implying that a natural theology is a way of obtaining some demonstrated truths concerning God.

The prevailing viewpoint is clearly expressed in two essays by Austin Farrer and I. M. Crombie. They agree that Ayer's main attack was directed not against the truth but against the significance of theistic convictions. Hence they conceive their task to be that of exhibiting the significance of theistic talk. They do not ignore the question of truth or try to settle that of significance entirely apart from claims to truth. But neither do they think that the question of theistic significance is bound up with any philosophical demonstration of the truth of propositions about God.

Farrer remarks dryly that, in our current atmosphere where nothing can be demonstrated and yet every manner of speaking finds its justification in its own use, the distinction largely disappears between revealed truths and rationally established doctrines about God.[6] Far from making a transposition of the demonstrative approach to God into an analytic framework, the actual procedure is to accept the method of clarification of meaning through the study of usage as a replacement for the demonstrative way to get truths bearing on God. Farrer seeks to be even more modest than Kant, since he abandons altogether the terrain of demonstration one way or the other concerning our philosophical ability to establish some truths about God. His appeals to experience are denominated "persuasions," in deliberate antithesis to determining anything in a demonstrative way about the statements we make concerning God. The theology to which his analytic techniques are proportioned is one in which the revealed and the naturally ascertainable doctrines are indistinguishably one, at least with respect to their source of validity which is located solely in the revealing God. So conceived, analytic theism studies the structure of our talk about God as molded by Christian belief and its interpretation of nature, but not as being regulated in any distinct way by the philosophical activity of making demonstrative inferences establishing the truth of some statements about God.

There are three decisive points at which Crombie strengthens this conception of theistic analysis. (1) He offers this practical negative rule about starting the study of the significance of theistic statements:

Let us begin by dismissing from our inquiry the troublesome statement 'There is a God' or 'God exists'. As every student of logic knows, all statements asserting the existence of something offer difficulties of their own, with which we need not complicate our embarrassment.[7]

If we do accept this rule, then a curious consequence follows. We are not permitted to make any try at a philosophical defense of the affirmation that God exists. And yet Crombie agrees that our statements about God's nature and His bonds with men and the world are laden with existential significance. If this significance is methodologically separated from any grounding in the demonstrative inference that

God exists, then the ultimate foundation of all existential affirmations concerning God consists either in an ontological deduction from the concept of His nature or in our act of religious faith in the self-revealing God. This is asking us to do more than admit the distinctive influence of religious belief upon philosophical thinking. It is asking us to confine our philosophical work to an analytic explication of the content and implications of revelation, with exclusion being made of any demonstrative philosophical knowledge about God whether reached in close union or not with one's religious faith.

(2) Crombie then offers this account of the logical structure of religious belief:

Theoretically, then, not in how it arises, but in its logical structure, religious belief has two parents; and it also has a nurse. Its logical mother is what one might call *undifferentiated theism*, its logical father is particular events or occasions interpreted as theophanic, and the extra-parental nurture is provided by religious activity.[8]

The notion of undifferentiated theism is specially interesting, since it permits Crombie to bring in some natural experiential sources of theistic conviction without conceding anything to a differentiated theism or natural theology in the sense of some demonstrative knowledge of the truth of statements about God. Undifferentiated theism includes our sense of contingency, our moral and religious experience, and our awareness of the order and beauty of nature. Lest it be supposed that these sources can furnish the basis for a differentiated and demonstrative approach to God in philosophy, Crombie assures us that

those who so interpret need not be so inexpert in logic as to suppose that there is anything of the nature of a deductive or inductive argument which leads from a premiss asserting the existence of the area of experience in question to a conclusion expressing belief in God. . . . Her [undifferentiated theism's] function is, not to prove to us that God exists, but to provide us with a 'meaning' for the word 'God'. . . . Often it has been held to be the task of natural theology to prove the existence of God. This seems to me to be a task which cannot, in any strict sense of 'prove' be accomplished. What however the arguments of the natural theologians do do is to reveal the intellectual pressures which lead people to talk about God; and, in so doing, they illuminate the meaning of such talk.[9]

This is a decisive passage for the question of relating analytic theism to the claim of demonstrative inference. Crombie uses the notion of undifferentiated theism to maintain that what the analytic theist analyzes turns out precisely not to be a demonstrative inference to God at all. He regards it as a sign of logical weakmindedness to try to work demonstratively from the experiential data to the truth about the existent God.

Hence he seeks to determine the meaning of the word "God" otherwise than through inspecting the outcome of a demonstrative inference and, indeed, in contradistinction to any effort to obtain demonstrative knowledge of the truth that God exists. That effort has to be treated therapeutically for what it will tell the analyst indirectly about the intellectual pressures which make people talk about God. These pressures include the experiential areas in undifferentiated theism, but they explicitly exclude any validly established inferential demonstrations in the philosophy of God. The analytic theist's account of the experiential significance of theistic discourse cannot be construed as a linguistic clarification of what the natural theologian is doing who does attempt to achieve the demonstrative mode of some knowledge about God. On the contrary, undifferentiated theism is used as a tool for completing the cleavage between meaning and demonstration, between our faith-guided response to experience and the efforts of some philosophers and men of faith to acquire a demonstrative kind of knowledge concerning God.

(3) An alliance between religious faith and an undifferentiated theism, in the sense indicated, is all that is required so that analytical theism can establish the meaningfulness of statements about God. "For, after all, all that is necessary for an utterance to be a meaningful statement is that it should be governed by rules which specify what it is about, and what it asserts about it." [10] In practice, however, Crombie and other analytic theists find it necessary to specify that the meaningfulness in question is cognitive and not merely emotive, and that its cognitive status is that of an assertion about existing reality rather than that of the moral-rule model proposed by Braithwaite.

Some naturalists and latter-day logical empiricists will generously accord significance to religious language, but will question whether it conveys any knowledge about the existing being of God. When they are told that the hiatus between an indeterminately meaningful and existentially informative statement is closed on the basis of one's faith in the revealing God, then they want to know whether it is any longer an affair in philosophy. They will not regard the fact that one's discourse follows logically ordering rules as sufficient warrant for the claim to have existentially significant assertions which can be weighed by natural canons of evidence. This is a legitimate objection, since our philosophical assent to the claim of existential significance requires a different backing from the assurance that one's use of language employs rules whose intent is to express such significance. We still have to inquire whether the evidence is rendered philosophically available for requiring us to accept this particular existential intent.

3. *Falsifiability of Theistic Statements*

The point of the discussion over the falsifiability of theistic statements is to inquire whether even the logical rules under which analytic theists operate allow for empirically significant statements about the divine attributes.[11] Some nontheistic analysts and naturalists press home the objection that we can only talk about God's creative power and providential goodness in such a way that they are conceived as holding good under any and all circumstances. If we cannot conceive of a state of affairs which would tell against these divine attributes, then our statements about them are not capable of being tested. They lie outside the realm of falsifiability and definite meaning, so that such assertions can be given neither proof nor disproof of their having existential cognitive significance. Theistic discourse may carry some meaning, but it is not of the sort that is amenable to determination as being cognitively meaningful. When tests are proposed, the statements about God are eroded by constant qualification or (in Antony Flew's phrase) die the slow death of a thousand qualifications.

Wrestling with this difficulty, Raphael Demos suggests that the all-pervasive belief in the intelligibility of natural events, upon which scientific research rests, is just as unfalsifiable as the convictions of theism.[12] This fits in with the view of Dooyeweerd that there is an act of faith supporting the entire scientific outlook. It has to be weighed against the naturalistic reply, however, that our working acceptance of the intelligible character of natural events is a broad hypothesis sustained by the actual history of science and yet open to revision in the light of future efforts at understanding the world. This or that scientist may strengthen his dedication through some kind of act of faith, but the logic of the situation of scientific research requires us to treat the accessibility of events to human scrutiny as a working hypothesis and not as an absolute postulate. It is here that Stephen Toulmin's examination of the mythic aspect of the poetic and scientific outlooks is relevant for illuminating at least the psychological conditions of scientific work, if not its logically minimal structure.

334

R. M. Hare takes the ingenious line that the question of falsifiability does not apply to one's religious belief, since the latter expresses the individual's *blik* or most general attitude of concern. It is not an explanation of any sort but is the inclusive frame of mind within which one actually determines which given facts shall count at all as worth considering for an explanation. On Hare's reckoning, one's theistic convictions would be pure expressions or performatory utterances lying beyond the domain of the falsifiable and verifiable. But their immunity is bought at the price of renouncing their direct intention of real assertion. This limitation would be satisfactory to nontheists, since they would regard it as a concession to their thesis about the lack of cognitive justification for the realistic bearing of theistic assertions. If the retort is made by Hare that all cognitively significant explanations require the framework of an utterance about what will be taken as counting as evidence about the real order, then the question has to be faced of how we are to go about deciding between counter-*bliks* and thus justifying any claim of "having the right *blik*." In the case of a radical disagreement about affirmations and negations concerning God, it is not enough to point again to the legislative rule for the interpretation of experience because the question may well concern opposing interpretative frameworks.

Basil Mitchell suggests that utterances about God as creating and loving us are indeed explanations, but have a unique structure. They are not scientific explanations in the sense of hypotheses undergoing constant verification and open to the possibility of eventual replacement. What keeps them distinct from such explanatory hypotheses is not that they are founded upon a demonstrative inference from experience but that they are held through the nonhypothetical commitment of faith. Mitchell does not explore any natural grounds in the appropriate philosophical inferences about God for refusing to classify theistic statements along with scientific hypotheses. But he does hold that such statements are not totally vacuous, since they do specify something about the shape of the experienced world. Their foundation in faith does not render them wholly pliable and indifferent to what actually occurs in our world, even though they are not themselves to be treated as empirical generalizations.

If what occurs in our experience does make some decisive difference for theistic statements, then they are not entirely removed from the sphere of the falsifiable and the empirically meaningful. I. M. Crombie develops this point with considerable thoroughness. Because he both locates the ground of assent to the truth of assertions about

God in the act of supernatural faith and directs them toward the unknown God, he will not grant that theistic statements can in principle find a fully conclusive falsification and verification in respect to experience. Yet he observes that there is no intrinsic linguistic rule governing the formulation of theological statements (including assertions of revealed doctrine as well as natural theism) which forbids us to put them to an experiential test. They are not logically structured in such fashion as to rule out the falsifying operation, but there are some factual hindrances against getting results of a strictly definitive nature. The hindrances are that we cannot penetrate the recesses of human subjectivity and cannot weigh the outcome in the afterlife, and still be able to include these relevant factors in our temporal testing for falsification. These factual obstacles do not render the logic of theistic statements liable to the objection that it structurally excludes the possibility of falsification in every respect.

Antony Flew contends that the theist practices double-think when he first uses words like "loving" in their common meaning, in order to give substance to statements about God, and then so qualifies and whittles away at the common meaning that he avoids difficulties only by emptying them of all definite assertive content. Crombie replies by making an alternative description of actual theistic practice. Affirmations about a loving, providential God are made within the situation of the parable.[18] These assertions are not generalized from experience but their meaning does function within the parable situation and hence requires the use of examples drawn from human relations. This human bearing enables us to conceive of what would constitute a decisive experiential objection against the intended meaning. Such an objection would be present if we experienced human life to consist in unalleviated misery, in suffering that is pointless, everlasting, and wholly irremediable. The statement about a loving God is falsifiable in some degree, since we do know of a possible state of the world which would be incompatible with our affirmation. Any instance of suffering does present a difficulty to which the theist must remain sensitively open. He cannot bring all the factors in the situation within range, but at least he can mark out a limit for his view of the actual world and can thus achieve some definite meaning for it.

Furthermore, although the fact of mystery remains and requires adjustments within the parable, this process does not rest on a total plasticity of concessions being made in just every quarter. There is a certain definite direction taken in the qualifications, such that they do *not* terminate in claiming that irremediable suffering would be

336

compatible with the loving God or that suffering of any sort presents no difficulty to acceptance of God. Thus the universal range of divine love is not reconcilable with just any arrangement of things. We do have to engage in a constant reinterpreting of the relation between experiential conditions and theistic belief. Yet, as G. C. Stead notes, this reinterpretation is not so much a whittling down as an enrichening of significance in agreement with the open texture of all our predications about God. We learn to see new facets of meaning and thus we deepen, rather than evacuate, our original affirmations about God.[14]

This description of the workings of the theistic mind is much closer to the concrete situation than are the dialectical accounts based upon Hume's treatment of the problem of evil. It suggests that the rules of falsification cannot be applied in a univocal way, as well as that the theist is not fatuously indifferent to the bitter facts of evil. Nevertheless, there are some difficulties in relating this phase of analytic theism to a philosophy of God in which the role of demonstrative inference from experience remains central.

It is noticeable, for instance, that the relation of the parable situation to experience is not such as to establish anything about the truth of statements about God. The assent to them as true comes from another source: the faith-act of accepting revelation. Hence the issue of falsification is confined by the analytic theists to the meaning of theistic statements, rather than extended to their truth, and concerns their meaning only in the degree that it is open to a phenomenalistic challenge. This is an apologetic approach which does not stake the truth of theistic convictions upon the outcome of the philosophical discussion, but defends their significance within the bounds of analytic objections. Hence the question of falsification is sufficiently treated by setting off a range of reference in experience where our theistic statements (already known by faith to be true) operate and exclude certain possible arrangements. But for a theism seeking some demonstrative knowledge, there is the problem of showing the grounds in experience for accepting some statements about God as true, in addition to furnishing some explanations correlated with the actual course of experience. Such a theism regards certain experiential findings as fully decisive for the philosophical project of obtaining some knowledge in the demonstrative mode, showing the truth or falsity of some statements about God. What makes the findings decisive is not a comparison between actual circumstances and a conceivable situation contradicting them, but rather the character of the principles found actually to be present in experienced things.

There is a pluralism of modes of falsification to take account of the differences between statement-groups that are explanatory by way of hypothesis, correlation, and causal demonstration. When the latter aim is involved, it is not sufficient to set up a range of reference for a pre-given linguistic pattern of assertions about God in which the question of the truth of the assertions is not raised. For a theism organized primarily around causal demonstration of the truth of our statements about God, the experienced world is not viewed mainly as a region for a marked-off reference but as the source of our warrant for making any existential assertions about God in philosophy. Since the question of valid meaning depends upon the outcome of the effort at demonstration, the process of falsification of correlated meanings is kept subordinate as far as concerns the development of a philosophy embodying some knowledge about God in the mode of demonstration.

4. *The Appropriate Oddness of Theistic Language*

The linguistic theists are particularly sensitive about the charge that all discourse concerning God is a tissue of category-mistakes, that it rests on the same kind of logical confusion which Ryle uncovered in talk about the mind. Should we not purge our thinking and talking of all references to the ghost-above-the-cosmos as well as to the ghost-in-the-machine? This question is dealt with most incisively by Crombie and I. T. Ramsey.

Crombie admits that there are some instructive anomalies in theological language, the most important of which is the use of the word "God" as a proper name.[15] This usage is puzzling, since we cannot lead anyone by the hand and introduce him directly to the being referred to by this term. Another anomalous feature is that we do not seem to allow any empirical facts to overrule entirely the predicates used in sentences about God. But such anomalies are the index of a certain paradox in human discourse about God rather than the sign of its incoherence. We make a paradoxical attempt to say something about the divine, to use the resources of our visible world as means of designating the invisible reality of God who transcends the world.

A strain is inevitably placed upon human language when a man tries to speak about the mystery of God. He seeks to say something meaningful in terms of his own experience about a reality which he does not directly experience and which he regards as something other than an extension of the world. The theistic predicament is to bring to linguistic expression some meanings about the being who is the transcendent, infinite spirit. Since language does not comfortably enshrine this referent, our talk about God always remains somewhat anomalous and elusive. The conclusion is not that theistic usage is hopelessly ambiguous, however, but that it reflects a distinctive human situation. If there is any category-mistake here, it is a deliberately made one and hence one that carries along its own corrective. Theists are engaged in exploring how far they can use words, whose origin they cannot dictate, to express meanings which transcend the situation of linguistic origin.

Crombie describes the theistic use of language as a response to a certain feeling or sense of things, a conviction that we live in a derived universe and that there may exist an underived being. We experience an intellectual dissatisfaction with the notion that our universe is complete and sufficient for itself. Furthermore, we feel that the conception of a transcendent spiritual being intimately related to our world, but distinct from it, could not leave us thus dissatisfied. Thus we are led to try to embody in fitting words our conviction about an infinite spiritual being. To ward off the objection that this explanation locates the springs of theism solely in a subjective feeling and thus renders theistic statements purely expressional or emotive, Crombie adds a further distinction between the notion of God which stimulates our theistic use of language and our ground for claiming that this notion holds good of the real world.

The conception of God, alone, can give rise to religious poetry and religious aspiration, but can supply no warrant for religious belief. For the latter one needs to be able to find, within experience, positive indications of the reality of God. . . . Christ, then, is the word of God to us; both the evidence of the reality of God, and also the declaration of Him to us.[16]

Thus the reality-claim for all statements about God is drawn from sacred history and the Incarnation. This is Crombie's basis for justifying the attachment of existential significance to the notion of God as the infinite spirit. A philosophy of God is not thereby eliminated, but its sole proper function becomes that of analyzing what we do say in human language about God. For the warrant behind our talk, we have to look to faith in Christ and to the shape of sacred history.

This approach offers one way in which to retain the living influence of religious faith upon our thinking about God, while still avoiding the ontological argument from the content of the notion of God. But it does not allow room for a theistic effort in philosophy which keeps an intimate relation with faith and yet seeks to gain some demonstrative knowledge about God. Crombie uncovers the very fruitful theme of the anomalous character of our discourse on God, but his fideism prevents him from tracing out those reasons for such discourse which spring from our natural and philosophical efforts at drawing some inferential support from the ordinary things of our experience. Hence he does not succeed in orienting the problem of anomalous theistic predication within the context of the human mind's activity of seeking to reach the truth of some propositions about God through demonstrative inference from our human reality and that of the world.

For his part, Ramsey asks Ryle to concede only one point: we cannot lay it down a priori that all true indicative sentences must describe existents or report occurrences essentially of the same kind and essentially in the same way. A policy of dogmatic univocity would incapacitate analytic philosophy for dealing with a major share of our ordinary, scientific, and moral statements. It would also prevent us from saying what we can about the theistic use of the object-language to state some aspects of religious conviction. That conviction consists fundamentally in the ontological claim that not all our human situations are confined to the spatio-temporal elements contained in them.[17] There are some distinctively religious situations in which we recognize not only the perceptual factors and their resultants but also the presence of something more. Then we have to find a language suitable for expressing this ontological claim. The anomalies of theistic discourse are not due to fuzzy and evasive thinking but to the persistent and rigorous effort to use ordinary language in a way that does justice to this claim and its consequences for man.

Given this logical purpose for religious talk, Ramsey concludes that it cannot avoid using language in a way that is logically odd from the perceptual standpoint. The materials of the religious way of discourse are taken from the ordinary object-language and yet are used to convey and explicate the claim that there is a reality transcending the perceptual objects. The oddness in question is thus a suitable one, since it responds perfectly to the religious task of disclosing a new depth of meaning within the context of familiar experiences. What makes religious language appropriately peculiar is the logical intent of so qualifying our ordinary words as to evoke recognition of there being something more in the perceptual situation than its spatio-temporal components.

Ramsey admits an affinity between his view of the distinctively religious situation and the existentialist discussion of authentic, participative situations. He regards the religious situation as the empirical basis for the theistic and religious use of language, and hence also as the basis in fact for the ontological claim regulating that use. The two factors setting off the religious situation are a discernment and a commitment.[18] Where Ramsey differs from the existentialists is in restricting his analysis of these factors as much as possible to the linguistic realm. What we discern is that there are perceptual situations with a difference, namely, ones where not everything is resolvable into the space-and-time elements. For instance, Joseph Butler states that we are aware of ourselves as not being only gross bodies, but as being living agents capable of self-awareness and responsible choice. Religious commitment is our practical response to such discernment, since it is a resolve to center our lives upon the spiritual reality of God.

Language is being used in a religious context when it aims at describing the religious situation of discernment and commitment in such a way as to provoke personal recognition. The key or apex words are used in logically odd ways as ultimates of explanation, as pointers leading beyond the observed world to God's spiritual reality. For instance, "immutable" functions as a guide for meditating on all-pervasive change, for stopping us short with the thought that some things do remain stable amid this change (the friend's loyalty persists despite his aging), and then for suggesting that the reality of God is wholly untouched by change. Another procedure is followed in calling God "one" or "perfect." These predicates direct our stories along the path of contrasting relations, somewhat in the manner of Bradley's dialectic. We work progressively through various sorts of manyness and unity until the mind is led to a disclosure of the theme of God as the supremely one being and the supremely perfect.

Perhaps the most interesting part of Ramsey's theory is his analysis of complex predicates, as when we talk about God as being "the first cause" or "the infinitely good." Ramsey distinguishes between the model-words ("cause" and "good") and the qualifier-words ("first" and "infinitely").[19] The function of the model-and-qualifier structure is to guide the placement of the apex word "God" with respect to a particular family of stories, say, those about powerful agencies or good persons. The model specifies the familiar empirical situation where we can make sentences about causal relations and good deeds. The qualifier tells us how to develop the situation in the direction of a less familiar situation where we will be able to make sentences concerning the being who is first in the causal order and infinitely good. Together, the model and qualifier gradually enable us to build up a pattern of terms and relations in story form, until perhaps a disclosure is made of the characteristically different religious situation and its significance for grasping something about God. We may play the causal game, for example, until someone must answer the causal question simply by saying that he decided to do something just because he is the man he is and has the will he does have. This brings the discourse within the region of the first-cause situation and suggests that we should employ the word "God" at the head of all our causal stories, through the predication of "first cause." The individual comes to see the fitness of this perceptually odd type of predication, since the religious situation demands that we use the term "God" in a logical position that is distinct, regulative, and a climax to all our causal stories.

The religious use of language is directed ultimately toward insight and not simply toward the perpetuation of the language game itself. Its aim is to provoke recognition of the religious situation as being unique and yet as appropriately supported by the ordinary situations from which our talk starts. The pattern of the model-and-qualifier not only guides a set of stories but places the mind of the participant in position for making its own discernment of, and commitment to, religious truth about God. The result is not achieved automatically through an incantative use of language, and the difference among minds requires a variety of language routes to the insight. But the pattern of talk may well place the mind within range of sharing for itself in the characteristically religious situation.

Ramsey's theory of appropriate linguistic oddness comes closest toward rejoining analytic theism with the metaphysically based philosophies of God. It defends the shift in the use of perceptual terms on the ground of its being a linguistic response suitable to an ontological claim. Now an ontological claim can be understood in two ways: as an assertion about the real order and as an assertion drawing its evidence and argument from the real order. The former meaning is common to most analytic theists, but Ramsey comes to the verge of reopening the ontological issue in the latter sense, in virtue of his views on the discernment factor present in the religious situation. He does state formally that his treatment remains within linguistic boundaries and postpones a metaphysical study for another occasion. But already in his book on *Religious Language* he is broaching the metaphysical issues by dealing not only with the appropriateness of the verbal placings in relation to the logical purpose of religious talk but also with the situational grounding of the logical purpose itself.

342

There are definite indications that the limits of linguistic gamesmanship are rather swiftly reached in defending the propriety of statements about God. Ramsey wants to show that there are good grounds for holding that the perceptual situation sometimes conveys something more than its spatio-temporal elements. He cites Butler's account of our awareness of the distinction between gross bodies and living, reflective, and responsible agents. This can be taken either as an analysis of still another set of statements for their linguistic properties or as an analysis intended to provoke a recognition of the truth about an experiential condition. The latter function fits in with the pattern of models and qualifiers.

Regarded as a way of leading us to see the empirical warrant for the ontological claim, the citation of Butler on the awareness of a distinctive mode of reality in human reality is a first step within metaphysics. It encourages us to accept as true the separative judgment that the real is not confined to the perceptual factors and their resultants. This is not yet enough, however, to show that the perceptual situation can be opened sufficiently to give us some assurance about the transcendent spiritual reality of God. There is still the question of showing why we persist in using several causal stories which are organized in a definite direction and toward a definite climax. The function of the qualifiers in theistic discourse is not just to set up rules about the usage but to give an orientation to stories that are ordered toward and justified by an inference about the spiritual reality of God. This peculiar directional feature of the talk also requires a warrant which is just as firmly grounded in an aspect of our experience as is the minimal ontological claim about our own spiritual reality.

Ramsey himself points out that "God" serves not only as an elucidating term but as an explaining, unifying, and controlling one. This stretches to the breaking point the slogan that the job of philosophy is to understand and not to explain. Ramsey appeals to the use of nicknames and Gestalt diagrams as parallels for the process of bringing out of a relatively narrow perceptual basis some meanings that transcend it and explain a wider range. Yet, since he does not identify these procedures with that involved in our use of stories controlled by the placement of "God," he still has the problem of showing the specific grounds for the use of infinite qualifiers in such stories. If the justification comes from the factor of discernment, then it must be established that the discernment reaches not only to our human reflective mode of reality but also to the transcendent spiritual reality of God.

343

The man who does use stories about causal agencies or good persons to provoke a specific recognition of the appropriateness of talking about "first cause" or "infinitely good," can be reasonably expected to show that he himself is responding to a discernment of the grounds for accepting God as first cause and the infinitely good person. Otherwise, his handling of stories will seem not merely odd but unjustifiably queer and baseless. He has to furnish some evidence outside the model-and-qualifier pattern itself why he can reasonably adopt it in his talk about God. This means that he knows not only that there is another viewpoint than the perceptual one but, more specifically, that there is a viewpoint in which we are warranted in holding to the truth of the statement that the first cause and infinite spiritual person does exist. The "something more" which regulates his use of infinite qualifiers and his ordination of stories with respect to the presiding term "God" is evidence about the infinite reality of God. Without it, the handling of the stories can be regarded as a response to private whim or to the logic of a jointly shared delusion.

5. *Theistic Causal Demonstration as a New Field for Analysis*

Our purpose in this chapter has been a strictly limited one. We have confined ourselves to an examination of some actual instances of analytic work in the area of theism, in order to determine how analytic theism is related to a realistic philosophy of God based on the search after demonstrative knowledge. The investigation shows that, up to now, the representatives of analytic theism are not engaged in clarifying the linguistic conditions under which men operate when they seek to make causally based demonstrative inferences concerning the truth of statements about God. On the contrary, the situation under analysis is that in which Christian religious belief is taken as the sole basis of the truth-claim and natural theism acts as a means of illustrating and correlating the doctrine on God with aspects of our experience, so as to establish a foothold for empirical meaning rather than the grounds of demonstration. This adaptation of analytic techniques to a nondemonstrative approach to statements about God is striking in the case of the problem of God's existence, but it is also consistently followed in treating the key issues of falsifiability and linguistic oddness. Analytic theism tries to overcome the older position of logical positivism in regard to the meaningfulness of statements about God, but it still remains within the confines of phenomenalism as far as concerns the philosophical demonstration of the truth of statements about God. The analysts have not yet examined the distinctive use of language within the context and intention of theistic realism, taken as a philosophically ordered inference to God.

From these findings, we cannot infer that all future work done by analytic theists must conform with the pattern prevailing until now. There is no evidence to show that the use of analytic resources in treating the problem of God is bound up essentially and exclusively with the standpoint which we have been describing. Rather, it would seem that the actual direction of analytic theism has been determined so far by philosophical and theological considerations which are distinct from the whole analytic enterprise. The influence of extra-analytic factors holds good for all the parties to the discussion, both the theists and the nontheists. They have proportioned their analytic work to a situation in which no claim is made for demonstrating the truth of the statement that God exists and hence in which such a truth-claim exercises no dominating role. It is very helpful to have analytic explorations of this nondemonstrative situation and the problems involved in maintaining that nevertheless our statements about God are empirically significant. But there seems to be no compelling reason for confining analytic theism to such materials.

As soon as one begins to talk about the topics of theism with those naturalists and phenomenalists who do raise the question of the truth as well as the meaning of statements about God, one discovers some good reasons for hoping that there will be a development of analytic theism relevant directly to the work of a realistic philosophy seeking some causally based, demonstrative kind of knowledge concerning God. Our present study shows that such help is not already at hand, since the leading analytic theists have not been describing linguistic patterns of what we do when we try to demonstrate the truth of our statements about God. Hence we can expect that the modifications involved in the proposed analysis will be quite radical and not restricted to some slight changes in the present standpoints. There is a pressing need for describing the language structure regulated by the metaphysical intent of obtaining some demonstrative knowledge about God, that is, of showing the causal foundation for the truth of some of our statements about God. But this need is not already supplied by what the analytic theists examined here have been doing.

This also suggests that the current analytic theists have not exhaustively studied all the ways in which the Christian faith influences the philosophical search after God. It would be just as arbitrary to limit the relation of faith and philosophical inquiry about God to the particular situation described by the analytic theists as it would be to confine the meaning of philosophy of God to the one presupposed by them. A difference in conceiving how the philosopher backs up his statements about God is bound up intimately with a difference over how one's religious faith is relevant to the philosophy of God. The way of demonstrative inference suggests that the philosopher's religious faith does not rule out, but instead may encourage, the search after a causal basis in our experienced world for demonstrating the truth of some propositions concerning God. Our previous studies in Gabriel Marcel and Edith Stein point in the same direction. Here is another reason why a radical revision of the analytic framework is required to take full account of philosophical ways to God that have not yet been investigated by analytic theism.

In this context, it is instructive to see how Ramsey defends the view that an analytic theism operating within the climate of logical empiricism can do justice both to that climate and to the theological tradition.

We might well admit that in principle we are only doing what, for example, St. Thomas Aquinas was doing, though we are not thereby committed (for better or worse) to his ontology and system. We may perhaps say that logical empiricism offers us a possible *generalization* of Thomism for bringing new life to old and complex controversies. . . . God and his worship: logical empiricism, put to the service of theology, starts and ends there. Need we trouble if we discover meanwhile that a whole heap of metaphysical furniture—'underlying substances,' 'indelible characteristics,' and so on—which some might have supposed to be indispensable, has in fact belonged only to a confusing dream? [20]

The metaphysical lumber to be thrown out as now useless also includes all references to being, potency, essence, and accident. This is the price to be paid for realizing the ideal of logical empiricism as *ancilla theologiae*. Whether or not the price is too steep does not depend fundamentally on our touchiness over traditional terms or even on our quandary over how to fit this plan in with the notion of generalizing Thomism. The basic point is whether we can still do the business of natural theology as a search after demonstrative knowledge concerning God, without using whatever aspects of reality may have been indicated by these terms.

Furthermore, we will have to find out why Ramsey and other analytic theists grant special privileges to the term "cause," when they eliminate so many other terms which have been used historically to elucidate its meaning.[21] They do not have a metaphysical theory of causality, such as is used in a demonstrative theism. Particularly in the case of joining the causal model with an infinite qualifier, it will have to be inquired whether any of the considerations intended by the outmoded metaphysical furniture help to validate this junction. The answer will probably depend upon the way we view the range of experience and the manner in which a philosophy of God is related to it. It will not suffice simply to say that "cause" is used by way of correlation and evocation, rather than with demonstrative intent, since this is precisely the point where the present form of analytic theism is being challenged as a fully adequate account of what the human mind does in seeking some truths about God. And if the appeal to a residual logical empiricism is strictly intended, then we are openly moving beyond the linguistic frontiers in order to justify our use of certain terms and our rejection of others. In bringing out the difference between current analytic theism and the way of causal-demonstrative inference to God, we can see more clearly that the former position is too closely bound up with special commitments on faith and phenomenalism to have provided the general pattern for philosophical inquiry about God. Both the requirements of inference and the new possibilities of theistic analysis point toward a fresh study of the causal basis of our knowledge and discourse about God, as shaped by realistic theism.[22]

CHAPTER 14

HUSSERL AND THE BOND
OF NATURAL BEING

MY AIM in this chapter is to examine a few metaphysical aspects
of man's relationship with nature, and to do so by inspecting Edmund
Husserl's theory of nature. There are several considerations which
prompt me to make this approach to the problem of the starting point
of metaphysics, a problem which has to be renewed by each generation in terms of its own concerns and commonplaces. Today, it is difficult to distinguish metaphysics from philosophical anthropology, since
we are so centrally preoccupied with man and his way of being. There
is considerable discussion about the self and its world of meanings,
but the bearing of such discussion upon natural reality as ordinarily
experienced and as treated by the scientist and the philosopher is
often left obscure. By placing some stress upon man's connection with
nature, it may be possible not only to bring out an indispensable way
of describing his being but also to sharpen the formulation of the
question of metaphysical knowledge about man and the rest of the
natural world.

To develop this question with constant reference to Husserl's teaching rests, however, upon two further reasons connected with our present way of philosophizing. The more general point is that phenomenology continues to make some headway in America, without yet
achieving wide support among philosophers. This is due in part to a
continued failure to find a common ground of inquiry, despite some
similarities that have been pointed out between phenomenology and
analytic philosophy. One common theme which is seldom stressed is
an interest in the meaning of nature and the validity of philosophical
naturalism. At least as far as Husserl is concerned, this is not an easy
topic or one that can be handled once for all, without finding any

questions left over to nag the mind. Rather, it is one which he finds it necessary constantly to reopen and rework in the light of new ideas and new emphases in his thought.

Part of the responsibility for the only halfway emergence of phenomenology so far in American philosophy must be borne by those of us who are friends of phenomenology, not only for giving a rather curt and routine treatment to this major portion of Husserl's doctrine but also for failing to keep his whole philosophy distinct from that of other European phenomenologists. It is very easy for us to slip from a precise discussion of Husserl to an imprecise appeal to phenomenology in general. The latter often becomes little more than a descriptive manner of stating one's own convictions and clothing them in unusual forms of language. The history of philosophy provides us with many instances where metaphysics is developed in the manner of a free fantasy on the part of a school, and where some rigor is recovered only by paying scrupulous attention to the actual argumentation of the great minds at the fountainhead. The return from Cartesianism to Descartes or from Hegelianism to Hegel is difficult but not impossible, and the same prospect holds for the return from a generalized phenomenology to Husserl and the other major sources. Unless their distinctive positions are respected, the valuable studies made by phenomenologists in particular areas of experience will be undeservedly neglected and their exact bearing upon metaphysics never determined.

Such a movement involves one in some minimal historical work, however, and this is the remaining point of my approach. Husserl is just sufficiently removed from the present generation to require us to use the resources of historical analysis, if we want our references to him to count as something more than conventional evocations of a name. We are just starting to grasp the details and the general sweep of his writings. His philosophy furnishes a concrete instance of the intermingling of the past and the present in metaphysical speculation, since it confronts us both as a source to be studied and as a strongly argued case for how to work phenomenologically today. We are accustomed to say that doing history is fine, as long as you take a definite stand. Yet it is also true that taking a definite stand is fine, as long as you permit the relevant portions of history to contribute toward it.

1. *The Elucidating Intent*

This problem of permitting historical findings to impinge upon one's speculations is acute in metaphysics. The creative thinker wants to be able to shape his thought freely in the light of what he personally sees, without being weighted down by past teachings and the responsibility of examining them in advance of reaching his own conclusions. He is also vividly aware of the unique influence exerted by philosophers who are speaking with their own living voice. What counts right now in a philosophical discussion is what is well thought and well said right now, almost regardless of what has been said on the subject in the past. And yet the responsible thinker does not fail to insert the qualifying adverb "almost," even though he may allow it to remain ineffective as far as his own work is concerned. For his speculation aims at determining a truth of some durability, one which can stand up under more meditative testing than is possible in the passing discussion. At some phase in the long testing process undertaken by the philosophical community, his arguments will be compared with those contained in positions previously taken in the history of his problem, and the comparison will be bound to affect the judgments then being formed about his work. In varying proportions, then, there is a tension between one's responsibility toward the urgent contemporary argument and toward the quiet but powerful tide of reasons coming to bear from the past.

Working within his contemporary frame, the metaphysician enjoys the advantage of determining within certain limits the extent and quality of his relationship with previous inquirers. He knows that he cannot entirely escape their historical influence, that in one sense they constitute the fate with which he must struggle. They furnish him with a language, a set of problems, and a dossier of evidence, all of which can tyrannize over his mind and never so completely as when he ignores their origins. He must expend a good deal of effort in reforging the meanings of his technical language, restating the topical questions in terms of his own method, and thus reducing the likelihood of his serving merely as an echo of a well-worn melody. By these reflective measures, the metaphysician can achieve the integrity of his own mind and, along with it, a certain control over his further engagement with the history of metaphysics. He may try to limit himself to taking samples of philosophic discourse from past thinkers, so

350

that he can have materials for analysis at a technical level. Or else he may restrict his interest to the definition and classification of typical positions on the main issues, so that he can more readily characterize his own views by reference to these generalizations.

This process of controlling one's engagement with the historical aspects of metaphysics cannot be carried on in complete isolation, however, and with regard solely for one's own systematic constructions. The work still goes on within the community of philosophers, at least some of whom may be expected to introduce some further points. It is a specially perilous thing to introduce extensive statements taken from the great philosophical sources. Philosophers in any age talk the way they do in order to do justice to the look of things, as seen from their own vantage point. To restore their discourse is also to restore their vein of evidence and their beam of vision. In and through their language, the metaphysicians of the past find a way of entering our room and engaging us in some counter-analysis. Moreover, they file into our room one by one, that is, each man speaks in his own fashion and calls attention precisely to what he grasps in his peculiar statements. He is likely to register a protest against being reduced to a variant case of some abstract position, under which he has been herded. If we give the slightest foothold of a contemporary reading to the historical sources in metaphysics, they will compel us to admit that it is better to make a biting encounter with the actual argumentation of some individual thinker than to rest with pure generalized positions.

One area where the metaphysician is well advised to take account of previous developments is the problem of nature and natures. This is one of the permanent routes leading either to a metaphysical position or to a specific criticism of such positions. Aristotle defended first philosophy by showing that there is some kind of substance which is not intrinsically subject to change and hence whose study does not fall within the scope of the philosophy of nature. The conflict between Descartes and Spinoza pivoted largely around the metaphysical significance of nature and God's relation to it. The centrality of the problem of nature for determining the possibility of metaphysical knowledge continued in the case of Kant and Hegel. Both in making his attack upon transcendental metaphysics and in defending a type of metaphysical analysis of scientific and moral knowledge, Kant made prominent use of the concepts of world and nature. And one helpful way of following the transition from Kant to Hegel is to observe how the meaning of a metaphysics of nature shifted from being primarily an epistemological account of a priori factors to being an ontological account of the connection between natural forms and the developing absolute spirit. Whenever the foundation of metaphysics has been discussed, it has involved some definite conception of nature, natures, and human knowledge thereof.

Philosophers in our century have not been exceptions to this intimate association of problems. There is a special concern with the meaning of nature on the part of the three men of the immediately past generation who have most strongly influenced our metaphysical thinking—Dewey, Whitehead, and Husserl. In the case of the first two of these thinkers, their preoccupation with nature and man's relation to it is striking and well known. It is a major theme in Husserl as well, and he develops it in a somewhat corresponding way. He is more concerned than is Dewey with the mathematical contribution to our conception of nature, and agrees with his two contemporaries about the explanatory power of the evolutionary theory, especially as concentrated in genetic psychology. Yet Husserl tries to determine the context and limits of the scientific conception of nature by relating it to the acts of intending consciousness which make it meaningful. His key question about nature is not how to achieve a Whiteheadian blending of essences and not how to achieve a Deweyan transaction with the environment, but rather how to achieve the signifying act whose fulfillment is precisely the natural world. Although the factors of blending and transaction are by no means absent from his account of nature, they are consistently ordered toward a dominant relationship of the self and its domain of objectivity. This way of treating the question of man and nature disposes Husserl toward a first philosophy organized around the intending self and its world, rather than toward a metaphysics of natural being.[1]

If we were looking for some contemporary work being done on the problem of man and nature by phenomenologically based thinkers, we would probably want to consult Heidegger and Merleau-Ponty. Heidegger is somewhat less readily accessible than Husserl, however, since his treatment of this topic is quite intricately bound up with his interpretation of the pre-Socratics, Hölderlin, and now in an increasing degree Nietzsche. Merleau-Ponty is in quite a different situation, since he takes his point of departure from the juncture made between Husserl and modern psychologies. In the last book which he was able to edit, however, he went out of his way to emphasize the Husserlian context for his own discussions on nature.[2] As it were, he was saying that it is risky to use his writings as a first premise which settles the question of the method of reduction and authorizes a metaphysical use of the notion of the world of living experience. It may be possible to criticize the method of reduction and use the notion of the life world in a phenomenological metaphysics, but this cannot be done in a rigorous way without personally going over the basic argumentation with Husserl himself.

Nevertheless, a roadblock seems to be erected by Husserl himself against pursuing this task with the aid of our ordinary historical procedures. He includes historical thinking, especially as it functions in the philosophical sphere, as a form of psychologism since it relativizes our speculations to some transient cultural situation. The more faithfully we respect the particular form of a philosopher's thought, the more surely do we seem to restrict its significance to his own few decades of activity and thus relieve ourselves of having to take his arguments very seriously, at least in their historical mode of presentation. Hence Husserl explicitly includes the historical approach to philosophical topics within the scope of his method of suspension of assent. Furthermore, he offers an objection that is almost moral in import, namely, that the historical attitude in philosophy breeds a type of historicism which scandalously prefers to describe facts about the past rather than wrestle directly with difficulties in the present world. It is not surprising that, among the meanings prominently assigned by Husserl to his imperative of going back to the things themselves, there is one which advises us to move our center of attention from historical systems to the present analysis of issues and evidences.

These criticisms are salutary and should be included in every philosopher's working kit. They are reminders that, when he has to approach a philosophical teaching across a temporal horizon and thus in some kind of historical mode, he is still responsible for the intent which shapes his study of it. Husserl's objections tell against making a substitutional use of historical interests to divert oneself from dealing directly with the issue and from forming one's own philosophical judgment about it. Instead of this substitutional intent, however, one may deliberately guide his historical work by what I will call *the elucidating intent*. Its methodic aim is to insure a close integration between obtaining a faithful understanding of the sources and bringing out their relevance for one's contemporary treatment of problems. A double elucidation can thus be achieved, when the philosopher's own speculative difficulties sharpen his study of previous thinkers and when, in turn, their arguments are seen to touch upon our common experience and thus establish their present import. Both historicism and the evasion of one's philosophical vocation can be avoided, when the elucidating intent is permitted to govern the study of our philosophical past.

Indeed, Husserl himself was eventually led by his reflections on temporality and the continuous reworking of meanings within the human community to stress the essentially historical nature of philosophical reason. Without becoming involved in matters of erudition and textual analysis, he did make room for a critical history of ideas in their intentional genesis and did try to characterize his phenomenology by reference to some modern philosophers and their ideal for speculation. His own doctrine on the nature-man relationship is available to us in our turn, provided only that we try to quicken the main problems and treat them in the light of our own experience. I intend to concentrate upon just two of the many facets of this doctrine: the theory of the natural attitude and the intentional analysis of nature and man. In both instances, special attention will be paid to any meaning for natural being which is relevant for the founding of a metaphysics of existent beings and a realistic influence to God.

2. *The Natural Attitude and the Ingressive Method*

One of Husserl's best known accomplishments is his description and criticism of the natural attitude.[3] This is a deceptive topic, because it can be stated quite simply for introductory purposes in the exposition of phenomenology and then never re-examined for the unexpected complications it does contain. The natural attitude is present in all of us when we take for granted the reality of things around us, when we regard the natural world simply as being there in a way that arouses no questions. We tend to regard our environing world merely as a massive fact which is unproblematically with us and remains there, regardless of the perspectives we may take upon it. This attitude of unquestioning acceptance of the obvious reality of our world is shared by unsophisticated minds and scientifically trained ones alike. However much the scientists may be aware of their own contribution to constructs and theories, they nevertheless refer their explanations back eventually to a domain of real things and events, to nature as the testing ground and ultimate place for resolving our conceptual schemes and interpretations. Nature consists of a vast objective field of things, dynamically related in space and time, to which we must ultimately refer our thoughts and evaluations for verification. The frame of mind and pattern of judging which permit us to regard this natural domain as too obviously real for serious discussion comprise the natural attitude.

The philosopher's obligation is to pry us loose from this massively naive commitment, or at least to do so in the degree that we make any pretensions at philosophizing. As Husserl is careful to observe, there is nothing objectionable in maintaining the natural attitude in our everyday affairs, where its coherence and practical value are recommendations for leaving it undisturbed. And as long as it does not interfere with the free elaboration of hypotheses and the methodological recognition of the human mind's initiative in the study of nature, it can also be legitimately maintained by the working scientist. To shape one's life in accord with the natural attitude is no ultimate defect in anyone except the philosopher, whose vocation is to carry out a radical questioning which should not stop short of including our ordinary belief in the already present real world. For him to permit this belief to remain operative and even to be decisive for the basis of his philosophy is a failure touching upon his very integrity of thought and purpose.

Husserl and the phenomenologists who follow in his steps on this issue spell out explicitly the three consequences of not putting out of play, at the very outset of philosophizing, both the act of believing and that of disbelieving in the solid given reality of the natural world. First, the mind never attains to the radical kind of reflectiveness demanded of the philosopher. There are various kinds of reflectiveness possible for people other than philosophers, but the touchstone for the philosophical kind is to remove from any foundational role the entire issue about the real world accepted as being already there for us to look at. Secondly, anyone who does keep his assent operative at this point is inevitably bound to develop some form of philosophical naturalism. In its narrower meaning for Husserl, naturalism is a philosophy which applies to man himself the methods and concepts elaborated for the scientific investigation of the physical world, and which adds that these procedures are the sole valid cognitive means for studying man and nature. In the wider sense, however, any philosophy which operates within the assumption contained in the natural attitude is in principle a form of naturalism, although perhaps not yet developed in a consequential and thorough way to that extreme in philosophy.

And thirdly, there is a common liability visited upon any effort at philosophizing within the premise of the natural attitude: it is fully vulnerable to a skeptical attack. Our existential statements about the real world are contingent ones, falling into what Leibniz and Hume call the class of statements of fact. Their contradictory opposite is coherent and cannot be removed by any necessary, essential argumentation. Hence such existential statements are open to doubt and yield no philosophical certitude. We must either accept a skeptically motivated suspension of assent or else remove the entire question of the foundation of philosophy from the context of the thesis about the reality of the world to that of the relation between intending consciousness and its object. Nothing is lost in making the latter transfer, since Husserl's program is to reconstitute every aspect of the natural belief in things, including their trait of real existence.[4]

It seems to me that evaluation of this theory about the natural attitude hardens too rapidly into two conventional kinds of response. The one sort is to repeat that, whatever the consequences, our only cognitively reliable tools are those furnished by a generalized logic of the sciences and an evolutionary approach to consciousness and the language about the self. The other response is to accept the critique just as it stands, since it opens up the only path for avoiding an unreflective, naturalistic, and skeptically demolishable position in philosophy today. My present criticism is restricted to the latter view, with the aim of showing that the alternatives to skepticism are not narrowed down as drastically as it supposes. The difficulty is to keep Husserl's own discussion about the deficiencies of an obvious natural attitude from itself becoming too obvious and unproblematic to warrant critical examination, especially on the part of those who seek to become philosophically reflective in a more inclusive manner than the logic of science can provide.

Husserl himself does not recommend in a general way that we become reflective and put our speculations upon a non-naturalistic and non-skeptical footing. Rather, the barb in his argument is that, apart from his specific way of dealing with the natural attitude, there can be no genuinely critical philosophy and hence no effective alternative to naturalism and skepticism. It is indeed necessary to distinguish the several ways in which we can realize our human power for becoming reflective. The kinds of self-awareness achieved by the poet and the moral agent, the biologist and the statesman, cannot be reduced by rule to a flat level of uniformity or treated merely as preludes to the philosopher's grasp upon himself in his situation. But the question now is whether there are also several ways of becoming reflective within philosophy itself or whether every presumed philosopher remains fundamentally pre-reflective, until he accepts the Husserlian method of disengaging the mind from belief in the real world and directing it to the life of the intending self and its objects.

356

Husserl regards any position which is not constituted by these two acts as being irretrievably naive and sunk in the natural attitude. It is notorious, however, that one man's naiveté is another man's reasoned stand. The criterion of naiveté employed here is highly determinate and already defined in terms of Husserl's own reduction of philosophical analysis to a study of the transcendental ego and its activities and objects. At the outset of philosophy, this standard need not be accepted. An ordinary type of reflectiveness is attainable by attending to the grounds of our major assents, by remaining vigilant about the presuppositions we introduce into arguments, and by recognizing the need to inquire persistently into the relationship between the inquiring man and the things he values, seeks, and knows. Whether or not this initial sort of philosophical reflection contains a germ which must lead to adoption of the Husserlian method is a matter to be shown, not a first principle of the logic of naiveté. As far as an ultimately adequate reflection is concerned, this must be an argued matter if we are to be able to follow the reasoning and weigh its worth.

It may seem to be an intrusion upon the argument to continue the references to naturalism and skepticism. Yet Husserl makes it very clear that he is not treating of the natural attitude simply for its own sake, but as an instrumental theme whose purpose is to compel us to accept the dilemma between these positions and his own transcendental phenomenology. Nevertheless, it is worthwhile to make the experiment of giving a direct analysis of the natural attitude, by de-instrumentalizing it and viewing it apart from the perspective of that dilemma. There is no perfect equivalence between the natural attitude and philosophical naturalism. The former is a much broader position, embracing the everyday view of men and the standpoint of many scientists. Their ways of sharing in the natural attitude or accepting the reality of the natural world are not philosophical, even though they may furnish the materials for a philosophical analysis. Even if the everyday and scientific modes of the natural attitude contain some philosophical significance which can be rendered explicit, there are several philosophical interpretations which can be made. There is no necessary ordination of the natural attitude toward philosophical naturalism, taken in a determinate sense, unless one already presupposes that it is the only positive alternative in philosophy to transcendental phenomenology.

It is helpful for us to distinguish between three meanings which are given to the natural attitude. Basically, it signifies the act of accepting the reality of our world as being too obvious to require consideration, too overwhelmingly self-warranted to make our relationship to the world significant for critical study in this respect. Sometimes closely associated with this first sense is a second meaning for the natural attitude, one that is best exemplified by psychologism and some forms of positivism. Here, man is regarded simply as one more physical entity among others in the world, with the consequence that cognitive statements about human reality are limited to those which can be made with the methods and categories devised for studying the physical world. A third way of taking the natural attitude is as a methodological commitment to the standpoint of objectivity, a program for dealing with the whole scope of reality solely in terms of the structure and relations present in objects of experience.

There is no inevitable and exclusive passage from one of these meanings to the other. Maintaining the natural attitude in the first sense may be a condition for the development of psychologism, but it need not lead in that direction. Within psychology itself, refinements in the understanding of methods and concepts for the study of man provide a corrective for the psychologistic postulate even on the part of people who are still living within the natural attitude in its initial form. When we realize that man is a being who grasps, fashions, and communicates meanings, and that he shows a certain freedom in the process, we are then in possession of some directly relevant grounds for developing new methods and concepts, distinct from those which deal with the physical world. There are good reasons here for not applying unchanged to man the categories found useful elsewhere, and hence of not expanding the natural attitude to include the second mode of it. This is not to say that the analysis of man cannot be carried out in terms of relations, causality, and substance, but that their meaning has to be rethought in order to take into account the human manner of being and acting. Reflection upon man may result not only in a critique of the second mode of the natural attitude but also in a grasp of the inadequacy of the third mode, namely, that which restricts the study of man to the common features shared by things in their condition as objects. The experience of men as agents and makers of symbols can, apart from a reference to any transcendental source of objectivity, prevent the acceptance of the third sort of natural attitude as a necessary climax.

Because there is no necessary link between these three forms of the natural attitude, criticism of that attitude need not result in accepting the dilemma between Husserl's phenomenology and philosophical naturalism. The definite meanings for the latter position correspond roughly with the second and third modes of the natural attitude. But they are not generated by the first mode with any necessity which would force one either to accept them or else adopt Husserl's own theory of the transcendental ego and its kind of intentionality. The only way in which there can be a rigorous dilemma here is to treat "naturalism" as a descriptive term covering all the philosophies which do not make the Husserlian reduction to the transcendental ego. Used in this manner, the term is too broad to specify the different methods for criticizing that reduction and also too contingent to establish the case for identifying a terminal philosophical reflectiveness with Husserl's philosophy.

Still, there is another face to his problem of the natural attitude which continues to assure its fruitfulness for philosophical study. Instead of approaching it through the method of transcendental regression, however, we can use *the ingressive method*.[5] It requires an act of reorientation on the part of the inquirer. Instead of giving the unquestioned primacy to the question of the transcendental conditions of possibility for an aspect of experience, he directs his attention initially toward the components actually involved in that phase of experience which evokes his questioning. The ingressive method requires him to move by gradual analysis to a more determinate understanding of the factors directly contained within the situation itself. The outcome of this analysis will then determine the appropriate type of question to ask thereafter about the implications of the experiential situation. Whether those subsequent questions be concerned with conditions of possibility, actual causal principles, or membership in a community of being, will be determined in the specific instance by the ingressive clarification rather than by a purely methodological decision favoring a regression to the pure ego.

In the present instance, this procedure requires us to consider more closely the two drawbacks in the first modality of the natural attitude. They are the tendency to give a conventional, thoughtless assent to the world's reality, and to do so with the connotation that the only thing which matters is this massive fact of the world as being there regardless of our reaction to it. The defective features concern the manner of the assent and the range of awareness of the relationships directly involved in making the assent. The ingressive approach is to work toward a removal of these defects at the level of the assent itself, rather than to put the assent out of play and then be forced to transfer the analysis to the plane of a pure ego and its constituting operations. A heedless conventional response to real things can be removed by making the requirement of a personal inspection of evidence apply even to our primary judgments and other experiential relations with existing beings. The way to overcome a foolish claim of obviousness is not to withdraw the presence of the actualities we experience, but rather to make our grasp upon them a personal act which nourishes itself reflectively upon the beings which present themselves. And in doing so, we need not become forgetful of ourselves but should try to comprehend the full situation. The judgment of real existence is made by the human inquirer about some actual existents with which he is complexly related. The more fully he becomes aware of his relations of interacting-desiring-knowing-possessing with respect to the existent beings, the more fully can he understand the nature of the beings affirmed to be really existent.

Analyzed ingressively, the problem of the natural attitude leads to a reflective condition which retains the existential assent to real beings in our world. The analysis permits us to distinguish between the actual being of the natural things, the human natural experiences whereby we engage in a living communion with these things, and the reflective existential judgment of natural being which we make about the existent things and ourselves as related to them. Taken together, these components constitute the bond of natural being, which furnishes a basis for metaphysical reflection. But we do not reach a comfortable shelter simply by moving from the natural attitude to the more fundamental natural acts of being and natural experiential judgment. For at this point, Husserl suggests that the whole position is open to a skeptical attack which would render it foundationally useless for the purposes of philosophy.

Husserl often points out his special kinship with Descartes and Hume. It is well displayed in their joint sensitivity to the skeptical challenge in philosophy and their skillful use of this challenge to consolidate their own starting points. When Husserl calls his philosophy an integral rationalism, he means among other things that it appeals to the skeptical arguments about actual existents in order to remove from any foundational role the entire question of belief or disbelief in the existing natural world. Just as Descartes requires a reduction to the thinking thing and Hume a reduction to the phenomenal object as an evidential basis, so Husserl requires a disengagement of the mind from the contingently circumscribed natural things so as to reach the transcendental ego and its life of intending acts. Here he finds a doubt-resistant footing which cannot be affected by the skeptical strategy, but which imposes itself with essential necessity upon our reflection. This return to the pure ego achieves both the rationalistic ideal of a primary evidence, which is scientifically necessary in virtue of its lack of basic commitment toward perceived actual beings, and also the framework for reconstructing the experienced world out of this first evidence. The meaning and being of the experienced, existing things will not be lost, but they will be permitted to function only within a certain order of constitution by the intending ego and hence only as a reduced and constituted achievement, not as the foundation of philosophical reflection. The entire Husserlian recovery of existential significance depends upon this dialectic of a transferred basis of evidence.

Husserl's stringent, deliberately adopted style of skeptical argumentation as the prelude to his own doctrine is notably lacking from many subsequent essays in phenomenology. That may be why they fail to wrestle seriously with the question of the transcendental reduction or to regard integral rationalism as a central issue in phenomenology. But when Husserl himself is read with an elucidating intent, he makes these questions too urgent to be evaded or given a secondary treatment. He invokes the skeptical tropes to show that we cannot build a philosophy upon the assent to contingently existing things, since we can think coherently about them as non-existent and thus can reduce the whole issue to a suspensive probability.

We can consider that assent in its own structure, however, rather than refer it at once to the technique of equipollence or the counterbalancing and neutralizing of judgments. The perceptual existential judgment does not affirm a mere content or bare subject of isolated meaning but a subject in actual being or a thing perceived as existing. The assent is regulated by our perceptual and other experiences of the thing as actually existing and, when reflectively considered, takes into account these relationships with the being. These determinants of the meaning and ground of our judgment about the perceived actual existent are not revoked, transmuted, or reduced to indetermination, even when we may think coherently about the content of meaning as non-existent. Even when the play of alternatives is refined by the technique of an imaginative variation of conditions, it does not remove the actual perception and hence does not dissolve the reflectively held judgment about the perceived existing being. Our imaginative variation is effective for discovering an essential structure amid contingent circumstances, but not for dissolving the structured existent and our basal assent to it.

The ingressive method tries, therefore, to find a middle path between naive or deliberate disregard of the difficulties on the one side and a necessary appeal to the transcendental reduction on the other. It subjects the natural attitude to analytic reflection, yet without making the assumption that reflectiveness cannot be achieved in philosophy anywhere this side of a theory about the pure ego and its intending objectivities. The inquirer has to become reflective about the complex situation of man and the natural world, without regarding our judgments on it as being naive in principle until founded upon the constituting operations of the pure ego. To attempt to study the being of man and other natural things in their experienced actuality and powers, without treating that actuality primarily as an index pointing to the transcendental life of the ego, is a way of describing the human point of departure for metaphysics in terms familiar to Husserl himself. A start can be made in this manner in order to obtain some reflective understanding of ourselves and other beings involved and implicated in human experience, apart from the method of constituting their philosophically valid meaning and being within Husserl's intentional analysis of the regional ontology of man and nature. We must now inquire whether his theory of man and nature resembles his theory of the natural attitude on the score of raising some questions which point toward a metaphysics of reflectively examined, but not transcendentally constituted, existent beings.

3. *From Man-Object to Man the Natural Existent*

One of the richest veins in Husserl's intentional analysis deals with the meaning of nature and objectivity, with specific reference to the contributions made by the physical, psychological, and social sciences.[6] He accepts their methods and objects, and then brings out other ways of interrogating nature and the belief in nature which demand a distinctive philosophical treatment. It is impossible here to do real justice to his investigations on this topic, the particular features of which retain their worth even when there are difficulties about the general interpretation given to them. My business is to concentrate upon the broad theory of nature with the aim of determining man's role within it. Thereby, I hope to furnish some reasons for developing metaphysics out of the human experience and judgmental recognition of man and other things as existing and acting beings, not as objectifications of pure subjectivity.

It is a phenomenological maxim that we must regard every objective reality as a sign pointing toward an objectifying activity on the part of the intending self. Hence the classical modern view of nature as an objective order of real bodies, acting under calculable laws of motion, suggests that there is a guiding idea of nature which enables us to abstract and specify some aspects of perceptual life along this line. Stating Husserl's procedure in this question very schematically, it consists of five major steps toward determining the full idea and context of nature.

His first move is to equate nature in a general way with the realm of factual things or thing-objects, which supply the more inclusive meaning for "a natural thing." In order to put our perceptual life at the service of a scientific study of thing-objects, we methodically set aside the aspects of value, affectivity, and practical desire, in order to focus upon those of measurement, functional correlation, and experiment. The factual things or thing-objects in nature are then regarded as those objective components in our experience which submit to such conditions of theoretical explanation, entirely apart from human considerations of value and practical appreciation. We learn to accept this domain of natural thing-objects as real by permitting the ideal of natural research to discipline our perceptual life and desires.

As a second step, Husserl then distinguishes within the wider field of nature the two major kinds of objects which comprise it: inanimate things or material nature and animate things or psychic nature. This part of his theory of nature is similar to what Whitehead says about the bifurcation of nature, and Dewey about its internal dualism. Inanimate things provide the narrower meaning for "a natural thing." The mathematizing of nature is most readily accomplished in terms of material or lifeless nature, but the same types of explanation are then used as guides for studying the psychic order. The third point is that the psyche is regarded as a thinking thing, a residual reality remaining after we account for the mathematicized, extended thing of Descartes' natural philosophy. The perceptual life and values of the psychological self are acknowledged within the perspective of natural reality only when they can be stated in conformity with the thing-objects in nature and their explanatory methods.

Fourthly, however, there is not a total submergence of objective reality into the thing-objects of nature, because of the stubborn presence of such human achievements as works of art, political and social institutions, and powerful historical traditions. The order of objectivity is wider than that of nature, since the former includes not only the two classes of natural thing-objects (material and psychic nature) but also the cultural activities embodying an order of values, affectivity, and practical desires. Objectivity embraces both natural being and cultural being as its chief modes.

Having brought his analysis of nature and cultural objectivity this far, Husserl then makes the final move of rooting both of them in the pure subject or transcendental ego. The whole realm of objectivity, in both its natural and its cultural aspects, is an achievement of the intending ego and its objectifying activities. The living ego constitutes itself along with constituting the meaning and philosophically ascertainable being of natural things and cultural objects. Husserl does not specify this achieving and constituting in causal terms, since he includes the whole causal language within the sphere of constituted natural reality. But he does give an active meaning to intentionality and establishes the primary reference as being one between the pure subject and the modes of objectivity which manifest its life and guide its genetic analyses. Beings in their existential act are then given philosophical standing only by prior reference to the intending operations and achieved objectivity of the pure ego.

The one salient question which can now be raised is this: How does man fit into this account? He is not directly mentioned in the schema of physical objects in nature, the psyche, and cultural objects. Yet this schema cannot be scrutinized for very long, without recognizing how closely it implicates the being and activities of man. The physical objects are constructed out of human living experience and by means of humanly devised methods. The psyche is not simply a residual entity but has a living body and employs language in the human manner. And the world of cultural objects testifies to the meaningful work of man, as he fashions symbolically the means provided by natural materials. Husserl's own investigations underline this distinctive ordering of all the modes of objectivity to man, who is distinguished from them by reason of his complex personal reality, out of which are developed the scientific approaches to nature and the entire contrast between the psyche and other natural things. Man is a subject present in nature. Yet man is also set apart from the pure subjectivity by his perceptual acts and hence by his need for an incarnate mode of being and acting.

Husserl's own aim of supplying philosophy with a formally necessary certitude, as its scientific foundation against skeptical arguments, compels him to base his theory of man and objectivity ultimately upon the functions they serve within the intending life of the transcendental ego, as it constitutes the meaning of the world. Nevertheless, there are some aspects in his analysis of man which suggest to me that the direct relationship between man and the world of natural things and cultural works remains central, and that this bond of natural being can furnish the appropriate starting point for a humanly developed metaphysics. Specifically, there are three methodological points where a prospect opens for this metaphysical interpretation of human reality and thus for a restatement of the meaning of natural things apart from Husserl's framework. These topics concern man's ambiguity, his position at the crossroads, and his relation to poles and attitudes.

(a) *Ambiguity.* Man is a natural being, existing and acting under spatial and temporal conditions, sharing in the common changes, and expressing his powers in objective forms. In these traits, he is one among the many factors involved in natural causality and the community of living organisms. He is not only a component member of the world of natural processes, however, but also the organizer of the meaningful perspectives for understanding, using, and appreciating what happens. Things have the significance of belonging in our biological, economic, and esthetic environing worlds by reference to our intentions in these modes of experience. Human reality can therefore be studied both through the common explanatory concepts used in or taken from physical science and also through those which consider in a reflective way the elaboration of human methods and meanings.

As a consequence, Husserl and other phenomenologists develop the theme of the ambiguity of man. It is well to maintain a distinction, however, between two sorts of ambiguity which are relevant to this matter. One is the ambiguity of propositions made about man, insofar as they can be referred to different contexts of interpretation for their significance and limitation in understanding man. The other is the capacity of man himself to regard his own complex reality in various ways and thus to develop the plurality of methods governing the interpretation of propositions about our human being. The ambiguity is both propositional and existential. These two senses of ambiguity are distinct and ordered, even though they are as inseparable as language is from man's way of being.

Propositional ambiguity does not refer primarily to a framework set by a detached observer or by the pure subjectivity. Rather, it is a trait of human statements and refers basically to the going methods whereby man tries to understand and develop his own reality, in relation to the other beings which exist together with him. It is only because our human being is complex and variously related to natural things that the methods and statements whereby we develop our diverse capacities and relationships in the natural world have an ambiguous character. In and through our linguistic acts, we achieve and communicate the several perspectives concerning our range of experiencing natural reality. Reflection upon this situation centers around the human interpreter thus complexly developing his relations with natural things, without any need for treating either type of ambiguity as an index leading to the objectifying work of the pure ego.

(b) *Crossroads.* When man is treated mainly in terms of the thing-psyche-value-and-pure-subjectivity schema, his own actuality and unity slip through our net. He is viewed as a crossroads in the traffic of meanings, having only that sort of uniqueness in being which belongs to a point of intersection or vacuous inactuality. There is a long tradition in philosophy which places man at the cutting edge where flesh and spirit intermingle, where time and timeless meanings communicate. To me, this is one sound way of giving a situational description of man. But it should not be permitted to reduce man to a moment of transition from the one order to the other, thus missing the problem of his actual unity as an existent being. When human reality is studied primarily within the context of Husserl's schema, taken as the basic way to determine the meaning of man's being, the tendency is to convert a useful situational description into an essential definition of man in terms of his crossroads functions. The metaphor looms larger than life and eventually swallows up the being which it is intended to illuminate.

Husserl is strongly aware of the uniqueness of the human person. He treats its composite reality in reference to a twofold act: that whereby the pure intending ego "realizes" itself, in the sense of attaining to objectivity and the condition of a natural reality, and that whereby the realm of inanimate things arrives at life and interiority. The human person is constituted by these two lines of action, which are different aspects of the intentional operation of the pure subjectivity. Husserl adds that it is the same ego which is present as the pure intending subject, the psyche, and the man.

The problem is that the confluence of these two operations in man can be understood in quite different ways, as far as the meaning of human being is concerned. It can be taken to mean either that man's reality simply designates a certain conjunctive climax in the double movement of the pure ego's intentional activity or else that man is the being whose nature develops itself in relational operations. In the first interpretation, human reality does not take its proper significance from itself but only from its being the meeting point in the march of spirit toward objectivity and of bodily modes toward reflectivity. Yet man displays himself as an insistent actuality in nature, not as a stage in the naturalization of the pure ego and not as a stage in the animation and spiritualization of the bodily world as such. He does perform some bridgemaking functions which enable him to give incarnate form to meanings and to bring the physical modes and qualities to the condition of value and judgment. But these are *his* operations as a composite personal existent, and not those of the pure ego found present in him and in the psyche through an active and a passive genesis.

Man's relational work of developing his various modes of desiring, valuing, and knowing the experienced natural world retains its human character and ordering by reference to his own substantial and existent being. This does not disrupt our relational and operational experience, but specifies it at least minimally in reference to the present discussion. The continuity of relations is not fundamentally that of a series of moments in a web of intentional forms, achieving the life of a transcendental subjectivity. Meanings are actually shaped and realized by men in the course of their personal living through and reflecting upon the many bonds in experience which actively join them with the other existing and operating beings.

(c) *Poles and attitudes.* That the relationship of men with other natural things is the decisive one for determining a metaphysical point of departure can be brought out in another way. Like his contemporaries, Whitehead and Dewey, Husserl relies heavily upon a polar metaphor. This he does in order to assign some limits to the trend toward objectifying everything, including man. In this context, his distinction between the ego-pole and the object-pole is not merely a variation of that between the intending act and its object. The ego-pole signifies precisely the pure subjectivity which is to be set off from everything in the order of nature and objective cultural values. The contrast is best expressed as one holding between the transcendental ego-pole and the totally naturalized and objectified man, standing as a unified symbol for all the forms of natural and objective meaning. Husserl realizes that he has arrived at one of those end-of-the-road situations to which he often pushes his investigations. The cleavage which it introduces into the order of meaning is too radically conceived to be healed dialectically by invoking the phenomenological commonplace about the correlation between self and world. Poles may imply and require one another, but in this case the entire polar relationship is subjected to conflicting interpretations on the part of the integral rationalist and the naturalist, representing the positions of the pure ego and the man-object. Hence it is insufficient to say, with

Husserl, that the self and the world are being jointly constituted through the polarized intentional activities.

A return has to be made to human reality itself with the aim of clarifying its relationship with this polar schema. Man remains distinct from Husserl's pure ego-pole, not chiefly by being rendered into an objectified thing in nature but by reason of the close relationship between perception, judgment, and the other modes of experiencing which belong to a being that is at once bodily and reflective. A descriptive analysis of this complex actuality increases our self-understanding, without lessening the intimate influence of perceptual activity upon all the other human ways of experiencing natural being. Man's way of being is also resistant to becoming identified with an object-pole, no matter how comprehensively it may be conceived. The object-pole includes both the thing-psyche-value pattern and the method of objectifying whereby that pattern is established. Both the method and its resultant interpretation are elaborated by the human inquirer as a means of understanding and appraising his own experience in the scientific and cultural contexts. To regard natural and cultural being as the two modes of objectivity within which he lives and develops, is a work of interpretation achieved by man himself and reflectively used for his purposes.

Hence in any development of the theme of man's naturalization and objectification, it is helpful to distinguish between a certain *conception* of man and the human *existents* themselves as the source of this conception. What can get scientifically objectified (but perhaps never totally so) is only the particular conception of man which is specified by the use of the so-called "realizing" method, directed by the standard of valid statements in physical science. The human existent or reflective agent retains his capacity for recognizing the limited significance of this conception of man and hence for providing other methods of exploring the human way of being and acting. Human reality does not exhaust itself in the objectifying process. The same distinction can also be brought to bear upon the theory of the ego-pole. The latter is another way of enlarging the conception of man through the use of a distinctive method. It is one philosophical route followed for developing the distinction between man as a free searcher after and creator of meanings and his achieved meanings themselves, including those referring to his own being. Yet the human subject retains its own act of existing as a composite personal being, rather than as an aspect of the pure ego.

The human existent does not cease to have his own unifying act of being and his reflective life, therefore, even when he permits these polar conceptions to shape his speculative interest and practical concerns. In the very act of submitting to them, he remains their originative source and can recover their reference to his own experience. He may find it useful to use a polarizing method organized around the pure subjectivity and the man-object. But they remain conceptions or principles of interpretation measured by their aid in grasping the relations between existing men and other things involved in human experience. Men can never convert themselves into their own polarizing principles or entirely forget the human origin and founding reference for these instruments.

Thus we are brought to much the same conclusion as resulted from our previous study of the natural attitude. Husserl does not take a primarily psychological view of attitudes, but regards them as settled ways of fulfilling intentions through the organization of our judgments and modes of experiencing. Yet it is not enough to say that the same self is present in the transcendental ego, the psyche, and the man. Quite emphatically, *man* is the intending being who develops various methods and kinds of meaning (including a theory of selves) for understanding and practically transforming his situation. He elaborates the intention, forms the governing attitude in function of the intentional pattern, and makes the attitude effective in his active life and reflection. Thus the several attitudes coming within phenomenological analysis are achievements of the exploring human existent, rather than of a pure subjectivity or pure ego. When Husserl himself refers to the transcendental position as a style and attitude, by way of contrast with the naturalistic and objectivistic styles and attitudes, he opens the path for considering the pure ego or transcendental subjectivity as a methodological development of precisely a human intention.[7] This is not a matter of anthropologism versus transcendentalism, but a rooting of the activity of intentional analysis in the human existent as an irreducible being.

In recovering the actuality of man as a foundation out of which and for the sake of which the distinction between subject and object is drawn, we can also make a similar recovery of the being of other natural things.[8] It is with them that we are primarily related through our several experiential modes of acting and reflecting. Considered in reference to our practical and interpretative methods, they have an appropriate aspect of objectivity. But it is not constituted by a global comparison with a pure subjectivity. Things have an objective status through their determinable relations to the various methods of human work, appraisal, and research. Man can treat himself objectively in terms of these methods, without thereby losing his own act of being or his recognition of it. Similarly, he can treat the things, relations, and changes within his experience by various methods, without transforming them into their objective condition and without losing sight of the existent reality of the things concerned.

There can be, therefore, no simple equivalence between thing and object, any more than between man and object. At least those things which we acknowledge in our perceptual existential judgments have a unified structure and existential act of their own. They are involved in human experience and the common course of change, without ceasing to remain centers of actuality, initiative, and perhaps surprise for us. They do not present themselves to us in a bare and isolated way, but always within the context of a real use of powers and a relationship to other existents, thus responding to our guiding idea of the contexting world. This suggests that, just as things in their existing being cannot be bound down by a transcendental theory of objectivity, neither can they be restricted to a theory which identifies natural being with the condition of pure objectivity and isolation from values. Natural being is opened up to include men and other things in their several relationships, including our way of experiencing things as valuable for us. The value aspect is not confined to the works of culture, but has its roots in our fundamental experience of natural things.

4. A Metaphysics of Natural Beings

I must now try to draw together these strands into a conclusion relevant for the basis of metaphysics. As Hegel reminds us, the problem of the starting point of metaphysics is a perpetually renewable one. It can be restated profitably with reference to Husserl, because he is formally concerned with the theme of the beginning of philosophy and because he seeks to specify the beginning of his own philosophy in a way that would rule out an existentially founded metaphysics. Nevertheless, his analysis of the natural attitude and the region of nature raises questions which at least point toward the possibility of another founding procedure for philosophy, one that would permit the development of a metaphysics of existent beings.

(a) *The elucidating intent and the crisis of humanism.* The terms of the problem are not only analytical but also historical in their significance. Phenomenologists in America are not likely to make much

370

solid headway until they abandon the shelter of the so-called common ground of phenomenology. The latter notion can be maintained only at a high level of abstraction from the actual and determinate context of the particular philosophies in question. Whenever an attempt is made to carry out a specific piece of phenomenological analysis and then show its philosophical import, some distinctive meaning must be given to intentionality, self, world, and the other concepts being used. They have to be referred to a definite position on how the meaning of being is determined in our experience and our act of philosophizing. At this point, the differences which radically mark the several phenomenological philosophies become visible and assert their primary importance for inquiry.

A return to the headwaters in Husserl is fruitful only if it leads to a recovery and discussion of his entire teaching. His philosophy cannot be limited to his early methodological work at the one extreme or to his very latest discussion of man, history, and the life world at the other end of his productive life. There is a strong continuity binding together the several phases in his doctrine. Especially in his treatment of the split between the humanistic and scientific outlooks—the two cultures more recently described for us by C. P. Snow—he is intent upon relating the factors in the crisis to his own program for an integral rationalism.[9] He does not consider it sufficient to show that the crisis is generated by confusing successful scientific abstractions with the concrete meanings of things, and that such a confusion is only possible because the original intentions embodied in geometrical concepts and physical methods have been buried over and lost from view. He deliberately transposes this entire analysis (which, as it stands, is a common theme among twentieth-century philosophers) into the dominant context of his own search for apodictic knowledge on the basis of the pure intending ego.

The transposition is accomplished by the familiar use of the skeptical style of thought. A search for the intentional genesis of the ruling ideas in our culture runs the risk of terminating in historicism. Even if a pattern is found to run throughout the founding meanings, it can be taken as signifying only a broad "outlook" limited to some historical situation. The life world of our perceptual experience is similarly vulnerable. In making his own use of the critical history of ideas, Husserl is careful to state that this world of living experience is explicitly called into doubt, as far as its validity for understanding being is concerned, by the modern tradition of the skeptics, Descartes and Hume. Hence Husserl himself extends his own philosophical questioning into this life world, in order to remove the last shred of naiveté from acceptance of it as a privileged access to reality. It is more concrete than the constructs and methods of the sciences, but this is only a relative advantage. There are many life worlds in the plural, and hence for anyone sensitive to Husserl's argument their study still raises the question of the transcendental ego and its intending operations. Any pattern of a priori forms which may be present among the several life worlds of actual men can still be regarded as an index pointing to the pure ego and its achievement of forms and experiences.

In his final period, Husserl was not confident about working out all the lines of intentional genesis and thereby displaying the evidence for his philosophy in a coercive way. But he did maintain that a study of the crisis between Western sciences and humanism leads to three unavoidable conclusions. First, the cultural crisis is being generated by the philosophical dilemma between objectivism or naturalism and transcendentalism. Next, the remedy for this situation is not to be found in some higher synthesis but in recognizing that the proper intent of modern philosophy is to achieve that integral rationalism or transcendental doctrine of the intending ego and its world which is fundamental in Husserl's own thought. And finally, it is one and the same thing to accept this integral rationalism, to maintain the self-founding will to rationality or practico-transcendental faith in reason, and to realize an authentic humanism.

In critically reorienting Husserl's theory about man and the realm of objectivity, however, I am also suggesting that his philosophical account of the humanistic crisis cannot be left unaltered. The dilemma which he specifies is a prolongation of that between the pure ego and objectified man. Transcendentalism and naturalistic objectivism are judgmental attitudes elaborated by men. Neither one of them is exhaustive in its descriptive and analytic power, and the limitation can be determined by reflecting upon the situation of men as existing in relation with other experienced beings. Hence we are not forced to accept an intentional sort of transcendentalism as the only philosophical basis for limiting naturalism (in Husserl's sense) and securing the order of human values. He performs a good service in emphasizing the interest which reason has in the work of clarifying and transforming the quality of human experience, as well as the need for a practical adhesion to the methods which will control this work. But practical fidelity to philosophical reason and the demands of humanly grasped evidence is not the same as acceptance of integral rationalism and the strict dichotomy upon which Husserl's specific analysis of the crisis rests. Here, as well as in our previous scrutiny of Dewey and Marx, it is necessary to measure the particular version of humanism by our reflective grasp upon man's complex reality and natural context.

(b) *Natural beings and metaphysics.* Philosophic and scientific investigators into nature are always faced with an overabundance of meanings, some of them not easily reconcilable with others. Whether it be Aristotle or Descartes, Boyle or Heisenberg, however, the responsible thinker makes his first step to be a study of the actual usages of the word "nature" in comparison with his own experience, rather than an initial legislation of a preferred meaning. This is an instance of the use of the ingressive method, which seeks to penetrate the linguistic and experiential situation directly in terms of its own components, as specified through a reflective analysis rather than as referred at the outset to some other principle or set of definitions.

This procedure is used in the present study of some prominent meanings of nature found in Husserl's phenomenology. Two of its main themes concern the natural attitude and the region of natural things. The two senses of "natural" assigned there by Husserl have a recognized standing both in other philosophies and in that protean sphere called ordinary usage. The natural attitude covers our strong tendency to convert longstanding conventions into an unyielding order of real things imposing themselves upon man, and to convert common sayings into obviously evidenced truths. The region of natural things concerns the objects and events specified according to the physical methods and their variations in psychology and social sciences. Furthermore, Husserl's critical handling of these two meanings agrees in a general way with that of many non-phenomenological philosophers. He removes the natural attitude from the opportunity of supplying certitudes to philosophy, by arousing an awareness of the contributions made by our human attitudes, beliefs, and searchings after evidences. And he tries to indicate the limits within which the physical methods operate, the importance of the valuational aspects of being, and the operation of reason in determining the conditions for objective statements. On all these scores, he has made some incisive and permanent contributions to the philosophical discussion.

Yet skepticism and phenomenalism cannot be used as levers compelling us to transpose the findings into the framework set by the transcendental ego and its intending operations. Instead, a study of Husserl's two usages for "the natural" furnishes some reasons for trying to base metaphysics upon the actual existents and relationships to which the ingressive analysis leads. A critical look at both the natural attitude and the regions of natural and cultural objectivity centers upon the complex actuality of man, as existing along with other things and living in his several modes of experiencing them. These experiences are natural, not in the two senses criticized by Husserl, but in the sense that they disclose to our reflection and practical activity the bond of being which joins men and other existent things in a community of changes under perceptual conditions.[10] This community of natural beings furnishes the subject for metaphysical analysis and inference.

As far as the method used here is able to determine, metaphysics must begin with a careful inspection of these natural things in their own existential act and structure, their co-implicated powers, and their ways of changing and getting related. Metaphysics would be distracted from this task, if it were to regard men and the world of things as pointers or index figures of the pure subjectivity. The initial work of metaphysics is to study their complex actuality along with the actual and possible orders of change which bind them together. A way may then be found to follow any implications of the natural community of beings which will lead to some knowledge about the distinct being and causal activity of God, but this cannot be done at the outset without confusing the being of God with certain a priori structures of the transcendental ego.

Finally, the limits of the ingressive method are evident from the task for which it is fitted and the two metaphysical issues which it cannot settle by itself alone. It can deal critically with a situation where our attention must be drawn steadily toward the components of a question as they are related to the human way of existing and experiencing. In the present instance, it enables us to determine the meaning of natural being by reference to man and other actual things which come in principle within the range of our perceptual judgment of existence, which are actively involved in changes making for their mutual intercourse and influence, and whose variously patterned powers and qualities help to specify the practical, cognitive, and affective modes of human experiencing. Within this comprehensive meaning, the familiar contrasts of nature with man and art, convention and chance, can then be regarded as subordinate distinctions. They help to articulate the actual and possible relations and changes within natural being.

By the ingressive method, the bond of natural being can be specified as furnishing the soil for metaphysical reflection. But the inquiring mind must then make a fresh analysis in order to determine precisely how the metaphysical judgment of being is formed by reference to our human experience of men and other existent things.[11] The metaphysical conception of being is developed by the human mind on the groundwork of natural beings, but also through a distinctive judgment of reflection upon the actualities provided in our natural experiences. As a consequence of this limitation, the ingressive approach is also unable by itself to determine the relation between experience, natural being, and reality in the inclusive sense. Neither the impatient naturalist nor the impatient theist can resolve the question of God and nature beforehand by equating experience with reality or by giving a special description of religious experiences. The last service of the ingressive method is to point out that this question really does remain open, until the inquiry establishes whether or not it is necessary to retain a distinction between the analysis of components within human experience and the inference to a being implied by that experience.

Metaphysics makes its proper start with the integral human experience of the community of existing natural beings. It is here that we obtain the foundational meaning for the concretely real. Our act of acknowledging natural existents in their active relations is more basic for metaphysics than the contrasts which we draw in relatively abstract and limitative ways for purposes of analysis and inference concerning the concrete natural beings. Among these abstractive contrasts are that in the order of philosophical disciplines between the theories of nature and man, and that in the order of philosophical methods between the analysis of sense-data objects and the analysis of the experiencing self and its life. These distinctions enable us to sift, evaluate, and make inferences about the actually experienced natural beings. But it is the latter which furnish the basis of reference for grounding and controlling our distinctions and modes of intelligible explanation.[12] The life of metaphysical reflection develops steadily at the heart of this experience of natural beings, and seeks in every generation of human history to understand the structures and further the potencies for good at least a little more adequately than was previously achieved. This development depends upon a sustained use of the two basic functions in metaphysics: a descriptive analysis or elucidation of the community of natural beings, and a causal inference to God, whose actuality we are led to affirm by following out the existential implications of natural things.

CHAPTER 15

THOMISM IN THE COLLEGE

THIS final chapter is quite restricted in its scope. For one thing, it does not deal directly with philosophical issues but with some problems in higher education which involve philosophy. Another restriction is that, even within the educational context, the main concern is with the teaching of philosophy under the prevailing conditions in American Catholic colleges. This means that major attention must be given to Thomism, which is the predominant form in which philosophy is presented to students in the American Catholic college. One of the interesting developments of recent years is that the philosophical horizons of the students in this type of college have been immensely broadened. Students are gaining a fairly close understanding of the many philosophies which are historically important, as well as those which are strictly contemporary with us. Under these encouraging circumstances, we have to inquire about the relationship between Thomism and these other philosophies considered precisely within the college situation. This is one way in which to deal concretely with the study of divergent views on God, the distinction between a factual plurality and a pluralism-in-principle among philosophies, and the function of a realistic philosophy in the college whose goal is the liberal education of young men and women.

1. *Tasks for the Theistic Philosopher*

We could deal very abruptly with the theme of the theistic philosopher's responsibility in our world by saying that he has the same responsibility as anyone else in the guild—simply to do a good job at philosophizing. Nothing more need be said after that, provided we really understand what it takes to do the job. There are some disagreements about what it does take, however. It may be useful, therefore, to spell out some of the philosopher's responsibilities.

We have, for example, a share in the responsibility for long-range preparation of college students who show an interest in becoming philosophers. It seems to me we could improve our counseling of such students when we talk to them about the study of modern languages and the choice of a major subject.

In order to avoid wasting valuable time at the graduate level and to insure a real use of language resources in later life, the undergraduate who plans to work in philosophy should master both French and German. For students of the sciences, translations of new research are systematically furnished, and their main objective is simply to make information available. Philosophical reading, however, demands something more than the transfer of information; the reader must eventually make a close study of sources. Norman Kemp Smith has provided fine renditions of Descartes and Kant, but the student who wants to become an effective philosopher must be able to consult the original French and German—and Latin—of Descartes and Kant. He cannot be fully confident about the bases of modern thought without making a personal source-study of the pattern and nuance of Descartes and Kant, which elude even a well-turned translation.

More is at stake here than background erudition. Language deficiencies often limit the course of studies and thus hamper the comparative work which should be done in the contemporary field. Often, a student will embrace some current trend in British or American analytic philosophy simply because he lacks the linguistic skill to explore any other regions. And then he goes along with the trend of many analytic philosophers to become rapidly impoverished in thought content, because they fail to consult other ways of thinking which are not reducible to questions about English usage or formal systems. A counterpart case is furnished by the student who knows French well but is vague about German; he then spends his graduate program in assimilating only the French approach to such philosophies as phenomenology and existentialism. His understanding of the roots of these movements is likely to remain forever slightly out of focus; he cannot make the thorough evaluation of them for which we are looking.

Another domestic responsibility we have is to counsel prospective philosophers about the proper value of non-philosophical studies. I would prefer to see these students do their major undergraduate work in something other than philosophy, and thus develop a lifelong habit of cultivating other fields of interest. There is nothing so barren as a mind which has tried to specialize too early and too exclusively in philosophy, especially in the School philosophies, which introduce one into a formalized world of terms and syllogistic rules.

The fact is that it takes time and experience to ripen the philosophical temper of mind, and to date there is no way available for artificially stepping up the process of maturation. Hence, while the undergraduate and graduate student is learning the rudiments of philosophy, he should also be feeding his mind with large doses of literature and the sciences, history and the arts. In doing so, he will discover his own way of overcoming the isolation that initially separates the tradition-based philosophical mind from contemporary modes of inquiry. Sometimes it is suggested that desperate measures must be taken to remove the isolation. Some educators recommend sloughing off the entire philosophical tradition in philosophy, and simply combining one's religious faith with some currently important tendency in philosophy. I am convinced that this procedure results in more of a net loss than a gain, particularly when the individual is asked to compare the merits of the philosophy of his choice with other alternatives and finds himself unable to do so by means of a philosophical comparison and judgment. What we should do is, rather, to try the indirect route of deepening our hold on both the philosophical tradition and the liberal heritage in the sciences and humanities, to the point where the mind begins to feel confident about bringing them to bear upon some present issues. This is a very steep demand to make of the maturing philosopher, but the road to philosophical competence is an unusually steep one in any case.

There is one definite advantage in cultivating an interplay between one's philosophy and the other cultural components. It gives the theistic philosopher sufficient familiarity with problems in other fields to enable him to speak with wisdom about them.

The complaint is often heard today from jurists, directors of foundations, and other administrators that they consult the philosophers in their midst for guidance on major human issues—but do so in vain. The analytic philosophers, who are in the majority, are quite adept at describing the logic of courses of action already taken and at pointing out flaws in all plans for future action. But they regard even their work in the moral area as a meta-ethics, which usually means a theoretical analysis that does not result in any definite practical recommendation or norms of choice.

On the other hand, the philosopher with a religious background is apt to be embarrassingly rich in general recommendations, which he does not know how to make concretely applicable to the particular shape of the problem confronting the practical man. Here, the individual thinker has to rely upon his own fund of experience drawn from his personal studies in the relevant natural and humane sciences.

An example of my point is furnished by the theme of the public interest. In our country, this question becomes practically important due to our urgent need to set up some working standards for determining when there is a genuine conflict between the private connections of a public officer and his official responsibilities. There is a good deal of murkiness about the meaning of the public interest and about the grounds for upholding and promoting it, even at cost of sacrificing a political administrator's private advantage. Some independent rethinking of the "conflict of interests" issue is required, and it must be done with resources drawn both from political philosophy and from acquaintance with relevant materials in political history and present-day economic situations. The theme of the common good may be more productive in this inquiry than the general topic of natural law. There is no easy equivalence between the common good and the public interest, any more than there is between moral good in general and moral value. But there is a definite relevance of the doctrine about the common good to what underlies our present talk about the public interest and the obligation to uphold it. One of the theistic philosopher's prime tasks is to show this bearing and make his findings available in public conference and readable prose.

We are beginning to realize that, in our world of many philosophies, more is required than agreement on some practical courses of action. We see a need for dialogue or intelligent communication between widely divergent general interpretations of human existence and the roots of obligation. I think, however, that the time is overdue for taking a critical look at the nature and limits of dialogue itself. There is a danger that it may be praised out of all proportion, and hence a danger that we may demand more of it than we can reasonably expect it to yield.

Recent probes into the role of religion in American society show the need not only of carrying on a persistent dialogue, but also of clarifying the nature of dialogue. Suppose that we want to understand and develop our human nature to the fullest. Can we do so if we consider only the the individual man in isolation or as related solely to the world of impersonal things? A negative answer is required because isolated man merely talks to himself, and man, the shaper of things, does not profit by independent criticism. For full use of his capacities

379

and for full understanding of what they are, the individual man has to enter into the society of persons. Only then can a man open himself to another (as well as to himself) on a person-with-person basis. This interpersonal relation constitutes the situation of the dialogue, which is a mainspring for humanizing our social bonds.

For over a century now, philosophers have been examining this dialogal relation among men. From the time of Feuerbach and Kierkegaard down to Buber and Marcel, a remarkably broad zone of agreement has been developing among otherwise quite divergent thinkers. They refer to man's attitude toward nonpersonal things as an I-and-it relation, and they observe that this non-dialogal relation is a powerful but one-sided realization, since it leaves out the challenge of a free response from another person. The human individual is made for something more than dominion over things; he looks for a sharing in the goods of interpersonal life. This is possible only in the form of an I-and-Thou bond among persons engaged in dialogue, whether the other person be a fellow man or God. Dialogal analysis is the philosophical study of the traits that unfold when a man reaches out to other persons and seeks to produce conditions of mutual understanding, critical integrity and, perhaps, love. The dialogue itself is the interlacing of several mutual interpersonal efforts.

One of the lasting achievements of our century is to uncover the values of interpersonal communication, both among men and between man and God. But I would like to see the basic findings of existentialism and psychiatry about the unique reality of the I-Thou relation and dialogal intercourse kept distinct from the mass of loose variations and overextensions of these insights. At least two critical limitations should be respected. First, although a dialogal relationship establishes the conditions most favorable for studying questions about the human person and the acts of freedom, it does not automatically generate the evidence which will lead to sound conclusions about them or to firm agreement among the participants in the dialogal situation. Second, there is a wide range of significant philosophical issues, especially those concerning scientific methods and the domain of nature, which must be investigated by non-dialogal means. Philosophy itself reaches farther than analysis of the dialogal situation, some of whose implications can be followed through only with the aid of other philosophical approaches. In other words, philosophical discussion involves argument as well as dialogue, clash as well as openness, evidence as well as personal respect.

In a televised study of Western ideals which was sponsored by the

380

Rockefeller Foundation, two of the participants, Arnold Toynbee and Reinhold Niebuhr, described the West's commitment to respect for personal integrity, moral courage, and the constant search after justice in society. The discussion became highly charged, however, when a dissenting observation was quietly introduced by the third participant, the only professional philosopher in the group, Professor Charles Frankel of Columbia University.

While approving of the dialogally congenial traits of the Western mind that Toynbee and Niebuhr described, Professor Frankel said that he missed any mention of another outstanding trait—the search for truth and the readiness to accept objective evidence, regardless of where it leads. Frankel then pressed home the point that one of the triumphs of the Western mind is its investigation of the structures rationally attainable in nature. He left the impression that Greek and Judaeo-Christian humanisms contained some strong convictions, but that it was the task of the Enlightenment and the scientific method to sift these convictions, identify the sound ones and eliminate any views conflicting with a scientifically grounded humanism.

We may readily sympathize with the judgment, expressed in Crane Brinton's *History of Western Morals,* that Frankel takes too simplistic a view of the relation between the scientific mind and rational structures, as well as between the Enlightenment and Christianity. There is much more constructural activity, and hence more need for decision and a basis of intelligibility, on the part of the scientist than Frankel admits. There is also a much broader basis of intellectual content and independent, self-critical activity on the part of the Judaeo-Christian mind than he allows.

The main criticism which suggests itself to me, however, tells against all the participants in the discussion: it is unfortunate that anyone should be permitted to pit the values of dialogal existence against the truths about nature as embodied in a scientific ordering. The theist's acceptance of God as the creative source of both personal and nonpersonal realms of being, as well as his acceptance of the value of all our sources of experience, requires him to overcome this dichotomy.

The realistic philosopher is clearly obliged to keep open the meaning of philosophy, so that it can include the method of *object*-analysis as well as that of *dialogal* analysis, the world of nature as well as the society of personal centers. He may well specialize in one of these modes of philosophizing and be thorough in working out its interpretation of human experience. But he should not succumb to the temptation of absolutizing only one of these approaches and to reduce the other to a subordinate function.

The theistic realist's respect for nature as well as man fits him for healing the split which has made intellectual strangers out of the existentialists and the naturalists, the phenomenologists and the analysts. His critical integrity will prevent him from following the momentary fashion of pretending that these two groups are saying the same thing in different ways. The problem of bringing unity and order into our philosophical world is much too genuine and complex to tolerate such an eirenic illusion for very long. But the theistic realist can work deliberately and steadily to bring these two approaches within range for examination of the complex evidence which will benefit philosophy as a whole. Under human conditions, the theistic realist can neither separate the study of nature and the cultivation of the dialogal situation from each other nor regard either one of them as an adequate fulfillment. His temporal existence involves them both, but does so under permanent conditions of search after God under both these aspects of our existence.

2. *Thomism and the Varieties of Philosophical Experience*

It is always revealing when a key term takes on a new meaning, and doubly significant when the word begins to acquire some quite divergent meanings during the same period. Something of this sort seems to be happening to the word "Thomism" and its variants. As it now occurs in interfaith discussions, it is often used as a polite synonym for a Catholic position. No matter whether the Catholic intellectual in question be of an Augustinian type of mind, a convinced Scotist, a cultivator of existentialism or analytic philosophy, or even a student of St. Thomas, he is called a Thomist. This usage is here to stay, and it does not do much good to cite academic cases of men who are Thomistic in a philosophical sense and yet who are not Catholics.

Such a use of words is disconcerting for those who like to keep philosophical questions distinct from other types, and who also like to keep the several philosophical positions distinct from one another. But it is even more disconcerting when combined with a new trend among Catholics themselves. Some people engaged in Catholic higher education tend to associate a rather baleful meaning with Thomism, as though it were a highly dogmatic and conservative standpoint which is being taught more because of official decrees than because of its intrinsic evidence or the conviction of those who present it to college students. On the basis of this usage, we are hearing some dramatic outbursts about how fine it is that Thomism is falling from its high estate and is being rejected even among teachers in American Catholic colleges.

During the past several years, it has been my privilege to discuss with many younger instructors in philosophy at widely scattered colleges our common problems of studying and teaching the subject. These conversations convince me that the present situation is new, complex, and ultimately more hopeful for a sound Thomistic philosophy than the negative critics realize. Thomism is not involved in the throes of internal collapse and dissolution, but neither is it being permitted to stand still in placid contentment. The fact is that American Thomists are engaged in a process of *transition,* even though some of them do not seem to be fully aware of its depth and sweep. They are beginning to feel the impact of some convergent circumstances which are bound to affect the character and presentation of their philosophy work within Catholic education. We can point to several markers which chart the course from the pre-1945 atmosphere to what is coming to a head in the 1960's.

One new factor is the great expansion of educational opportunities at the graduate level. A noticeable proportion of those Catholics who receive fellowship grants elect to do their advanced work in the area of philosophy. Many young men fresh out of college or seminary training receive splendid fellowships for studying philosophy at the great university centers here and abroad. They quickly find it necessary to learn about and adapt their minds to the modes of thinking, the vocabulary, the favored questions, and the kinds of evidence which form the common atmosphere of the intellectual community to which they now belong. Their enthusiasm is fired in many instances by direct and intimate relationship with leading philosophers, men who are at the forefront of research and writing in a particular school of thought. More than likely, they choose a doctoral topic well within the field of interest of their professor and develop it in a spirit which is congenial to their particular department and their recent lines of reading. A new doctor of philosophy then emerges whose approach to philosophical questions agrees with the current trends in logic or analytic philosophy, phenomenology or one of the philosophies of science.

Ordinarily, the young scholar now returns to a Catholic college for his teaching career. He is welcomed for his specialty in a phase of contemporary philosophy, but he is also expected to do his share of teaching in the systematic undergraduate courses in Thomism. At this point, several patterns can develop. Some people have no difficulty in combining Thomism with their contemporary interests, since they recognize the former as being always open to growth and the latter as being open to the influence of fundamental philosophizing. These minds can then move ahead to do fruitful work both in education and in research. Other men find it difficult to make any sort of correlation between St. Thomas or Aristotle and their specific field. This is to be expected, because such a communication between tradition and modernity is neither obvious nor easy to attain. If the quality of the particular instance of Thomism known to these men is low in intellectual daring, they are especially apt to isolate the two poles because of discouragement and lack of concrete guidance.

American Catholics who work in the field of philosophy are highly responsive to the need for participating fully in the cultural concerns of the nation. Their problem, however, is that they are still learning how to do so within their own area of competence. There simply are no ready-made patterns available for showing how the Christian philosopher is to translate the general counsel of cultural participation into the concrete modes proper to his own profession. He is, indeed, caught up in the same predicament as are almost all Catholics who engage in specialized intellectual work. He belongs fully to an age that is experimenting with various ways of synthesizing the demands of faith with those of a chosen discipline.

Yet there is something unique about the philosopher's condition. He is not working in a field like pure mathematics which, although highly intellectual in method and content, is not directly concerned with the central issues about God, man, and the meaning of our existence. Nor is his work the exegesis of documents and sacred texts after the manner of the historian and the scriptural scholar. In his formal arguments, he cannot even appeal to the pronouncements of authority to furnish the basis of his philosophical judgments, so that his task remains distinct from that of the theologian. The philosopher must concern himself with the direct evidence which our experience of man and the world provides for shaping the mind's assent on basic matters of knowing, choosing, and being. Thus his standpoint cannot be assimilated easily to that of any other type of learning. Hence his patterns of solution for sharing in American intellectual life and its practical decisions must be worked out in creatively new ways, which respect the peculiar structure of his own discipline.

This is still a highly tentative enterprise, and a new one for American Thomists. Until now, their energies have been consumed in preparing the classroom lectures and the textbooks which can present Aristotle and Aquinas, Maritain and Gilson, to the American Catholic college student. This is an indispensable work, but it is not the same thing as taking part in contemporary discussions, whether in the strictly professional zone of philosophy or in the larger field of our national concerns. Only a hasty critic who has not experienced some of the labors involved in assimilating and re-presenting philosophical traditions could conclude that the Thomists are incapable of this further reach of intellectual activity. But criticism may have the beneficial effect of prodding them into these new responsibilities and, above all, of forcing a recognition that there must be some new explorations on the part of the Christian philosophical intelligence. Whether or not these new explorations can be carried on in continuity with the themes in Thomism depends upon the quality of the response which individual Thomists give to this challenge, not upon administrative regulations—a point already made in our study of Leo XIII and philosophical modernity.

We are now in position to see the main aspect of the transitional process. Lately there has been a good deal of fashionable talk and some nonsense about pluralism in American society. But pluralism assumes many forms, and the kind which is relevant here sometimes goes unnoticed. In discussing whether Catholics can accept the conditions of the democratic civil life, we tend to envisage the Catholic group as fairly homogeneous within itself and, at most, open to relatively superficial differences of political allegiance and cultural taste. Yet there is a middle zone between theological unity and cultural diversity where different standpoints do exist and where they really matter. This zone lies in the sphere of philosophy, where there are some pronounced and important differences among Catholics. Here is a type of intraconfessional pluralism in serious intellectual matters—the existence of several contrasting philosophies among men who commonly accept the Catholic faith.

That such factual plurality of philosophies among Catholics is the usual and expected condition can be easily verified by looking over a history of medieval philosophy or by taking a trip to European Catholic centers of intellectual work. These sources will show that there seldom has been or is unanimity among Christian philosophers, especially with regard to their integral philosophical approaches, even though many of their detached conclusions are in agreement. From this historical fact of philosophical diversity, however, no strict inference

385

can be drawn that in principle this condition is necessary and inevitably beneficial in terms of philosophical inquiry itself. Taking it simply at the factual level, it is none the less significant that the pluralistic condition which has always characterized the European Catholic scene is now becoming established in America, with the important difference that Americans are inclined to choose among a variety of contemporary philosophies rather than among a variety of traditional scholastic schools.

Given these circumstances which define the course of the intellectual transition in which American Thomists are unavoidably implicated, what measures can this group take in order to grow along with the college situation and meet it most intelligently? It would be foolish and unseemly to offer a neat formula, but there are four lines of action which tentatively suggest themselves to me.

1. Full recognition should be given to the *factual plurality* of philosophies which now exists. From our previous discussion of perennial philosophy, however, we can see that there is no need to construct a theory justifying any *pluralism-in-principle*, on the ground that it is a necessary condition for the wider attainment of philosophical truth. Yet, the factual plurality should impel Thomists to reconsider their presentation and make special attempts to reveal the experiential basis for their philosophical positions. They should try more carefully to give the better students the invaluable experience of philosophizing under the direction of teachers who are thoroughly at home with Aristotle and St. Thomas, and who can convey their doctrines in a living way. Less stress should be placed on covering a long syllabus, so that the time can be spent in developing key theories in full view of the class through a steady analysis of our common experience. In other words, the situation of factual plurality does not require the Thomist to become less attached to his doctrines, but rather to make sure that his own attachment springs from a reflective grasp of the evidence and that his students' assent has a similar grounding, right from the start.

2. Students must be prepared for their personal task of integrating the traditional and the new factors. The day has long since passed when a person could be regarded as liberally educated in the history of philosophy on the basis of a slapdash semester wildly crowded with the names, dates, and abbreviated theses of all the philosophers from Thales to Toulmin. If a college student is serious enough about philosophy to want to study it beyond the minimum, then teachers have the responsibility of providing him with the two or three semes-

ters of hard work in ancient and medieval, modern and contemporary, philosophies which his inquiring mind needs. This introduction to the major thinkers should take place within the same intellectual community in which the undergraduate is learning the systems of Aristotle and Aquinas. The intellectual atmosphere shaping a young person's first acquaintance with the history of philosophy makes a more lasting imprint on his mind than this or that particular idea he may examine in the course.

Moreover, those students who intend to do graduate work in philosophy should be counseled to do some graduate studies centering around Plato and Aristotle, Augustine and Aquinas, Descartes and Hume, Kant and Hegel, before concentrating upon contemporary theories. The undergraduate in the honors program can be encouraged to do some reading in and especially to take part in some guided discussion of these great sources. If he is at a university, he may be permitted to attend some graduate seminars dealing with these central thinkers or he may be counseled to do a master's program that is based upon them. In any case, the individual who plans to work professionally in philosophy should have some personal experience with classical philosophy precisely as it is taught at the graduate level.

One purpose of this policy would be to prevent a complete imbalance between the quality of one's knowledge of Aristotle or St. Thomas and one's grasp of a contemporary philosophy. Often, the intellectual difficulties arise from trying to combine junior-year Thomism with postgraduate analytic philosophy or phenomenology. If one's knowledge of St. Thomas is deliberately kept in the frozen state of an undergraduate memory, then the very hope of integrating it with some current position seems fantastic and impossible to realize. The practical rule is to advise the student to devote at least a portion of his graduate years to an advanced study of the great sources, so that his understanding of them will be as mature and progressive as his grasp of a contemporary movement.

3. There is the need to clarify various ways of becoming truly contemporary in matters philosophical. Those who attend meetings of the different philosophical associations soon realize that there are two main ways of establishing rapport. One path is to become an ardent party man behind some currently popular trend. This insures a quick entrance into a particular treadmill but not a basis for understanding and respect. The other approach is to take part in discussions on the common philosophical heritage provided by the greatest minds of ancient, medieval, and modern philosophy. A knowledge of these

387

sources is the surest way to insure philosophical communication with others and some degree of common understanding on the main issues.

Paradoxically, the man who plunges into a study of contemporary ideas without acquiring a classical background is likely to become isolated in an esoteric enclave, which is soon out of fashion and out of contact with the philosophical community. What makes a philosopher genuinely contemporary is not his adherence to a passing fad but his exercise of responsible and reflective judgment in the present hour. Contemporaneity is found only in this act, and it is one which is available to us all. In the light of this ultimate act of philosophical judgment, all doctrines and methods—whether formulated centuries ago or in yesterday's journal—become matter for reappraisal. We can lose our philosophical identity and cease to judge for ourselves just as readily by uncritical adherence to a 20th-century position as to a 13th-century one.

This stress upon personal reflection as the most proper activity shared by all philosophers brings out the immense difference between relating oneself to Aristotle and St. Thomas by sheer memorial recall, mediated by a textbook tradition, and relating oneself to them by means of a personal reading of the sources, a direct rethinking of the issues, and a judgmental mastery of the clues in evidence. To move from the former to the latter mode of thinking is the transitional problem facing Thomists. To the degree that they are able to develop in this direction, they not only come to appreciate Aristotle and St. Thomas better but also learn how to approach contemporary philosophies in a sympathetic fashion.

This does not mean that the thought of Aquinas is being downgraded, but only that the Thomist is discovering how to evaluate a theory by referring it primarily to the judgmental act about the being of things and the modes of human interpretation. Loyalty to this procedure is the soundest way of becoming contemporary and of remaining open to the new volume of evidence and the new refinements of method being explored in our time, without losing sight of those already shown to be indispensable. It also serves to remove from "Thomism" the ring of a party name and a power move, by imposing upon the Thomist the common obligation of responding in an appreciative and critical way to every new suggestion that has its roots in our human experience.

4. Thomists should become more reflective on the meaning of criticism in philosophy. In past years, the tendency was to be excessively quick and negative in criticizing contemporary theories. The pendulum

seems to be swinging to the other extreme at present. Many Catholics working in philosophy suffer a total paralysis of the critical power. Their condition is induced by a peculiar way of interpreting the rule that one should respect the integrity of another's philosophical position. They infer that anyone who engages in detailed and incisive criticism is thereby violating the integrity of the view under investigation and is using it merely as a punching bag.

Such an attitude rests on a fundamental misconception of philosophical work. This intellectual labor begins with a faithful understanding of what a philosopher teaches and why he does so, but it cannot end there. Sympathetic understanding is the first step in good philosophical work, but eventually there must be a personal evaluation of the doctrine. In the philosopher's case, the step from dialogue to critical discussion cannot be postponed. A new theory must be compared with the propositions one already accepts, so that one can direct his whole study to a philosophical judgment on the truth of the matter. One cannot indefinitely postpone bringing his inquiry to this point without gradually exchanging the philosopher's vocation for that of the connoisseur of new modes of thought. Along with everyone else in the commonwealth of philosophy, the Thomist has the right and the obligation to advance from expository analysis to critical assimilation and evaluation of doctrines. It is thus that he adds to the store of truth.

3. *Thomistic Philosophy and a Liberal Education*

A long address by Father Gustave Weigel on "American Catholic Intellectualism" contained a widely quoted section on the teaching of philosophy in Catholic colleges. This he described as being chiefly a deadening form of indoctrination, with the stress placed upon memorizing verbal formulas, reducing new and vital problems to old classifications, and achieving apologetic proficiency in debate. Philosophy teachers at all levels will recognize in this picture an all too accurate account of what happens in many classrooms. Many of them will add, however, that at least the intention of a growing number of instructors is to present philosophical problems in a more challenging way, so that something of the real philosophical life will be communicated to the student.

It is scarcely a secret that among Thomists themselves there is sharp disagreement at present, rather than unanimity, concerning the role of Thomistic philosophy in the college program. This is only to be expected, because there is no way of settling the issue solely on the philosophical side without taking into account the special conditions and needs of the college tradition itself. An abstract schema of the sciences, drawn from the writings of Aristotle and Aquinas, is an insufficient guide here, since what is in question is the actual teaching of philosophy within the particular context of the Catholic liberal college in America. There are no neat and a priori solutions available for easy application. The individual Thomist must think out the problem of educational order at his own risk, taking into account the purposes of the college, his own philosophical convictions and teaching experience, and the counsel of his colleagues. I know of no quick route for bypassing these sources.

Philosophy is sometimes recommended in the Catholic college for the wrong reason. As justification for the high number of required course hours in philosophy, it is sometimes treated as a necessary means to salvation, if not intrinsically then at least under present circumstances. But in sober fact, Thomistic philosophy is careful to avoid any claim to being an essential condition of faith. It is a human science and natural wisdom, acquired through the human use of our intelligence. From apostolic times to our own day, there have been Christian saints and men of deep faith, whether steeped in humanistic learning or not, who have done their proper work without having acquired the philosophical state of mind. The Thomistic philosopher himself is the first to want clear thinking and plain speaking on this crucial point.

It is not by any direct nexus with the Catholic faith, but by reason of its function in the college situation, that philosophy becomes indispensable in the teaching program. For the American Catholic who is pursuing a liberal intellectual formation and who will normally be associating with cultivated minds, the study of philosophy is a basic and integrating task. For it encourages and disciplines his intellect in exploring the reaches of being, in reflecting critically upon the various modes of knowledge open to man, and in defending the natural truths and moral values which provide the educated man's milieu for the life of faith. It seems to be characteristic of our human condition, nevertheless, that the last-named role of philosophy cannot be cultivated apart from the intrinsic intellectual activities of examining reality and reflecting upon the ways of knowing. The liberal mind learns to study philosophy for its own sake. Whenever philosophy is conceived of chiefly as an apologetic weapon, the weapon eventually breaks in the educator's hands for lack of integrity within itself and orientation to the problems of our age.

One major hindrance to the vigorous growth of Thomism in the Catholic colleges is a common confusion between seminary methods and college methods of teaching philosophy. College work in philosophy is sometimes treated as a cut-down version of the seminary program, an adjustment of the seminary curriculum to the narrower limits of the collegian's schedule. It is assumed that the problem is only a quantitative and linguistic one of teaching all the main theses, and doing so in English rather than Latin. In practice, this means demanding a very high number of course hours, a curriculum involving all the parts of philosophy, and at least a surface coverage of the chief terms and conclusions in these parts. This Anglicized dehydration of the seminary approach leads to short-snippet courses and the ideal of verbal dexterity, at least while the student is still in course. But it does not serve the long-term needs of the Catholic layman or prepare him to make an effective cultural contribution to American life. And it falls short precisely because it does not respect the different aims of the seminary and the college. This difference reaches down into every portion of the teaching program, including philosophy.

It is not a question of two philosophies, that of the seminary and that of the college, but of two ways of teaching and learning philosophy, in accordance with the social purposes of the two institutions. Philosophical instruction fails when the norms and methods devised for the one type of institution are transferred to the other, with only superficial modifications.

The seminary program in philosophy is a professional one, rightly demanding a ready recall of all the theses and terms needed for professional training in theology and for later practical duties. But college work in Thomism is not regulated by these goals, and hence should not ape the seminary methods. One would normally expect, therefore, that a student transferring from college to seminary, or vice versa, will encounter difficulties and will have to make a new orientation that goes deeper than language and detail.

There are two valid senses in which the teaching of Thomism in the college is not professionally oriented: it is directed neither toward the training of priests nor toward the supplying of experts in philosophy. Occasionally, an individual college student will be inspired by his philosophy course to seek the priesthood or pursue graduate studies in philosophy. These are excellent consequences; nevertheless, the courses themselves should not be organized formally toward achieving such results, and should not be deemed a failure for not producing them.

Hence the philosophy instructor need not be disappointed if the college student is unfamiliar with some technical terms and fails to have a thesis ready to cover every problem. But the teacher will have to admit failure, if the student does not have some personal conviction and reliable knowledge in principle concerning the fundamental natural truths about man, God and our world. These aims are his proper contribution toward the college's purpose of helping laymen to achieve mature human perfection, especially through sound intellectual culture.

The educational goal of generating an integrated outlook is another fertile source of misunderstanding about the office of Thomistic philosophy in the college. The former view was that philosophy courses will somehow provide an automatic and one-way intellectual principle of integration. The other extreme, currently fashionable, reduces philosophy to some brief introductory work in logic and the philosophy of nature, to be undertaken at the outset of college study. These exaggerated positions have in common an underlying premise: that there is some single, mechanically applied principle for the ordering of liberal knowledge. The integrated mind remains a basically analogous ideal, however, which is realized in different ways in different types of educational institutions, in accordance with the types of knowledge and the approaches taken to them.

Precisely what distinguishes a liberal education from professional training is the complexity of the knowledges that a liberal education involves. Because they are many and capable of being unified in various ways, it is impossible to apply here any univocal norm of technical proficiency or to impose a homogeneous pattern upon all the strands of learning.

The integration of the studies in the liberal college is an unavoidably multiform enterprise. The student is challengingly introduced to the patterns of order provided by the humanities, by philosophy and the sciences, and by the Catholic faith. In order to avoid both a chaotic diversity and a deceptive uniformity, the student must learn to respect the structural integrity of each of these centers and its distinctive way of unifying his knowledge. The very realism of Thomistic philosophy and its closeness to the human condition compel it, operating within the college context, to encourage this rich complexity as a condition for its own basic work of ordering the mind. It cannot supplant or impoverish the other integrating principles without rendering its own activities fraudulent and misdirected. This balanced modesty

392

within the educational universe was succinctly summed up in the remark of one scholar that Thomistic metaphysics does not provide salvation, and it does not exercise any imperialism over the other sciences.

The *humanistic* perspective supplied by literature and history has
recently been described by Henri Marrou, the historian of Greek and
early Christian education, as "this longing for human wholeness." [1]
Humanism engages all of our knowing powers in the search for a concrete and rounded view of man in his world. Here is the realm of the
historian's stubborn fact and the poet's green thought in a green shade.
We admire a Hilaire Belloc tramping the battlefields of Europe or a
Samuel Eliot Morison sailing again the route of Columbus. They remind us vividly that one must pursue the truth with one's whole being,
and that the conditions of existence involve the fact perceived and
the moral decision taken.

Shakespeare, Pascal, and Pope play upon the theme of man, and we
learn—as we could learn in no other way—about the fermenting life of
the metaphor and the thousand individual shapes of the human heart.
This humanistic world has its own consistent fabric of methods, data,
and standards of appropriateness. The student introduced to it is stimu-
lated to bring his powers of imagination, concrete intelligence, and
emotion into play and thus achieve one sort of integration of the
realities of life in this world.

Yet it is also part of the liberal education to become aware that
the humanistic mode of knowledge is peculiarly vulnerable to criticism
that uses abstract arguments and comparative cases. The contemporary
college student wonders why humanistic values are thus vulnerable;
whether logical positivism and cultural anthropology really undermine
these values; whether a religious interpretation of man expressed in
humanistic terms is similarly threatened; and what positive framework
of general truths can be guaranteed as an intellectual setting. These
are proper questions to arise in the student's mind, and it is the distinctive responsibility of philosophy to point out where their resolution lies.

Using the example of history, Jacques Maritain has indicated the
ground of limitation of humanistic knowledge:

The explanation given by an historian, as historian, is an explanation of the
individual by the individual—by individual circumstances, motivations or
events. The historical elucidation, being individual, participates in the potential infinity of matter; it is never finished; it never has (in so far as it is elucidation) the certainty of science. It never provides us with a *raison d'être*
drawn from what things are in their very essence. [2]

This is a philosophical analysis, explaining the nature and essential limitations of the humanistic mode of integration. Because humanism is the kind of knowledge it is, it cannot be self-sufficient for the educated mind, but demands completion by other kinds of knowledge. Just as the humanistic view supplies concrete insights into man and his milieu which it alone can furnish to the eager student, so it points beyond itself to other unique ways of seeing reality. This limitation and self-transcendence also hold for the Christian form of humanism whose study is advocated strongly by Christopher Dawson.

The dynamic growth of the college-trained mind is partly measured by its gradually becoming aware of the need for a knowledge which *is* framed in terms of what things are, and which does possess the valuable traits of universal, abstract intelligibility. Philosophy, then, becomes relevant for the humanities, both in defending their values and in providing them with that setting in intellectual depth and stability which comes from knowing the permanent truths about man's spiritual principle, his freedom, and his direction toward God. But in meeting this need, philosophy does not arrogate to itself the right to dictate to the humanistic disciplines within their own sphere, or to weaken their characteristic way of integration.

The modern physical, biological, and social *sciences* do provide some sort of general laws, and produce an abstract structure of their own. This is the source of their intellectual fascination for the college student, along with an awareness of their shaping presence in all the practical tendencies of our civilization. Here again, the function of Thomism is not to stipulate the methods of research or the content and mode of teaching to qualified scientists. What is required in the college situation is not an extrinsic framework for incorporating the sciences into natural philosophy, but rather an authentic interpretation of scientific thinking as it actually displays itself today. A Thomistic analysis of science will fail to convince the college student, unless it arises internally from critical reflection upon current scientific procedures in at least some areas with which the philosopher has a first-hand acquaintance. He must be able to show with confidence that the internal constitution of modern scientific research requires a careful distinction between the constructural statements in the sciences and the philosophical statements concerning the act of real being and the essential nature of beings.

Today's collegians have a no-nonsense attitude which befits denizens of the age of consolidation. Yet the disturbing question is whether there is any ultimate "sense," any permanent truth about man and God that is worth consolidating through one's intellectual assent and the moral ordering of one's life. Catholic college students are not exempt from the common difficulties arising from the rapid turnover in basic scientific concepts, or from the naturalistic inference that there has to be a corresponding revolution in our moral values and religious beliefs. This inference suggests itself inevitably and has its skilled philosophical advocates.

Instead of suppressing the issue or weakening the science program, however, the Thomist can use the occasion for preparing his students for the transition from an uncritical and indiscriminate use of scientific methods to a reflective philosophical study of their proper scope and inherent limits. Just as the vulnerability of the humanities can be made the beginning of philosophical wonder, so too can the difficulties aroused by the current tendency to use scientific methods as tools for resolving philosophical and religious matters. There is no better starting point for aiding the student to view science not only "as a formal system, nor simply as a way of knowing, nor even as a vast theory for practical achievements but now as an enterprise of human beings, like mountain climbing, falling in love or fighting wars." [3] There can be no sound philosophical appraisal of the sciences, apart from a personal grounding in a particular science and its supporting basis in human intentions.

Yet to bring home forcefully and personally to the student the difference between scientific and philosophic explanation, there must also be some direct experience of the *philosophical* mode of knowing. It is no longer enough to recommend philosophy as a formal training in thinking or even as a theory of scientific methodology. Its primary significance must be seen to be the penetration of the real, the mind's natural way of access to some general truths about the being of man and God.

Whatever its relative functions in the sphere of the humanities and the sciences, the main responsibility of Thomism lies in awakening the student to the core problems of reality, clarifying his difficulties, and assisting him to discover the intellectual evidence available to us. Without pretending to be forming technical philosophers, Thomism should aim at arousing the ability to make a disciplined examination of the real data about man's spiritual principle, his freedom and moral responsibility, and the existence of God. The knowledge in principle which the college student can gain about these truths must become a deeply held personal conviction, leading in later years to further reflection and reading and to effective conversation with other people concerning them. This awakening of the mind and heart to the central themes in our natural universe is the most rigorous and genuine test of a program in Thomistic philosophy.

Philosophical knowledge is worth cultivating for its own sake, as a basic perfecting of the human intellect. In terms of real finality, however, it does not furnish the ultimate integration of Catholic education. Both the concrete knowledge of the humanities and the abstract truth of philosophy and the sciences are ordered, from the standpoint of the actual end of man, to supernatural sharing in the life of God. Thus *theology* and religious faith provide a unification for the liberally educated mind. The humanities can strengthen this Christian integration through their own vigorous examination of the unique nature of man and the scale of values in his intellectual, emotional and moral universe. Thomistic philosophy makes its contribution also by performing its proper work of orienting the humanities, evaluating the methods of the sciences, and establishing the truth about the spiritual mode of being and God's existence. By remaining faithful to its own functions, Thomism thus helps to keep the human spirit open to God and responsive to His call.

Two definite curricular recommendations emerge from this concept of the role of Thomism in the college. The first is a caution against the two extremes of multiplying short courses in all branches of philosophy and of reducing philosophy to some rapid indoctrinations of the freshman class. Philosophy cannot perform its critical and integrative work until the student has acquired a certain college maturity in the humanistic and scientific areas. Hence the second suggestion— to begin the main philosophy instruction at the midpoint of the college years. The pivotal work should consist of an intensive introduction to a metaphysics leading to the truth of God's existence, a philosophy of man centered around his spiritual and free nature, and a philosophy of conduct which makes moral obligation clearly continuous with its metaphysical roots in God and human nature.

As a culmination, the final year should be devoted to a comparative synthesis of the various types of knowledge already encountered in college education, and to a more explicit development of the several lines of integration initiated in the separate philosophy courses. Here, there can also be a stress upon modern and contemporary philosophies. Undoubtedly the greatest burden of this program is placed upon the teacher himself, who has to learn how to philosophize genuinely, though in an introductory way, with the young minds engaged in

396

the college adventure. The effective teacher of philosophy is the practical point of insertion for theistic realism, both for helping the student to interpret his complex world and for encouraging those new thrusts of intelligence which this philosophy needs for its continued development in our time.

NOTES

(See Bibliography for more complete information on titles cited.)

Chapter 1 ART AND THE EXISTENTIALISTS

1. Herbert Spiegelberg, "French Existentialism: Its Social Philosophies," *The Kenyon Review*, 16 (1954), 446-462.

2. Paul Tillich, "Existentialist Aspects of Modern Art," in *Christianity and the Existentialists*, edited by C. Michalson, 128-147.

3. Samuel Beckett, *Waiting for Godot*, 51.

4. See Jean-Paul Sartre, *No Exit and Three Other Plays*, 44, 45 (*No Exit*), for the dialogue given here.

5. For comments on Faulkner and Dos Passos, see Jean-Paul Sartre, *Literary and Philosophical Essays*, 73-96. Sartre's literary significance is studied by Hazel Barnes, *The Literature of Possibility*.

6. Cf. Karl Jaspers, *Existentialism and Humanism*, 35-64, on Goethe's humanism; the quotation from Faust is quoted here, p. 42.

7. This quotation appears in the epigraph for the essay, "Hölderlin and the Essence of Poetry," in Martin Heidegger, *Existence and Being*, 293.

8. This quotation is given in Edgard Sottiaux, *Gabriel Marcel: Philosophe et dramaturge*, 11. There is an excellent discussion in English on Marcel's plays made by F. Temple Kingston, *French Existentialism: A Christian Critique*.

9. See the entire second volume of Marcel's *The Mystery of Being*.

10. This quotation will be found in the long and important essay, Gabriel Marcel, "Rilke: A Witness to the Spiritual," *Homo Viator*, 234. Marcel is influenced by Romano Guardini's stimulating commentaries on Rilke's vocation in the modern world. See Romano Guardini, *Rilke's Duino Elegies*.

11. *Homo Viator*, 159.

Chapter 2 JASPERS' CONCEPTION OF MODERN SCIENCE

1. For instance, see *Way to Wisdom*, 8 ff., 74 ff., 168 f.; *Reason and Existenz*, 71-73; *Existenzphilosophie*, 10 f.; *Reason and Anti-Reason in Our Time*, 30-35.

2. *Philosophie*, 279; "On My Philosophy," in *Existentialism from Dostoevsky to Sartre*, edited by Walter Kaufmann, 139-140.

3. *Man in the Modern Age*, 144-151; *The Origin and Goal of History*, 83 ff.

4. *Reason and Existenz*, 146-147; *The Perennial Scope of Philosophy*, 29-30; *Existenzphilosophie*, 9.

5. These characteristics are conveniently analyzed together in *The Origin and Goal of History*, 83 ff.

6. Consult "On My Philosophy" (Kaufmann, 132-133); "Philosophical Auto-

biography," in *The Philosophy of Karl Jaspers*, edited by Paul A. Schilpp, 8-9, 16-25; *Rechenschaft und Ausblick*, 170-172; *Existenzphilosophie*, 2-5.

7. For Jaspers' estimate of Husserl, see *Rechenschaft und Ausblick*, 327-328.

8. *Descartes und die Philosophie*, 56-64; "On My Philosophy" (Kaufmann, 157).

9. *The Origin and Goal of History*, 93-94. Since scientism eliminates the dimension of transcendence, Jaspers regards the absolutizing of the natural world not only as a type of superstition but also as a form of unbelief; cf. *The Perennial Scope of Philosophy*, 119.

10. *Nietzsche: Einführung in das Verständnis seines Philosophierens*, 176-184. I do not discuss here the historical accuracy of Jaspers' portraits of Descartes and Nietzsche, but in *The Lure of Wisdom* I bring out Descartes' respect for wisdom and its modes. Jaspers gives a compact religious view of Nietzsche's love of truth in *Nietzsche and Christianity*.

11. *Von der Wahrheit*, 595-597.

12. For synoptic treatments of these three standpoints, cf. *Man in the Modern Age*, 163-174; *Reason and Anti-Reason in Our Time*, 8-37.

13. *Von der Wahrheit*, 96.

14. Jaspers offers a summary of the Kantian basis of his theory of knowledge in *The Perennial Scope of Philosophy*, 8-9, 25-26. On the subject-object relationship, cf. *Psychologie der Weltanschauungen*, 21-28.

15. *Philosophie*, 4-5, 74-75, uses the Kantian distinction between the indeterminate object or counterpart (*Gegenstand*) and the determinate object in knowledge (*Objekt*). Kant's thought is analyzed and criticized by Jaspers in *The Great Philosophers*, 230 ff.

16. On the Kantian distinction between restraints (*Schranken*) and boundaries (*Grenze*), see *The Origin and Goal of History*, 94; *Von der Wahrheit*, 96. Jaspers gives an excellent condensation of his teaching on the nature and limits of science, as well as its relations with philosophy, in *The Idea of the University*, 7-27 (including a bibliographical note on where he has treated the subject elsewhere).

17. *Way to Wisdom*, 75-76; *Reason and Anti-Reason in Our Time*, 27-30; *Philosophie*, 73-110; *Von der Wahrheit*, 96-103; *Descartes und die Philosophie*, 47-48.

18. "On My Philosophy" (Kaufmann, 157-158); *Philosophie*, 128-130, 144, 232-240. The general conditions for a systematic of the sciences are outlined in *Psychologie der Weltanschauungen*, 17-20; *Allgemeine Psychopathologie*, 625-628.

19. On inner awareness or *Innewerden*, see *Existenzphilosophie*, 18-24; *Von der Wahrheit*, 155, 346-347. The contrast between viewing man as a scientific object and as a free, existing subject is developed in *The Perennial Scope of Philosophy*, 54-62; *Way to Wisdom*, 63-65; *Existentialism and Humanism*, 68-69. One special difficulty in Jaspers' epistemology is to explain how thought and reason can serve as the common foundation both for scientific knowledge and for inner awareness, without requiring us to admit an analogical meaning for the modes of knowledge, with sufficient scope to include inner awareness as a kind of knowing.

20. *The Perennial Scope of Philosophy*, 174-176; *Way to Wisdom*, 140-141. Because of the sharp contrast, Jaspers sometimes denies that philosophy can rightly be said to progress. He would agree with Gabriel Marcel that linear progress characterizes the movement of science among its problems, whereas permanent reflection on the same central themes is the proper life of philosophy in dealing with what Jaspers regards as ambiguities and Marcel as mystery.

21. His position is concisely stated in the essay, "Philosophy and Science," included in *Way to Wisdom*, 147-167.

22. On their mutual service, consult *Philosophie*, 272-282; *Existenzphilosophie*,

7-10; *Allgemeine Psychopathologie,* 641-644; *Von der Wahrheit,* 156-157. In *ibid.,* 322-323, Jaspers considers whether science is *wertlos,* as well as *wertfrei.*

23. *The Perennial Scope of Philosophy,* 90-92; *Von der Wahrheit,* 733-738.

24. The entire third book of *Philosophie* (675 ff.) is devoted to a study of metaphysical thinking, which is defined as an effort to express transcendence within the sphere of empirical being. Cf. Hans Kunz, "Critique of Jaspers' Concept of Transcendence," in *The Philosophy of Karl Jaspers* (Schilpp, 499-522).

25. "On My Philosophy" (Kaufmann, 145); *Von der Wahrheit,* 104-105.

26. The naturalistic position will be described in Part Two, below.

27. Jacques Maritain, *Philosophy of Nature,* 73-88.

28. See Jaspers' "Reply to My Critics," in *The Philosophy of Karl Jaspers* (Schilpp, 797-800; 845-846), containing his reply to my critique as offered in the Schilpp volume.

Chapter 3   THE RELIGIOUS THEME IN EXISTENTIALISM

1. James K. Feibleman, "The Social Adaptiveness of Philosophies," *Ethics,* 70 (1960), 146-154.

2. The examples cited here are: R. Allers, *Existentialism and Psychiatry; Existence,* edited by R. May, E. Angel, and H. F. Ellenberger; H. E. Barnes, *The Literature of Possibility;* Paul Tillich, *Dynamics of Faith;* "Existentialism and Literature," *Chicago Review,* 13 (1959), 3-202.

3. This background is described in James Collins, *The Existentialists: A Critical Study,* chapter one. The religious implications of existentialism are set forth in D. E. Roberts, *Existentialism and Religious Belief.*

4. Sartre discusses his relationship with these three predecessors most rewardingly in *Question de méthode.* The edition of this work cited here is the one placed at the beginning of *Critique de la raison dialectique,* tome I. Each of these works is cited here by its own title, even though the page references are to the one volume in which they are jointly published. For the comparison in question, see *Question de méthode,* 18-22.

5. Bad faith "stands forth in the firm resolution *not to demand too much,* to count itself satisfied when it is barely persuaded, to force itself in decisions to adhere to uncertain truths." Sartre, *Being and Nothingness,* 68.

6. *Question de méthode,* 22-24, 30-32, 107-111. In discussing the relation of his existentialism to Marxism, Sartre uses the Hegelian terminology about a sublated position and the Marxian terminology about the withering-away of the state. He also surmises that there will not be need for a distinctive Marxist philosophy (even one which incorporates existentialism) in the perfect condition of productive freedom.

7. *Critique de la raison dialectique,* 247-249.

8. *Being and Nothingness,* 566; 615. Sartre's general difficulty about relating his basic project of freedom to any particular free choices crops up again in his view that the general meaning for the basic human project is that of being God. He calls this meaning an abstract structure which does not itself constitute the basic project of man, but nevertheless the project is structured always with this general meaning. Sartre's description of human reality is thus permeated with a religious significance, but one which functions as an oppressive doom rather than as a liberation and realization for human aspirations.

9. *Critique de la raison dialectique,* 248, 249.

10. This point is well made in the course of John Macquarrie's sober comparative study, *An Existentialist Theology: A Comparison of Heidegger and Bultmann.*

11. *Letter on Humanism*, in *Philosophy in the Twentieth Century*, edited by W. Barrett and H. D. Aiken, II, 270-302.

12. This is the common theme of Heidegger's recent shorter treatises: *The Question of Being* and *What Is Philosophy?*

13. Critical evaluation of this finitizing theory of being in Heidegger's recent writings is made by J. B. Lotz, S.J., "Denken und Sein nach den jüngsten Veröffentlichungen von M. Heidegger," *Scholastik*, 33 (1958), 81-97, and by Rudolf Allers, "Heidegger on the Principle of Sufficient Reason," *Philosophy and Phenomenological Research*, 20 (1960), 365-373, with emphasis upon the underlying univocal notion of being.

14. Heidegger, *An Introduction to Metaphysics*, 17. On the problem of poetic and philosophical language, cf. Heidegger, *Unterwegs zur Sprache*.

15. Friedrich Hölderlin, "The Archipelago," English translation by S. Stepanchev, in *An Anthology of German Poetry from Hölderlin to Rilke*, edited by Angel Flores, 18-19. See the essay by S. R. Hopper, "On the Naming of the Gods in Hölderlin and Rilke," in *Christianity and the Existentialists*, edited by Carl Michalson, 148-190.

16. *An Introduction to Metaphysics*, 7. The incapacity of philosophy for reaching God is reaffirmed in Heidegger's critique of the onto-theological position of Hegel; see *Essays in Metaphysics*, 35-67.

17. Consult Bultmann's 1930 article, "The Historicity of Man and Faith," in *Existence and Faith: Shorter Writings of Rudolf Bultmann*, edited by S. M. Ogden, 92-110. Commentaries are made on the Heidegger-Bultmann relationship by John Macquarrie (above, note 10) and by L. Malevez, S.J., *The Christian Message and Myth*. For his part, Karl Jaspers criticizes Bultmann for hoping to find a non-ambiguous, absolute center of human truth in Scripture with the help of the Heideggerian theory of human reality. See Karl Jaspers and Rudolf Bultmann, *Myth and Christianity*.

18. Karl Jaspers outlines his position on religion in *The Perennial Scope of Philosophy;* cf. Paul Hossfeld, "Karl Jaspers and Religion," *Philosophy Today*, 3 (1959), 277-280.

19. Marcel, *L'Homme problématique*, 35.

20. The intimate continuity between problem and mystery is suggested even in the well-known definition which Marcel proposed for a mystery. "A mystery is a problem which encroaches upon its own data, invading them and thereby transcending itself as a simple problem." *On the Ontological Mystery*, in *Philosophy in the Twentieth Century* (Barrett and Aiken, II, 370, modified).

21. *L'Homme problématique*, 63. Norman Malcolm's *Ludwig Wittgenstein: A Memoir*, 70-72, recalls three features in Wittgenstein's sparse comments on the possibility of religion. He expressed wonder at the existence of the world, at there being anything existing at all; he made sense of the idea of a judging and redeeming God, corresponding to man's sense of sin and guilt; and he could make no sense of a creating and causing God, a cosmological Deity apart from the religious bond. Marcel would regard wonder, a sense of guilt, and a need for redemption as basic witnesses to religion; but he would treat creation in a religious, noncausal way.

22. *L'Homme problématique*, 67-71. Marcel appeals to Bergson for support of his contention that neither the order of freedom nor that of grace can be translated into the language of causality. It is more precise to say that these orders cannot be translated into the spatial determinism which Bergson found in Spencer and nineteenth-century physics. But neither the scientific nor the philosophical conceptions of causality and its methodology have stood still in the time since Bergson's analysis was made. For a phenomenological approach, read Maurice

Natanson, "Causation as a Structure of the *Lebenswelt*," *The Journal of Existential Psychiatry*, 1 (1960), 346-366.

23. This is the chief topic in Marcel's *The Mystery of Being*, vol. I: *Reflection and Mystery*.

24. *Ibid.*, I, 52-55.

25. These religious modalities are well described in *Homo Viator: Introduction to a Metaphysics of Hope*, and in the second volume of Gifford Lectures, *The Mystery of Being*, vol. II: *Faith and Reality*.

26. The entire second half of *L'Homme problématique*, 81 ff., is devoted to a report on human inquietude as a question for the Stoic sages and the Gospels, for Augustine and Pascal, for Goethe and Gide and Sartre.

27. J. H. Newman, *Parochial and Plain Sermons*, I, 56; IV, 293. For a comparison between Newman and existentialism, see D. Gorce, "Newman existentialiste?" in *Newman Studien*, III, edited by H. Fries and W. Becker, 203-224.

28. Newman, *Parochial and Plain Sermons*, II, 213.

29. See the discussion between J. M. Le Blond, S.J., "L'Usage théologique de la notion de causalité," and Gabriel Marcel, "Dieu et la causalité," in *Recherches de Philosophie*, 3-4 (1958), 15-26, 27-33. On the similar refusal of Husserl to apply a physically oriented notion of causality to God, cf. S. Strasser, "Das Gottesproblem in der Spätphilosophie Edmund Husserls," *Philosophisches Jahrbuch*, 67 (1959), 130-142.

30. The resources of such a study can be estimated by consulting A. C. Bouquet, *Comparative Religion*, and August Brunner, S.J., *Die Religion*.

Chapter 4 FAITH AND REFLECTION IN KIERKEGAARD

1. Although the topic of faith and reflection is one of Kierkegaard's constant, major preoccupations, the essence of his position is given in four books. Two of them are concerned mainly with keeping a firm distinction between philosophical and religious reflection: *Philosophical Fragments* and *Concluding Unscientific Postscript*. The other two basic treatments try to build up a positive awareness of the meaning and cost involved in the religious and the specifically Christian type of faith and reflection: *For Self-Examination and Judge for Yourselves!* and *Training in Christianity*. In reading the other works of Kierkegaard, it is important to hold these major writings firmly in mind as a context. J. H. Thomas, *Subjectivity and Paradox*, is both a helpful study of Kierkegaard's conception of faith and also an interesting restatement of it in terms of the analytic theism which will engage us later on. An acute comparison is made between Kierkegaard and St. Thomas on the question of faith and reason by Cornelio Fabro, C.P.S., "Faith and Reason in Kierkegaard's Dialectic," in *A Kierkegaard Critique*, 156-206.

Both the Introduction and the Commentary by Niels Thulstrup to the second English edition of Kierkegaard's *Philosophical Fragments* provide valuable guides on the question of Christian faith and reflection.

Chapter 5 EDITH STEIN AS A PHENOMENOLOGIST

1. *Zum Problem der Einfühlung.* For biographical details, see H. C. Graef, *The Scholar and the Cross: The Life and Work of Edith Stein*.

2. Edmund Husserl, "Philosophy as a Strict Science," *Cross Currents*, 6 (1956), 239-240, 244-245. In the last of his *Cartesian Meditations*, 120 ff., Husserl gives his mature notion of a phenomenological kind of community awareness, as an aid in the problem of intersubjectivity and the constitution of nature and society.

3. See her critical remarks in *Zum Problem der Einfühlung*, 2, 10, 72-73.

4. "Beiträge zur philosophischen Begründung der Psychologie und der Geisteswissenschaften. Erste Abhandlung: Psychische Kausalität; Zweite Abhandlung: Individuum und Gemeinschaft," *Jahrbuch für Philosophie und phänomenologische Forschung*, 5 (1922), 1-116, 116-283.

5. *Ibid.*, 2-7; cf. *Zum Problem der Einfühlung*, p. 80, n. 1.

6. "Beiträge," 21.

7. *Ibid.*, 31-32; 84-106.

8. *Ibid.*, 34-41. The section from this essay dealing with motivation and freedom has been translated in *Writings of Edith Stein*, edited by H. C. Graef, 177-197.

9. "Beiträge," 72-79, 106.

10. *Ibid.*, 120.

11. *Ibid.*, 123. Cf. the important insertion which Husserl made in his *Cartesian Meditations*, p. 52, n. 1, concerning the need to relate the intending and reductive acts to "the Ego given in experience of myself as a man." This question will be restudied from Husserl's standpoint in chapter 14.

12. "Beiträge," 175. Here, Edith Stein disagrees explicitly with the view of Max Scheler that individual freedom exists only by reference to the primary freedom of the community. For Stein, there is responsible use of power by the social reality only because of its constituted reference to the human persons intending a common purpose.

13. "Beiträge," 236-246.

14. *Ibid.*, 258.

15. "Eine Untersuchung über den Staat," *Jahrbuch für Philosophie und phänomenologische Forschung*, 7 (1925), 1-123.

16. *Ibid.*, 7, 42, 75. See the study by P. Lenz-Médoc, "L'Idée de l'État chez Edith Stein," *Les Études Philosophiques*, 11 (1956), 451-457.

17. Edith Stein has a geo-anthropological concept of race, rather than a biological one. She regards a race as a personal type which reflects the character of a particular terrain or region on the earth. When members of a racial group, taken in this sense, join together in a communal life having a distinctive culture, they then constitute a people or folk. Thus there is no direct relationship between a race and a state, and no primarily biological basis for the race elements which do enter into a state. See "Untersuchung," 87-88.

18. *Ibid.*, 11-12.

19. "Untersuchung," 22, 119.

20. *Ibid.*, 113-117.

21. *Ibid.*, 117-123.

22. "Husserls Phänomenologie und die Philosophie des hl. Thomas v. Aquin," *Festschrift Edmund Husserl zum 70. Geburtstag gewidmet. Ergänzungsband zum Jahrbuch für Philosophie und phänomenologische Forschung*, 315-338.

23. *Ibid.*, 323.

24. *Ibid.*, 325-326.

25. *Festschrift*, 330-332.

26. *Endliches und ewiges Sein*. This is the second volume in *Edith Steins Werke*, edited by L. Gelber and R. Leuven, O.C.D.

27. *Endliches und ewiges Sein*, 31-59.

28. *Ibid.*, 433-454, where Edith Stein refers to Gredt as an authority on the Thomistic doctrine on matter and the individual. This textbook approach hinders the real comparative study of Aquinas and Husserl.

29. *Ibid.*, 307.

30. *Endliches und ewiges Sein*, 303-305.

31. *Ibid.*, 53-59. Also, "The Knowledge of God," in *Writings of Edith Stein*, 61-96.

32. *Endliches und ewiges Sein*, 21, n. 33. In this book, Stein acknowledges her debt to Heidegger and makes a critique of his views on the relation between being and temporality. For her, the understanding of being is more comprehensive than the understanding of the finite-temporal modalities of human being. There is a brief account of Edith Stein's place in the development of phenomenology in Herbert Spiegelberg's *The Phenomenological Movement*, I, 223-224. However, her use of a Thomistic vocabulary leads Spiegelberg to overstate her acceptance of Thomism, to overlook her extensive criticism of the textbook Thomism of Gredt and others, and to minimize her continued use and development of many phenomenological concepts and procedures in discussing the traditional problems.

Chapter 6 ROOTS OF SCHELER'S EVOLUTIONARY PANTHEISM

1. The first quotation is from George N. Shuster, "Introductory Statement to: 'Symposium on the Significance of Max Scheler for Philosophy and Social Science,'" *Philosophy and Phenomenological Research*, 2 (1942), 270. The next quotation is translated from P. Wolff, ed., *Christliche Philosophie in Deutschland, 1920 bis 1945*, 9.

2. Dietrich von Hildebrand, "Max Scheler als Persönlichkeit," *Hochland*, 26 (1928-1929). This essay, along with another on "Max Schelers Stellung zur katholischen Gedankenwelt," is reprinted in Dietrich von Hildebrand's book, *Zeitliches im Lichte des Ewigen*. His interpretation of Scheler is followed in J. M. Oesterreicher, *Walls are Crumbling*, 135-198.

3. Nicolai Hartmann, "Max Scheler," *Kantstudien*, 33 (1928), xv, where he calls Scheler a "thinker of problems," rather than a "producer of systems."

4. The Thomistic and other Catholic evaluations are described by James Collins, "Catholic Estimates of Scheler's Catholic Period," *Thought*, 19 (1944), 671-704.

5. The exception is Erich Przywara's brilliant comparison of the religious positions of Scheler and Cardinal Newman, *Religions-begründung: Max Scheler— J. H. Newman*, which goes straight to the problem of what method should be used in a metaphysics and philosophy of religion which study God.

6. The books considered here are: *On the Eternal in Man, Philosophical Perspectives*, and *Die Stellung des Menschen im Kosmos*. These three works are referred to here respectively as: *Eternal, Perspectives*, and *Stellung*. An English translation of *Stellung* will be published soon by the Beacon Press of Boston. Scheler's widow, Maria Scheler, is now engaged in editing Max Scheler's *Gesammelte Werke*. The original text of *Eternal* is published in this collection as vol. 5: *Vom Ewigen im Menschen*. The original texts of *Perspectives* (*Philosophische Weltanschauung*) and *Stellung* will be in volume nine of this edition.

7. Edmund Husserl, "Philosophy as a Strict Science," *Cross Currents*, 6 (1956), 227-246, 325-344, with notes by the translator, Quentin Lauer, S.J. Scheler discusses this project in *Eternal*, 80-83.

8. Martin Heidegger, "What is Metaphysics?", in *Existence and Being*, 356, 387.

9. *Eternal*, 93-94.

10. See the description of scientific knowledge and power over nature, in *Perspectives*, 3-5, where it is distinguished from Husserl's knowledge of essences, and Scheler's own metaphysics or salvational knowledge. Scheler would reduce not only the natural and the scientific attitude, but also that of Husserlian study of essences, to his own salvational knowledge of the unity of God and the world

in man. He analyzes the scientist's moral attitude of self-mastery for the sake of mastery over the contingent world, in order to establish necessary limits for science (*Eternal*, 96-97).

11. *Eternal*, 97, 330-331.

12. *Ibid.*, 74. For a careful, orderly introduction to Scheler's philosophy, as developed around this definition of philosophizing, cf. Johannes Hessen, *Max Scheler: Eine kritische Einführung in seine Philosophie.*

13. The theory of the moral attitude of upsurge as animating the philosopher's work is set forth in *Eternal*, 89-98.

14. *Stellung*, 51.

15. Unlike Hegel and Nicolai Hartmann, Scheler does not make a special distinction between actuality and reality, *Wirklichkeit* and *Realität*. Because of his voluntarist and vitalist theory of actuality, Scheler was once called a Catholic Nietzsche by Ernst Troeltsch.

16. *Eternal*, 92, n. 1; *Stellung*, 49-50.

17. *Eternal*, 98-102.

18. Spinoza, "On the Improvement of the Understanding," in *Spinoza Selections*, edited by J. Wild, 15.

19. *Eternal*, 149-150; cf. *ibid.*, 139-140.

20. *Ibid.*, 150.

21. *Ibid.*, 90-91, 151.

22. *Eternal*, 150-151.

23. *Stellung*, 7; cf. *Perspectives*, 9-12.

24. *Eternal*, 103.

25. In *Eternal*, 260-264, Scheler infers the existence of God from our religious acts. He calls this inference a disclosure-type of demonstration and a confirmation, but not a proof in the strict sense. Scheler's views on the religious act and the nature of the divine are analyzed by Maurice Dupuy, *La Philosophie de la religion chez Max Scheler.*

26. Compare *Eternal*, 240, and *Stellung*, 58, on the impotence of mind or spirit, and the reciprocal need for the spiritualization of life and the vitalization of spirit. The basic continuity in Scheler's thought is emphasized in the major study of his philosophy by Maurice Dupuy, *La Philosophie de Max Scheler: Son Évolution et son unité.*

27. *Stellung*, 65. "Man, a brief holiday in the tremendous expanse of time, of universal growth of life, thus *means* something in the development of God himself. Man's history is not merely a spectacle for an eternal, perfect, and divine spectator and judge, but is interwoven into the growth of God himself." *Perspectives*, 30.

28. Scheler's split between spirit and life is criticized from a neo-Kantian standpoint in Ernst Cassirer's essay, " 'Spirit' and 'Life' in Contemporary Philosophy," in *The Philosophy of Ernst Cassirer*, 857 ff.

29. *Eternal*, 101.

30. *Ibid.*, 339.

31. On his moral philosophy, see Q. Lauer, S.J., "The Phenomenological Ethics of Max Scheler," *International Philosophical Quarterly*, 1 (1961), 273-300. Scheler's treatise, *The Nature of Sympathy*, shows him at his best in using the phenomenological method to elucidate fellow-feeling, states of love and hatred, and our relations with other persons. This same skill at descriptive elucidation of human situations (taken apart from their metaphysical implications) is exhibited in his valuational study, *Ressentiment*, edited by L. A. Coser, including a comparison of an ethics based on *ressentiment* with both the Christian and the modern humanitarian motifs of fellow love.

Chapter 7 DARWIN'S IMPACT ON PHILOSOPHY

1. J. Royce, *The Spirit of Modern Philosophy*, 286.

2. See the witty opening chapter of W. Irvine, *Apes, Angels, and Victorians*.

3. G. West, *Charles Darwin: A Portrait*, 78, reports that Darwin knew Paley's *Natural Theology* by heart and admired its logic.

4. On this distinction in general, see R. L. Faricy, S.J., "The Establishment of the Basic Principle of the Fifth Way," *The New Scholasticism*, 31 (1957), 189-208. The critical comments of Hume, Kant, and Mill on the physico-theological argument are examined in J. Collins, *God in Modern Philosophy*, 120-21, 164-66, 179-80, 288-92. Cf. G. P. Klubertanz, S.J., "St. Thomas' treatment of the Axiom, '*Omne Agens Agit Propter Finem*,'" in *An Etienne Gilson Tribute*, ed. by C. J. O'Neil, 101-117.

5. For this problem in Great Britain during the background years 1790-1850, read C. C. Gillispie, *Genesis and Geology*. "During the seven decades between the birth of modern geology and the publication of *On the Origin of Species*, the difficulty [between science and religion] as reflected in scientific literature appears to be one of religion (in a crude sense) *in* science rather than one of religion *versus* science" (ix).

6. W. Paley, *Natural Theology*, 20. See J. C. Greene's chapter on "Darwin and Natural Theology," in *Darwin and the Modern World View*, 39-87.

7. F. Darwin and A. C. Seward, editors, *More Letters of Charles Darwin*, I, 154, 155. Darwin's few guarded statements on religion are gathered in F. Darwin, *The Life and Letters of Charles Darwin*, I, 274-86. His preoccupation with Paley crops out in his remark that "the old argument from design in Nature, as given by Paley, which formerly seemed to me so conclusive, fails, now that the law of natural selection has been discovered" (*Ibid.*, I, 278). He adds that physical evil is more compatible with natural selection than with a providential God, that it once seemed to him unlikely that the whole universe came from blind chance and necessity, but nevertheless that the animal origin of our mind probably incapacitates us for answering these questions with certainty. See M. Mandelbaum, "Darwin's Religious Views," *Journal of the History of Ideas*, 19 (1958), 363-378. The publication of the integral text of the *Autobiography of Charles Darwin*, edited by N. Barlow, does not greatly alter the picture of a gradual fading away of Darwin's theism and interest in natural religious belief. But it does make available his critical remarks on Christianity and the account of his relatively early loss of the Christian faith. His interchange of views on religion with other scientists is studied by J. C. Greene, "Darwin and Religion," *Proceedings of the American Philosophical Society*, 103 (1959), 716-25.

8. L. Eiseley, *Darwin's Century*, 197. R. J. Nogar, O.P., "The Darwin Centennial: A Philosophical Intrusion," *The New Scholasticism*, 33 (1959), 411-45, argues that Darwin's theory of evolution inherently denies real intrinsic finality. But his theory is sufficiently complex to bar the flat alternative that he must either accept or reject this finality. His thought involves a threefold reference: (1) to the natural world of the organisms, (2) to the explanatory scheme of his own concepts, and (3) to the notion of design found in current works on physico-theology. Darwin's remarks on purpose belong within this threefold context and do not constitute a simple denial of finality in its metaphysical meaning.

9. Huxley's private waverings come out most clearly in correspondence with Charles Kingsley and are examined in Irvine, *Apes, Angels, and Victorians*, 127-34. William Irvine has also described the turmoil aroused in Tennyson, Hardy, and other poets by evolutionary views of nature: "The Influence of Darwin on Literature," *Proceedings of the American Philosophical Society*, 103 (1959), 616-28.

10. D. Duncan, *Life and Letters of Herbert Spencer*, III, 319. (The text is from Spencer himself, who wrote about his own development in an impersonal mode.) For scholarly research on the pre-Darwinian history of evolutionary theories, H. F. Osborn's *From the Greeks to Darwin* has long been outmoded by the work of Lovejoy, Zirkle, and others; Eiseley gives a good description of the two generations of scientific thought before Darwin in *Darwin's Century;* a new reading of the sources is made by W. Zimmermann, *Evolution: Die Geschichte ihrer Probleme und Erkenntnisse.* But the best report of recent historical findings is the collection of essays by B. Glass and others: *Forerunners of Darwin, 1745-1859.*

11. In Duncan, *Life and Letters of Herbert Spencer*, II, 334.

12. *Ibid.*, II, 313-14, 323, 326 (against Huxley); Herbert Spencer, *First Principles,* 502.

13. H. Bergson, *Écrits et paroles,* tome I, 234.

14. *First Principles,* 501; cf. 484, 492-93, 505-06. S. F. Mason, "The Idea of Progress and Theories of Evolution in Science," in *Essays on the Social History of Science,* edited by S. Lilley, 90-106, shows that evolutionary thought has given rise to various theories of progress, but he does not stress the anti-progress and cyclic inferences that have also been made from it.

15. On Nietzsche's ambivalence toward Darwinism, cf. W. Kaufmann, *Nietzsche,* 126-27, 288-89. Nietzsche approved of its stress on universal change and man's animal origin, but he criticized it for not seeing that only a few choice spirits rise above the species level and for not facing up to eternal recurrence.

16. The influence of natural and revealed faith is studied by J. Baillie, *The Belief in Progress.*

17. Relevant sections from *The Descent of Man* are conveniently presented in the source readings edited by F. J. Teggart (with introduction by G. H. Hildebrand), *The Idea of Progress,* 448-53. The theme of J. C. Greene's *The Death of Adam* is that scientists applied evolutionary ideas only gradually and reluctantly to man, and that Darwin's own view of man remained basically ambiguous about the moral quality of man's future developments.

18. "Evolution and Ethics," reprinted in the joint volume by T. H. Huxley and Julian Huxley, *Touchstone for Ethics,* 93. Even the positivist historian, J. B. Bury, was so impressed by Thomas Huxley's view that he admitted that evolutionary theory remains neutral and "lends itself to a pessimistic as well as to an optimistic interpretation." Bury, *The Idea of Progress,* 345.

19. For the Christian and naturalistic background of modern millennialism, consult E. L. Tuveson, *Millennium and Utopia.*

20. R. Hofstadter, *Social Darwinism in American Thought,* discusses the vogue of Spencer, the ethical influence of Huxley, and the reaction of James and Dewey. A broader account of evolutionary ideas in America is provided in the essays edited by S. Persons, *Evolutionary Thought in America,* especially the chapters on the rise of evolutionism and its effect on ethics and theology.

21. The best study of this group is P. P. Wiener's *Evolution and the Founders of Pragmatism.* Also informative are the briefer accounts by H. W. Schneider, *A History of American Philosophy,* 321-437, and by M. H. Fisch, "Evolution in American Philosophy," *The Philosophical Review,* 56 (1947), 357-73. The two latter authors stress the application of evolutionary ideas to man, whereas the viewpoint of the present chapter is directed toward the underlying problems in methodology and causality which remain lively issues today. For the rearguard action of the older Scottish school, see J. McCosh, *The Religious Aspect of Evolution.*

22. His core ideas on science and evolution are available in *The Philosophical Writings of Chauncey Wright,* edited by E. H. Madden, 12-42. On Darwinism

and earlier philosophies of science, consult A. Ellegard, "The Darwinian Theory and Nineteenth-Century Philosophies of Science," *Journal of the History of Ideas,* 18 (1957), 362-93.

23. *The Philosophical Writings,* 24, 25.

24. *The Philosophical Writings,* 21.

25. *Loc. cit.*

26. C. Wright, *Philosophical Discussions,* 403; R. B. Perry, *The Thought and Character of William James,* I, 524-28, and II, 718-21. Perry gives an interchange between Wright and William James on the former's nihilism of scientific method. Here as everywhere in treating of American philosophy since 1860, we have to return to the documents provided by Perry on James and the men surrounding him. Perry devotes a chapter (I, 474-93) to James's criticism of Spencer's "teatable elysium" and "orgy of ambiguity," as well as to James's position that the evolutionary origin of man is acceptable as long as it allows for the mind's originality and freedom.

27. C. Wright, *Philosophical Discussions,* 400.

28. *Values in a Universe of Chance: Selected Writings of Charles S. Peirce (1839-1914),* edited by P. P. Wiener, 148-49 (against Spencer), 263, 268. Wiener's selection of materials is excellent for studying Peirce's views on scientific method and evolutionary philosophy, and will be referred to hereafter as *Values.* Most of the sources can also be found in vols. 1, 5, 6, and 7 of the *Collected Papers of Charles Sanders Peirce,* edited by C. Hartshorne, P. Weiss, and A. Burks. A close analysis is given in the chapter on Peirce in Wiener, *Evolution and the Founders of Pragmatism,* 70-96.

29. *Values,* 299-300; cf. 81-84. Hume is outmoded by evolutionary thought, since his standpoint in the isolated perceiver cannot explain either the evolving patterns in nature or the social development of science itself. Whitehead would accept Peirce's criticism of Hume.

30. *Ibid.,* 94-95, 174-78, 247.

31. *Ibid.,* 174; cf. 217, 429.

32. *Values,* 158-59. A. O. Lovejoy's criticism is found as Appendix E, in Wiener's *Evolution and the Founders of Pragmatism,* 227-30. Peirce had already replied to Paul Carus' similar objection by noting that the initial condition is "an indefinite specifiability, which is nothing but a tendency to the diversification of the nothing." Peirce, *Collected Papers,* 6.612.

33. *Values,* 291; cf. 300, 316. The context for this definition is an essay on "The Laws of Nature and Hume's Argument against Miracles," which, as the accompanying correspondence reveals, was composed under frustrating intellectual and financial conditions for S. P. Langley of the Smithsonian Institution.

34. *Values,* 199. Peirce retained several theories of evolution in order to account for the several ways in which science advances: by chance discovery (Darwin), by persistent habitual effort (Lamarck), and by the violent influx of new evidence upsetting the old habits of thought (Clarence King, the American geologist). Thus he gave a plurimodal evolutionary explanation of the history of science itself (*Ibid.,* 149-50, 257-60).

35. J. Dewey, *The Influence of Darwin on Philosophy and Other Essays in Contemporary Thought,* 14.

36. H. Bergson, *The Creative Mind,* 10-13; H. Bergson, *Creative Evolution,* 395-402. The latter work concludes with a criticism of Spencer's mechanist or extrinsic method and an affirmation of Bergson's own internal method. "It is within the evolutionary movement that we place ourselves, in order to follow it to its present results, instead of recomposing these results artificially with fragments of themselves. . . . It is the study of becoming in general, it is true evolutionism and consequently the true continuation of science" in the Bergsonian philosophy

of duration. *Creative Evolution*, 402. On the grounds for reading Darwin teleologically with Bergson rather than mechanistically with Dewey, see G. Himmelfarb, *Darwin and the Darwinian Revolution*, 325-30. But Himmelfarb does not distinguish clearly enough between Darwin's own outlook and limitations and those of his later interpreters.

37. Scholastic critics were sometimes arguing at cross purposes with Bergson, since his doctrine on intuition and more fluid concepts was not inspired primarily by anti-intellectualism in the broad meaning of intelligence, but by a positive effort to reach the heart of evolutionary reality through an attention to life in its temporal course. "The movement will not be grasped from without and, as it were, from where I am, but from within, inside it, in what it is in itself." *The Creative Mind*, 188.

38. Bergson has been criticized for his remarks on relativity theory, but sometimes without seeing that his main purpose was to show that present physical theory neither supports nor attacks his philosophy of evolutionary duration. Cf. *ibid.*, pp. 301-03, n. 5.

39. R. A. Fisher, *Creative Aspects of Natural Law*, 4-6 (his meaning for creative evolution), 6-11, 14-15 (on Bergson). Fisher is more sympathetic toward the holistic doctrine propounded by J. C. Smuts, *Holism and Evolution*. Smuts deliberately left the philosophical elaboration of his position to others, however, and hence did not face the full brunt of the evolutionary problem at the level of methodology.

40. *The Spirit of Modern Philosophy*, 306, 307. The repetition of the word "pretends" is reminiscent of Hegel on the cunning of reason, as is the reference to sin and ignorance. For an adjustment of Hegel's theory of the contingent and irrational factors in nature with Darwin on the variability in natural selection, read D. G. Ritchie, *Darwin and Hegel*, 56-58.

41. Royce develops these views in *The World and the Individual*, I, 501 ff., and II, 209-33, 315-23; and in his article, "The Mechanical, the Historical and the Statistical," *Science*, N.S., 39 (1914), 551-66. He wants to demonstrate the idealistic hypothesis that evolutionary laws of irreversible processes *"are in their most general type, common to Matter and to Mind, to the physical and to the moral world." The World and the Individual*, II, 218.

42. J. W. Buckham and G. M. Stratton, *George Holmes Howison, Philosopher and Teacher: A Selection from His Writings with a Biographical Sketch*, 163-64, 184.

43. *Ibid.*, 169; cf. 177.

44. E. Harris, *Nature, Mind, and Modern Science*, 328-55.

45. *Ibid.*, 202-06, 373-74.

46. *Nature, Mind, and Modern Science*, 442.

47. *Loc. cit.*

48. See his essay on "The Evolutionary Process," in *Evolution as a Process*, edited by J. Huxley, A. C. Hardy, and E. B. Ford, 1-13. The factual data and theories in the various sciences supporting the Neo-Darwinian account of evolution are presented by G. G. Simpson, *The Meaning of Evolution;* W. K. Gregory, *Evolution Emerging;* L. C. Cuénot, *L'évolution biologique*. In their concluding sections, Simpson and Gregory take a position close to the naturalism and evolutionary humanism of Julian Huxley, yet Gregory holds that evolutionary steps are irrevocable but not irreversible. Cuénot is even more cautious and does not absolutize the evolutionary factors. Huxley's address on "Man and the Future of Evolution" dominated the Chicago centennial meeting; cf. S. Tax (ed.), *Evolution after Darwin*.

49. J. Huxley, *Evolution: The Modern Synthesis*, 578. Evolutionary humanism is applied to all human spheres in *The Humanist Frame*, edited by J. Huxley.

50. On the biological basis for the concept of evolutionary progress, see *Evolution: the Modern Synthesis*, 556-69, and J. Huxley, *Evolution in Action*, 124-51.

51. *Ibid.*, 152-76; *Evolution: the Modern Synthesis*, 570-78; *Evolution as a Process*, 11-13. Huxley adopts a Bergsonian accent in holding that "the evolutionary process, as now embodied in man, has for the first time become aware of itself, is studying the laws of its own unfolding." *Evolution as a Process*, 13.

52. This statement concludes Julian Huxley's own Romanes Lecture on "Evolutionary Ethics," in T. H. Huxley and J. Huxley, *Touchstone for Ethics*, 156; cf. 199, 228. Julian Huxley presents his synthesis of atheistic naturalism and a religious attitude in *Religion without Revelation*. Of special interest is his personal confession of combining a highly religious response to nature with only the most casual acquaintance with any intellectual evidence for theism. See 65-96. Cuénot, *L'évolution biologique*, 568-69, sees little difference between a pantheistic and a naturalistic approach to nature in religious terms.

53. T. Dobzhansky, *The Biological Basis of Human Freedom*, 131. He makes a similar point in *Mankind Evolving*, 341-45.

54. P. A. Moody, *Introduction to Evolution*, 432. A similar point is made philosophically by C. A. Hartshorne, "Outlines of a Philosophy of Nature. Part II," *The Personalist*, 39 (1958), 385-89, with a use of Peirce's logic of chance against Huxley's antifinalism.

55. M. Grene, "Two Evolutionary Theories," *The British Journal for the Philosophy of Science*, 9 (1958), 192, 193. G. P. Klubertanz, S.J., in "The Influence of Evolutionary Theory upon American Thought," *Gregorianum*, 32 (1951), 582-90, shows the difference between describing some lines of descent and furnishing a total causal explanation.

56. S. Toulmin, "Contemporary Scientific Mythology," *Metaphysical Beliefs*, by S. Toulmin, R. W. Hepburn, and A. MacIntyre, 50-65.

57. S. C. Pepper, *The Sources of Value*, 625. Pepper restates his case succinctly in his *Ethics*, 199-223, but does not clarify the naturalistic basis of obligation.

58. A brief sketch is made in English by A. Knodel, "An Introduction to the Integral Evolutionism of Teilhard de Chardin," *The Personalist*, 38 (1957), 347-55. Longer studies have been written by C. Tresmontant, *Pierre Teilhard de Chardin: His Thought*, and by Claude Cuénot, *Pierre Teilhard de Chardin: Les grandes étapes de son évolution*. A bibliography of writings by and on Teilhard was compiled by Leo Larkin, S.J., for *Woodstock College Library Chapbook* (1958), 7-15.

59. This and the following quotation are from Pierre Teilhard de Chardin, S.J., "Spiritualistic Evolution," *Ibid.*, 17, 18. Two brief statements of some philosophical and theological issues raised by evolution, especially as it applies to man, are made by L. Dufault, O.M.I., "The Philosophical and Biological Implications of Evolution," *Proceedings of the American Catholic Philosophical Association*, 26 (1952), 66-80, and by C. Vollert, S.J., "Evolution of the Human Body," *The Catholic Mind*, 50 (1952), 135-54.

Recent theological interest in time and history should avoid two pitfalls. One is the confusion sometimes made between a rigorously cyclic theory of cosmic change and the spiral sort of advance envisioned by Vico and Teilhard. The other danger is that of over-simplifying the problem of the roots of contemporary concern for time and history to the point where all positive conceptions are treated merely as a secularizing and mythologizing of the Christian outlook. Although evolutionary thought is much more ambiguous about historical progress than is usually recognized, this does not lessen the fact that some aspects of evolutionism do furnish an irreducible source of our present awareness of time and history which is not just a transposition of theological themes.

In English, we have two major books by Pierre Teilhard de Chardin: his evolutionary synthesis, *The Phenomenon of Man*, and his specifically Christian conception of life, *The Divine Milieu*. Julian Huxley's own opinion of Teilhard will be found in the Introduction to *The Phenomenon of Man*, 11-28. A moderate critique is made by Olivier Rabut, O. P., *Teilhard de Chardin*.

Chapter 8 HOW DEWEY BECAME A NATURALIST

1. Referring to previous philosophical meanings for "nature," Dewey once remarked that "few terms used in philosophy have a wider or a looser use, or involve greater ambiguity." Article by John Dewey on "Nature," in *Dictionary of Philosophy and Psychology*, edited by J. M. Baldwin, II, 139.

2. "Soul and Body," *Bibliotheca Sacra*, 43 (1886), esp. 244-248. Dewey explained his later functionalist interpretation in an article which is important for the history of American psychology: "The Reflex Arc Concept in Psychology," *Psychological Review*, 3 (1896), 357-370.

3. "Soul and Body," 240.

4. "The Psychological Standpoint," *Mind*, 11 (1886), 1-19; "Psychology as Philosophic Method," *Mind*, 11 (1886), 153-73. The former article contains a criticism of Spencer's evolutionary realism. For the role of these articles in Dewey's general development, see M. G. White, *The Origin of Dewey's Instrumentalism*, 34-48.

5. "Psychology as Philosophic Method," 170-73.

6. *Ibid.*, 164.

7. *Loc. cit.* We have noted and criticized a similar view of time in the idealism of E. E. Harris; cf. above, chapter 7, n. 47.

8. The "Biography of John Dewey," edited by Jane M. Dewey, included in *The Philosophy of John Dewey*, edited by P. A. Schilpp, is still invaluable for information on the intellectual influences on Dewey. On the Vermont days, consult the two articles by L. S. Feuer: "H. A. P. Torrey and John Dewey: Teacher and Pupil," *American Quarterly*, 10 (1958), 34-54; "John Dewey's Reading at College," *Journal of the History of Ideas*, 19 (1958), 415-21. See also, G. Dykhuizen, "John Dewey: The Vermont Years," *Journal of the History of Ideas*, 20 (1959), 515-44.

9. "Ethics and Physical Science," *The Andover Review*, 7 (1887), 582. Similar in approach is his 1904 essay, "Herbert Spencer," reprinted in *Characters and Events*, I, 45-62. On the relation between Dewey's ethical naturalism and other American criticism of Spencer's ethics, cf. W. F. Quillian, Jr., "Evolution and Moral Theory in America," in *Evolutionary Thought in America*, edited by S. Persons, 398-419.

10. "Ethics and Physical Science," 579, 580. What made George Santayana's *The Life of Reason* so important for the genesis of American naturalism was its presentation of a naturalistic sense in which nature does indeed give birth to an ideal. Dewey himself insists that it is only through giving rise to man that nature performs this function.

11. "Christianity and Democracy," in *Religious Thought at the University of Michigan*, 60-69. A preliminary description of the published, but little known, Michigan writings by Dewey is made by W. Savage, "The Evolution of John Dewey's Philosophy of Experimentalism as Developed at the University of Michigan." The connection between democracy and religion is examined on the basis of these same materials by John Blewett, S.J., "Democracy as Religion: Unity in Human Relations," in *John Dewey: His Thought and Influence*, edited by John Blewett, S.J., 33-58.

12. "Green's Theory of the Moral Motive," *The Philosophical Review*, 1 (1892), 610. Dewey is here repeating the view expressed in "Christianity and Democracy," 64, 65.

13. "Green's Theory of the Moral Motive," 610. Dewey's 1908 essay, "Religion and Our Schools," reprinted in *Characters and Events*, makes this important naturalistic religious suggestion about the increase of scientific knowledge of nature: "Possibly if we measured it from the standpoint of the natural piety it is fostering, the sense of the permanent and inevitable implication of nature and man in a common career and destiny, it would appear as the growth of religion." *Characters and Events*, II, 515-16. This is a good definition of the Deweyan naturalistic meaning for the religious attitude. On the religious availability of humanistic naturalism, see G. R. Geiger, *John Dewey in Perspective*, 219-24.

14. "Reconstruction," *The Monthly Bulletin* of the Students' Christian Association of the University of Michigan, 17 (1893-94), 149-56.

15. "Christianity and Democracy," 64.

16. "Reconstruction," 154

17. *The Influence of Darwin on Philosophy and Other Essays*, 12; henceforth this book is referred to as *Influence of Darwin*. For theism, however, God is not outside of the natural process but is distinct from it in such a way that it embodies a causal reference to God. Hence Dewey must suppress this causal reference from his description of the conditions, objects, and consequences involved in natural process. See below, note 23.

18. *Influence of Darwin*, 19. J. H. Randall, Jr., "Dewey's Interpretation of the History of Philosophy," in the Schilpp volume, *The Philosophy of John Dewey*, 77-102, distinguishes sympathetically between destruction and critical reconstruction of historical materials. But he also observes that Dewey is interested more in power than in justice as a motive in using history of philosophy, and that his tolerance of previous views stops short of any doctrine defending a transcendent reality beyond nature. G. Boas, "Instrumentalism and the History of Philosophy," in *John Dewey: Philosopher of Science and Freedom*, edited by S. Hook, maintains that anyone faithful to temporalism must accept the obsolescence of doctrines on a transcendent reality, and adds: "I see no way of an Instrumentalist's answering the question of why obsolete ideas survive except anthropologically" (85). Faithfulness to the *temporal* character of nature is different from fidelity to *temporalism*, however, since the former does not stipulate that the temporal and eternal ways of being must be incompatible. Hence there is more to the persistence of the problem of God than is provided by an anthropological explanation: it is a question raised for human intelligence precisely by the temporality of our experience of natural things and human societies.

19. *Influence of Darwin*, 259.

20. *Ibid.*, 24-25.

21. *Ibid.*, 8-9. In a letter to William James (March 27, 1903), Dewey states that his own instrumental analysis of active process in nature and scientific inquiry results in the subordination of both idea and fact, both idealism and pragmatism, to a naturalism stressing the ongoing active process of nature and inquiry. The letter is found in R. B. Perry, *The Thought and Character of William James*, II, 522-23; also see 528. His philosophy is thus viewed as fulfilling and moving beyond the previous trends in modern science and philosophy.

22. *Influence of Darwin*, 10.

23. Dewey finally rejects the view that causation involves a productive efficient agency and necessarily determining force. Thus he hopes to remove the philosophical inference to either a powerful God or an absolute self-consciousness, as well as the appeal of Spencer to natural causal tendencies as the basis of

ethics. See John Dewey: "The Superstition of Necessity," *The Monist*, 3 (1892-93), 362-79; "The Ego as Cause," *The Philosophical Review*, 3 (1894), 337-41. In the latter article, Dewey uses the reduction of causality to uniform conditions in order to close off the inference to the ego as a separate causal agent.

24. *Influence of Darwin*, 44.

25. *Influence of Darwin*, 262, 269.

26. M. R. Cohen, *Studies in Philosophy and Science*, 140, objects that Dewey's naturalism is too anthropocentric and that "it offers no vistas of nature beyond the human scene." But Dewey does maintain that the traits of nature found within our experience and required for scientific inquiry are also characteristic of the rest of nature. The pertinent criticism is that the integrity of these traits and their philosophical importance do not depend necessarily upon any closure of inquiry within the man-and-nature circuit. On Dewey's effort to identify this closure with the experimental way in philosophy, consult C. W. Hendel, "The New Empiricism and the Philosophical Tradition," in *John Dewey and the Experimental Spirit in Philosophy*, edited by C. W. Hendel, 1-31.

27. See especially the first and last chapters of *Experience and Nature*.

Chapter 9 HUMANISTIC NATURALISM IN MARX AND DEWEY

1. The major philosophical sections of Marx's early *Economic and Philosophical Manuscripts* are translated by T. B. Bottomore, as the second part of Erich Fromm's book, *Marx's Concept of Man*, 87-196. One cannot rely upon Fromm for a precise and adequate interpretation of Marx's philosophical position, however, but must turn for this to Robert Tucker, *Philosophy and Myth in Karl Marx*. Tucker shows that eventually Marx's humanism is internally weakened by being regulated by the dialectical myth about the proletariat as embodying all human potentialities. For a descriptive report, cf. H. P. Adams, *Karl Marx in His Earlier Writings*. The fundamental philosophical issues faced by Marx and Engels prior to 1848 are described at length, and from a sympathetically Marxian viewpoint, by Auguste Cornu, *Karl Marx et Friedrich Engels*. Cornu has summarized his findings in the brief but pointed monograph, *The Origins of Marxian Thought*.

2. The best analysis is made by George Cottier, *L'Athéisme du jeune Marx*, who stresses the Hegelian origins of Marx's atheism and criticizes the latter for offering us the model of atheistic man without troubling to furnish the verification for the validity of this model. From a Marxist position, Luc Somerhausen stresses the intimate link between atheism and Marxian humanism, in *L'Humanisme agissant de Karl Marx*.

3. On the relation between Marx and Feuerbach, see Sidney Hook, *From Hegel to Marx*, 220-307. Here, and especially in his *Towards the Understanding of Karl Marx*, Hook reformulates Marx's thought in order to show its affinity on many points with that of Dewey.

4. The connection between Marx's humanism and his application of the estrangement theory to religion and property is brought out firmly in H. Bartoli, *La Doctrine économique et sociale de Karl Marx*, especially part one. A Marxist presentation of the biographical materials which make this connection understandable is made by M. Rubel, *Karl Marx: Essai de biographie intellectuelle*. In English, Isaiah Berlin's *Karl Marx: His Life and Environment* remains a fine account.

5. Most of the philosophical texts of Marx on man in nature and society are collected in *Marx and Engels: Basic Writings on Politics and Philosophy*, edited by L. S. Feuer. The Marxist theory of man is explained and evaluated favorably

in terms of a nontheistic humanism by Vernon Venable, *Human Nature: The Marxian View.*

6. For a Christian phenomenological appreciation and criticism of this theme in Marx, cf. R. C. Kwant, O.S.A., *Philosophy of Labor,* 59-91.

7. The humanistic element in Marx's social and economic analyses is underlined by Pierre Bigo, S.J., *Marxisme et humanisme: Introduction à l'oeuvre économique de Karl Marx,* who then criticizes Marxian humanism by showing how it depends upon a frozen view of property. Much the same kind of criticism could be made of Marxian humanism, insofar as it presupposes a frozen view of religion.

8. The continuing difficulties of Soviet theoreticians in trying to maintain some definite type of materialism, while not renouncing humanistic initiative, are brought out by Gustav Wetter, S.J., *Dialectical Materialism: A Historical and Systematic Survey of Philosophy in the Soviet Union.*

9. The dialectical structure of Marxian philosophy is carefully explained and evaluated by Jean Calvez, S.J., *La Pensée de Karl Marx.*

10. Cf. M. M. Bober, *Karl Marx's Interpretation of History.* There is an interesting criticism of Marx for confusing causal and structural meanings for the laws of history, in A. G. Meyer, *Marxism: The Unity of Theory and Practice.*

11. This is the tenor of Dewey's essay in *Naturalism and the Human Spirit,* edited by Y. H. Krikorian, a co-operative volume of essays by the leading American naturalists.

12. This restricted experimentalist pluralism is best stated in *Experience and Nature,* and is prolonged in *Art as Experience.*

13. The social-biological pattern of his philosophical method is maturely stated in Dewey's *Logic: The Theory of Inquiry.* For a personalist and theist criticism of Dewey's experimentalist naturalism, see John E. Smith, "John Dewey: Philosopher of Experience," in *John Dewey and the Experimental Spirit in Philosophy,* edited by C. W. Hendel, 93-119.

14. Dewey's polemic against the eternalistic spectator attitude predominates his Gifford Lectures, *The Quest for Certainty.*

15. Dewey, in *A Common Faith,* 51-52, recommended that the word "God" should stand for the active union between the ideal and the actual in our social life. Some people mistakenly concluded that he was admitting a minimal theism thereby, but he replied that he was only giving a recommendation for a proper definition. Cf. Corliss Lamont, "New Light on Dewey's *Common Faith,*" *The Journal of Philosophy,* 58 (1961), 21-28, where Dewey is quoted as saying in a letter to Lamont: "I have come to think of my own position as cultural or humanistic Naturalism. Naturalism, properly interpreted, seems to me a more adequate term than Humanism. . . . As to the Humanistic Society [supported by Lamont himself], as I told you before, I limit my acceptance of Humanism to religious matters where its meaning in opposition to supernaturalism is definite in significance." (26, 27) Dewey liked the Humanist Society's repudiation of the reality of God and the supernatural, but he also felt the need for joining this humanism with a rigorous naturalistic logic and theory of nature and society. Consult the debate between J. A. Auer and J. Hartt, *Humanism versus Theism,* on whether theism is compatible with humanism.

16. There is a good deal of discussion at present concerning the ethical implications of humanistic naturalism, as found in Dewey and the contributors to the Krikorian volume, *Naturalism and the Human Spirit.* A naturalistic defense is made by Patrick Romanell, *Toward a Critical Naturalism.* There are two penetrating critical appraisals of American naturalism and its ethical consequences. Eliseo Vivas' *The Moral Life and the Ethical Life* charts a philosophical course which began in naturalism (Vivas was a contributor to the Krikorian volume)

and which moved gradually toward axiological realism, with the aid of a highly personal use of the phenomenological method to establish the reality of values and ethical demands. In *Ethical Naturalism and the Modern World-View*, E. M. Adams maintains that "value-requiredness is a unique categorial feature of reality known to us through our affective-conative experiences, which I contend are cognitive in nature. . . . Metaphysical naturalism (and thus ethical naturalism as well) is wrong, I argue, precisely because it counts only our sensory experiences and thought confirmable in terms of them as cognitive." (ix) Thus the ethical issue cannot be treated without raising the ultimate questions in method and metaphysics about nature and the knowable. The epistemological basis for a non-naturalistic theory of being and value is treated in E. W. Hall's *Our Knowledge of Fact and Value*. The contemporary case for naturalism is most ably argued in Sidney Hook's collection of essays, *The Quest for Being*. Yet he does not recognize the crucial distinction between God and an idea of God drawn from the Hegelian theory of the absolute, and does not satisfactorily account for the unity and purposive striving of beings by referring them solely to human interests.

Chapter 10 THE PROBLEM OF A PERENNIAL PHILOSOPHY

1. Maurice De Wulf, *History of Mediaeval Philosophy*, II, 333-350. Etienne Gilson's conception of medieval philosophy is best stated in *History of Christian Philosophy in the Middle Ages*.
2. See Erich Przywara's two books: *Polarity* and *Analogia Entis*. Reports on continental theological and philosophical uses of perennial philosophy are made in two articles by R. F. Harvanek, S.J.: "Philosophical Pluralism and Catholic Orthodoxy," *Thought*, 25 (1950), 21-52, and "The Church and Scholasticism," *Proceedings of the American Catholic Philosophical Association*, 32 (1958), 215-225.
3. Immanuel Kant, *Critique of Pure Reason*, N. K. Smith translation, 666-669.
4. Karl Jaspers gives two summaries of his conception of a perennial philosophy: *The Perennial Scope of Philosophy*, 173-176, and *Way to Wisdom*, 159-163. In chapter two above, we have seen how Jaspers bases his distinction between science and philosophy partly on the difference between scientific progress and philosophic perenniality.
5. For Heidegger's position, see J. Collins, *The Existentialists: A Critical Study*, 176-185.
6. Urban summed up his position in two notable chapters in two different books: "The Return to Perennial Philosophy: The Conditions of Philosophic Intelligibility," *The Intelligible World: Metaphysics and Value*, 171-205; and "Realism, Idealism and *Philosophia Perennis*," *Beyond Realism and Idealism*, 239-63.

Urban's version of the Perennial Philosophy or the Great Tradition is an axiological idealism, which attempts to overcome the conflict between idealism and realism. These alternatives are overcome, however, only by reinterpreting realism to mean that the ultimate object of knowledge is idea or essence. Once this postulate is accepted, there is no difficulty in conflating realism with objective idealism. Urban admits that this sort of realism is incompatible with the Thomistic emphasis upon the physical world as a point of departure, upon sensation as a principle of human knowledge and metaphysics, and upon the existential and sensuous import of the distinctively human type of intellectual intuition. "An intellectual intuition can be only of ideas or essences, and this is the very heart of idealism in the traditional sense; only an ideal world is ultimately intelligible" (*Beyond Realism and Idealism,* 254). Between such a position and an existential realism there is a genuine and irreducible metaphysical opposition.

7. P. Häberlin, *Philosophia Perennis: Eine Zusammenfassung,* 15-18.

8. S. Radhakrishnan, general editor, *History of Philosophy Eastern and Western,* II, 443-48. Cf. the conclusion of the chapter on St. Thomas and note 11 (II, 167-68), stressing that God's essence remains unknown to us.

9. F. S. Northrop, *The Meeting of East and West: An Inquiry Concerning World Understanding;* A. Huxley, *The Perennial Philosophy.*

10. Consult, for instance, Leibniz's *Discourse on Metaphysics,* section 11, "That the opinions of the theologians and of the so-called scholastic philosophers are not to be wholly despised," in *Leibniz Selections,* edited by P. P. Wiener, 303-304; see also 302-303, 318-20.

11. For an attempt to give a theistic restatement of Hegel's view of the history of metaphysics, read F. Sawicki, "Die Geschichtsphilosophie als philosophia perennis," in *Philosophia Perennis,* edited by F. J. von Rintelen, I, 513-25.

12. In "Métaphysique et relativité historique," *Revue de Métaphysique et de Morale,* 57 (1952), 381-414, L. B. Geiger, O.P., defends the transhistorical stability of the basic metaphysical truths of being and of the threefold principle of resolution for philosophical knowledge (resolution to sense, to being, and to the principle of contradiction). Far from being incompatible with historicity, these ontological data alone make change meaningful and genuinely historical. They are permanent and accessible to all men, because they express what is common to all historical situations and individual differences. But acceptance of them does not entail acceptance of the normative theory of a perennial philosophy.

13. An instance of irreducible philosophical opposition is provided by Wilbur Urban. He excludes the Aristotelian-Thomistic epistemology from the genuine tradition of the perennial philosophy, to the extent that this epistemology accepts sensation as a primary source and reliable norm of knowledge, takes the physical existent object as the starting point of philosophy, and reaches God only through a demonstration from the data of the sensible world. On all these scores, he regards idealism as the standard of perennial philosophy. "It takes God, not man, as its starting point, being, not sensation, as its initial option" (*Beyond Realism and Idealism,* 258). The only kind of realism which Urban succeeds in reconciling with this sort of perennial idealism is one that surrenders precisely the distinguishing marks of a realistic theism. Clearly, this question concerns primarily the nature of metaphysical thinking itself. It cannot be settled by a normative appeal to the notion of a perennial philosophy, since the metaphysical conflict leads to irreconcilable conceptions of what a perennial philosophy is. Here, as everywhere else that the question of a perennial philosophy is discussed, what is at stake is precisely the meaning of perennial philosophy. Such radical questioning can only be resolved by having recourse to some extra-perennialist considerations about human knowledge and the history of philosophy.

14. Cf. Johannes Hirschberger, *The History of Philosophy.*

Chapter 11 TOWARD A PHILOSOPHICALLY ORDERED THOMISM

1. Etienne Gilson, *The Christian Philosophy of St. Thomas Aquinas,* 442-443, n. 33.

2. Émile Bréhier, *Histoire de la philosophie,* tome I: *L'Antiquité et le moyen âge.*

3. Jacques Maritain, *An Essay on Christian Philosophy,* 11-31.

4. Maritain, *On the Philosophy of History,* 39, n. 25.

5. Gilson, *The Spirit of Mediaeval Philosophy,* 18.

6. Gilson, *Christianity and Philosophy*, 131, n. 9.

7. See Michael Foster, *Mystery and Philosophy*, and Hermann Dooyeweerd, *A New Critique of Theoretical Thought*.

8. Gilson, *The Christian Philosophy of St. Thomas Aquinas*, 14-15.

9. *Ibid.*, 21-22.

10. *Ibid.*, 29. A recapitulation of Gilson's position is made by A. C. Pegis, "Thomism as a Philosophy," in *The McAuley Lectures, 1960: Saint Thomas Aquinas and Philosophy*, by E. Gilson and A. C. Pegis, 15-30.

11. *The Christian Philosophy of St. Thomas Aquinas*, chapter one, "Existence and Reality," 29-45.

12. *Ibid.*, 94.

13. Cf. Maritain, *On the Philosophy of History*, 24-34.

14. Gilson, *Christianity and Philosophy*, 101.

15. See the chapters on Malebranche and Pascal in Gilson and Langan, *Modern Philosophy from Descartes to Kant*. An autobiographical approach to the question is taken in Gilson's *The Philosopher and Theology*.

Chapter 12 LEO XIII AND THE PHILOSOPHICAL APPROACH TO MODERNITY

1. The most durable commentary continues to be that by F. Ehrle, S.J., *Zur Enzyklika "Aeterni Patris": Text und Kommentar*, newly edited by F. Pelster, S.J., 110-113. Ehrle observes that the encyclical seeks to quicken Christian philosophy as a way of treating modern questions, not merely to reproduce the thought of the past.

2. Propositions 11 and 14 in the Syllabus of Errors, appended to Pius IX's encyclical *Quanta Cura*. There is a convenient translation in *The Papal Encyclicals in Their Historical Context*, edited by Anne Fremantle, 144-145. Compare Propositions 10, 144. For Leo's relationships with his age, see R. H. Schmandt, "The Life and Work of Leo XIII," in *Leo XIII and the Modern World*, edited by E. T. Gargan, 15-48. B. O'Reilly's old-fashioned *Life of Leo XIII*, 226-35, gives excerpts from Archbishop Pecci's 1864 Lenten pastoral on current errors.

3. The translation of *Aeterni Patris* annotated by E. Gilson is used here. Page references are made to the translation as printed in J. Maritain, *St. Thomas Aquinas*, because Appendix III (179-266) of this book contains the major recent papal documents on St. Thomas and Christian philosophy. For the quoted text, see *Aeterni Patris*, paragraph 2 (Maritain, 184-85). Also, Pope Leo's Letter "Dum vitiatae," *Acta Sanctae Sedis*, 13 (1880-81), 3.

4. *Aeterni Patris*, par. 29 (Maritain, 206-207). See also, Leo XIII, "Ut mysticam Sponsam," *Motu Proprio A.S.S.*, 23 (1890-91), 523; Pius XII, *Humani Generis*, par. 29 (text in Maritain, *St. Thomas Aquinas*, 257-58).

5. Along with the texts cited below in notes 7 and 16, see the Allocution "Pergratus Nobis," *A.S.S.*, 12 (1879-80), 487; and the Letter "Quod in novissimo," *Acta Leonis XIII*, 2 (1883-87), 263.

6. This recent development is explained in J. Collins, *The Existentialists: A Critical Study*, 212-20.

7. *Aeterni Patris*, par. 9 (Maritain, 192). It should be noted that Pope Leo is relating the act of philosophizing with the influence of the Christian faith, without requiring the use of the theological order of development. For a different reading of the text and its implications, consult E. Gilson, "What Is Christian Philosophy?" in *A Gilson Reader*, 185-87.

8. *Aeterni Patris*, par. 24 (Maritain, 203-204); *Immortale Dei*, par. 10, translation in J. Husslein, S.J., *Social Wellsprings*, Vol. I: *Fourteen Epochal Documents*

418

by Pope Leo XIII, 76. Apart from *Aeterni Patris,* Leo's translated encyclicals are cited from Husslein's volume.

9. *Aeterni Patris,* par. 8, 29-30 (Maritain, 191, 207-208); Pius XI, *Studiorum Ducem* (text in Maritain, St. Thomas Aquinas, 231-32). See the Apostolic Letter "Cum hoc sit" (in the form of a Brief signed by Cardinal Mertel), which establishes St. Thomas as patron of all Catholic schools. There (*A.S.S.,* 13 [1880-81], 57-58), we are assured that St. Thomas's way of relating reason and the Christian faith results in a noble service of philosophical intelligence rather than a demeaning servitude, since he retains the distinction of offices between philosophical demonstration of truths from a study of natural things and faith as an acceptance of truths coming from God as their author. The contrast between *servitus* and *obsequium* is reminiscent of the views of M. Liberatore, S.J.

10. Read, for instance, the Letter "Susceptum a Nobis," reprinted conveniently along with Pope Leo's other letters on the Thomistic chair and Institute of Philosophy at Louvain in the Appendices to L. de Raeymaeker, *Le Cardinal Mercier et l'Institut Supérieur de Louvain,* 241-243.

11. This is brought out in three historical studies devoted, respectively, to epistemology, metaphysics, and ethics: G. Van Riet, *L'épistémologie thomiste,* 32-133; J. Gurr, S.J., *The Principle of Sufficient Reason in Some Scholastic Systems, 1750-1900,* 121-158; R. Jacquin, *Taparelli,* 51-57, 168-74. The decisive influence of Leo XIII and *Aeterni Patris* is recognized by all three scholars. B. Bonansea, O.F.M., "Pioneers of the Nineteenth-century Scholastic Revival in Italy," *The New Scholasticism,* 28 (1954), 1-37, is mainly a summary of Van Riet. For the theological side of the same story, see E. Hocedez, S.J., *Histoire de la théologie au XIXe siècle,* I, 49-60; II, 347-364; III, 41-52, 351-394.

12. *Aeterni Patris,* par. 31 (Maritain, 208). See the interpretative remarks of E. Soderini, *The Pontificate of Leo XIII,* 129-130. The passage in *Pascendi* where Pius X quotes this text of his predecessor is presented in Maritain, *St. Thomas Aquinas,* p. 136. In the same tradition, Pius XII mentions the ways in which Christian philosophy can be enriched today, even in regard to fundamental doctrines: *Humani Generis,* par. 30 (Maritain, 258-59).

13. *Immortale Dei,* par. 19 (Husslein, 85); *Libertas Praestantissimum,* par. 20 (Husslein, 132). See R. Fülöp-Miller, *Leo XIII and Our Times,* 41.

14. The text is given in *Philosophical Readings in Cardinal Newman,* edited by James Collins, 283.

15. Letter "Iampridem," *A.S.S.,* 12 (1879-80), 227; Letters "Instituto" and "Per alias literas," reprinted in De Raeymaeker, *op. cit.,* 231, 237 (especially the second sentence in each letter); Letter "Quod in novissimo," *Acta Leonis XIII,* 2 (1883-87), 262-63. Also, Pius XII, *Humani Generis,* par. 9-10 (Maritain, 248).

16. *Aeterni Patris,* par. 24 (Maritain, 204). Cf. Letter "Quod opera," *Acta Leonis XIII,* 3 (1887-89), 292.

17. De Raeymaeker, *op. cit.,* gives the record of Mercier's achievements at Louvain.

18. A ready introduction to Maréchal is provided in *Mélanges Joseph Maréchal,* I, 3-101, containing a sketch of his work, a genetic essay, a bibliography, and Marechal's own summary of the argument in his chief work, *Le Point de départ de la métaphysique.* For a restatement in terms of modern science, see B. J. Lonergan, *Insight.*

19. See J. Collins, "Olgiati's Conception of Modern Philosophy," *Thought,* 18 (1943), 478-504. Beginning with the third volume of his *History of Philosophy,* F. C. Copleston, S.J., treats of Renaissance and modern thinkers. His *Contemporary Philosophy* deals critically and constructively with logical positivism and existentialism. Copleston's noteworthy series of articles on "Man and Metaphysics," in the first volume of *The Heythrop Journal* (1960), provides a modern defense of metaphysical inference.

20. Maritain's range of thought is described in two co-operative volumes of essays: *The Maritain Volume of The Thomist*, 5 (1943), and *The Social and Political Philosophy of Jacques Maritain*, edited by J. W. Evans and Leo R. Ward.

21. This problem is explored particularly in respect to existential phenomenology by A. Dondeyne, *Contemporary European Thought and Christian Faith*.

22. *Aeterni Patris*, par. 24 (Maritain, 204).

23. *James* 1, 5; quoted in *Aeterni Patris*, par. 32 (Maritain, 209). In his study of *La Philosophie catholique en France au XIXᵉ siècle avant la renaissance thomiste et dans son rapport avec elle* (1800-1880), especially 237-68, L. Foucher suggests that the issuance of *Aeterni Patris* corresponded with the view of tradition-minded French Catholic philosophers of the nineteenth century that the spiritual authority of the Church should provide some decisive guidance in unifying Christian intellectual life around a sound, enduring philosophy of a nonrationalistic kind and open to the wisdom of the faith.

Chapter 13 ANALYTIC PHILOSOPHY AND DEMONSTRATIVE THEISM

1. This remark is made by W. P. Alston in his review of E. L. Mascall, *Words and Images*. See *The Philosophical Review*, 68 (1959), 410. What makes Mascall's book disappointing is its failure to stress the different analytic procedures required for different notions of the philosophy of God. The background of the analytic movement is well described by M. J. Charlesworth, *Philosophy and Linguistic Analysis*.

2. A. J. Ayer and F. C. Copleston, S.J., "Logical Positivism—A Debate," in *A Modern Introduction to Philosophy*, edited by P. Edwards and A. Pap, 586-618.

3. John Hospers, *An Introduction to Philosophical Analysis*, 331.

4. "The Nature of Theological Discourse," a symposium by Jason Xenakis, J. Collins, J. Wisdom, V. C. Aldrich, and P. Wheelwright, in *The Christian Scholar*, 41 (1958), 601-13.

5. "Can God's Existence be Disproved?" a symposium by J. N. Findlay, G. E. Hughes, and A. C. A. Rainer, in *New Essays in Philosophical Theology*, edited by A. Flew and A. MacIntyre, 47-75.

6. Austin Farrer, "A Starting-Point for the Philosophical Examination of Theological Belief," in *Faith and Logic*, edited by B. Mitchell, 9-30.

7. I. M. Crombie, contribution to "Theology and Falsification," in *New Essays in Philosophical Theology*, 110.

8. *Ibid.*, 111.

9. *Ibid.*, 112, 116; I. M. Crombie, "The Possibility of Theological Statements," in *Faith and Logic*, 56.

10. *Ibid.*, 35.

11. "Theology and Falsification," a symposium by A. Flew, R. M. Hare, B. Mitchell, and I. M. Crombie, in *New Essays in Philosophical Theology*, 96-130.

12. R. Demos, "The Meaningfulness of Religious Language," *Philosophy and Phenomenological Research*, 18 (1957-58), 96-106. W. E. Kennick, "The Language of Religion," *The Philosophical Review*, 65 (1956), 56-71, subordinates the cognitive element in religious language to the prime function of evoking attitudes which are all-pervasive and deemed most important. S. Toulmin, "Contemporary Scientific Mythology," in *Metaphysical Beliefs*, by S. Toulmin, R. W. Hepburn, and A. MacIntyre, 13-81, probes into some mythic aspects of the scientific outlook which also have an evocative function to perform. For R. M. Hare's theory of the *blik*, see *New Essays in Philosophical Theology*, 99-103.

13. "Theology and Falsification," in *New Essays in Philosophical Theology*, 108 (Flew on Orwell's notion of doublethink), 118 f. (Crombie on the parable situa-

tion). A. MacIntyre, "Faith and the Verification Principle," in *Metaphysical Beliefs*, 181-83, criticizes Crombie for having an incomplete verification and hence a tentative religious adherence, as well as for overlooking the case where the harsh side of nature clears the way for assent to God. But Crombie does not base the truth-adherence to theological statements on the verification process, so that the latter's incompleteness only preserves mystery without reducing the doctrine itself to a hypothesis.

14. G. C. Stead, "How Theologians Reason," in *Faith and Logic*, 114-16.

15. I. M. Crombie, "The Possibility of Theological Statements," in *Faith and Logic*, especially 39-56.

16. *Ibid.*, 67-68.

17. "Here is the one ontological claim on which he [the religious philosopher] cannot yield. *To have distinctively religious language at all, there must be situations not restricted to the spatio-temporal elements they contain*" (I. T. Ramsey, "Empiricism and Religion. A Critique of Ryle's *Concept of Mind*," *The Christian Scholar*, 39 [1956], 162).

18. I. T. Ramsey, *Religious Language*, 11-48.

19. *Ibid.*, 49-89, based on the language of natural theology. In the remainder of the book, Ramsey extends this analysis to the language of the Bible and of Christian doctrine.

20. I. T. Ramsey, *Religious Language*, 185 (one quotation mark is modified). See his further remarks on this point in "Empiricism and Religion," *art. cit.*, 163.

21. The need for more precise thinking on the theistic aspect of the causal problem is evident from the attempt made in the unsigned article on "Theism" in *The Concise Encyclopedia of Western Philosophy and Philosophers*, edited by J. O. Urmson, to have it both ways. The writer of the article criticizes every causal inference to God on the ground that "Hume has shown that it only makes sense to speak of causal relations as holding between observable states of affairs." (377) Then he goes on to observe that "the chief difficulty in advancing a proof of, or argument for, the existence of God lies not in the difficulties over such concepts as those of causality, but in the elementary logical point that in a valid proof nothing can appear in the conclusion which was not already contained in the premises. A valid proof of God's existence could therefore be nothing other than the making explicit of a belief which was implicit in the premises." (378) The first criticism is based on a conventional acceptance of Hume's phenomenalism. But the point at issue in causal theory is precisely whether every knowable causal dependence must be stated only in phenomenalistic terms or whether it refers basically to the composed character of experienced beings. Realistic theism explores this second meaning for causal statements, and hence any analysis of theistic discourse along this second path must come back to an extra-linguistic and metaphysical discussion of causality. And if the latter meaning for the causal relation is admitted as governing some theistic discourse, then the elementary logical point cited in the second quotation does not settle anything. The theistic realist may or may not adhere to God through an act of religious faith. In either case, his philosophical work on the problem of God is not structured as an explicitation of his religious faith. That faith may be implicit or quite explicit in his mind as he engages in the theistic inquiry. But insofar as the inquiry of the theistic realist is a philosophically based and ordered one, his task is to ascertain whether or not the causal analysis of experienced beings requires him to accept a dependence of their being upon the being of the uncomposed cause, God. The proposition about God's existence can be included in his philosophy as a well grounded truth only through the outcome of such inquiry. That is why the previously discussed issue of achieving philosophical order as well as evidence in one's philosophy of God is crucial for a realistic theism which must treat such arguments as this.

The distinctively metaphysical and non-phenomenalistic meaning of causality is explored by W. Norris Clarke, S.J., "Causality and Time," in *Experience, Existence, and the Good*, edited by I. C. Lieb, 143-157.

22. Frederick Ferré's *Language, Logic and God* makes an able summary of the various positions already taken on the analysis of theistic language, and recognizes the presence of a manifold logic in theism. Just as there are many ways to God, so there must be many modes of analysis which respect the differently intended patterns of discourse on God. However, Ferré views the plurality of modes of logical analysis as being governed by various ways in which theological statements and imagery illuminate our understanding of the world. Realistic theism includes the function of illumination within the more radical question of the philosophically ascertainable validity and inferential basis for statements about God which claim our philosophical assent. As is pointed out by Joseph Owens, C.Ss.R., "St. Thomas and Elucidation," *The New Scholasticism*, 35 (1961), 421-444, a realistic theism sets itself the task of integrating the analytic elucidation of meaning with the metaphysical validation of causal inference bearing on God. For an analytic approach to God and the causal problem in St. Thomas, see G. E. M. Anscombe and P. T. Geach, *Three Philosophers: Aristotle, Aquinas, Frege*, 109-125. An attempt is made there to reach God as maker of the world as a whole, without considering the different kinds of causal acts required for particular existent things in experience. The metaphysical reconstruction of the theistic argument which must be done when one passes from the theological setting in St. Thomas to a consideration of Kantian and analytic difficulties is outlined in Edward Sillem's *Ways of Thinking about God*. Sillem leaves unsettled the extent to which St. Thomas himself furnishes some properly philosophical aids for this reconstruction, even within his own theological context.

The naturalistic contributors to the symposium, *Religious Experience and Truth*, edited by Sidney Hook, press the need to consider verifiable truth, as well as self-consistent linguistic usage and meaningful human experience, in the question of God and religion. The special worth of M. C. D'Arcy's *No Absent God* is its suggestion that the truth as well as the meaning of theism is verified in the theist's growth of self and of a capacity to interpret human life.

Chapter 14   HUSSERL AND THE BOND OF NATURAL BEING

1. Husserl develops the contrast between his own first philosophy of the transcendental ego and its intentional life and an existential metaphysics in his Freiburg lectures, *Erste Philosophie (1923/24)*, edited by Rudolf Boehm. In the first volume, he applies his own technique of a critical history of ideas to the notions about a first philosophy advanced since the time of Plato and Aristotle. Whereas J. S. Mill's first philosophy is psychology, Husserl's first philosophy is a transcendental intentional logic.

2. Maurice Merleau-Ponty, *Signes*, 201-228. His critical remarks on the meanings of "the natural attitude" are relevant for the following section of this paper.

The weakness in John Wild's "The Exploration of the Life-World," *Proceedings and Addresses of the American Philosophical Association*, 1960-1961, 5-23, lies in its failure to follow Husserl and Merleau-Ponty in taking seriously the skeptical and phenomenalist interpretations of the life world itself.

3. This is a major topic in these two writings by Husserl: "Philosophy as a Strict Science," translated with notes by Quentin Lauer, S.J., in *Cross Currents*, 6 (1956), 227-246, 325-344; *Ideen zu einer reinen Phänomenologie und phänomenologischen Philosophie, Erstes Buch*, edited by Walter Biemel.

4. See Aron Gurwitsch, "The Problem of Existence in Constitutive Phenomenology," *The Journal of Philosophy*, 58 (1961), 625-632.

5. I employ this method also in treating the modern conceptions of wisdom, in *The Lure of Wisdom*, 141-48.

6. This theme is developed in detail in Husserl's *Ideen zu einer reinen Phänomenologie und phänomenologischen Philosophie, Zweites Buch* and *Drittes Buch*, edited by Marly Biemel.

7. In *Die Krisis der europäischen Wissenschaften und die transzendentale Phänomenologie*, edited by Walter Biemel, 70-71, Husserl distinguishes transcendental subjectivity from naturalistically interpreted man, but also notes the historical development of a subjectivism in the transcendental style.

8. The concept of thing is studied in terms of object by R. O. Johann, S.J., "Subjectivity," *The Review of Metaphysics*, 12 (1958), 200-234. That it is more fundamental in metaphysics to consider men and things as existents or subjects-in-being than as epistemological subject and object is argued by Kenneth Schmitz, "Toward a Metaphysical Restoration of Natural Things," in *An Etienne Gilson Tribute*, edited by C. J. O'Neil, 245-262. The distinction between person and physical thing can be drawn within the broad meaning of thing as a determinately existing subject in being. See J. E. Smith, *Reason and God*, 130-133, on extending existence beyond man to other beings.

9. This is the aim of part three of *Die Krisis* and of the shorter pieces printed with it.

10. For an analytic comparison of Husserl with Hegel and Marx in respect to our natural experiences, cf. Alphonse De Waelhens, *La Philosophie et les expériences naturelles*, with stress upon the grasp of being implied in particular temporal works of man. But De Waelhens does not permit his phenomenology to make any inference to the being of God.

11. At this point, the questions asked in the three following articles can be formally considered in human experiential terms, without regarding our humanity as a realizing of the *a priori* structures in transcendental reason: L. J. Eslick, "What Is the Starting Point of Metaphysics?" *The Modern Schoolman*, 34 (1956-57), 247-263; G. P. Klubertanz, S.J., "Where Is the Evidence for Thomistic Metaphysics?" *Revue Philosophique de Louvain*, 56 (1958), 294-315; R. J. Henle, S.J., "A Phenomenological Approach to Realism," in *An Etienne Gilson Tribute*, 68-85. Henle's method of reflection on experience is not a Husserlian sort of phenomenology, and the ordinary knowledge which he analyzes remains distinct in principle from scientific knowledge and hence is not the same as the natural attitude dealt with here.

12. Whitehead moves in the direction of this controlling natural reality with his reformed subjectivist principle, uniting the Cartesian subjectivist experience of the self with the Humean objectivist data in actual perception. See *Process and Reality*, 238-254. But the metaphysical reform must be carried out more radically than the subject-object distinction permits by centering the reflective judgment upon natural beings as existing, acting, and tending, in their diverse sorts of actuality. The modern values of scientific objectivity and philosophical subjectivity must be retained and deepened within the reformed principle of existent being which is proposed here as the basic referent for philosophical reflection.

Chapter 15 THOMISM IN THE COLLEGE

1. H. I. Marrou, *A History of Education in Antiquity*, 220.
2. Jacques Maritain, *On the Philosophy of History*, 3.
3. Robert J. Henle, S.J., "Science and the Humanities," *Thought*, 35 (1960), 531-532.

BIBLIOGRAPHY

This List supplies the bibliographical information concerning the books, articles, and other items mentioned in the *Notes*. Thus it can be used as a checklist for some of the major contributions on the contemporary topics dealt with in the book.

I. *Books*

Adams, E. M. *Ethical Naturalism and the Modern World-View*. Chapel Hill: University of North Carolina Press, 1960.

Adams, H. P. *Karl Marx in His Earlier Writings*. London: Allen and Unwin, 1940.

Allers, Rudolf. *Existentialism and Psychiatry*. Springfield: Thomas, 1961.

Anscombe, G. E. M., and P. T. Geach. *Three Philosophers: Aristotle, Aquinas and Frege*. Ithaca: Cornell University Press, 1961.

Auer, J. A., and J. Hartt. *Humanism versus Theism*. Yellow Springs, Ohio: Antioch Press, 1951.

Baillie, John. *The Belief in Progress*. New York: Scribner, 1951.

Baldwin, J. M. *Dictionary of Philosophy and Psychology*. 3 volumes. New York: Macmillan, 1902.

Barlow, N., editor. *Autobiography of Charles Darwin*. New York: Harcourt, Brace, 1958.

Barnes, Hazel E. *The Literature of Possibility*. Lincoln: University of Nebraska Press, 1959.

Barrett, W., and H. D. Aiken. *Philosophy in the Twentieth Century*. 2 volumes. New York: Random House, 1962.

Bartoli, H. *La Doctrine économique et sociale de Karl Marx*. Paris: Éditions du Seuil, 1950.

Beckett, Samuel. *Waiting for Godot*. New York: Grove Press, 1954.

Bergson, H. *Creative Evolution*. New York: Modern Library, 1944.

———. *The Creative Mind*. New York: Philosophical Library, 1946.

———. *Écrits et paroles*. Tome I. Paris: Presses Universitaires, 1957.

Berlin, Isaiah. *Karl Marx: His Life and Environment*. New York: Oxford University Press, 1939.

Bigo, Pierre. *Marxisme et humanisme: Introduction à l'oeuvre économique de Karl Marx*. Paris: Presses Universitaires, 1954.

Blewett, John, editor. *John Dewey: His Thought and Influence*. New York: Fordham University Press, 1960.

Bober, M. M. *Karl Marx's Interpretation of History*. Revised second edition. Cambridge: Harvard University Press, 1948.

Bouquet, A. C. *Comparative Religion*. Fourth revised edition. Baltimore: Penguin Books, 1953.

Bréhier, Émile. *Histoire de la philosophie*. Volume I. Paris: Alcan, 1927.

425

Brunner, August. *Die Religion*. Freiburg: Herder, 1956.

Buckham, J. W., and G. M. Stratton. *George Holmes Howison, Philosopher and Teacher: A Selection from His Writings with a Biographical Sketch*. Berkeley: University of California Press, 1934.

Bury, J. B. *The Idea of Progress*. Reprint edition. New York: Dover, 1955.

Calvez, Jean. *La Pensée de Karl Marx*. Paris: Éditions de Seuil, 1956.

Charlesworth, M. J. *Philosophy and Linguistic Analysis*. Pittsburgh: Duquesne University Press, 1959.

Cohen, M. R. *Studies in Philosophy and Science*. New York: Holt, 1949.

Collins, James. *The Existentialists: A Critical Study*. Chicago: Regnery Gateway edition, 1959.

——. *God in Modern Philosophy*. Chicago: Regnery, 1959.

——. *The Lure of Wisdom*. Milwaukee: Marquette University Press, 1962.

——, editor. *Philosophical Readings in Cardinal Newman*. Chicago: Regnery, 1961.

Copleston, F. C. *Contemporary Philosophy*. Westminster: Newman Press, 1956.

——. *History of Philosophy*. Volumes III-VI. Westminster: Newman Press, 1953-1960.

Cornu, Auguste. *Karl Marx and Friedrich Engels*. 2 volumes. Paris: Presses Universitaires, 1955-58.

——. *The Origins of Marxian Thought*. Springfield, Ill.: Thomas, 1957.

Cottier, George. *L'Athéisme du jeune Marx*. Paris: Vrin, 1959.

Cuénot, L. C. *L'Évolution biologique*. Paris: Masson, 1951.

Cuénot, Claude. *Pierre Teilhard de Chardin: Les grandes étapes de son évolution*. Paris: Plon, 1958.

D'Arcy, M. C. *No Absent God*. New York: Harper and Row, 1962.

Darwin, F. *The Life and Letters of Charles Darwin*. 2 volumes. New York: Appleton, 1898.

Darwin, F., and A. C. Seward, editors. *More Letters of Charles Darwin*. 2 volumes. London: Murray, 1903.

De Waelhens, Alphonse. *La Philosophie et les expériences naturelles*. The Hague: Nijhoff, 1961.

De Wulf, Maurice. *History of Mediaeval Philosophy*. Third English edition. 2 volumes. New York: Longmans, Green, 1938.

Dewey, John. *Art as Experience*. New York: Putnam, 1934.

——. *Characters and Events*. 2 volumes. New York: Holt, 1929.

——. *A Common Faith*. New Haven: Yale University Press, 1934.

——. *Experience and Nature*. Reprint edition. New York: Dover Publications, 1958.

——. *The Influence of Darwin on Philosophy and Other Essays*. Reprint edition. New York: Peter Smith, 1951.

——. *Logic: The Theory of Inquiry*. New York: Holt, 1938.

——. *The Quest for Certainty*. London: Allen and Unwin, 1930.

—— et al. *Religious Thought at the University of Michigan*. Ann Arbor: Inland Press, 1893.

Dobzhansky, T. *The Biological Basis of Human Freedom*. New York: Columbia University Press, 1956.

——. *Mankind Evolving*. New Haven: Yale University Press, 1962.

Dondeyne, A. *Contemporary European Thought and Christian Faith*. Pittsburgh: Duquesne University Press, 1958.

Dooyeweerd, Hermann. *A New Critique of Theoretical Thought*. 4 volumes. Philadelphia: Presbyterian and Reformed Publishing Co., 1953-58.

Duncan, D. *Life and Letters of Herbert Spencer*. 2 volumes. New York: Appleton, 1908.

426

Dupuy, Maurice. *La Philosophie de la religion chez Max Scheler*. Paris: Presses Universitaires, 1959.

———. *La Philosophie de Max Scheler: Son évolution et son unité*. 2 volumes. Paris: Presses Universitaires, 1959.

Edwards, P., and Pap, A., editors. *A Modern Introduction to Philosophy*. Glencoe: The Free Press, 1957.

Ehrle, F. *Zur Enzyklika "Aeterni Patris": Text und Kommentar*, newly edited by F. Pelster, S.J. Rome: Edizioni di storia e letteratura, 1954.

Eiseley, L. *Darwin's Century*. New York: Doubleday, 1958.

Evans, J. W., and Ward, L. R., editors. *The Social and Political Philosophy of Jacques Maritain*. New York: Scribner, 1955.

Ferré, Frederick. *Language, Logic and God*. New York: Harper, 1961.

Feuer, L. S., editor. *Marx and Engels: Basic Writings on Politics and Philosophy*. New York: Doubleday Anchor, 1959.

Fisher, R. A. *Creative Aspects of the Natural Law*. Cambridge: Cambridge University Press, 1950.

Flew, A., and MacIntyre, A., editors. *New Essays in Philosophical Theology*. London: SCM Press, 1955.

Flores, Angel, editor. *An Anthology of German Poetry from Hölderlin to Rilke*. New York: Doubleday Anchor, 1960.

Foster, M. *Mystery and Philosophy*. London: SCM Press, 1957.

Foucher, L. *La Philosophie catholique en France au siècle avant la renaissance thomiste et dans son rapport avec elle (1800-1880)*. Paris: Vrin, 1955.

Fremantle, Anne, editor. *The Papal Encyclicals in Their Historical Context*. New York: Putnam, 1956.

Fries, H., and Becker. W., editors. *Newman Studien, III*. Nuremberg: Glock and Lutz, 1957.

Fromm, Erich. *Marx's Concept of Man*. With a translation from Marx's *Economic and Philosophic Manuscripts* by T. B. Bottomore. New York: Ungar, 1961.

Fülöp-Miller, R. *Leo XIII and Our Times*. New York: Longmans, Green, 1937.

Gargan, E. T., editor. *Leo XIII and the Modern World*. New York: Sheed and Ward, 1961.

Geiger, G. R. *John Dewey in Perspective*. New York: Oxford University Press, 1958.

Gillispie, C. C. *Genesis and Geology*. Cambridge: Harvard University Press, 1951.

Gilson, Etienne. *The Christian Philosophy of St. Thomas*. New York: Random House, 1956.

———. *Christianity and Philosophy*. New York: Sheed and Ward, 1939.

———. *The Philosopher and Theology*. New York: Random House, 1962.

———. *The Spirit of Mediaeval Philosophy*. New York: Scribner, 1936.

Gilson, E., and T. Langan. *Modern Philosophy from Descartes to Kant*. New York: Random House, 1962.

——— and Pegis, A. C. *The McAuley Lectures, 1960: Saint Thomas and Philosophy*. West Hartford: Saint Joseph College, 1961.

Glass, B., et al. *Forerunners of Darwin, 1745-1859*. Baltimore: Johns Hopkins Press, 1959.

Goudge, T. A. *The Ascent of Life*. Toronto: University of Toronto Press, 1961.

Graef, H. C. *The Scholar and the Cross: The Life and Work of Edith Stein*. Westminster: Newman Press, 1955.

———, editor. *Writings of Edith Stein*. Westminster: Newman Press, 1956.

Greene, J. C. *Darwin and the Modern World View*. Baton Rouge: Louisiana State University Press, 1961.

———. *The Death of Adam*. Ames, Iowa: The Iowa State University Press, 1959.

Gregory, W. K. *Evolution Emerging*. 2 volumes. New York: Macmillan, 1951.

Guardini, Romano. *Rilke's Duino Elegies*. Chicago: Regnery, 1961.

Gurr, J. *The Principle of Sufficient Reason in Some Scholastic Systems, 1750-1900*. Milwaukee: Marquette University Press, 1959.

Häberlin, P. *Philosophia Perennis: Eine Zusammenfassung*. Berlin: Springer, 1952.

Hall, E. W. *Our Knowledge of Fact and Value*. Chapel Hill: University of North Carolina Press, 1961.

Harris, E. *Nature, Mind, and Modern Science*. New York: Macmillan, 1954.

Hartshorne, C., P. Weiss, and A. Burks, editors. *Collected Papers of Charles Sanders Peirce*. 8 volumes. Cambridge: Harvard University Press, 1931-1958.

Heidegger, Martin. *Being and Time*. New York: Harper and Row, 1962.

———. *Essays in Metaphysics*. New York: Philosophical Library, 1961.

———. *Existence and Being*. Chicago: Regnery, 1949.

———. *An Introduction to Metaphysics*. New Haven: Yale University Press, 1959.

———. *The Question of Being*. New York: Twayne, 1958.

———. *Unterwegs zur Sprache*. Pfullingen: Neske, 1959.

———. *What is Philosophy?* New York: Twayne, 1958.

Hendel, C. W., editor. *John Dewey and the Experimental Spirit in Philosophy*. New York: Liberal Arts Press, 1959.

Hessen, Johannes. *Max Scheler: Eine kritische Einführung in seine Philosophie*. Essen: Chamier, 1948.

Hildebrand, Dietrich von. *Zeitliches im Lichte des Ewigen*. Regensburg: Habbel, 1932.

Himmelfarb, G. *Darwin and the Darwinian Revolution*. New York: Doubleday, 1959.

Hirschberger, Johannes. *The History of Philosophy*. 2 volumes. Milwaukee: Bruce, 1959.

Hocedez, E. *Historie de la théologie au XIXe siècle*. 3 volumes. Paris: Desclée De Brouwer, 1947-52.

Hofstadter, R. *Social Darwinism in American Thought*. Revised edition. Boston: Beacon Press, 1955.

Hook, Sidney. *From Hegel to Marx*. New York: Reynal and Hitchcock, 1936.

———, editor. *John Dewey: Philosopher of Science and Freedom*. New York: Dial, 1950.

———. *The Quest for Being*. New York: St. Martin's Press, 1961.

———, editor. *Religious Experience and Truth*. New York: New York University Press, 1961.

———. *Towards the Understanding of Karl Marx*. New York: Day, 1933.

Hospers, John. *An Introduction to Philosophical Analysis*. New York: Prentice-Hall, 1953.

Husserl, Edmund. *Cartesian Meditations*. The Hague: Nijhoff, 1960.

———. *Erste Philosophie (1923/24)*, edited by Rudolf Boehm. 2 volumes. The Hague: Nijhoff, 1956-59. *Husserliana*, volumes VII and VIII.

———. *Ideen zu einer reinen Phänomenologie und phänomenologischen Philosophie, Erstes Buch, Zweites Buch, und Drittes Buch*. Walter and Marly Biemel, editors. The Hague: Nijhoff, 1950-52. *Husserliana*, volumes III, IV, and V.

———. *Die Krisis der europaischen Wissenschaften und die transzendentale Phänomenologie*, edited by Walter Biemel. The Hague: Nijhoff, 1954. *Husserliana*, volume VI.

Husslein, J. *Social Wellsprings*. 2 volumes. Milwaukee: Bruce, 1940.

Huxley, A. *The Perennial Philosophy*. New York: Harper, 1945.

Huxley, J. *Evolution in Action*. New York: Harper, 1953.

——. *Evolution: The Modern Synthesis*. New York: Harper, 1942.

——, editor. *The Humanist Frame*. London: Allen and Unwin, 1961.

——. *Religion without Revelation*. Revised edition. New York: Harper, 1957.

Huxley, J., A. C. Hardy, and E. B. Ford, editors. *Evolution as a Process*. London: Allen and Unwin, 1954.

Huxley, T. H., and Huxley, Julian. *Touchstone for Ethics*. New York: Harper, 1947.

Irvine, W. *Apes, Angels and Victorians*. New York: McGraw-Hill, 1955.

Jacquin, R. *Taparelli*. Paris: Lethielleux, 1943.

Jaspers, Karl. *Allgemeine Psychopathologie*. Fifth edition. Berlin and Heidelberg: Springer, 1948.

——. *Descartes und die Philosophie*. Second edition. Berlin: Walter de Gruyter, 1948.

——. *Existenzphilosophie*. Berlin: Walter de Gruyter, 1938.

——. *Existentialism and Humanism*. New York: R. F. Moore Company, 1952.

——. *The Great Philosophers*. New York: Harcourt, Brace, and World, 1962.

——. *The Idea of a University*. Boston: Beacon Press, 1959.

——. *Man in the Modern Age*. New York: Doubleday Anchor Books, 1957.

Jaspers, Karl, and Bultmann, R. *Myth and Christianity*. New York: Noonday Press, 1958.

Jaspers, Karl. *Nietzsche: Einführung in das Verständnis seines Philosophierens*. Third edition. Berlin: Walter de Gruyter, 1950.

——. *Nietzsche and Christianity*. Chicago: Regnery Gateway, 1961.

——. *The Origin and Goal of History*. New Haven: Yale University Press, 1953.

——. *The Perennial Scope of Philosophy*. New York: Philosophical Library, 1949.

——. *Philosophie*. Second edition. Berlin and Heidelberg: Springer, 1948.

——. *Psychologie der Weltanschauungen*. Third edition. Berlin: Springer, 1925.

——. *Reason and Anti-Reason in Our Time*. New Haven: Yale University Press, 1952.

——. *Rechenschaft und Ausblick*. Munich: Piper, 1951.

——. *Von der Wahrheit*. Munich: Piper, 1957.

——. *Way to Wisdom*. New Haven: Yale University Press, 1951.

Johnson, H. A., and Thulstrup, N., editors. *A Kierkegaard Critique*. New York: Harper, 1962.

Kant, Immanuel. *Critique of Pure Reason*, translated by N. K. Smith. Second English edition. London: Macmillan, 1933.

Kaufmann, Walter, editor. *Existentialism from Dostoevsky to Sartre*. New York: Meridian Books, 1956.

Kaufmann, Walter. *Nietzsche*. Princeton: Princeton University Press, 1950.

Kierkegaard, Søren. *Concluding Unscientific Postscript*. Princeton: Princeton University Press, 1941.

——. *For Self-Examination and Judge for Yourselves!* New York: Oxford University Press, 1941.

——. *Philosophical Fragments*. Second edition. Princeton: Princeton University Press, 1962.

——. *Training in Christianity*. New York: Oxford University Press, 1941.

Kingston, F. Temple. *French Existentialism: A Christian Critique*. Toronto: University of Toronto Press, 1961.

Krikorian, Y. H., editor. *Naturalism and the Human Spirit*. New York: Columbia University Press, 1944.

Kwant, R. C. *Philosophy of Labor*. Pittsburgh: Duquesne University Press, 1960.

Lieb, I. C., editor. *Experience, Existence, and the Good*. Carbondale: Southern Illinois University Press, 1961.

Lilley, S., editor. *Essays on the Social History of Science*. Copenhagen: Munksgaard, 1953.

Lonergan, B. J. *Insight: A Study of Human Understanding*. New York: Philosophical Library, 1956.

Macquarrie, John. *An Existentialist Theology: A Comparison of Heidegger and Bultmann*. New York: Macmillan, 1955.

Malcolm, Norman. *Ludwig Wittgenstein: A Memoir*. New York: Oxford University Press, 1958.

Malevez, L. *The Christian Method and Myth*. Westminster: Newman Press, 1958.

Marcel, Gabriel. *L'Homme problématique*. Paris: Aubier, 1955.

———. *Homo Viator: Introduction to a Metaphysics of Hope*. Chicago: Regnery, 1951.

———. *The Mystery of Being*. 2 volumes. Chicago: Regnery, 1950.

———. *Position et approches concrètes du mystère ontologique*. Louvain: Nauwelaerts, 1949.

Maritain, Jacques. *An Essay on Christian Philosophy*. New York: Philosophical Library, 1955.

———. *On the Philosophy of History*. New York: Scribner, 1957.

———. *Philosophy of Nature*. New York: Philosophical Library, 1951.

———. *St. Thomas Aquinas*. Revised second English edition. New York: Meridian Books, 1958.

Marrou, H. I. *A History of Education in Antiquity*. New York: Sheed and Ward, 1956.

May, R., E. Angel, and H. F. Ellenberger, editors. *Existence*. New York: Basic Books, 1958.

McCosh, J. *The Religious Aspects of Evolution*. Revised edition. New York: Scribner, 1890.

Merleau-Ponty, Maurice. *Signes*. Paris: Gallimard, 1960.

Meyer, A. G. *Marxism: The Unity of Theory and Practice*. Cambridge: Harvard University Press, 1954.

Michalson, Carl, editor. *Christianity and the Existentialists*. New York: Scribner, 1956.

Mitchell, B., editor. *Faith and Logic*. Boston: Beacon Press, 1957.

Moody, P. A. *Introduction to Evolution*. New York: Harper, 1953.

Newman, J. H. *Parochial and Plain Sermons*. New Impression, 8 volumes. New York: Longmans, Green, 1908-1920.

Northrop, F. S. *The Meeting of East and West: An Inquiry Concerning World Understanding*. New York: Macmillan, 1946.

Oesterreicher, J. M. *Walls Are Crumbling*. New York: Devon-Adair, 1952.

Ogden, S. M. *Existence and Faith: Shorter Writings of Rudolf Bultmann*. New York: Living Age Books, 1960.

O'Neil, C. J., editor. *An Etienne Gilson Tribute*. Milwaukee: Marquette University Press, 1959.

O'Reilly, B. *Life of Leo XIII*. Revised edition. Philadelphia: Winston, 1903.

Osborn, H. F. *From the Greeks to Darwin*. Revised second edition. New York: Scribner, 1929.

Paley, W. *Natural Theology*. Thirteenth edition. London: Faulder, 1811.

Pegis, A. C., editor. *A Gilson Reader*. New York: Doubleday, 1957.

Pepper, S. C. *Ethics*. New York: Appleton-Century-Crofts, 1960.

430

Pepper, S. C. *The Sources of Value*. Berkeley and Los Angeles: University of California Press, 1958.

Perry, Ralph Barton. *The Thought and Character of William James*. 2 volumes. Boston: Little, Brown, 1935.

Persons, S., editor. *Evolutionary Thought in America*. New Haven: Yale University Press, 1950.

Przywara, Erich. *Analogia Entis*. Munich: Pustet, 1932.

———. *Polarity*. London: Oxford University Press, 1935.

———. *Religions-begründung: Max Scheler—J. H. Newman*. Freiburg im Breisgau: Herder, 1923.

Rabut, O. *Teilhard de Chardin: A Critical Study*. New York: Sheed and Ward, 1961.

Radhakrishnan, S., editor. *History of Philosophy Eastern and Western*. 2 volumes. London: Allen and Unwin, 1953.

Raeymaeker, L. de. *Le Cardinal Mercier et l'Institut Supérieur de Louvain*. Louvain: Publications Universitaries, 1952.

Ramsey, I. T. *Religious Language*. London: SCM Press, 1957.

Rintelen, F.-J. von, editor. *Philosophia Perennis*. 2 volumes. Regensburg: Habbel, 1930.

Ritchie, D. G. *Darwin and Hegel*. New York: Macmillan, 1893.

Roberts, D. E. *Existentialism and Religious Belief*. New York: Oxford University Press, 1957.

Romanell, Patrick. *Toward a Critical Naturalism*. New York: Macmillan, 1958.

Royce, Josiah. *The Spirit of Modern Philosophy*. Reprint edition. New York: Braziller, 1955.

———. *The World and the Individual*. 2 volumes. New York: Macmillan, 1900-01.

Rubel, M. *Karl Marx: Essai de biographie intellectuelle*. Paris: Rivière, 1957.

Santayana, George. *The Life of Reason*. New York: Scribner, 1954.

Sartre, Jean-Paul. *Being and Nothingness*. New York: Philosophical Library, 1956.

———. *Critique de la raison dialectique*. Tome I. Paris: Gallimard, 1960. Also contains *Question de méthode*.

———. *Literary and Philosophical Essays*. New York: Criterion Books, 1955.

———. *No Exit and Three Other Plays*. New York: Viking Books, 1955.

Scheler, Max. *Gesammelte Werke*. Edited by Maria Scheler. Bern: Franke, 1954 ff.

———. *On the Eternal in Man*. New York: Harper, 1960.

———. *Philosophical Perspectives*. Boston: Beacon Press, 1958.

———. *Ressentiment*. Edited by L. A. Coser. New York: The Free Press of Glencoe, 1961.

———. *Die Stellung des Menschen im Kosmos*. Munich: Nymphenverlag, 1947.

———. *The Nature of Sympathy*. New Haven: Yale University Press, 1954.

Schilpp, Paul A., editor. *The Philosophy of Ernst Cassirer*. Evanston: Library of Living Philosophers, 1949.

———, editor. *The Philosophy of John Dewey*. Second edition. New York: Tudor, 1951.

———, editor. *The Philosophy of Karl Jaspers*. New York: Tudor, 1957.

Schneider, H. W. *A History of American Philosophy*. New York: Columbia University Press, 1946.

Simpson, G. G. *The Meaning of Evolution*. New Haven: Yale University Press, 1949.

Smith, J. E. *Reason and God*. New Haven: Yale University Press, 1961.

Smuts, J. C. *Holism and Evolution*. London: Macmillan, 1926.

Soderini, E. *The Pontificate of Leo XIII*. London: Burns, Oates and Washbourne, 1934.

Somerhausen, Luc. *L'Humanisme agissant de Karl Marx*. Paris: Richard-Masse, 1946.

Sottiaux, E. *Gabriel Marcel: Philosophe et dramaturge*. Louvain: Nauwelaerts, 1956.

Spencer, Herbert. *First Principles*. Sixth edition. Akron, Ohio: Werner, 1900.

Spiegelberg, Herbert. *The Phenomenological Movement*. Two volumes. The Hague: Nijhoff, 1960.

Spinoza Opera, edited by C. Gebhardt. 4 volumes. Heidelberg: Winter, 1923-24.

Stein, Edith. *Endliches und ewiges Sein*. Volume II of *Edith Steins Werke*. Edited by L. Gelber and R. Leuven. Louvain: Nauwelaerts, 1950.

——. *Zum Problem der Einfühlung*. Halle: Waisenhause, 1917.

Tax, S., editor. *Evolution after Darwin*. 3 volumes. Chicago: University of Chicago Press, 1960.

Teggart, F. J., editor. *The Idea of Progress*. Revised edition. Berkeley and Los Angeles: University of California Press, 1949.

Teilhard de Chardin, Pierre. *The Divine Milieu*. New York: Harper, 1960.

——. *The Phenomenon of Man*. New York: Harper, 1959.

Thomas, J. H. *Subjectivity and Paradox*. New York: Macmillan, 1957.

Tillich, Paul. *Dynamics of Faith*. New York: Harper, 1957.

Toulmin, S., R. W. Hepburn, and A. MacIntyre. *Metaphysical Beliefs*. London: SCM Press, 1957.

Tresmontant, C. *Pierre Teilhard de Chardin: His Thought*. Baltimore: Helicon Press, 1959.

Tucker, Robert. *Philosophy and Myth in Karl Marx*. New York: Cambridge University Press, 1961.

Tuveson, E. L. *Millennium and Utopia*. Berkeley and Los Angeles: University of California Press, 1949.

Urban. *Beyond Realism and Idealism*. London: Allen and Unwin, 1949.

——. *The Intelligible World: Metaphysics and Value*. New York: Macmillan, 1929.

Urmson, J. O., editor. *The Concise Encyclopedia of Western Philosophy and Philosophers*. New York: Hawthorne, 1960.

Van Riet, G., *L'Épistémologie thomiste*. Louvain: Éditions de l'Institut Supérieur, 1946.

Venable, Vernon. *Human Nature: The Marxian View*. New York: Knopf, 1946.

Vivas, Eliseo. *The Moral Life and the Ethical Life*. Chicago: University of Chicago Press, 1950.

West, G. *Charles Darwin: A Portrait*. New Haven: Yale University Press, 1938.

Wetter, Gustav. *Dialectical Materialism: A Historical and Systematic Survey of Philosophy in the Soviet Union*. New York: Praeger, 1958.

White, M. G. *The Origin of Dewey's Instrumentalism*. New York: Columbia, 1943.

Whitehead, Alfred North. *Process and Reality*. New York: Macmillan, 1929.

Wiener, P. P. *Evolution and the Founders of Pragmatism*. Cambridge: Harvard University Press, 1949.

——, editor. *Leibniz Selections*. New York: Scribner, 1951.

——, editor. *Values in a Universe of Chance: Selected Writings of Charles S. Peirce (1839-1914)*. Stanford: Stanford University Press, 1958.

Wild, J., editor. *Spinoza Selections*. New York: Scribner, 1930.

Wolff, P., editor. *Christliche Philosophie in Deutschland 1920 bis 1945*. Regensburg: Habbel, 1949.

432

Wright, Chauncey. *Philosophical Discussions.* New York: Holt, 1878.
——. *The Philosophical Writings of Chauncey Wright.* Edited by E. H. Madden. New York: Liberal Arts Press, 1958.
Zimmermann, W. *Evolution: Die Geschichte ihrer Probleme und Erkenntnisse.* Freiburg and Munich: Verlag Karl Alber, 1953.

II. *Articles*

Allers, Rudolf. "Heidegger on the Principle of Sufficient Reason," *Philosophy and Phenomenological Research,* 20 (1960), 365-73.
Bonansea, B. "Pioneers of the Nineteenth-century Scholastic Revival in Italy," *The New Scholasticism,* 28 (1954), 1-37.
Clark, M. "The Contributions of Max Scheler to the Philosophy of Religion," *The Philosophical Review,* 43 (1934), 577-47.
Collins, James. "Catholic Estimates of Scheler's Catholic Period," *Thought,* 19 (1944), 671-704.
——. "Olgiati's Conception of Modern Philosophy," *Thought,* 18 (1943), 478-504.
Copleston, F. C. "Man and Metaphysics," *The Heythrop Journal,* 1 (1960).
Demos, R. "The Meaningfulness of Religious Language," *Philosophy and Phenomenological Research,* 18 (1957-58), 96-106.
Dewey, John. "The Ego as Cause," *The Philosophical Review,* 3 (1894), 337-41.
——. "Ethics and Physical Science," *The Andover Review,* 7 (1887), 239-263.
——. "Green's Theory of the Moral Motive," *The Philosophical Review,* 1 (1892), 593-612.
——. "The Psychological Standpoint," *Mind,* 11 (1896), 153-73.
——. "Reconstruction," *The Monthly Bulletin* of the Students' Christian Association of the University of Michigan, 17 (1893-94), 149-56.
——. "The Reflex Arc Concept in Psychology," *Psychological Review,* 3 (1896), 357-70.
——. "Soul and Body," *Bibliotheca Sacra,* 43 (1886), 239-263.
——. "The Superstition of Necessity," *The Monist,* 3 (1892-93), 362-79.
Dufault, L. "The Philosophical and Biological Implications of Evolution," *Proceedings of the American Catholic Philosophical Association,* 26 (1952), 66-80.
Dykhuizen, G. "John Dewey: The Vermont Years," *Journal of the History of Ideas,* 20 (1959), 515-44.
Ellegard, A. "The Darwinian Theory and Nineteenth-century Philosophies of Science," *Journal of the History of Ideas,* 18 (1957), 362-93.
Eslick, L. J. "What is the Starting Point of Metaphysics?" *The Modern Schoolman,* 34 (1956-57), 247-63.
Faricy, R. L. "The Establishment of the Basic Principle of the Fifth Way," *The New Scholasticism,* 31 (1957), 189-208.
Feibleman, James K. "The Social Adaptiveness of Philosophies," *Ethics,* 70 (1960), 146-54.
Feuer, L. S. "H. A. P. Torrey and John Dewey: Teacher and Pupil," *American Quarterly,* 10 (1958), 34-54.
——. "John Dewey's Reading at College," *Journal of the History of Ideas,* 19 (1958), 415-21.
Fisch, M. H. "Evolution in American Philosophy," *The Philosophical Review,* 56 (1947), 357-73.
Geiger, L. B. "Métaphysique et relativité historique," *Revue de Métaphysique et de Morale,* 17 (1952), 381-414.

Greene, J. C. "Darwin and Religion," *Proceedings of the American Philosophical Society*, 103 (1959), 716-25.

Grene, M. "Two Evolutionary Theories," *The British Journal for the Philosophy of Science*, 9 (1958), 110-27, 185-93.

Gurwitsch, Aron. "The Problem of Existence in Constitutive Phenomenology," *The Journal of Philosophy*, 58 (1961), 625-32.

Hartmann, Nicolai. "Max Scheler," *Kantstudien*, 33 (1928), IX-XVI.

Hartshorne, C. A. "Outlines of a Philosophy of Nature, Part II," *The Personalist*, 39 (1958), 385-89.

Harvanek, R. F. "The Church and Scholasticism," *Proceedings of the American Catholic Philosophical Association*, 32 (1958), 215-25.

——. "Philosophical Pluralism and Catholic Orthodoxy," *Thought*, 25 (1950), 21-52.

Henle, Robert J. "Science and the Humanities," *Thought*, 35 (1960), 513-536.

Hossfeld, Paul. "Karl Jaspers and Religion," *Philosophy Today*, 3 (1959), 277-80.

Husserl, Edmund. "Philosophy as a Strict Science," *Cross Currents*, 6 (1956), 227-46; 325-44.

Irvine, William. "The Influence of Darwin on Literature," *Proceedings of the American Philosophical Society*, 103 (1959), 616-28.

Johann, R. O. "Subjectivity," *The Review of Metaphysics*, 12 (1958), 200-234.

Kennick, W. E. "The Language of Religion," *The Philosophical Review*, 65 (1956), 56-71.

Klubertanz, G. P. "The Influence of Evolutionary Theory upon American Thought," *Gregorianum*, 32 (1951), 582-90.

——. "Where is the Evidence for Thomistic Metaphysics?" *Revue Philosophique de Louvain*, 56 (1958), 294-315.

Knodel, A. "An Introduction to the Integral Evolutionism of Teilhard de Chardin," *The Personalist*, 38 (1957), 347-55.

Lamont, Corliss. "New Light on Dewey's *Common Faith*," *The Journal of Philosophy*, 58 (1961), 21-28.

Lauer, Quentin. "The Phenomenological Ethics of Max Scheler," *International Philosophical Quarterly*, 1 (1961), 273-300.

Le Blond, J. M. "L'Usage théologique de la notion de causalité," *Recherches de Philosophie*, 3-4 (1958), 15-26.

Lenz-Médoc, Paulus. "L'Idée de l'État chez Edith Stein," *Les Études Philosophiques*, 11 (1956), 451-57.

Lotz, J. B. "Denken und Sein nach den jüngsten Veröffentlichungen von M. Heidegger," *Scholastik*, 33 (1958), 81-97.

Mandelbaum, M. "Darwin's Religious Views," *Journal of the History of Ideas*, 19 (1958), 363-78.

Marcel, Gabriel. "Dieu et la causalité," *Recherches de Philosophie*, 3-4 (1958), 27-33.

Natanson, Maurice. "Causation as a Structure of the *Lebenswelt*," *The Journal of Existential Psychiatry*, 1 (1960), 346-66.

Nogar, R. J. "The Darwin Centennial: A Philosophical Intrusion," *The New Scholasticism*, 33 (1959), 411-445.

Owens, Joseph. "St. Thomas and Elucidation," *The New Scholasticism*, 35 (1961), 421-444.

Ramsey, I. T. "Empiricism and Religion. A Critique of Ryle's *Concept of Mind*," *The Christian Scholar*, 39 (1956), 159-63.

Royce, Josiah. "The Mechanical, the Historical, and the Statistical," *Science*, N.S., 39 (1914), 551-66.

Shuster, George N. "Introductory Statement to: 'Symposium on the Significance of Max Scheler for Philosophy and Social Science'," *Philosophy and Phenomenological Research*, 2 (1942), 270.

Spiegelberg, Herbert. "French Existentialism: Its Social Philosophies," *The Kenyon Review*, 16 (1954), 446-62.

Stein, Edith. "Beiträge zur philosophischen Begründung der Psychologie und der Geisteswissenschaften. Erste Abhandlung: Psychische Kausalität; Zweite Abhandlung: Individuum und Gemeinschaft," *Jahrbuch für Philosophie und phänomenologische Forschung*, 5 (1922), 1-116; 116-283.

——. "Husserls Phänomenologie und die Philosophie des hl. Thomas v. Aquin," *Festschrift Edmund Husserl zum 70. Geburtstag gewidmet. Ergänzungsband zum Jahrbuch für Philosophie und phänomenologische Forschung* (1929), 315-338.

——. "Eine Untersuchung über den Staat," *Jahrbuch für Philosophie und phänomenologische Forschung*, 7 (1925), 1-123.

Strasser, S. "Das Gottesproblem in der Spätphilosophie Edmund Husserls," *Philosophisches Jahrbuch*, 67 (1959), 130-142.

Vollert, C. "Evolution of the Human Body," *The Catholic Mind*, 50 (1952), 135-54.

Wild, John, "The Exploration of the Life-World," *Proceedings and Addresses of the American Philosophical Association, 1960-1961.*

Xenakis, Jason, J. Collins, J. Wisdom, V. C. Aldrich, and P. Wheelwright. "The Nature of Theological Discourse," *The Christian Scholar*, 41 (1958), 601-13.

III. *Varia*

Acta Leonis XIII, 2 (1883-87), 3 (1887-89).

Acta Sanctae Sedis, 12 (1879-80), 13 (1880-81), 23 (1890-91).

Chicago Review, 13 (1959), number 2, "Existentialism and Literature," 3-202.

Mélanges Joseph Maréchal. 2 volumes; Paris: Desclée De Brouwer, 1950.

Savage, W. "The Evolution of John Dewey's Philosophy of Experimentalism as Developed at the University of Michigan," Unpublished University of Michigan doctoral dissertation; Ann Arbor: University Microfilms, 1950.

The Thomist, 5 (1943), the Maritain volume.

Woodstock College Library Chapbook (1958), 7-15. Contains a bibliography of writings by and on Teilhard de Chardin compiled by Leo Larkin, S.J.

INDEX

INDEX

439

441